# Lecture Notes in Computer Science

*Commenced Publication in 1973*
Founding and Former Series Editors:
Gerhard Goos, Juris Hartmanis, and Jan van Leeuwen

Annie Cuyt   Walter Krämer
Wolfram Luther   Peter Markstein (Eds.)

# Numerical Validation in Current Hardware Architectures

International Dagstuhl Seminar
Dagstuhl Castle, Germany, January 6-11, 2008
Revised Papers

 Springer

Volume Editors

Annie Cuyt
Universiteit Antwerpen
Department of Mathematics and Computer Science
Middelheimlaan 1, 2020 Antwerpen, Belgium
E-mail: annie.cuyt@ua.ac.be

Walter Krämer
Bergische Universität Wuppertal
Wissenschaftliches Rechnen/Softwaretechnologie
Gaussstrasse 20, 42097 Wuppertal, Germany
E-mail: kraemer@math.uni-wuppertal.de

Wolfram Luther
Universität Duisburg-Essen, Fakultät Ingenieurwissenschaften
Abteilung Informatik und Angewandte Kognitionswissenschaft
47048 Duisburg, Germany
E-mail: luther@inf.uni-due.de

Peter Markstein
160 Redland Road, Woodside, CA 94062, USA
E-mail: peter@markstein.org

Library of Congress Control Number: Applied for

CR Subject Classification (1998): G.1, G.4, D.2, F.2.1, D.3

LNCS Sublibrary: SL 1 – Theoretical Computer Science and General Issues

ISSN 0302-9743

ISBN 978-3-642-01590-8 Springer Berlin Heidelberg New York

springer.com

© Springer-Verlag Berlin Heidelberg 2009

Typesetting: Camera-ready by author, data conversion by Scientific Publishing Services, Chennai, India
Printed on acid-free paper     SPIN: 12659739     06/3180     5 4 3 2 1 0

# Preface

The major emphasis of the Dagstuhl Seminar on "Numerical Validation in Current Hardware Architectures" lay on numerical validation in current hardware architectures and software environments. The general idea was to bring together experts who are concerned with computer arithmetic in systems with actual processor architectures and scientists who develop, use, and need techniques from verified computation in their applications. Topics of the seminar therefore included:

- The ongoing revision of the IEEE 754/854 standard for floating-point arithmetic
- Feasible ways to implement multiple precision (multiword) arithmetic and to compute the actual precision at run-time according to the needs of input data
- The achievement of a similar behavior of fixed-point, floating-point and interval arithmetic across language compliant implementations
- The design of robust and efficient numerical programs portable from diverse computers to those that adhere to the IEEE standard
- The development and propagation of validated special-purpose software in different application areas
- Error analysis in several contexts
- Certification of numerical programs, verification and validation assessment

Computer arithmetic plays an important role at the hardware and software level, when microprocessors, embedded systems, or grids are designed. The reliability of numerical software strongly depends on the compliance with the corresponding floating-point norms. Standard CISC processors follow the 1985 IEEE norm 754, which is currently under revision, but the new highly performing CELL processor is not fully IEEE compliant. The draft standard IEEE 754r guarantees that systems perform floating-point computation that yields results independent of whether the processing is done in hardware, software, or a combination of the two. For operations specified in this standard, numerical results and exceptions are uniquely determined by the values of the input data, sequence of operations, and destination formats, all under user control. There was a broad consensus that the standard should include interval arithmetic.

The discussion focused on decimal number formats, faithful rounding, higher mantissa length, high precise standard functions, and linking of numerical and symbolic algebraic computation. This work is accompanied by new vector, matrix, and elementary or special function libraries (i.e., complex functions and continued fractions) with guaranteed precision within their domains. Functions should be correctly rounded and even last bit accuracy is available for standard functions. Important discussion points were additional features such as fast interval arithmetic, staggered correction arithmetic, or a fast and accurate multiply and accumulate instruction by pipelining. The latter is the key operation for a fast multiple precision arithmetic. An exact dot product (implemented in pipelined hardware) for floating point vectors would provide operations in vector spaces with accurate results without any time penalty. Correctly rounded results in these vector spaces go hand in hand with correctly rounded elementary functions. The new norm will be based on solid and interesting theoretical studies in integrated or reconfigurable circuit design, mathematics, and computer science.

In parallel to the ongoing IEEE committee discussions, the seminar aimed at highlighting design decisions on floating-point computations at run-time over the whole execution process under the silent consensus that there are features defined by the hardware standard, by language, or deferred to the implementation for several reasons. Hardware and software should support several (user-defined) number types, i.e., fixed width, binary, or decimal floating-point numbers or interval arithmetic. A serious effort is being made to standardize the use of intervals especially in the programming language C. Developers are prompted to write efficient numerical programs easily portable with small revisions to other platforms. C-XSC is a C++ Library for Extended Scientific Computing for developing numerical software with result verification. This library is permanently enlarged and enhanced as highlighted in several talks.

However, depending on the requirements on speed, input, and output range, or precision, special-purpose processors also use other number systems, i.e., fixed-point or logarithmic number systems and non-standard mantissa length. Interesting examples reported were a 16-bit interval arithmetic on the FPGA (Field Programmable Gate Array)- based NIOS-II soft processor and an online-arithmetic with rational numbers. Therefore, research on reliable computing includes a wide range of current hardware and software platforms and compilers.

Standardization is also asked for in inhomogeneous computer networks. The verification step should validate the partial results coming from the owners of parcels before combining them to the final result.

Our insights and the implemented systems should be used by people with various numerical problems to solve these problems in a comprehensible and reliable way and by people incorporating validated software tools into other systems or providing interfaces to these tools.

Thus, we want raise awareness of interval tools, the validated modeling and simulation systems, and computer-based proofs in science and engineering.

This book contains the proceedings (revised papers) of the Dagstuhl Seminar 08021 "Numerical Validation in Current Hardware Architectures" held during January 6-11, 2008. The 16 contributions are grouped into four sections:

1. Standardization/Hardware
2. Tools
3. Applications
4. Linear Systems

All papers were refereed by at least two of the referees listed here. We would like to thank all the referees for doing a very good job. We would also like to thank all authors for providing us with their excellent contributions and for their willingness to join in groups to present a coherent description of related research and software tools. We are also grateful to Springer for the fruitful cooperation when preparing this volume and, last but not least, to Michael Zimmer, for compiling the final version of the text.

January 2009

Annie Cuyt
Walter Krämer
Wolfram Luther
Peter Markstein

# Organization

## Organizers

Annie Cuyt            University of Antwerp
Walter Krämer         University of Wuppertal
Wolfram Luther        University of Duisburg-Essen
Peter Markstein       Woodside California

## Referees

G. Alefeld          U. Klatte          S. Oishi
E. Auer             W. Krämer          E. Popova
G. Bohlender        V. Kreinovich      J. Pryce
A. Cuyt             U. Kulisch         A. Rauh
A. Frommer          B. Lang            N. Revol
M. Grimmer          W. Luther          S.M. Rump
M. Hochbruck        G. Melquiond       B. Tibken
R.B. Kearfott       J.M. Muller        J. Wolff von Gudenberg
M. Kieffer          M. Neher

## Additional online information available from the Dagstuhl server

Dagstuhl Seminar Proceedings 08021 (DROPS), Numerical Validation in Current Hardware Architectures. A. Cuyt, W. Krämer, W. Luther, P. Markstein (Eds.), ISSN 1862 - 4405, see
http://drops.dagstuhl.de/portals/index.php?semnr=08021

# Table of Contents

## Standardization/Hardware

## Tools

## Applications

## Linear Systems

# Discussions on an Interval Arithmetic Standard at Dagstuhl Seminar 08021

R. Baker Kearfott[1], John Pryce[2], and Nathalie Revol[3]

[1] University of Louisiana at Lafayette
Box 4-1010
Lafayette, Louisiana 70504-1010
USA

[2] Department of Informatics and Simulation
Royal Military College of Science
Shrivenham
Wilts SN6 8LA
England

[3] Projet Arenaire
Laboratoire de l'Informatique du Parallélisme
École Normale Supérieure de Lyon
46 allée d'Italie
69364 Lyon Cedex 07
France

## 1 Background

Efforts have been made to standardize interval arithmetic (IA) for over a decade. The reasons have been to enable more widespread use of the technology, to enable more widespread sharing and collaboration among researchers and developers of the technology, and to enable easier checking that computer codes have been correctly programmed. During the late 1990's, the first author of this report led such a project to introduce an interval data type into the Fortran language. One reason for failure of that effort was the Fortran language standardization committee's lack of familiarity with interval technology and consequent caution. Another was misunderstanding between the Fortran standardization committee's basic tenets on standardizing interline optimization and some views expressed by members of the interval analysis community. A third was confusion over how extended IA (arithmetic dealing with division by intervals that contain zero) should be handled. This was coupled with a heavy committee load associated with other projects, such as standardizing an interface for interoperability with "C" language programs.

Since then, the interval analysis community has studied and gained additional understanding of extended IA. One such study is [10], a systematization of the options. Another, with a particular point of view, is Prof. Kulisch's contribution to this volume. Extended arithmetic remains a controversial part of efforts to standardize the arithmetic, particularly whether the underlying model should consider $-\infty$ and $\infty$ to be numbers in their own right or if $-\infty$ and $\infty$ should

A. Cuyt et al. (Eds.): Numerical Validation, LNCS 5492, pp. 1–6, 2009.

just be considered placeholders to describe unbounded sets of finite real numbers. A practical consequence is a difference in the value of $0 \times X$ when $X$ is an unbounded interval. Nonetheless, our understanding and thinking about this issue is clearer than a decade ago. This, coupled with the desire to have a standard, should lead to progress.

A proposal is concurrently being developed to add IA to the C++ standard library. This work is presently slated to become a technical report (something that is generally implemented by compiler developers and is expected to become an integral part of a future standard).

Meanwhile, perhaps the most widely used IA system is that underlying INTLAB [11], although various other systems, such as PROFIL/BIAS [3,4], FILIB++ [8,7] and BOOST [9], and the interval facilities in the Sun compilers, e.g. [12], as well as systems within the XSC languages, see [2] and http://www.xsc.de, also are in wide use. The above references are biased towards C/C++, but a number of Fortran IA systems are also well used. See also the extensive bibliography in [5].

## 2  Proceedings at the Seminar

The context of this meeting was that

- The IFIP Working Group 2.5 on Numerical Software (WG 2.5) had written in September 2007 to the IEEE 754 Revision committee (IEEE754R) strongly supporting the inclusion of IA in the forthcoming standard (P754).
- IEEE754R had asked WG 2.5 to produce a proposal for inclusion in the standard, which they had submitted in October 2007 with a minor revision in December 2007. This proposal is based on the interval model described in the recent book by Kulisch, [5], see also the paper [1] by Kirchner and Kulisch.
- From then up to and including at the Dagstuhl meeting, there was a division of views among leading workers in intervals, as well as members of IEEE754R. Several expressed broad support for the WG 2.5 proposal but felt it lacked some crucial detail and could not be included in the standard without further work. Others, however, still wished to address perceived defects before the IEEE754R deadline, supporting the Kulisch initiative. They felt that a separate standard for interval arithmetic would lack the impact of one that, being integral with P754, is recognised by the whole floating-point community. Members of this group, therefore, didn't sign the letter.

A first discussion on the topic was held at Dagstuhl on Thurs 10 Jan. The following aims to summarise this discussion. Speakers recorded are:

| | | | |
|---|---|---|---|
| JWvG | : Jürgen Wolff von Gudenberg | PM | : Peter Markstein |
| RBK | : R. Baker Kearfott | JDP | : John Pryce |
| UK | : Ulrich Kulisch | NR | : Nathalie Revol |
| RL | : Rudolf Lohner | SR | : Siegfried Rump |
| JMM | : Jean-Michel Muller | NS | : Neil Stewart |

RBK, leading the discussion, began by saying he believed there was a general view that the lack of consensus, and time constraints, made it impossible to include the WG 2.5 proposal in the current P754 revision. Instead, we should ask IEEE's authority for starting a new committee with wide participation from the interval community, to produce an IA standard in a longer timescale.

PM said that IA *had* been in the draft standard but too little of the detail was agreed by everyone so it was dropped. If we could agree on the WG 2.5 proposal or something close, we were in good shape to have it included in IEEE754 in a short time—provided we could muster enough people willing to work on the detail.

JMM said it was important to include people from IEEE754R, to ensure compatibility with that standard.

RBK proposed the motion:

"That the WG 2.5 proposal be supplied to IEEE754R as the basis for an initial draft of a free-standing IA standard, initially independent of    (1) P754, to be worked on by a new committee set up for the purpose."

If this were carried, we should write a suitable letter to IEEE with a preliminary list of people who had expressed interest in participating.

UK: He had already essentially done this when submitting his proposal on 10th October.

JDP: Then the purpose of this meeting was to obtain wider consensus.

NS: The new committee needed members with a wide range of expertise—hardware, software engineering, people from industry, numerical analysts, members of research teams, ...

Possible members were suggested, including people from

- Intel, say Herbert Cornelius, since the MK library includes IA.
- Current IEEE754R committee, say David Hough.
- Current WG 2.5 committee, say Van Snyder (who is also on Fortran standard committee).
- ISL (Interval Subroutine Library), say Baker Kearfott and John Pryce.
- INRIA, say Nathalie Revol and Guillaume Melquiond.

RL and JWvG were willing to serve on the committee. UK might do so.

SR raised a more general question about the work. There are several underlying mathematical models on which IA can be based. The WG 2.5 proposal only supported one of these. There were several that he regarded as an acceptable basis for practical interval computation. Should the committee study several models with the aim of (a) choosing the one it thought best and/or (b) creating a standard that supports more than one model? These were not mutually exclusive options.

RBK proposed wording:

"There are several well developed IA philosophies. The committee will study and *integrate* these, so that the resulting standard does not make    (2) it too difficult to implement any of them."

JMM: Probably the best IA philosophy to choose is

"The one that is easiest to build other models on top of." $\hspace{4cm}$ (3)

It was agreed that this should be put in the proposed letter.

NR mentioned the Hickey, Ju and van Emden interval model. The authors should be invited.

SR would consider who from the Hamburg group might take part.

RBK mentioned that members of the C++ interval standard group (Brönnimann, Melquiond, Pion) should all be invited.

The motion, as such, was dropped and it was agreed that a letter should be written proposing the new working group, with a remit based on (2, 3), and with a preliminary list of participants.

It was also agreed to start a discussion forum on the Reliable Computing mailing list, to find more participants, gather opinions, and clarify the points of consensus and most crucially the main points of disagreement.

The meeting closed. A letter was drafted by RBK, JDP and NR. Further discussions took place the following day and the letter was revised as a result. It was sent, dated 11th Jan 2008, to Dr Dan Zuras, Chair IEEE 754 Revision Committee, with a copy to Dr. R. F. Boisvert, Chair, IFIP Working Group 2.5. Signatories supporting the letter (listed in order of signing) were:

> R. Baker Kearfott, W. Luther, J.D. Pryce, Nathalie Revol, S.M. Rump, Guillaume Melquiond, Michel Kieffer, Vincent Lefèvre, C. Keil, Andreas Rauh, Jean-Michel Muller, Nicolas Louvet, Jean-Luc Lamotte, Markus Neher, Rudolf Lohner, Peter Markstein.

## 3   Subsequent Developments

Subsequently, the first and third authors of this note collected a list of electronic mail and postal addresses for interested persons. Fortunately, these persons included those who were unable to attend the final meeting, as well as those against formation of the new committee and in favor of trying to get IEEE to adopt the results of IFIP Working Group 2.5.

The three authors of this note worked with Bob Davis, chair of the IEEE Microprocessor Standards Committee, to frame the wording of, and submit, a Project Authorization Request through the IEEE New Standards Committee (NSC), for work on a stand-alone standard (separate from the floating point standard P754) for interval arithmetic. The Scope, Purpose, and Rationale of the project are as follows.

> 1. *Scope.* This standard will specify basic interval arithmetic operations selecting and following one of the commonly used mathematical interval models and at least one floating-point type defined by the IEEE-754/2008 standard. Exception conditions will be defined and standard handling of these conditions will be specified. Consistency with the model

will be tempered with practical considerations based on input from representatives of vendors and owners of existing systems.

The standard will provide a layer between the hardware and the programming language levels. It will not mandate that any operations be implemented in hardware. It will not define any realization of the basic operations as functions in a programming language.

2. *Purpose.* The standard's aim is to improve the availability of reliable computing in modern hardware and software environments by defining the basic building blocks needed for performing interval arithmetic. There are presently many systems for interval arithmetic in use, and lack of a standard inhibits development, portability, and ability to verify correctness of codes.

3. *Rationale.* There is presently no defined standard, although there are many systems in use today. However, due to the nature of applications of interval arithmetic in providing automatic verification, simplicity, predictability, and portability are doubly important in the underlying computations. The standard will provide the necessary ease of implementation, portability, and ability to check correctness of codes.

Authorization for the project passed unanimously at the NSC on June 11, 2008 and it was given the title *IEEE Working Group P1788, Standardization of Interval Arithmetic.* As the next step, an organizational meeting was held in conjunction with SCAN-2008 in El Paso, Texas, USA, September 29 to October 3, 2008.

The agenda for this meeting included election of officers and agreement on procedures for decision-making. Such procedures need to include all interested parties, and should be such that all will respect the decisions made according to the procedures. Through these procedures, we strive to gain wider and more unambiguous acceptance, at all levels, than of the document produced by IFIP Working Group 2.5.

Although the project is for a stand-alone document, a goal is to make it consistent with the floating point arithmetic standard P754, for eventual incorporation therein. Some (but not all) issues related to this are

- the underlying mathematical model for the real numbers,
- requirements that features be implemented in hardware (or not),
- the set of features that are implemented.

The time frame for the project is four years, although the aim and expectation is to complete the process sooner.

The P1788 membership (currently around 90 on the mailing list and 45 registered to vote) has approved the slate of officers as follows. Nathalie Revol, Chair (currently on maternity leave). R. Baker Kearfott and John Pryce, Vice chairs. William Edmonson, Secretary. Jürgen Wolff von Gudenberg, Web master. Guillaume Melquiond, Archivist. David Lester and John Pryce, Technical editors. George Corliss, Vote tabulator.

At the time of writing, the membership is voting on the Policies and Procedures document, which is based on standard IEEE practice. An active discussion of many aspects of the standard is underway on the electronic forum at stds-1788@LISTSERV.IEEE.ORG.

# References

1. Kirchner, R., Kulisch, U.W.: Hardware support for interval arithmetic. Reliable Computing, 225–237 (2006)
2. Klatte, R., Kulisch, U., Lawo, C., Rauch, M., Wiethoff, A.: C-XSC: A C++ Class Library for Extended Scientific Computation. Springer, Berlin (1993)
3. Knüppel, O.: PROFIL/BIAS – A fast interval library. Computing 53(3–4), 277–287 (1994)
4. Knüppel, O.: PROFIL/BIAS v 2.0. Bericht 99.1, Technische Universität Hamburg-Harburg, Harburg, Germany (February 1999),
   http://www.ti3.tu-harburg.de/profil_e
5. Kulisch, U.: Computer Arithmetic and Validity — Theory, Implementation, and Applications. De Gruyter Studies in Mathematics, vol. 33. Walter de Gruyter, Berlin (2008)
6. Kulisch, U.: Complete Interval Arithmetic and its Implementation on the Computer. In: Cuyt, A., et al. (eds.) Numerical Validation in Current Hardware Architectures (Dagstuhl Seminar 2008). LNCS, vol. 5492, pp. 7–26. Springer, Heidelberg (2009)
7. Lerch, M., Tischler, G., von Gudenberg, J.W.: filib—interval library specification and reference manual. Technical Report 279, Universität Würzburg, Germany (2001), http://www.math.uni-wuppertal.de/~xsc/software/filib.html
8. Lerch, M., Tischler, G., von Gudenberg, J.W., Hofschuster, W., Krämer, W.: filib++, a fast interval library supporting containment computations. ACM Transactions on Mathematical Software 32(2), 299–324 (2006)
9. Melquiond, G., Pion, S., Brönnimann, H.: Boost interval arithmetic library (2006), http://www.boost.org/doc/libs/1_37_0/libs/numeric/interval/doc/interval.htm
10. Pryce, J.D., Corliss, G.F.: Interval arithmetic with containment sets. Computing 78(3), 251–276 (2006)
11. Rump, S.M.: INTLAB–INTerval LABoratory. In: Csendes, T. (ed.) Developments in Reliable Computing: Papers presented at the International Symposium on Scientific Computing, Computer Arithmetic, and Validated Numerics, SCAN 1998, in Szeged, Hungary. Reliable Computing, vol. 5(3), pp. 77–104. Kluwer Academic Publishers, Dordrecht (1999), http://www.ti3.tu-harburg.de/rump/intlab/
12. Sun Microsystems. Interval arithmetic in the Forte[tm] C++ compiler (2000), http://www.sun.com/forte/cplusplus/interval/

# Complete Interval Arithmetic and Its Implementation on the Computer

Ulrich W. Kulisch

Institut für Angewandte und Numerische Mathematik
Universität Karlsruhe

**Abstract.** Let $I\!R$ be the set of closed and bounded intervals of real numbers. Arithmetic in $I\!R$ can be defined via the power set $P\!R$ of real numbers. If divisors containing zero are excluded, arithmetic in $I\!R$ is an algebraically closed subset of the arithmetic in $P\!R$, i.e., an operation in $I\!R$ performed in $P\!R$ gives a result that is in $I\!R$. Arithmetic in $P\!R$ also allows division by an interval that contains zero. Such division results in closed intervals of real numbers which, however, are no longer bounded. The union of the set $I\!R$ with these new intervals is denoted by $(I\!R)$. This paper shows that arithmetic operations can be extended to all elements of the set $(I\!R)$.

Let $F \subset I\!R$ denote the set of floating-point numbers. On the computer, arithmetic in $(I\!R)$ is approximated by arithmetic in the subset $(IF)$ of closed intervals with floating-point bounds. The usual exceptions of floating-point arithmetic like underflow, overflow, division by zero, or invalid operation do not occur in $(IF)$.

**Keywords:** computer arithmetic, floating-point arithmetic, interval arithmetic, arithmetic standards.

## 1 Introduction or a Vision of Future Computing

Computers are getting ever faster. On all relevant processors floating-point arithmetic is provided by fast hardware. The time can already be foreseen when the *PC* will be a teraflops computer. With this tremendous computing power scientific computing will experience a significant shift from floating-point arithmetic toward increased use of interval arithmetic. With very little extra hardware, interval arithmetic can be made as fast as simple floating-point arithmetic [3]. Nearly everything that is needed for fast interval arithmetic is already available on most existing processors, thanks to multimedia applications. What is still missing are the arithmetic operations with the directed roundings. Properly developed, interval arithmetic is a complete and exception-free calculus. The exceptions of floating-point arithmetic like underflow, overflow, division by zero, or operation invalidity do not occur in such interval arithmetic. This will be shown in the following.

For interval evaluation of an algorithm (a sequence of arithmetic operations) in the real number field a theorem by R. E. Moore [7] states that increasing the

A. Cuyt et al. (Eds.): Numerical Validation, LNCS 5492, pp. 7–26, 2009.

precision by $k$ digits reduces the error bounds by $b^{-k}$, i.e., results can always be guaranteed to a number of correct digits by using variable precision interval arithmetic (for details see [1], [9]). Variable length interval arithmetic can be made very fast by an exact dot product and complete arithmetic [4]. There is no way to compute a dot product faster than the exact result. By pipelining, it can be computed in the time the processor needs to read the data, i.e., it comes with utmost speed. Variable length interval arithmetic fully benefits from such speed. No software simulation can go as fast. With operator overloading variable length interval arithmetic is very easy to use.

The tremendous progress in computer technology should be accompanied by extension of the mathematical capacity of the computer. A balanced standard for computer arithmetic should require that the basic components of modern computing (floating-point arithmetic, interval arithmetic, and an exact dot product) be provided by the computer's hardware. See [5].

## 2   Remarks on Floating-Point Arithmetic

Computing is usually done in the set of real numbers $\mathbb{R}$. The real numbers can be defined as a conditionally complete, linearly ordered field. Conditionally complete means that every bounded subset has an infimum and a supremum. Every conditionally ordered set can be completed by joining a least and a greatest element. In case of the real numbers these are called $-\infty$ and $+\infty$. Then $\mathbb{R}^* := \mathbb{R} \cup \{-\infty\} \cup \{+\infty\}$ is a complete lattice. We remark, however, that the elements $-\infty$ and $+\infty$ are not elements of the field. The cancellation law $a + c = b + c \Rightarrow a = b$, for instance, does not hold for $c = \infty$.

A real number consists of a sign, an integral part, and a fractional part, for instance: $\pm 345.789123 \cdots \in \mathbb{R}$. The point may be shifted to any other position if we compensate for this shifting by a corresponding power of $b$ (here $b = 10$). If the point is shifted immediately to the left of the first nonzero digit: $\pm 0.345789123 \cdots \cdot 10^3$ the representation is called normalized. Zero is the only real number that has no such representation. It needs a special encoding. Thus a normalized real number consists of a signed fractional part $m$ (mantissa) and an integer exponent $e$ and we have $0.1 \leq |m| < 1$.

Only subsets of these numbers can be represented on the computer. If the mantissa in truncated after the $l^{th}$ digit and the exponent is limited by $e_{min} < e < e_{max}$ one speaks of a floating-point number. Let $F$ denote the set of floating-point numbers and $F^* := F \cup \{-\infty\} \cup \{+\infty\}$.[1]

Arithmetic for floating-point numbers may cause exceptions. Well known such exceptions are underflow, overflow, division by zero, or invalid operation. To avoid interruption of program execution in case of an exception the so-called IEEE floating-point arithmetic standard provides additional elements and defines operations for these, for instance, $4/0 := \infty, -4/0 := -\infty, \infty - \infty := NaN, 0 \cdot \infty := NaN, \infty/\infty := NaN, 0/0 := NaN, 1/(-\infty) := -0, (-0.3)/\infty :=$

---

[1] A rounding maps the complete lattice $\mathbb{R}^*$ on the complete sublattice $F^*$. Both lattices coincide in the least and the greatest element, see [4].

$-0$. It should be clear, however, that $-\infty, +\infty, NaN, -0,$[2] or $+0$ with their operations are not elements of the real number field.

# 3   Arithmetic for Intervals of $I\!R$ and $I\!F$

Interval arithmetic is another arithmetic tool. It solely deals with sets of real numbers. Neither the exceptions of floating-point arithmetic mentioned above nor the measures to deal with them occur or are needed in interval arithmetic. The symbol $I\!R$ usually denotes the set of closed and bounded intervals of $I\!\!R$. Arithmetic in $I\!R$ can be interpreted as a systematic calculus to deal with inequalities. We assume here that the basic rules for arithmetic in $I\!R$ with zero not in the divisor are known to the reader. It is a fascinating result that, in contrast to floating-point arithmetic, interval arithmetic even on computers can be further developed into a well rounded, exception-free, closed calculus. We briefly sketch this development here.

In floating-point arithmetic the crucial operation that leads to the exceptional strategic objects mentioned above is division by zero. So we begin our study of extended interval arithmetic by defining division by an interval that contains zero.

The set $I\!R$ is a subset of the power set $I\!\!PR$ (which is the set of all subsets) of real numbers. For $A, B \in I\!\!PR$ arithmetic operations are defined by

$$\bigwedge_{A,B\in I\!\!PR} A \circ B := \{a \circ b \mid a \in A \land b \in B\}, \text{ for all } \circ \in \{+, -, \cdot, /\}. \qquad (3.1)$$

The following properties are obvious and immediate consequences of this definition:

$$A \subseteq B \land C \subseteq D \Rightarrow A \circ C \subseteq B \circ D, \text{ for all } A, B, C, D \in I\!\!PR, \qquad (3.2)$$

and in particular

$$a \in A \land b \in B \Rightarrow a \circ b \in A \circ B, \text{ for all } A, B \in I\!\!PR. \qquad (3.3)$$

Property (3.2) is called *inclusion-isotony* (or *inclusion-monotonicity*). Property (3.3) is called the *inclusion property*. (3.2) and (3.3) are the fundamental properties of interval arithmetic. Under the assumption $0 \notin B$ for division, the intervals of $I\!R$ are an algebraically closed subset[3] of the power set $I\!\!PR$, i.e., an operation for intervals of $I\!R$ performed in $I\!\!PR$ always delivers an interval of $I\!R$.

In real analysis division by zero is not defined. In contrast to this, in interval arithmetic division by an interval that contains zero can be defined in a strict mathematical manner. The result again is a set of real numbers.

---

[2] In $I\!\!R$, 0 is defined as the neutral element of addition. From the assumption that there are two such elements 0 and $0'$ it follows immediately that they are equal: $0 + 0' = 0 = 0'$.

[3] As are the integers of the real numbers for addition, subtraction, and multiplication.

In accordance with (3.1) division in $I\!R$ is defined by

$$\bigwedge_{A,B\in I\!R} A/B := \{a/b \mid a \in A \wedge b \in B\}, \text{ for } 0 \notin B. \tag{3.4}$$

The quotient $a/b$ is defined as the inverse operation of multiplication, i.e., as the solution of the equation $b \cdot x = a$. Thus (3.4) can be written in the form

$$\bigwedge_{A,B\in I\!R} A/B := \{x \mid bx = a \wedge a \in A \wedge b \in B\}. \tag{3.5}$$

For $0 \notin B$ (3.4) and (3.5) are equivalent. While in $I\!R$ division by zero is not defined, the representation of $A/B$ by (3.5) allows definition of the operation and also interpretation of the result for $0 \in B$.

By way of interpreting (3.5) for $A = [a_1, a_2]$ and $B = [b_1, b_2] \in I\!R$ with $0 \in B$ the following eight distinct cases can be set out:

1   $0 \in A,$      $0 \in B.$
2   $0 \notin A,$     $B = [0,0].$
3 $a_1 \leq a_2 < 0, b_1 < b_2 = 0.$
4 $a_1 \leq a_2 < 0, b_1 < 0 < b_2.$
5 $a_1 \leq a_2 < 0, 0 = b_1 < b_2.$
6 $0 < a_1 \leq a_2, b_1 < b_2 = 0.$
7 $0 < a_1 \leq a_2, b_1 < 0 < b_2.$
8 $0 < a_1 \leq a_2, 0 = b_1 < b_2.$

The list distinguishes the cases $0 \in A$ (case 1) and $0 \notin A$ (cases 2 to 8). Since it is generally assumed that $0 \in B$, these eight cases indeed cover all possibilities. Since every $x \in I\!R$ fulfills the equation $0 \cdot x = 0$ we obtain in case 1: $A/B = I\!R = (-\infty, +\infty)$. Here the parentheses indicate that the bounds are not included in the set. In case 2 the set defined by (3.5) consists of all elements which fulfill the equation $0 \cdot x = a$ for $a \in A$. Since $0 \notin A$, there is no real number which fulfills this equation. Thus $A/B$ is the empty set, i.e., $A/B = \varnothing$.

In all other cases $0 \notin A$ also. We have already observed under case 2 that the element 0 in $B$ does not contribute to the solution set. So it can be excluded without changing the set $A/B$.

So the general rule for computing the set $A/B$ by (3.5) is to remove its zero from the interval $B$ and replace it by a small positive or negative number $\epsilon$ as the case may be. The resulting set is denoted by $B'$ and represented in column 4 of Table 1. With this $B'$ the solution set $A/B'$ can now easily be computed by applying the rules for closed and bounded real intervals. The results are shown in column 5 of Table 1. Now the desired result $A/B$ as defined by (3.5) is obtained if in column 5 $\epsilon$ tends to zero.

Thus in the cases 3 to 8 the results are obtained by the limit process $A/B = \lim_{\epsilon \to 0} A/B'$. The solution set $A/B$ is shown in the last column of Table 1 for all the eight cases. There, as usual in mathematics, parentheses indicate that the bound is not included in the set. In contrast to this, brackets denote closed interval ends, i.e., the bound is included.

**Table 1.** The eight cases of interval division $A/B$, with $A, B \in I\!R$, and $0 \in B$

| case | $A = [a_1, a_2]$ | $B = [b_1, b_2]$ | $B'$ | $A/B'$ | $A/B$ |
|------|------|------|------|------|------|
| 1 | $0 \in A$ | $0 \in B$ | | | $(-\infty, +\infty)$ |
| 2 | $0 \notin A$ | $B = [0, 0]$ | | | $\varnothing$ |
| 3 | $a_2 < 0$ | $b_1 < b_2 = 0$ | $[b_1, (-\epsilon)]$ | $[a_2/b_1, a_1/(-\epsilon)]$ | $[a_2/b_1, +\infty)$ |
| 4 | $a_2 < 0$ | $b_1 < 0 < b_2$ | $[b_1, (-\epsilon)]$ | $[a_2/b_1, a_1/(-\epsilon)]$ | $(-\infty, a_2/b_2]$ |
| | | | $\cup\ [\epsilon, b_2]$ | $\cup\ [a_1/\epsilon, a_2/b_2]$ | $\cup\ [a_2/b_1, +\infty)$ |
| 5 | $a_2 < 0$ | $0 = b_1 < b_2$ | $[\epsilon, b_2]$ | $[a_1/\epsilon, a_2/b_2]$ | $(-\infty, a_2/b_2]$ |
| 6 | $a_1 > 0$ | $b_1 < b_2 = 0$ | $[b_1, (-\epsilon)]$ | $[a_2/(-\epsilon), a_1/b_1]$ | $(-\infty, a_1/b_1]$ |
| 7 | $a_1 > 0$ | $b_1 < 0 < b_2$ | $[b_1, (-\epsilon)]$ | $[a_2/(-\epsilon), a_1/b_1]$ | $(-\infty, a_1/b_1]$ |
| | | | $\cup\ [\epsilon, b_2]$ | $\cup\ [a_1/b_2, a_2/\epsilon]$ | $\cup\ [a_1/b_2, +\infty)$ |
| 8 | $a_1 > 0$ | $0 = b_1 < b_2$ | $[\epsilon, b_2]$ | $[a_1/b_2, a_2/\epsilon]$ | $[a_1/b_2, +\infty)$ |

The operands $A$ and $B$ of the division $A/B$ in Table 1 are intervals of $I\!R$. The results of the division shown in the last column, however, are no longer intervals of $I\!R$. The result is now an element of the power set $I\!P\!R$. With the exception of case 2 the result is now a set which stretches continuously to $-\infty$ or $+\infty$ or both.

In two cases (rows 4 and 7 in Table 1) the result consists of the union of two distinct sets of the form $(-\infty, c_2] \cup [c_1, +\infty)$. These cases can easily be identified by the signs of the bounds of the divisor before the division is executed. For interval multiplication and division a case selection has to be done before the operations are performed anyhow, see [3]. In the two cases (rows 4 and 7 in Table 1) the sign of $b_1$ is negative and the sign of $b_2$ is positive.

A basic concept of mathematics is that of a function or mapping. A function consists of a pair $(f, D_f)$. It maps each element $x$ of its domain of definition $D_f$ on a unique element $y$ of the range $R_f$ of $f$, $f : D_f \rightarrow R_f$.

In real analysis division by zero is not defined. Thus a rational function $y = f(x)$ where the denominator is zero for $x = c$ is not defined for $x = c$, i.e., $c$ is not an element of the domain of definition $D_f$. Since the function $f(x)$ is not defined at $x = c$ it does not have any value or property there. In this strict mathematical sense, division by an interval $[b_1, b_2]$ with $b_1 < 0 < b_2$ is not well posed. For division the set $b_1 < 0 < b_2$ devolves into the two distinct sets $[b_1, 0)^4$ and $(0, b_2]$ and division by the set $b_1 < 0 < b_2$ actually means two divisions. The result of the two divisions consists of the two distinct sets shown in rows 4 and 7 of Table 1. It is highly desirable to perform the two divisions sequentially. Then the two cases (rows 4 and 7) of Table 1 where an operation delivers two distinct results can be eliminated. This simplifies Table 1 considerably. Division by the two sets $[b_1, 0]$ and $[0, b_2]$ is nevertheless defined in Table 1. In these cases only one division has to be performed. The result is a single extended interval. The six remaining cases are shown in Table 2.

---

[4] Since division by zero does not contribute to the solution set it does not matter whether a paranthesis or bracket is used here.

**Table 2.** The six cases of interval division with $A, B \in I\mathbb{R}$, and $0 \in B$

| case | $A = [a_1, a_2]$ | $B = [b_1, b_2]$ | $A/B$ |
|------|------------------|------------------|-------|
| 1 | $0 \in A$ | $0 \in B$ | $(-\infty, +\infty)$ |
| 2 | $0 \notin A$ | $B = [0, 0]$ | $\varnothing$ |
| 3 | $a_2 < 0$ | $b_1 < b_2 = 0$ | $[a_2/b_1, +\infty)$ |
| 4 | $a_2 < 0$ | $0 = b_1 < b_2$ | $(-\infty, a_2/b_2]$ |
| 5 | $a_1 > 0$ | $b_1 < b_2 = 0$ | $(-\infty, a_1/b_1]$ |
| 6 | $a_1 > 0$ | $0 = b_1 < b_2$ | $[a_1/b_2, +\infty)$ |

Thus only four kinds of result come from division by an interval of $I\mathbb{R}$ which contains zero:

$$\varnothing, \quad (-\infty, a], \quad [b, +\infty), \quad \text{and} \quad (-\infty, +\infty). \tag{3.6}$$

We call such elements extended intervals. The union of the set of closed and bounded intervals of $I\mathbb{R}$ with the set of extended intervals is denoted by $(I\mathbb{R})$. The elements of the set $(I\mathbb{R})$ are themselves simply called intervals. $(I\mathbb{R})$ is the set of closed intervals of $\mathbb{R}$. (A subset of $\mathbb{R}$ is called closed if its complement is open.)

Intervals of $I\mathbb{R}$ and of $(I\mathbb{R})$ are sets of real numbers. $-\infty$ and $+\infty$ are not elements of these intervals. It is fascinating that arithmetic operations can be introduced for all elements of the set $(I\mathbb{R})$ in an exception-free manner. This will be shown in the next section.

On a computer only subsets of the real numbers are representable. We assume now that $F$ is the set of floating-point numbers of a given computer. On the computer, arithmetic in $I\mathbb{R}$ is approximated by an arithmetic in $IF$. $IF$ is the set of closed and bounded intervals with bounds of $F$. An interval of $IF$ represents the continuous set of real numbers between the floating-point bounds. Arithmetic operations in $IF$ are defined by those in $I\mathbb{R}$ by rounding the result in $I\mathbb{R}$ on the least upper bound in $IF$ with respect to set inclusion as an order relation.

To transform the six cases of division by an interval of $I\mathbb{R}$ which contains zero into computer executable operations we assume now that the operands $A$ and $B$ are floating-point intervals of $IF$. To obtain a computer representable result we round the result shown in the last column of Table 2 into the least computer representable superset. For finite bounds that is, the lower bound of the result has to be computed with rounding downwards and the upper bound with rounding upwards. Thus on the computer the six cases of division by an interval of $IF$ which contains zero have to be performed as shown in Table 3.

Table 4 shows the same cases as Table 3 in another layout.

Table 3 and Table 4 display the six distinct cases of interval division $A \lozenge B$ with $A, B \in IF$ and $0 \in B$. On the computer the empty interval $\varnothing$ needs a special encoding. We explicitly stress that the symbols $-\infty$, $+\infty$ are used here only to represent the resulting sets. These symbols are not elements of these sets.

**Table 3.** The six cases of interval division with $A, B \in IF$, and $0 \in B$

| case | $A = [a_1, a_2]$ | $B = [b_1, b_2]$ | $A \Diamond B$ |
|------|------------------|------------------|----------------|
| 1 | $0 \in A$ | $0 \in B$ | $(-\infty, +\infty)$ |
| 2 | $0 \notin A$ | $B = [0, 0]$ | $\varnothing$ |
| 3 | $a_2 < 0$ | $b_1 < b_2 = 0$ | $[a_2 \mathbin{\underline{\nabla}} b_1, +\infty)$ |
| 4 | $a_2 < 0$ | $0 = b_1 < b_2$ | $(-\infty, a_2 \mathbin{\triangle} b_2]$ |
| 5 | $a_1 > 0$ | $b_1 < b_2 = 0$ | $(-\infty, a_1 \mathbin{\triangle} b_1]$ |
| 6 | $a_1 > 0$ | $0 = b_1 < b_2$ | $[a_1 \mathbin{\underline{\nabla}} b_2, +\infty)$ |

In Table 3 and Table 4 and in the following an operator symbol with a $\nabla$ upon it means an operation performed with rounding downward. Correspondingly an operation with a $\triangle$ upon it means an operation performed with rounding upward.

Table 3 and Table 4 show that division by an interval of $IF$ which contains zero on the computer also leads to extended intervals as shown in (3.6) with $a, b \in F$. The union of the set of closed and bounded intervals of $IF$ with such extended intervals is denoted by $(IF)$. $(IF)$ is the set of closed intervals of real numbers where all finite bounds are elements of $F$. Except for the empty set, extended intervals also represent continuous sets of real numbers.

Table 2 originated from Table 1 by elimination of rows 4 and 7. Division by an interval $[b_1, b_2]$ with $b_1 < 0 < b_2$ actually consists of two divisions by the distinct sets $[b_1, 0)$ and $(0, b_2]$ the result of which again consists of two distinct sets.

In the user's program, however, the two divisions appear as one single operation, as division by an interval $[b_1, b_2]$ with $b_1 < 0 < b_2$. So an arithmetic operation in the user's program delivers two distinct results. This is a totally new situation in computing. But computing certainly is able to cope with this situation.

A solution to the problem would be for the computer to provide a flag for *distinct intervals*. The situation occurs if the divisor is an interval that contains zero as an interior point. In this case the flag would be raised and signaled to the user. The user may then apply a routine of his choice to deal with the situation as is appropriate for his application.[5]

Newton's method reaches its ultimate elegance and strength in the extended interval Newton method. It computes all (single) zeros in a given domain. If a

---

[5] This routine could be: modify the operands and recompute, or continue the computation with one of the sets and ignore the other one, or put one of the sets on a list and continue the computation with the other one, or return the entire set of real numbers $(-\infty, +\infty)$ as result and continue the computation, or stop computing, or any other action.

A somewhat natural solution would be to continue the computation on different processors, one for each interval. But the situation can occur repeatedly. How many processors would we need? Future multicore units will provide a large number of processors. They will suffice for quite a while. A similar situation occurs in global optimization using subdivision. After a certain test several candidates may be left for further investigation.

**Table 4.** The result of the interval division with $A, B \in IF$, and $0 \in B$

|  | $B = [0,0]$ | $b_1 < b_2 = 0$ | $0 = b_1 < b_2$ |
|---|---|---|---|
| $a_2 < 0$ | $\varnothing$ | $[a_2 \triangledown b_1, +\infty)$ | $(-\infty, a_2 \triangle b_2]$ |
| $a_1 \leq 0 \leq a_2$ | $(-\infty, +\infty)$ | $(-\infty, +\infty)$ | $(-\infty, +\infty)$ |
| $0 < a_1$ | $\varnothing$ | $(-\infty, a_1 \triangle b_1]$ | $[a_1 \triangledown b_2, +\infty)$ |

function has several zeros in a given interval its derivative becomes zero in that interval also. Thus Newton's method applied to that interval delivers two distinct sets. This is how the extended interval Newton method separates different zeros from each other. If the method is continued along two separate paths, one for each of the distinct intervals it finally computes all zeros in the given domain. If the method continues with only one of the two distinct sets and ignores the other one it computes an enclosure of only one zero of the given function. If the interval Newton method delivers the empty set, the method has proved that there is no zero in the initial interval.

## 4   Arithmetic for Intervals of $(I\mathbb{R})$ and $(IF)$

For the sake of completeness, arithmetic operations now have to be defined for all elements of $(I\mathbb{R})$ and $(IF)$. Since the development of arithmetic operations follows an identical pattern in $(I\mathbb{R})$ and $(IF)$, we skip here the introduction of the arithmetic in $(I\mathbb{R})$ and restrict the consideration to the development of arithmetic in $(IF)$. This is the arithmetic that has to be provided on the computer.

First of all any operation with the empty set is again defined to be the empty set.

The general procedure for defining all other operations follows a continuity principle. Bounds like $-\infty$ and $+\infty$ in the operands $A$ and $B$ are replaced by a very large negative number $(-\Omega)$ and a very large positive number $(+\Omega)$ respectively. Then the basic rules for the arithmetic operations in $I\mathbb{R}$ and $IF$ are applied. In the following tables these rules are repeated and printed in bold letters. In the resulting formulas a very large negative number is then shifted to $-\infty$ and a very large positive number to $+\infty$.

As a short cut for obtaining the resulting rules very simple and well established rules of real analysis like $\infty * x = \infty$ for $x > 0$, $\infty * x = -\infty$ for $x < 0$, $x/\infty = x/ -\infty = 0$, $\infty * \infty = \infty$, $(-\infty) * \infty = -\infty$ can be applied together with variants obtained by applying the sign rules and the law of commutativity.

Two situations have to be treated separately. These are the cases shown in rows 1 and 2 of Table 1.

If $0 \in A$ and $0 \in B$ (row 1 of Table 1), the result consists of all the real numbers, i.e., $A/B = (-\infty, +\infty)$. This applies to rows 2, 5, 6 and 8 of Table 9.

If $0 \notin A$ and $B = [0,0]$ (row 2 of Table 1), the result of the division is the empty set, i.e., $A/B = \varnothing$. This applies to rows 1, 3, 4 and 7 of column 1 of Table 9.

We outline the complete set of arithmetic operations for interval arithmetic in $(IF)$ that should be provided on the computer in the next section. In summary it can be said that after splitting an interval $[b_1, b_2]$ with $b_1 < 0 < b_2$ into two distinct intervals $[b_1, 0)$ and $(0, b_2]$ the result of arithmetic operations for intervals of $(IF)$ always leads to intervals of $(IF)$ again. The reader should prove this assertion by referring to the operations shown in the tables of the following section.

For the development in the preceding sections it was essential to distinguish between parentheses and brackets. If a bound is adjacent to a parenthesis, the bound is not included in the interval; if a bound is adjacent to a bracket, the bound is included in the interval.

In the following tables an operator symbol with a $\triangledown$ upon it means an operation performed with rounding downward. Correspondingly an operation with a $\triangle$ upon it means an operation performed with rounding upward.

If during a computation in the real number field zero appears as a divisor the computation should be stopped immediately. In floating-point arithmetic the situation is different. Zero may be the result of an underflow. In such a case a corresponding interval computation would not deliver zero but a small interval with zero as one bound and a tiny positive or negative number as the other bound. In this case division is well defined by Table 1. The result is a closed interval which stretches continuously to $-\infty$ or $+\infty$ as the case may be.

From a theoretical point of view a note about the interval sets used in this paper and their relationships may be of interest. Basic to all considerations is the power set $\{P\!I\!R, \subseteq\}$. It is a complete lattice. The least element is the empty set $\varnothing$ and the greatest element is the set $I\!R = (-\infty, +\infty)$. The set $\{(I\!I\!R), \subseteq\}$ is an upper screen (a complete inf-subnet) of $\{P\!I\!R, \subseteq\}$. The set $\{(IF), \subseteq\}$ is a screen (a complete sublattice) of $\{(I\!I\!R), \subseteq\}$, see [4]. The sets $\{P\!I\!R, \subseteq\}$, $\{(I\!I\!R), \subseteq\}$, and $\{(IF), \subseteq\}$ have the same least and greatest element. With respect to set inclusion as an order relation upwardly directed roundings between the sets $P\!I\!R$ and $(I\!I\!R)$, and the sets $(I\!I\!R)$ and $(IF)$ are used to define arithmetic operations in $(I\!I\!R)$ and $(IF)$ via semimorphism. We briefly mention these properties here.

With the monotone upwardly directed roundings $\square : P\!I\!R \to (I\!I\!R)$ and $\diamondsuit : (I\!I\!R) \to (IF)$ arithmetic in $(I\!I\!R)$ and in $(IF)$ is uniquely defined by the following properties :

**(RG)** $A \;\boxdot\; B := \square\,(A \circ B)$, for all $A, B \in (I\!I\!R)$ and all $\circ \in \{+, -, \cdot, /\}$.

**(R1)** $\square\, A = A$, for all $A \in (I\!I\!R)$,
**(R2)** $A \subseteq B \Rightarrow \square\, A \subseteq \square\, B$, for $A, B \in P\!I\!R$,
**(R3)** $A \subseteq \square\, A$, for all $A \in P\!I\!R$.

**(RG)** $A \;\diamondsuit\; B := \diamondsuit\,(A \;\boxdot\; B)$, for all $A, B \in (IF)$ and all $\circ \in \{+, -, \cdot, /\}$.

**(R1)** $\diamondsuit\, A = A$, for all $A \in (IF)$,

**(R2)** $A \subseteq B \Rightarrow \diamondsuit A \subseteq \diamondsuit B$, for $A, B \in (I\!I\!R)$,
**(R3)** $A \subseteq \diamondsuit A$, for all $A \in (I\!I\!R)$.

The resulting calculi are free of exceptions. The proof of this assertion is given by the formulas in the following section.

## 5   Complete Arithmetic for Intervals of $(IF)$

The rules for the operations of extended intervals on the computer in Tables 5—9 look rather complicated. Their implementation seems to require many case distinctions. The situation, however, can be greatly simplified as follows.

On the computer actually only the basic rules for addition, subtraction, multiplication, and division for closed and bounded intervals of $IF$ including division by an interval that includes zero need to be provided. In Tables 5—9 these rules are printed in bold letters.

The remaining rules shown in the tables can automatically be produced out of these basic rules by the computer itself if a few well established rules for computing with $-\infty$ and $+\infty$ are formally applied. With $x \in F$ these rules are

$$\infty + x = \infty, \qquad\qquad -\infty + x = -\infty,$$
$$-\infty + (-\infty) = (-\infty) \cdot \infty = -\infty, \quad \infty + \infty = \infty \cdot \infty = \infty,$$
$$\infty \cdot x = \infty \text{ for } x > 0, \qquad \infty \cdot x = -\infty \text{ for } x < 0,$$
$$\frac{x}{\infty} = \frac{x}{-\infty} = 0,$$

together with variants obtained by applying the sign rules and the law of commutativity.

If in an interval operand a bound is $-\infty$ or $+\infty$ the multiplication with 0 is performed as if the following rules would hold

$$0 \cdot (-\infty) = 0 \cdot (+\infty) = (-\infty) \cdot 0 = (+\infty) \cdot 0 = 0. \qquad (5.1)$$

**Table 5.** Addition of extended intervals on the computer

| Addition | $(-\infty, b_2]$ | $[b_1, b_2]$ | $[b_1, +\infty)$ | $(-\infty, +\infty)$ |
|---|---|---|---|---|
| $(-\infty, a_2]$ | $(-\infty, a_2 \mathbin{\triangle} b_2]$ | $(-\infty, a_2 \mathbin{\triangle} b_2]$ | $(-\infty, +\infty)$ | $(-\infty, +\infty)$ |
| $[a_1, a_2]$ | $(-\infty, a_2 \mathbin{\triangle} b_2]$ | $[a_1 \mathbin{\triangledown} b_1, a_2 \mathbin{\triangle} b_2]$ | $[a_1 \mathbin{\triangledown} b_1, +\infty)$ | $(-\infty, +\infty)$ |
| $[a_1, +\infty)$ | $(-\infty, +\infty)$ | $[a_1 \mathbin{\triangledown} b_1, +\infty)$ | $[a_1 \mathbin{\triangledown} b_1, +\infty)$ | $(-\infty, +\infty)$ |
| $(-\infty, +\infty)$ | $(-\infty, +\infty)$ | $(-\infty, +\infty)$ | $(-\infty, +\infty)$ | $(-\infty, +\infty)$ |

**Table 6.** Subtraction of extended intervals on the computer

| Subtraction | $(-\infty, b_2]$ | $[b_1, b_2]$ | $[b_1, +\infty)$ | $(-\infty, +\infty)$ |
|---|---|---|---|---|
| $(-\infty, a_2]$ | $(-\infty, +\infty)$ | $(-\infty, a_2 \mathbin{\triangle} b_1]$ | $(-\infty, a_2 \mathbin{\triangle} b_1]$ | $(-\infty, +\infty)$ |
| $[a_1, a_2]$ | $[a_1 \mathbin{\triangledown} b_2, +\infty)$ | $[a_1 \mathbin{\triangledown} b_2, a_2 \mathbin{\triangle} b_1]$ | $(-\infty, a_2 \mathbin{\triangle} b_1]$ | $(-\infty, +\infty)$ |
| $[a_1, +\infty)$ | $[a_1 \mathbin{\triangledown} b_2, +\infty)$ | $[a_1 \mathbin{\triangledown} b_2, +\infty)$ | $(-\infty, +\infty)$ | $(-\infty, +\infty)$ |
| $(-\infty, +\infty)$ | $(-\infty, +\infty)$ | $(-\infty, +\infty)$ | $(-\infty, +\infty)$ | $(-\infty, +\infty)$ |

**Table 7.** Multiplication of extended intervals on the computer

| Multiplication | $[b_1,b_2]$ $b_2\leq0$ | $[b_1,b_2]$ $b_1<0<b_2$ | $[b_1,b_2]$ $b_1\geq0$ | $[0,0]$ | $(-\infty,b_2]$ $b_2\leq0$ | $(-\infty,b_2]$ $b_2\geq0$ | $[b_1,+\infty)$ $b_1\leq0$ | $[b_1,+\infty)$ $b_1\geq0$ | $(-\infty,+\infty)$ |
|---|---|---|---|---|---|---|---|---|---|
| $[a_1,a_2], a_2\leq0$ | $[a_2\triangledown b_2, a_1\triangle b_1]$ | $[a_1\triangledown b_2, a_1\triangle b_1]$ | $[a_1\triangledown b_2, a_2\triangle b_1]$ | $[0,0]$ | $[a_2\triangledown b_2,+\infty)$ | $[a_1\triangledown b_2,+\infty)$ | $(-\infty, a_1\triangle b_1]$ | $(-\infty, a_2\triangle b_1]$ | $(-\infty,+\infty)$ |
| $a_1<0<a_2$ | $[a_2\triangledown b_1, a_1\triangle b_1]$ | $[\min(a_1\triangledown b_2, a_2\triangledown b_1),\ \max(a_1\triangle b_1, a_2\triangle b_2)]$ | $[a_1\triangledown b_2, a_2\triangle b_2]$ | $[0,0]$ | $(-\infty,+\infty)$ | $(-\infty,+\infty)$ | $(-\infty,+\infty)$ | $(-\infty,+\infty)$ | $(-\infty,+\infty)$ |
| $[a_1,a_2], a_1\geq0$ | $[a_2\triangledown b_1, a_1\triangle b_2]$ | $[a_2\triangledown b_1, a_2\triangle b_2]$ | $[a_1\triangledown b_1, a_2\triangle b_2]$ | $[0,0]$ | $(-\infty, a_1\triangle b_2]$ | $(-\infty, a_2\triangle b_2]$ | $[a_2\triangledown b_1,+\infty)$ | $[a_1\triangledown b_1,+\infty)$ | $(-\infty,+\infty)$ |
| $[0,0]$ | $[0,0]$ | $[0,0]$ | $[0,0]$ | $[0,0]$ | $[0,0]$ | $[0,0]$ | $[0,0]$ | $[0,0]$ | $[0,0]$ |
| $(-\infty,a_2], a_2\leq0$ | $[a_2\triangledown b_2,+\infty)$ | $(-\infty,+\infty)$ | $(-\infty, a_2\triangle b_1]$ | $[0,0]$ | $[a_2\triangledown b_2,+\infty)$ | $(-\infty,+\infty)$ | $(-\infty,+\infty)$ | $(-\infty, a_2\triangle b_1]$ | $(-\infty,+\infty)$ |
| $(-\infty,a_2], a_2\geq0$ | $[a_2\triangledown b_1,+\infty)$ | $(-\infty,+\infty)$ | $(-\infty, a_2\triangle b_2]$ | $[0,0]$ | $(-\infty,+\infty)$ | $(-\infty,+\infty)$ | $(-\infty,+\infty)$ | $(-\infty,+\infty)$ | $(-\infty,+\infty)$ |
| $[a_1,+\infty), a_1\leq0$ | $(-\infty, a_1\triangle b_1]$ | $(-\infty,+\infty)$ | $[a_1\triangledown b_2,+\infty)$ | $[0,0]$ | $(-\infty,+\infty)$ | $(-\infty,+\infty)$ | $(-\infty,+\infty)$ | $(-\infty,+\infty)$ | $(-\infty,+\infty)$ |
| $[a_1,+\infty), a_1\geq0$ | $(-\infty, a_1\triangle b_2]$ | $(-\infty,+\infty)$ | $[a_1\triangledown b_1,+\infty)$ | $[0,0]$ | $(-\infty, a_1\triangle b_2]$ | $(-\infty,+\infty)$ | $(-\infty,+\infty)$ | $[a_1\triangledown b_1,+\infty)$ | $(-\infty,+\infty)$ |
| $(-\infty,+\infty)$ | $(-\infty,+\infty)$ | $(-\infty,+\infty)$ | $(-\infty,+\infty)$ | $[0,0]$ | $(-\infty,+\infty)$ | $(-\infty,+\infty)$ | $(-\infty,+\infty)$ | $(-\infty,+\infty)$ | $(-\infty,+\infty)$ |

**Table 8.** Division of extended intervals with $0 \notin B$ on the computer

| Division $0 \notin B$ | $[b_1, b_2]$ $b_2 < 0$ | $[b_1, b_2]$ $b_1 > 0$ | $(-\infty, b_2]$ $b_2 < 0$ | $[b_1, +\infty)$ $b_1 > 0$ |
|---|---|---|---|---|
| $[a_1, a_2], a_2 \leq 0$ | $[a_2 \triangledown b_1, a_1 \triangle b_2]$ | $[a_1 \triangledown b_1, a_2 \triangle b_2]$ | $[0, a_1 \triangle b_2]$ | $[a_1 \triangledown b_1, 0]$ |
| $[a_1, a_2], a_1 < 0 < a_2$ | $[a_2 \triangledown b_2, a_1 \triangle b_2]$ | $[a_1 \triangledown b_1, a_2 \triangle b_1]$ | $[a_2 \triangledown b_2, a_1 \triangle b_2]$ | $[a_1 \triangledown b_1, a_2 \triangle b_1]$ |
| $[a_1, a_2], a_1 \geq 0$ | $[a_2 \triangledown b_2, a_1 \triangle b_1]$ | $[a_1 \triangledown b_2, a_2 \triangle b_1]$ | $[a_2 \triangledown b_2, 0]$ | $[0, a_2 \triangle b_1]$ |
| $[0,0]$ | $[0,0]$ | $[0,0]$ | $[0,0]$ | $[0,0]$ |
| $(-\infty, a_2], a_2 \leq 0$ | $[a_2 \triangledown b_1, +\infty)$ | $(-\infty, a_2 \triangle b_2]$ | $[0, +\infty)$ | $(-\infty, 0]$ |
| $(-\infty, a_2], a_2 \geq 0$ | $[a_2 \triangledown b_2, +\infty)$ | $(-\infty, a_2 \triangle b_1]$ | $[a_2 \triangledown b_2, +\infty)$ | $(-\infty, a_2 \triangle b_1]$ |
| $[a_1, +\infty), a_1 \leq 0$ | $(-\infty, a_1 \triangle b_2]$ | $[a_1 \triangledown b_1, +\infty)$ | $(-\infty, a_1 \triangle b_2]$ | $[a_1 \triangledown b_1, +\infty)$ |
| $[a_1, +\infty), a_1 \geq 0$ | $(-\infty, a_1 \triangle b_1]$ | $[a_1 \triangledown b_2, +\infty)$ | $(-\infty, 0]$ | $[0, +\infty)$ |
| $(-\infty, +\infty)$ | $(-\infty, +\infty)$ | $(-\infty, +\infty)$ | $(-\infty, +\infty)$ | $(-\infty, +\infty)$ |

**Table 9.** Division of extended intervals with $0 \in B$ on the computer

| Division $0 \in B$ | $B =$ $[0,0]$ | $[b_1,b_2]$ $b_1 < b_2 = 0$ | $[b_1,b_2]$ $0 = b_1 < b_2$ | $(-\infty,b_2]$ $b_2 = 0$ | $[b_1,+\infty)$ $b_1 = 0$ |
|---|---|---|---|---|---|
| $[a_1,a_2], a_2 < 0$ | $\emptyset$ | $[a_2 \triangledown b_1, +\infty)$ | $(-\infty, a_2 \triangle b_2]$ | $[0,+\infty)$ | $(-\infty,0]$ |
| $[a_1,a_2], a_1 \leq 0 \leq a_2$ | $(-\infty,+\infty)$ | $(-\infty,+\infty)$ | $(-\infty,+\infty)$ | $(-\infty,+\infty)$ | $(-\infty,+\infty)$ |
| $[a_1,a_2], a_1 > 0$ | $\emptyset$ | $(-\infty, a_1 \triangle b_1]$ | $[a_1 \triangledown b_2, +\infty)$ | $(-\infty,0]$ | $[0,+\infty)$ |
| $(-\infty,a_2], a_2 < 0$ | $\emptyset$ | $[a_2 \triangledown b_1, +\infty)$ | $(-\infty, a_2 \triangle b_2]$ | $[0,+\infty)$ | $(-\infty,0]$ |
| $(-\infty,a_2], a_2 > 0$ | $(-\infty,+\infty)$ | $(-\infty,+\infty)$ | $(-\infty,+\infty)$ | $(-\infty,+\infty)$ | $(-\infty,+\infty)$ |
| $[a_1,+\infty), a_1 < 0$ | $(-\infty,+\infty)$ | $(-\infty,+\infty)$ | $(-\infty,+\infty)$ | $(-\infty,+\infty)$ | $(-\infty,+\infty)$ |
| $[a_1,+\infty), a_1 > 0$ | $\emptyset$ | $(-\infty, a_1 \triangle b_1]$ | $[a_1 \triangledown b_2, +\infty)$ | $(-\infty,0]$ | $[0,+\infty)$ |
| $(-\infty,+\infty)$ | $(-\infty,+\infty)$ | $(-\infty,+\infty)$ | $(-\infty,+\infty)$ | $(-\infty,+\infty)$ | $(-\infty,+\infty)$ |

These rules have no meaning otherwise.

We stress that (5.1) does not define new rules for the multiplication of 0 with $+\infty$ or $-\infty$. It just describes a short cut for applying the continuity principle mentioned earlier in this section.

# 6    An Alternative Approach

In two cases (rows 4 and 7) in Table 1 the result consists of the union of two distinct sets. In these two cases zero is an interior point of the divisor. In Section 3 we recommended splitting the interval $[b_1, b_2]$ with $b_1 < 0 < b_2$ into two distinct sets $[b_1, 0)$ and $(0, b_2]$ and performing the division sequentially. The result then consists of the two distinct sets $(-\infty, c_2]$ and $[c_1, +\infty)$.

This is not the usual way the division is performed in the literature. In the user's program division by an interval $[b_1, b_2]$ with $b_1 < 0 < b_2$ appears as one single operation. The division, therefore, is done at once. With existing processors only one interval can be delivered as the result of an interval operation. On the computer, therefore, the result is returned as an improper interval $[c_1, c_2]$ where the left hand bound is higher than the right hand bound $c_1 > c_2$.

This raises the question of whether arithmetic operations for improper intervals should be defined. This is not recommended. The situation can occur repeatedly. Zero can again be an interior point of one of the distinct intervals. The result of division would then consist of the union of three distinct sets and so on.

In the literature an improper interval $[c_1, c_2]$ with $c_1 > c_2$ occasionally is called an 'exterior interval'. On the number circle an 'exterior interval' is interpreted as an interval with infinity as an interior point. We do not follow this line here. Interval arithmetic is defined as an arithmetic for sets of real numbers. Operations for real numbers which deliver $\infty$ as their result do not exist. Here and in the following the symbols $-\infty$ and $+\infty$ are only used to describe sets of real numbers.

Independently of whether division by an interval $[b_1, b_2]$ with $b_1 < 0 < b_2$ is performed at once or sequentially in two steps the result consists of two distinct sets. Also, in our interpretation an improper interval describes the two distinct sets $(-\infty, c_2]$ and $[c_1, +\infty)$. In any case the flag that the result consists of two *distinct intervals* should be raised and signaled to the user. The user may then take measures to deal with the situation as is appropriate for his application.

# 7    Realization of Complete Interval Arithmetic on the Computer

For completeness we summarize in this section the formulas or rules that should be used to realize Complete Interval Arithmetic on the computer. These are the rules that should be required by an interval arithmetic standard.

Basic for all interval computations on the computer are the rules for addition, subtraction, multiplication and division including division by an interval that contains zero for closed and bounded intervals of $IF$:

**Addition**    $[a_1, a_2] + [b_1, b_2] = [a_1 \;\triangledown\; b_1, a_2 \;\triangle\; b_2].$

**Subtraction**    $[a_1, a_2] - [b_1, b_2] = [a_1 \;\triangledown\; b_2, a_2 \;\triangle\; b_1].$

| **Multiplication** | $[b_1, b_2]$ $b_2 \leq 0$ | $[b_1, b_2]$ $b_1 < 0 < b_2$ | $[b_1, b_2]$ $b_1 \geq 0$ |
|---|---|---|---|
| $[a_1, a_2], a_2 \leq 0$ | $[a_2 \triangledown b_2, a_1 \triangle b_1]$ | $[a_1 \triangledown b_2, a_1 \triangle b_1]$ | $[a_1 \triangledown b_2, a_2 \triangle b_1]$ |
| $a_1 < 0 < a_2$ | $[a_2 \triangledown b_1, a_1 \triangle b_1]$ | $[min(a_1 \triangledown b_2, a_2 \triangledown b_1),$ $max(a_1 \triangle b_1, a_2 \triangle b_2)]$ | $[a_1 \triangledown b_2, a_2 \triangle b_2]$ |
| $[a_1, a_2], a_1 \geq 0$ | $[a_2 \triangledown b_1, a_1 \triangle b_2]$ | $[a_2 \triangledown b_1, a_2 \triangle b_2]$ | $[a_1 \triangledown b_1, a_2 \triangle b_2]$ |

| **Division** $0 \notin B$ | $[b_1, b_2]$ $b_2 < 0$ | $[b_1, b_2]$ $b_1 > 0$ |
|---|---|---|
| $[a_1, a_2], a_2 \leq 0$ | $[a_2 \triangledown b_1, a_1 \triangle b_2]$ | $[a_1 \triangledown b_1, a_2 \triangle b_2]$ |
| $[a_1, a_2], a_1 < 0 < a_2$ | $[a_2 \triangledown b_2, a_1 \triangle b_2]$ | $[a_1 \triangledown b_1, a_2 \triangle b_1]$ |
| $[a_1, a_2], a_1 \geq 0$ | $[a_2 \triangledown b_2, a_1 \triangle b_1]$ | $[a_1 \triangledown b_2, a_2 \triangle b_1]$ |

| **Division** $0 \in B$ | $B =$ $[0,0]$ | $[b_1, b_2]$ $b_1 < b_2 = 0$ | $[b_1, b_2]$ $0 = b_1 < b_2$ |
|---|---|---|---|
| $[a_1, a_2], a_2 < 0$ | $\varnothing$ | $[a_2 \triangledown b_1, +\infty)$ | $(-\infty, a_2 \triangle b_2]$ |
| $[a_1, a_2], a_1 \leq 0 \leq a_2$ | $(-\infty, +\infty)$ | $(-\infty, +\infty)$ | $(-\infty, +\infty)$ |
| $[a_1, a_2], a_1 > 0$ | $\varnothing$ | $(-\infty, a_1 \triangle b_1]$ | $[a_1 \triangledown b_2, +\infty)$ |

A design for a hardware unit that realizes these operations is given in [3]. With it interval arithmetic would be about as fast as simple floating-point arithmetic.

Division by an interval that includes zero leads to extended intervals. Arithmetic operations for extended intervals of $(IF)$ can be performed on the computer if in addition a few formal rules for operations with $+\infty$ and $-\infty$ are applied in the computer. These rules are shown in the following tables.

Any operation with the empty set has the empty set as its result.

| **Addition** | $-\infty$ | $b$ | $+\infty$ |
|---|---|---|---|
| $-\infty$ | $-\infty$ | $-\infty$ | $-$ |
| $a$ | $-\infty$ | $-$ | $+\infty$ |
| $+\infty$ | $-$ | $+\infty$ | $+\infty$ |

| **Subtraction** | $-\infty$ | $b$ | $+\infty$ |
|---|---|---|---|
| $-\infty$ | $-$ | $-\infty$ | $-\infty$ |
| $a$ | $+\infty$ | $-$ | $-\infty$ |
| $+\infty$ | $+\infty$ | $+\infty$ | $-$ |

| **Multiplication** | $-\infty$ | $b < 0$ | $0$ | $b > 0$ | $+\infty$ |
|---|---|---|---|---|---|
| $-\infty$ | $+\infty$ | $+\infty$ | $0$ | $-\infty$ | $-\infty$ |
| $a < 0$ | $+\infty$ | $-$ | $-$ | $-$ | $-\infty$ |
| $0$ | $0$ | $-$ | $-$ | $-$ | $0$ |
| $a > 0$ | $-\infty$ | $-$ | $-$ | $-$ | $+\infty$ |
| $+\infty$ | $-\infty$ | $-\infty$ | $0$ | $+\infty$ | $+\infty$ |

| **Division** | $-\infty$ | $+\infty$ |
|---|---|---|
| $a$ | $0$ | $0$ |

# 8    Comparison Relations and Lattice Operations

Three comparison relations are important for intervals of $IF$ and $(IF)$:

$$equality, \quad less\ than\ or\ equal, \quad \text{and} \quad set\ inclusion. \qquad (8.1)$$

Let $A$ and $B$ be intervals of $(IF)$ with bounds $a_1 \leq a_2$ and $b_1 \leq b_2$ respectively. Then the relations *equality* and *less than or equal* in $(IF)$ are defined by:

$$A = B :\Leftrightarrow a_1 = b_1 \wedge a_2 = b_2,$$
$$A \leq B :\Leftrightarrow a_1 \leq b_1 \wedge a_2 \leq b_2.$$

Since bounds for intervals of $(IF)$ may be $-\infty$ or $+\infty$ these comparison relations are executed as if performed in the lattice $\{F^*, \leq\}$ with $F^* := F \cup \{-\infty\} \cup \{+\infty\}$.

With the order relation $\leq$, $\{(IF), \leq\}$ is a lattice. The *greatest lower bound* (glb) and the *least upper bound* (lub) of $A, B \in (IF)$ are the intervals

$$glb(A, B) := [min(a_1, b_1), min(a_2, b_2)],$$
$$lub(A, B) := [max(a_1, b_1), max(a_2, b_2)].$$

The greatest lower bound and the least upper bound of an interval with the empty set are both the empty set.

The inclusion relation in $(IF)$ is defined by

$$A \subseteq B :\Leftrightarrow b_1 \leq a_1 \wedge a_2 \leq b_2. \qquad (8.2)$$

With the relation $\subseteq$, $\{(IF), \subseteq\}$ is also a lattice. The least element in $\{(IF), \subseteq\}$ is the empty set $\varnothing$ and the greatest element is the interval $(-\infty, +\infty)$. The infimum of two elements $A, B \in (IF)$ is the intersection and the supremum is the interval hull (convex hull):

$$inf(A, B) := [max(a_1, b_1), min(a_2, b_2)] \text{ or the empty set } \varnothing,$$
$$sup(A, B) := [min(a_1, b_1), max(a_2, b_2)].$$

The intersection of an interval with the empty set is the empty set. The interval hull with the empty set is the other operand.

If in the formulas for $glb(A, B)$, $lub(A, B)$, $inf(A, B)$, $sup(A, B)$, a bound is $-\infty$ or $+\infty$ a parenthesis should be used at this interval bound to denote the resulting interval. This bound is not an element of the interval.

If in any of the comparison relations defined here both operands are the empty set, the result is true. If in (8.2) $A$ is the empty set the result is true. Otherwise the result is false if in any of the three comparison relations only one operand is the empty set.[6]

---

[6] A convenient encoding of the empty set may be $\varnothing = [+NaN, -NaN]$. Then most comparison relations and lattice operations considered in this section would deliver the correct answer if conventional rules for $NaN$ are applied. However, if $A = \varnothing$ then set inclusion (8.2) and computing the interval hull do not follow this rule. So in these two cases whether $A = \varnothing$ must be checked before the operations can be executed. However, to avoid confusion with the IEEE P754 exceptions we recommend to use another notation $\varnothing = [\varnothing_1, \varnothing_2]$ with similar properties.

A particular case of inclusion is the relation *element of*. It is defined by

$$a \in B :\Leftrightarrow b_1 \le a \wedge a \le b_2. \tag{8.3}$$

Another useful check is for whether an interval $[a_1, a_2]$ is a proper interval, that is, if $a_1 \le a_2$.

## 9  Evaluation of Functions

Interval evaluation of real functions fits smoothly into complete interval arithmetic as developed in the previous sections. Let $f$ be a function and $D_f$ its domain of definition. For an interval $X \subseteq D_f$, the range $f(X)$ of $f$ is defined as the set of the function's values for all $x \in X$:

$$f(X) := \{f(x) | x \in X\}. \tag{9.1}$$

A function $f(x) = a/(x - b)$ with $D_f = \mathbb{R} \setminus \{b\}$ is sometimes called singular or discontinuous at $x = b$. Both descriptions are meaningless in a strict mathematical sense. Since $x = b$ is not of the domain of $f$, the function cannot have any property at $x = b$.

In this strict sense a division $2/[b_1, b_2]$ by an interval $[b_1, b_2]$ that contains zero as an interior point, $b_1 < 0 < b_2$, means:
$$2/([b_1, 0) \cup (0, b_2]) = 2/[b_1, 0) \cup 2/(0, b_2] = (-\infty, 2/b_1] \cup [2/b_2, +\infty).$$

We give two examples:

$f(x) = 4/(x - 2)^2, \quad D_f = \mathbb{R} \setminus \{2\}, \quad X = [1, 4],$
$f([1, 2) \cup (2, 4]) = f([1, 2)) \cup f((2, 4]) = [4, +\infty) \cup [1, +\infty) = [1, +\infty).$

$g(x) = 2/(x - 2), \quad D_g = \mathbb{R} \setminus \{2\}, \quad X = [1, 3],$
$g([1, 2) \cup (2, 3]) = g([1, 2)) \cup g((2, 3]) = (-\infty, -2] \cup [2, +\infty),$
Here the flag *distinct intervals* should be raised and signaled to the user. The user may then choose a routine to apply which is appropriate for the application.

It has been suggested in the literature that the entire set of real numbers $(-\infty, +\infty)$ be returned as result in this case. However, this may be a large overestimation of the true result and there are applications (Newton's method) which need the accurate answer. To return the entire set of real numbers is also against a basic principle of interval arithmetic—to keep the sets as small as possible. So a standard should have the most accurate answer returned.

On the computer, interval evaluation of a real function $f(x)$ for $X \subseteq D_f$ should deliver a highly accurate enclosure of the range $f(X)$ of the function.

Evaluation of a function $f(x)$ for an interval $X$ with $X \cap D_f = \varnothing$, of course, does not make sense, since $f(x)$ is not defined for values outside its domain $D_f$. The empty set $\varnothing$ should be delivered and an error message may be given to the user.

There are, however, applications in interval arithmetic where information about a function $f$ is useful when $X$ exceeds the domain $D_f$ of $f$. The interval $X$ may also be the result of overestimation during an earlier interval computation.

In such cases the range of $f$ can only be computed for the intersection $X' := X \cap D_f$:

$$f(X') := f(X \cap D_f) := \{f(x)|x \in X \cap D_f\}. \tag{9.2}$$

To prevent the wrong conclusions being drawn, the user must be informed that the interval $X$ had to be reduced to $X' := X \cap D_f$ to compute the delivered range. A particular flag for *domain overflow* may serve this purpose. An appropriate routine can be chosen and applied if this flag is raised.
We give a few examples:

$l(x) := log(x), \quad D_{log} = (0, +\infty),$
$log((0, 2]) = (-\infty, log(2)].$
But also
$log([-5, 2]') = log((0, 2]) = (-\infty, log(2)].$
The flag *domain overflow* should be set. It informs the user that the function has been evaluated for the intersection $X' := X \cap D_f = [-5, 2] \cap (0, +\infty) = (0, 2]$.

$h(x) := sqrt(x), \quad D_{sqrt} = [0, +\infty),$
$sqrt([1, 4]) = [1, 2],$
$sqrt([4, +\infty)) = [2, +\infty).$
$sqrt([-5, -1]) = \varnothing$, an error message *sqrt* not defined for $[-5, -1]$, may be given to the user.
$sqrt([-5, 4]') = sqrt([0, 4]) = [0, 2].$
The flag *domain overflow* should be set. It informs the user that the function has been evaluated for the intersection $X' := X \cap D_f = [-5, 4] \cap [0, +\infty) = [0, 4]$.

$k(x) := sqrt(x) - 1, \quad D_k = [0, +\infty),$
$k([-4, 1]') = k([0, 1]) = sqrt([0, 1]) - 1 = [-1, 0].$
The flag *domain overflow* should be set. It informs the user that the function has been evaluated for the intersection $X' := X \cap D_f = [-4, 1] \cap [0, +\infty) = [0, 1]$.

## 10   Final Remarks

The basis of all technical computing is the set of real numbers $I\!R$. In general, however, real numbers are not representable and operations for them are not executable. On the computer the real numbers are mapped on a finite subset $F$, floating-point numbers. Floating-point arithmetic and interval arithmetic are different tools that approximate arithmetic for real numbers.

Floating-point arithmetic has been used very successfully. A lot of mathematics is used in conventional Numerical Analysis. Nevertheless the result of a long floating-point computation always carries some uncertainty. In contrast to this interval mathematics even on the computer is supposed to deliver results with guarantees. This is only possible if it is strictly kept on mathematical grounds.

It has been shown in this paper that arithmetic operations and comparison relations for closed intervals of $(I\mathbb{R})$ and $(IF)$ can be derived in a strict mathematical manner. Arithmetic operations of $(I\mathbb{R})$ are defined as power set operations. Formulas for the operations for extended intervals of $(I\mathbb{R})$ are obtained by a continuity principle via the operations for closed and bounded intervals of $I\mathbb{R}$. Formulas for the operations of $(IF)$ are obtained from those of $(I\mathbb{R})$ by rounding the result in $(I\mathbb{R})$ on the least upper bound in $(IF)$ with respect to set inclusion as an order relation. The tables in Section 5 show that the result of any operation for operands of $(IF)$ leads to an element of $(IF)$ again, i.e., arithmetic in $(IF)$ is free of exceptions. In Section 7 it is shown that only a small set of operations suffices to realize all arithmetic operations for operands of $(IF)$ on the computer.

Interval arithmetic solely deals with closed and connected sets of real numbers. $-\infty$ and $+\infty$ do not occur as elements of intervals. They are only used as bounds of intervals. This is essential for the entire calculus to be free of exceptions.

While in the real number field division by zero is not defined, in IEEE floating-point arithmetic division by zero is defined to be $+\infty$ or $-\infty$. In interval arithmetic there is no need for this definition. Here division of a number $a \neq 0$ by zero is well defined. The result is the empty set.

The tremendous progress in computer technology and the great increase in computer speed should be accompanied by extension of the mathematical capacity of the computer. Today floating-point arithmetic is hardware supported on every powerful processor. This should also hold for interval arithmetic. With very very little additional arithmetic circuitry interval arithmetic can be made available at the speed of simple floating-point arithmetic. See [3] and the letter of the IFIP Working Group 2.5 to IEEE754R [5]. Hardware support for the interval operations summarized in Section 7 would greatly simplify a future interval arithmetic standard.

Floating-point numbers and floating-point intervals are objects of contrasting quality. A floating-point number is an approximate representation of a real number, while an interval is a precisely defined object. An operation mixing the two, which ought to yield an interval, may not be precisely specified. It is thus not reasonable to define operations between floating-point numbers and intervals. The two calculi should be kept strictly separate. If a user does indeed need to perform an operation between a floating-point number and a floating-point interval, he may do so by using a transfer function which transforms its floating-point operand into a floating-point interval. In doing so, the user is made aware of the possible loss of quality of the interval as a precise object. The transfer function should check whether a given pair of floating-point values is a correct interval. Prohibiting an automatic type transfer from floating-point numbers to floating-point intervals also prevents exceptions of the IEEE floating-point arithmetic standard from being introduced into interval arithmetic. A strict separation of the two calculi would not slow down the runtime of interval computations if the operations summarized in Sections 7 are realized in hardware.

Of course, computing with result verification often makes use of floating-point computations.

Interval arithmetic for a fixed precision should be accompanied by a variable length interval arithmetic. For definition see [4]. The basic tool to achieve this is an exact multiply and accumulate (i.e., continued addition) operation for the data format double precision. Pipelining gives it high speed and exactitude brings very high accuracy into computation. There is no way to compute a dot product faster than the exact result. By pipelining it can be computed in the time the processor needs to read the data, i.e., it could not be done faster. Variable length interval arithmetic fully benefits from such speed. No software simulation can go as fast. With operator overloading variable length interval arithmetic is very easy to use. The exponent range can be kept very flexible, see [4] and the literature listed there.

# References

1. Alefeld, G., Herzberger, J.: Introduction to Interval Computations. Academic Press, New York (1983)
2. Kahan, W.: A More Complete Interval Arithmetic. Lecture Notes prepared for a summer course at the University of Michigan, June 17-21 (1968)
3. Kirchner, R., Kulisch, U.: Hardware support for interval arithmetic. Reliable Computing 12(3), 225–237 (2006)
4. Kulisch, U.W.: Computer Arithmetic and Validity – Theory, Implementation and Applications. De Gruyter, Berlin (2008)
5. IFIPWG-IEEE754R: Letter of the IFIP WG 2.5 to the IEEE Computer Arithmetic Revision Group (2007)
6. Moore, R.E.: Interval Analysis. Prentice Hall Inc., Englewood Cliffs (1966)
7. Moore, R.E.: Methods and Applications of Interval Analysis. SIAM, Philadelphia (1979)
8. Ratz, D.: On Extended Interval Arithmetic and Inclusion Isotony, Institut für Angewandte Mathematik, Universität Karlsruhe (preprint, 1999)
9. Rump, S.M.: Kleine Fehlerschranken bei Matrixproblemen. Dissertation, Universität Karlsruhe (1980)

# Continued Fractions for Special Functions: Handbook and Software

Annie Cuyt, Franky Backeljauw, Stefan Becuwe, Michel Colman, Tom Docx, and Joris Van Deun

Universiteit Antwerpen, Department of Mathematics and Computer Science
Middelheimlaan 1, B-2020 Antwerpen, Belgium
{annie.cuyt,franky.backeljauw,stefan.becuwe,
tom.docx,joris.vandeun}@ua.ac.be
http://www.cant.ua.ac.be

**Abstract.** The revived interest in continued fractions stems from the fact that many special functions enjoy easy to handle and rapidly converging continued fraction representations. These can be made to good use in a project that envisages the provably correct (or interval) evaluation of these functions. Of course, first a catalogue of these continued fraction representations needs to be put together.

The *Handbook of continued fractions for special functions* is the result of a systematic study of series and continued fraction representations for several families of mathematical functions used in science and engineering. Only 10% of the listed continued fraction representations can also be found in the famous NBS Handbook edited by Abramowitz and Stegun. More information is given in Sect. 1.

The new handbook is brought to life at the website www.cfhblive.ua. ac.be where visitors can recreate tables to their own specifications, and can explore the numerical behaviour of the series and continued fraction representations. An easy web interface supporting these features is discussed in the Sects. 2, 3 and 4.

## 1 Introduction

### 1.1 Handbooks and Software on Special Functions

Special functions are pervasive in all fields of science. The most well-known application areas are in physics, engineering, chemistry, computer science and statistics. Because of their importance, several books and websites and a large collection of papers have been devoted to these functions.

Of the standard work on the subject, the *Handbook of mathematical functions with formulas, graphs and mathematical tables* edited by Milton Abramowitz and Irene Stegun [1], the American National Institute of Standards and Technology (formerly National Bureau of Standards) claims to have sold over 700 000 copies (over 150 000 directly and more than fourfold that number through commercial publishers)!

A. Cuyt et al. (Eds.): Numerical Validation, LNCS 5492, pp. 27–40, 2009.

But the NBS Handbook, as well as the Bateman volumes written in the early fifties [2,3,4], are currently out of date due to the rapid progress in research and the revolutionary changes in technology. Already in the nineties several projects were launched to update the principal handbooks on special functions and to make them available on the web and extend them with computational facilities.

However, up to this date, even environments such as Maple, Mathematica, MATLAB and libraries such as IMSL, CERN and NAG offer no routines for the provably correct evaluation of special functions. The following quotes concisely express the need for new developments in the evaluation of special functions:

- *"Algorithms with strict bounds on truncation and rounding errors are not generally available for special functions. These obstacles provide an opportunity for creative mathematicians and computer scientists."* Dan Lozier, general director of the DLMF project, and Frank Olver [5,6].
- *"The decisions that go into these algorithm designs — the choice of reduction formulae and interval, the nature and derivation of the approximations — involve skills that few have mastered. The algorithms that MATLAB uses for gamma functions, Bessel functions, error functions, Airy functions, and the like are based on Fortran codes written 20 or 30 years ago."* Cleve Moler, founder of MATLAB [7].

Fortunately a lot of well-known constants in mathematics, physics and engineering, as well as elementary and special functions enjoy very nice and rapidly converging continued fraction representations. In addition, many of these fractions are limit-periodic. We point out how series and limit-periodic continued fraction representations can form a basis for a scalable precision technique allowing the provably correct evaluation of a large class of special functions. Our software is based on the use of sharpened a priori truncation and round-off error upper bounds. The implementation is validated, meaning that it returns a sharp interval enclosure for the requested function evaluation, at the same cost as the evaluation.

In order to get started we must of course first set up a systematic and encyclopedic study of continued fraction representations of special functions. The *Handbook of continued fractions for special functions* [8] is the result of such an endeavour. We emphasise that only 10% of the continued fractions contained in the new handbook, can also be found in the Abramowitz and Stegun project or at special functions websites!

### 1.2    Limit-Periodic Continued Fraction Representations

Let us consider a convergent continued fraction representation of the form

$$f = \cfrac{a_1}{1 + \cfrac{a_2}{1 + \dots}} = \mathop{\mathbf{K}}_{n=1}^{\infty} \left( \frac{a_n}{1} \right), \quad a_n := a_n(x), \quad f := f(x). \tag{1}$$

The symbol $\mathbf{K}$ (from German) for the continued fraction (1) is the analogue of the symbol $\Sigma$ for infinite sums. Sometimes (1) is also written as

$$\frac{a_1}{1} + \frac{a_2}{1} + \cdots .$$

Here $a_n$ is called the $n$-th partial numerator. The continued fraction is said to be limit-periodic if the limit $\lim_{n\to\infty} a_n$ exists (it is allowed to be $\pm\infty$). We respectively denote by the $N$-th approximant $f_N(x; w_N)$ and $N$-th tail $t_N(x)$ of (1), the values

$$f_N(x; w_N) = \mathop{\mathbf{K}}_{n=1}^{N-1} \left(\frac{a_n}{1}\right) + \frac{a_N}{1 + w_N},$$

$$t_N(x) = \mathop{\mathbf{K}}_{n=N+1}^{\infty} \left(\frac{a_n}{1}\right).$$

We restrict ourselves to the case where a sequence $\{w_n\}_n$ can be chosen such that $\lim_{n\to\infty} f_n(x; w_n) = \lim_{n\to\infty} f_n(x; 0)$. The value $w_N$ is called a modification.

The tails $t_N(x)$ of a convergent continued fraction can behave quite differently compared to the tails of a convergent series which always go to zero. We illustrate the different cases with an example. Take for instance the continued fraction expansion

$$\frac{\sqrt{1 + 4x} - 1}{2} = \mathop{\mathbf{K}}_{n=1}^{\infty} \left(\frac{x}{1}\right), \qquad a_n = x, \qquad x \geq -\frac{1}{4}.$$

Each tail $t_N(x)$ represents the value $1/2(\sqrt{1 + 4x} - 1)$ as well and hence the sequence of tails is a constant sequence. More remarkable is that the sequence of even-numbered tails of the convergent continued fraction

$$\sqrt{2} - 1 = \mathop{\mathbf{K}}_{n=1}^{\infty} \left(\frac{(3 + (-1)^n)/2}{1}\right)$$

converge to $\sqrt{2} - 1$ while the sequence of odd-numbered tails converge to $\sqrt{2}$ (hence the sequence of tails does not converge), and that the sequence of tails $\{t_N(x)\}_N = \{N + 1\}_N$ of

$$1 = \mathop{\mathbf{K}}_{n=1}^{\infty} \left(\frac{n(n + 2)}{1}\right)$$

converges to $+\infty$. When carefully monitoring the behaviour of these continued fraction tails, very accurate approximants $f_N(x; w_N)$ for $f$ can be computed by making an appropriate choice for $w_N$. For instance, when $-1/4 \leq \lim_{n\to\infty} a_n = a < +\infty$ then a rough estimate of the $N$-th tail is given by $(\sqrt{1 + 4a} - 1)/2$.

## 2   A Handbook of Continued Fractions and Its Live Version

The idea to write [8] originated more than 15 years ago in the mind of W. B. Jones, but the project only got started end of 2001 under the guidance of the first author. By that time the plan to produce merely a printed version of the continued fraction catalogue was outdated. We started to think of a more dynamic webversion accompanying a printed encyclopedic list of continued fraction representations. The recently published printed handbook splits naturally into three parts.

Part I comprises the necessary theoretic background about continued fractions. We deal with three term recurrence relations, linear fractional transformations, equivalence transformations, limit periodicity, continued fraction tails and minimal solutions. The connection between continued fractions and series is worked out in detail, especially the correspondence with formal power series at 0 and $\infty$. The different continued fraction representations are grouped into families. Classical convergence results are given, formulated in terms of element and value regions. The connection with Padé approximants, two-point Padé approximants, moment problems, Stieltjes integral transform representations and orthogonal polynomials are discussed.

In Part II the reader is offered algorithms to construct various continued fraction representations of functions, known either by one or more (formal) series representations or by a set of function values. When evaluating a continued fraction representation, only a finite part of the fraction can be taken into account. Several algorithms exist to compute continued fraction approximants. Each of them can make use of an estimate of the continued fraction tail to improve the convergence. A priori and a posteriori truncation error bounds are developed and accurate roundoff error bounds are given.

The families of special functions discussed in the separate chapters of Part III form the bulk of the handbook. We present series and continued fraction representations for several mathematical constants, the elementary functions, functions related to the gamma function, the error function, the exponential integrals, the Bessel functions and several probability functions. All can be formulated in terms of either hypergeometric or confluent hypergeometric functions. We conclude with a brief discussion of the q-hypergeometric function and its continued fraction representations.

Since, in practice, it is the initial convergence behaviour of a series or continued fraction representation that matters and not the asymptotic one, we illustrate the convergence rate empirically by the presentation of tables, where we evaluate different representations for a large range of arguments. This is where the handbook comes to life! Besides the tables shown in Part III of the printed version, the `tabulate` facility at the website `www.cfhblive.ua.ac.be` offers the possibility to create table output satisfying a reader's personal requirements. An illustration of the use of `tabulate` is given in Fig. 1. The resulting table is found in Table 1.

All tables are composed in the same way. The two leftmost columns contain the function argument and the function value. The function value is the correctly

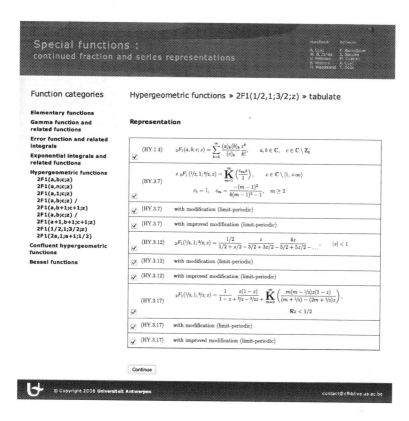

Fig. 1.

rounded mathematical value (to a small number of digits), verified in a variety of computer algebra environments. In case the function value $f(z)$ is a complex value, only its signed modulus

$$|f(z)|_s = \text{sgn}\left(\Re f(z)\right) |f(z)| \tag{2}$$

is returned. The sign of $\Re(f(z))$ indicates whether the complex value $f(z)$ lies in the right or the left half-plane. The other columns in a table contain the relative truncation error

$$\left| \frac{f(z) - f_N(z)}{f(z)} \right| \tag{3}$$

incurred when using a certain partial sum or continued fraction approximant $f_N(z)$ for the function $f(z)$. The continued fraction approximant $f_N(z)$ can be either a classical approximant $f_N(z; 0)$ or a modified approximant $f_N(z; w_N)$.

The function arguments are best selected in the intersection of the domains associated with each of the formulas evaluated in the table. The evaluation of the special function for the selected arguments is exactly rounded to 7 decimal digits and the truncation errors are upward rounded to 2 decimal digits. Since

## Table 1.

**Input**

| parameters | none | |
|---|---|---|
| base | 10 | |
| approximant | 10 | (1 ≤ approximant ≤ 999) |
| z | .1,.15,.2,.25,.3,.35,.4,.45 | |
| output in tables | $\mathfrak{C}$ relative error $\mathfrak{C}$ absolute error | |

**Output**

10th approximant (relative error)

| z | $_2F_1(1/2,1;3/2;z)$ | (HY.1.4) | (HY.3.7) | (HY.3.7) | (HY.3.7) | (HY.3.12) | (HY.3.12) | (HY.3.12) | (HY.3.17) | (HY.3.17) | (HY.3.17) |
|---|---|---|---|---|---|---|---|---|---|---|---|
| 0.1 | 1.035488e+00 | 4.6e−13 | 2.4e−16 | 6.4e−19 | 3.0e−21 | 1.5e−10 | 4.5e−13 | 8.5e−15 | 7.5e−11 | 3.9e−12 | 5.4e−14 |
| 0.15 | 1.055046e+00 | 4.1e−11 | 1.8e−14 | 5.0e−17 | 3.6e−19 | 8.3e−09 | 2.8e−11 | 8.4e−13 | 7.6e−09 | 4.0e−10 | 8.6e−12 |
| 0.2 | 1.076022e+00 | 1.0e−09 | 4.3e−13 | 1.2e−15 | 1.2e−17 | 1.4e−07 | 5.4e−10 | 2.3e−11 | 2.4e−07 | 1.3e−08 | 4.0e−10 |
| 0.25 | 1.098612e+00 | 1.2e−08 | 5.4e−12 | 1.6e−14 | 2.1e−16 | 1.3e−06 | 5.5e−09 | 3.1e−10 | 4.2e−06 | 2.5e−07 | 9.8e−09 |
| 0.3 | 1.123054e+00 | 9.5e−08 | 4.6e−11 | 1.4e−13 | 2.3e−15 | 7.9e−06 | 3.8e−08 | 2.7e−09 | 5.1e−05 | 3.3e−06 | 1.7e−07 |
| 0.35 | 1.149640e+00 | 5.4e−07 | 3.0e−10 | 9.1e−13 | 1.9e−14 | 3.6e−05 | 1.9e−07 | 1.7e−08 | 4.9e−04 | 3.6e−05 | 2.4e−06 |
| 0.4 | 1.178736e+00 | 2.5e−06 | 1.6e−09 | 5.1e−12 | 1.3e−13 | 1.3e−04 | 8.3e−07 | 9.1e−08 | 4.0e−03 | 3.8e−04 | 3.4e−05 |
| 0.45 | 1.210806e+00 | 9.4e−06 | 7.5e−09 | 2.5e−11 | 7.4e−13 | 4.1e−04 | 3.0e−06 | 4.0e−07 | 3.1e−02 | 4.6e−03 | 6.7e−04 |

the modulus of the truncation error (3) is always positive, the sign is omitted here.

When evaluating the approximants of a limit periodic continued fraction of which the partial numerators do not tend to zero, use of one or more modifications may be appropriate. In that case the evaluations without modification and with use of the different modifications is offered.

When the upward rounded relative truncation error, denoted by $C$, satisfies

$$C := \triangle \left( \left| \frac{f(z) - f_N(z)}{f(z)} \right| \right) \leq 5 \times 10^{-s}, \qquad s \in \mathbb{N}, \tag{4}$$

then the approximation $f_N(z)$ guarantees $s$ significant decimal digits compared to the exact value $f(z)$. When $C \simeq 10^k$ with $k \geq 0$, care must be taken in interpreting the quality of the approximation $f_N(z)$. For $k > 1$ we find $|f_N(z)| \simeq 10^k |f(z)|$, while for $k = 0$ we can very well have $|f_N(z)| \ll |f(z)|$. In both cases $f_N(z)$ can be way off, even missing to predict the magnitude of $f(z)$. In general

$$|f(z) - f_N(z)| \leq C|f(z)| \implies |f_N(z)| \in |f(z)| \, [1 - C, 1 + C].$$

As an example let us consider

$$_2F_1 \left( 1/2, 1; 3/2; z \right) = \frac{1}{2\sqrt{z}} \mathrm{Ln} \left( \frac{1 + \sqrt{z}}{1 - \sqrt{z}} \right).$$

In [8] the series representation labeled (HY.1.4) and three continued fractions labeled (HY.3.7), (HY.3.12) and (HY.3.17) are listed. From Fig. 1 we see that the intersection of the domain of $f(z) = {}_2F_1(1/2, 1; 3/2; z)$ with the convergence domains of the three continued fractions is the set

$$(\{z : |z| < 1\} \cap \{z : \Re z < 1/2\}) \setminus \{z : \mathrm{Arg}\, z = \pi\}.$$

So we can choose arguments:

- on the positive real axis in the interval $[0, 1/2)$,
- in all four quadrants as long as we remain inside the unit circle and have the real part less than $1/2$,
- and on the imaginary axis in the interval $(-\mathtt{i}, \mathtt{i})$.

Because of the symmetry property $f(x + \mathtt{i}x) = f(x - \mathtt{i}x)$, we can even restrict ourselves to the upper half-plane. The evaluation of the continued fractions can further be improved with the modifications

$$w_N(z) = w(z) = 1/2 \left( \sqrt{1-z} - 1 \right)$$

or

$$w_N^{(1)}(z) = w(z) + \frac{a_{N+1}z + z/4}{1 + 2w(z)} \, .$$

Generally, use of the given modifications results in better accuracy. Exceptionally, when the limiting behaviour expressed in the modification does not reflect $t_N$ well, the modifications are not recommended.

At the www.cfhblive.ua.ac.be website, Table 1 can for instance be created, which is different from the tables printed in the handbook.

## 3   Exploring the Special Function Representations

The generation of the tables displaying relative errors (and on the website also absolute errors), is possible thanks to a Maple package developed to complement the handbook [9]. It offers all the basic support required to handle continued fractions on the one hand, and implements all series and continued fraction representations listed in [8] on the other hand. The package requires Maple 9 or above and can be downloaded from www.cfsf.ua.ac.be. The development of this continued fraction package was necessary because the built-in support for continued fractions in computer algebra systems is rather inadequate. For instance, Maple's numtheory[cfrac] command lacks the functionality to deal with limit-periodic continued fractions. As we know, many continued fraction expansions for special functions are defined by a repetition of a limited number of general elements in terms of a running index, such as in

$$\exp(z) = 1 + \frac{2z}{2-z} + \frac{z^2/6}{1} + \overset{\infty}{\underset{m=3}{\mathbf{K}}} \left( \frac{a_m z^2}{1} \right),$$

$$a_m = \frac{1}{4(2m-3)(2m-1)}, \qquad z \in \mathbb{C} \quad (5)$$

and

$$\frac{\Gamma(a, z)}{z^a e^{-z}} = \frac{1}{z} + \overset{\infty}{\underset{m=1}{\mathbf{K}}} \left( \frac{m-a}{1} + \frac{m}{z} \right), \qquad a \in \mathbb{C}, \qquad |\text{Arg } z| < \pi. \quad (6)$$

Yet `numtheory[cfrac]` does not allow to create continued fraction representations of that form. In addition, `numtheory[cfrac]` does not offer the possibility of equivalence transformations, transformations between series and continued fractions or any functionality to work with continued fraction tails.

The newly developed Maple package supports all continued fraction representations that can be written in the form

$$
b_0 + \frac{a_1}{b_1 +} \cdots + \frac{a_m}{b_m +} \overset{\infty}{\underset{k=0}{\mathbf{K}}} \left( \frac{a_{m+1+kt}}{b_{m+1+kt} +} \cdots + \frac{a_{m+1+(k+1)t-1}}{b_{m+1+(k+1)t-1}} \right). \tag{7}
$$

Here the partial numerators $a_1, \ldots, a_m$ and the partial denominators $b_1, \ldots, b_m$ at the start do not yet follow the general expression for the elements $a_n$ and $b_n$ of the $t$ limit-periodic continued fraction (7). For instance, the continued fraction given in (5) can be constructed using the statement:

```
> expCF := create( contfrac,
  front = 1,
  begin = [ [2*z, 2-z], [z^2/6, 1] ],
  general = [ [z^2/(4*(2*m-3)*(2*m-1)), 1] ]
  );
```

and the continued fraction for the complementary incomplete gamma function $\Gamma(a, z)$ from (6) with the following statement:

```
> CIGammaCF := create( contfrac,
  label = "CIGammaCF",
  factor = z^a * exp(-z),
  begin = [ [1,z] ],
  general = [ [(m/2)-a,1], [(m-1)/2,z] ],
  parameters = a,
  constraints =  abs(functions:-argument(z)) < Pi
  );.
```

When visiting our life handbook on the web, a user doesn't have to create any of these continued fractions though. A full library of series and continued fraction representations for special functions is provided. An easy interface to the available formulas is provided in the **approximate** option on the webpage `www.cfhblive.ua.ac.be` (experienced Maple programmers can of course download the full package and its manual [9]).

Users can request the $N$-th partial sum of a series or the $N$-th approximant of a chosen continued fraction, with or without one of the automatically computed modifications $w_N$ that approximate the tail $t_N$. The latter is possible through Maple's `assuming` facility, which allows to compute the limiting behavior of the partial numerators $a_n$ and obtain several formulas suitable as a replacement for the tail. The web interface outputs the requested tail estimate together with the $N$-th approximant. An illustration of the use of **approximate** is found in Fig. 2 with the accompanying output displayed in Fig. 3.

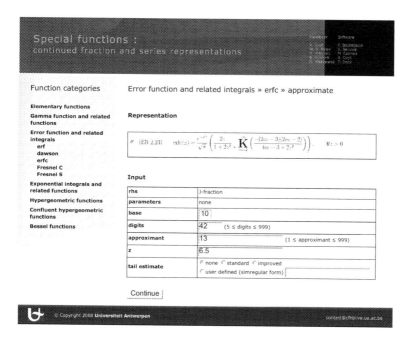

Fig. 2.

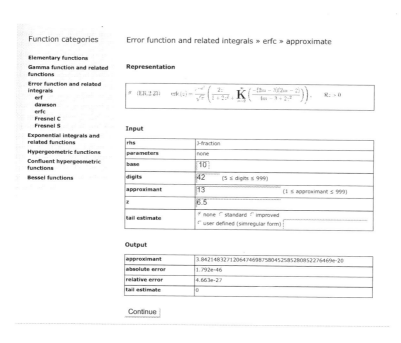

Fig. 3.

From the website's menu we choose the continued fraction representation

$$\operatorname{erfc}(z) = \frac{e^{-z^2}}{\sqrt{\pi}} \left( \frac{2z}{1 + 2z^2} + \underset{m=2}{\overset{\infty}{\mathbf{K}}} \left( \frac{-(2m-3)(2m-2)}{4m-3+2z^2} \right) \right), \qquad \Re z > 0, \quad (8)$$

of which we want to inspect the 13-th approximant using the `approximate` option. This approximant (and the factor $e^{-z^2}/\sqrt{\pi}$ in front) is computed symbolically and afterwards evaluated at $z = 6.5$ using Maple's built-in decimal arithmetic. For the latter we choose the decimal precision $t = 42$. The particular choices $N = 13$ and $t = 42$ allow an easy comparison with the results from Sect. 4. At this moment we do not want to emphasize the role of the continued fraction tail. For this option we select `none`. The output screen lists 42 digits of the thus obtained value, as well as the absolute and relative error, where the exact value of $\operatorname{erfc}(6.5)$ is replaced by a very high precision evaluation (computed in Maple at a multiple of the chosen precision $t$). Apparently the 13-th approximant yields 27 significant digits at $z = 6.5$. A posteriori, we see that a proper choice for the decimal precision $t$ should be larger than 27. We recommend to use a sufficiently large precision when inspecting $N$-th approximants, at least a multiple of $N$.

Information about the domain of convergence of a series or continued fraction is obtained from the `constraints` argument, which is used for instance in the construction of (6). In the web interface we distinguish between violating a parameter constraint and the case where the variable is taken outside the domain of convergence. In the latter, a result is still returned with the warning that it may be unreliable. This approach allows the user to observe the behaviour of the representation outside its domain. In the former, when a parameter constraint is violated, no value is returned.

When a user suspects the discovery of a new continued fraction representation, its equivalence with the existing continued fractions supported in the Maple library can be checked using the `equivalent` function. The function checks if the sequences of approximants are the same. Since we are dealing with limit-periodic continued fractions, this comes down to comparing all approximants up to the least common multiple of the numbers of general elements increased with the maximum number of begin elements. This can only be done in the Maple programming environment, not via the webpage. In Maple the library can also be searched for the predefined continued fractions and series using the `query` command. Predefined formulas can be retrieved using the `formula` command.

## 4   Evaluating the Special Functions Reliably

In the wake of the continued fraction handbook, again making use of series and continued fraction representations, a numeric software library for the provably correct evaluation of a large family of special functions is being developed as well. For the time being use of this library is restricted to the real line. So in the sequel we denote the function variable by $x$ rather than by $z$. We only summarize the workings here and refer to [10] for more detailed information. The library will be made available on the handbook's website and will be accessible via the web interface under the option `evaluate`.

Let us assume to have at our disposal a scalable precision IEEE 754-854 compliant [11] floating-point implementation of the basic operations, comparisons, base and type conversions, in the rounding modes upward, downward, truncation and round-to-nearest. Such an implementation is characterized by four parameters: the internal base $\beta$, the precision $t$ and the exponent range $[L, U]$. We target implementations in $\beta = 2$ at precisions $t \geq 53$, and implementations for use with $\beta = 2^i$ or $\beta = 10^i$ at all precisions $t$.

We denote by $\oplus, \ominus, \otimes, \oslash$ the exactly rounded (to the nearest) floating-point implementation of the basic operations $+, -, \times, \div$ in the chosen base $\beta$ and precision $t$. Hence these basic operations are carried out with a relative error of at most $1/2\beta^{-t+1}$ which is also called $1/2$ ulp in precision $t$:

$$\left| \frac{(x \circledast y) - (x * y)}{x * y} \right| \leq \frac{1}{2}\beta^{-t+1}, \qquad * \in \{+, -, \times, \div\}.$$

In the other three rounding modes the upper bound on the relative error doubles to 1 ulp. The realization of an implementation of a function $f(x)$ in that floating-point environment is essentially a three-step procedure:

1. For a given argument $x$, the evaluation $f(x)$ is often reduced to the evaluation of $f$ for another argument $\tilde{x}$ lying within specified bounds and for which there exists an easy relationship between $f(x)$ and $f(\tilde{x})$. The issue of argument reduction is a topic in its own right and mostly applies to only the simplest transcendental functions [12]. In the sequel we skip the issue of argument reduction and assume for simplicity that $x = \tilde{x}$.
2. After determining the argument, a mathematical model $F$ for $f$ is constructed, in our case either a partial sum of a series or an approximant of a continued fraction, and a truncation error

$$\frac{|f(x) - F(x)|}{|f(x)|} \tag{9}$$

comes into play, which needs to be bounded. In the sequel we systematically denote the approximation $F(x) \approx f(x)$ by a capital italic letter.
3. When implemented, in other words evaluated as $\mathsf{F}(x)$ by replacing each mathematical operation $*$ by its implementation $\circledast$, this mathematical model is also subject to a round-off error

$$\frac{|F(x) - \mathsf{F}(x)|}{|f(x)|} \tag{10}$$

which needs to be controlled. We systematically denote the implementation $\mathsf{F}(x)$ of $F(x)$ in capital typewriter font.

The technique to provide a mathematical model $F(x)$ of a function $f(x)$ differs substantially when going from a fixed finite precision context to a finite scalable precision context. In the former, the aim is to provide an optimal mathematical model, often a so-called best approximant, satisfying the truncation error bound imposed by the fixed finite precision and requiring as few operations as possible. In the latter, the goal is to provide a generic technique, from which a mathematical model yielding the imposed accuracy, is deduced at runtime. Hence best approximants are not an option since these models have to be recomputed every time the precision is altered and a function evaluation is requested. At the same time the generic technique should generate an approximant of as low complexity as possible.

We also want our implementation to be reliable, meaning that a sharp interval enclosure for the requested function evaluation is returned without any additional cost. If the total error $|f(x) - \mathsf{F}(x)|/|f(x)|$ is bounded by $\alpha\beta^{-t+1}$, then a reliable interval enclosure for the function value $f(x)$ is

$$[\mathsf{F}(x) - \alpha\beta^{e+1-t+1}, \mathsf{F}(x) + \alpha\beta^{e+1-t+1}], \qquad \lfloor \log_\beta |\mathsf{F}| \rfloor = e.$$

To make sure that the total error $|f(x) - \mathsf{F}(x)|/|f(x)|$ is bounded by $\alpha\beta^{-t+1}$ we must determine $N$ such that for the mathematical model $F(x)$, being either a partial sum of degree $N$ or an $N$-th approximant of a continued fraction, the truncation error satisfies

$$\left| \frac{f(x) - F(x)}{f(x)} \right| \leq \alpha_1 \beta^{-t+1}$$

and evaluate $F(x)$, in a suitable working precision $s$ larger than the user precision $t$, such that the computed value $\mathsf{F}(x)$ satisfies

$$\left| \frac{F(x) - \mathsf{F}(x)}{f(x)} \right| \leq \alpha_2 \beta^{-t+1}$$

with $\alpha_1 + \alpha_2 = \alpha$ ($\alpha_{1,2} = \alpha/2$ is not a bad choice).

How this can be guaranteed for series and continued fraction models is described in [10], where it is also illustrated with some examples. We content ourselves here with a teaser of the web interface to the `evaluate` option in the Figs. 4 and 5. In its `verbose` mode the web interface also returns the computed $N$ (obtained from the tolerated truncation error), the working precision $s$ (obtained from the tolerated round-off error), the tail estimate $w_N$ (if applicable) and the at runtime computed theoretical truncation and round-off error bounds (see [13]).

We choose to evaluate the complementary error function at $x = 6.5$ and request the total relative error (truncation and round-off acccumulated, taking into account any errors in the computation of the factor $e^{-x^2}/\sqrt{\pi}$ as well) to be bounded above by one decimal unit ($\beta = 10$) in the 40-th digit (not counting any leading zeroes). In other words we expect to receive a computed value $\mathsf{ERFC}(6.5)$ that satisfies

$$\left| \frac{\text{erfc}(6.5) - \mathsf{ERFC}(6.5)}{\text{erfc}(6.5)} \right| \leq 10^{-39}$$

In the option `evaluate` the base is not restricted to 10. It can be set to $10^i$ ($1 \leq i \leq 7$) or $2^i$ ($1 \leq i \leq 24$). We have made the choice $\beta = 10$ here in order to

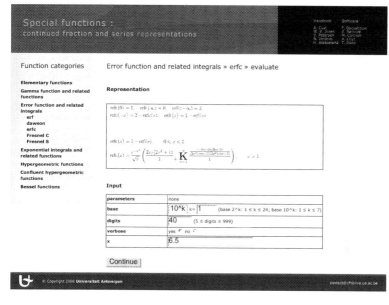

Fig. 4.

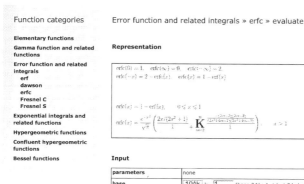

Fig. 5.

compare the output to the one from Fig. 3. The program returns the requested 40 digits with the information (verbose mode) that $N = 13$, $s = 42$, $t_N \approx -0.037$. Needless to say that the effortless but appropriate choice of the tail $t_N$ has greatly improved the accuracy of the result, from 27 to 40 significant digits!

## 5  Future Work

The project is an ongoing project and future work includes the inventory and symbolic implementation of representations for the Coulomb wave functions, the Legendre functions, the Riemann zeta function and other frequently used special functions. As they become available, the list of functions available in the tabulate (Sect. 2) and approximate (Sect. 3) options on the web is enlarged.

As far as the option evaluate (Sect. 4) is concerned, an interface to this numeric library from within Maple and from MATLAB is under development, and a similar implementation in the complex plane is the subject of future research. As the work evolves, the webpage www.cfhblive.ua.ac.be will be updated.

## References

1. Abramowitz, M., Stegun, I.: Handbook of mathematical functions with formulas, graphs and mathematical tables. U.S. Government Printing Office, NBS, Washington, D. C (1964)
2. Erdélyi, A., Magnus, W., Oberhettinger, F., Tricomi, F.: Higher transcendental functions, vol. 1. McGraw-Hill, New York (1953)
3. Erdélyi, A., Magnus, W., Oberhettinger, F., Tricomi, F.: Higher transcendental functions, vol. 2. McGraw-Hill, New York (1953)
4. Erdélyi, A., Magnus, W., Oberhettinger, F., Tricomi, F.: Higher transcendental functions, vol. 3. McGraw-Hill, New York (1955)
5. Cipra, B.A.: A new testament for special functions? SIAM News 31(2) (1998)
6. Lozier, D.: NIST Digital Library of Mathematical Functions. Annals of Mathematics and Artificial Intelligence 38(1–3) (May 2003)
7. Moler, C.: The tetragamma function and numerical craftmanship. MATLAB News & Notes (2002)
8. Cuyt, A., Brevik Petersen, V., Verdonk, B., Waadeland, H., Jones, W.B.: Handbook of Continued Fractions for Special Functions. Springer, Heidelberg (2008)
9. Backeljauw, F., Cuyt, A.: A continued fraction package for special functions. ACM Transactions on Mathematical Software (submitted, 2008)
10. Backeljauw, F., Becuwe, S., Cuyt, A.: Validated evaluation of special mathematical functions. In: Autexier, S., Campbell, J., Rubio, J., Sorge, V., Suzuki, M., Wiedijk, F. (eds.) AISC 2008, Calculemus 2008, and MKM 2008. LNCS (LNAI), vol. 5144, pp. 206–216. Springer, Heidelberg (2008)
11. Floating-Point Working Group: IEEE standard for binary floating-point arithmetic. SIGPLAN 22, 9–25 (1987)
12. Muller, J.-M.: Elementary functions: Algorithms and implementation. Birkhäuser, Basel (1997)
13. Cuyt, A., Verdonk, B., Waadeland, H.: Efficient and reliable multiprecision implementation of elementary and special functions. SIAM J. Sci. Comput. 28(4), 1437–1462 (2006)

# A Modified Staggered Correction Arithmetic with Enhanced Accuracy and Very Wide Exponent Range

Frithjof Blomquist, Werner Hofschuster, and Walter Krämer

Bergische Universität Wuppertal, Scientific Computing/Software Engineering, Gaußstraße 20, D-42097 Wuppertal, Germany
{Blomquist,Hofschuster,Kraemer}@math.uni-wuppertal.de
http://www.math.uni-wuppertal.de/~xsc

**Abstract.** A so called staggered precision arithmetic is a special kind of a multiple precision arithmetic based on the underlying floating point data format (typically IEEE double format) and fast floating point operations as well as exact dot product computations. Due to floating point limitations it is not an arbitrary precision arithmetic. However, it typically allows computations using several hundred mantissa digits.

A set of new modified staggered arithmetics for real and complex data as well as for real interval and complex interval data with very wide exponent range is presented. Some applications will show the increased accuracy of computed results compared to ordinary staggered interval computations. The very wide exponent range of the new arithmetic operations allows computations far beyond the IEEE data formats.

The new modified staggered arithmetics would be extremely fast if an exact dot product was available in hardware (the fused accumulate and add instruction is only one step in this direction).

This paper describes work in progress. Updates of the software as well as additional documentation may be downloaded from our web site http://www.math.uni-wuppertal.de/~xsc

**Keywords:** staggered correction, multiple precision, C-XSC, interval computation, wide exponent range, reliable numerical computations, complex interval functions.

**AMS classification:** 65G20, 65G30, 65Y99, 37M99, 30-04.

## 1   Introduction

Staggered correction arithmetics [3,4,6,27,28,36,49,51] are based on exact dot product computations of floating point vectors [10,32]. (Please refer to [36] for some historical remarks on the implicit/explicit usage of staggered numbers [3,9,25,28,34,35,47]). A staggered correction number is given as the (exact and unevaluated) sum of the components of a list of floating point numbers (components of a floating point vector). Thus the maximum precision of arithmetic operations depends strongly on the exponent range of the floating-point screen. Staggered correction numbers close to the underflow range are typically not as accurate as numbers with larger exponents. For the IEEE double

A. Cuyt et al. (Eds.): Numerical Validation, LNCS 5492, pp. 41–67, 2009.

precision format [2], the range for positive numbers is about 4.9E-324 to 1.7E+308. Thus, up to 630 (decimal) mantissa digits may be handled using staggered precision variables.

To get high accuracy in numerical calculations, (intermediate) underflow and/or overflow situations must be avoided, i.e. an appropriate scaling of the operands of arithmetic operations is necessary. To this end we represent our modified staggered number as a pair $(e, x)$. We refer to such pairs as extended staggered numbers. The integer $e$ denotes an exponent with respect to the base 2 and $x$ denotes an ordinary staggered number (i. e. a vector of floating point numbers). The value $v$ of the modified staggered variable $(e, x)$ is $v = (e, x) := 2^e \cdot \text{sum}(x)$. Here, $\text{sum}(x)$ means the exact sum of all floating point components of the staggered variable $x$. The pair-representation allows the handling of very small and very large numbers: 1.3E-487564, 4.1E9999999, or numbers with even larger exponents may be used in numerical calculations. We are aware of several test cases, where multiple-precision calculations using computer algebra packages like Maple and/or Mathematica fail, whereas our extended staggered software returns the expected results, see e.g. Subsection 5.2.

Our new package [6] offers real interval and complex interval arithmetic operations and also a rather complete set of mathematical functions for the new data types `lx_interval` (extended real staggered intervals) and `lx_cinterval` (extended complex staggered intervals). Many functions, like trigonometric and inverse trigonometric, hyperbolic and inverse hyperbolic, as well as several other functions are provided for (rectangular) extended complex staggered intervals.

Some details of the arithmetic operations as well as some details on the implementation of elementary transcendental mathematical functions will be discussed in this paper. Applications (logistic equation, limit calculations, complex Interval Newton method) will be presented to demonstrate the ease of use and to show the superior numerical behavior of the new arithmetics over the more traditional one with almost no expense of efficiency in performance. We will also discuss hardware requirements needed to get the staggered arithmetic working extremely fast.

The source code of the new package is distributed under the GNU general public license. Up to now, it is an independent supplement to our C-XSC library. The source code is available online, see `http://www.math.uni-wuppertal.de/~xsc/ xsc/cxsc_software.html`

We close this section with some references to different kinds of (multiple precision) arithmetics [10,14,16,17,19,27,30,31,41,43] and some general references to (high precision) function evaluations [7,11,13,15,17,37,38,39,45,46,48,50]. More specific citations are given in the text below.

## 2   (Extended) Staggered Data Types

Real, complex, real interval and complex interval staggered data types are realized as arrays of floating point numbers [27,36,6]. E.g. a real staggered variable is represented by an array of floating point values. The exact (but unevaluated) sum of these floating point numbers is the numerical value of the staggered number. The implementation of arithmetic operations for staggered numbers uses extensively the possibility to compute the value (the exact sum of its floating point components) of a staggered number error free . But exact summation is a special case of exact dot product computations. As we will see in a moment, this operation (which may be realized e. g. using a so called long accumulator [31]) is also extensively used to implement staggered operations.

Some general remarks are appropriate: Summation of numbers is the most sensitive operation in floating point arithmetic [10]. By this operation scalar products of floating point vectors, matrix products etc. can be computed without any error in infinite precision arithmetic, making an error analysis for those operations superfluous. Many algorithms applying this operation systematically have been developed. For others, the limits of applicability are extended by using this additional operation. Furthermore, the exact dot product speeds up the convergence of iterative methods (cited from [31,32]). XSC languages (e.g. C-XSC [22,24]) provide exact dot products via software simulation (hardware support should increase the computation speed by 2 orders of magnitude, see [32]). Computing $x \cdot y$ for floating point vectors $x$, and $y$ in C-XSC results in the best possible floating point result (exact mathematical result rounded to the nearest floating point number; correctly rounded result). Using the C-XSC data type `dotprecision` (so called long accumulator), the user can even store the result of dot products of floating point vectors with even quintillions of components errorfree.

Let us introduce staggered numbers in a more formal way [6,27,36]. An ordinary staggered interval number $x$ is given by

$$x := \sum_{i=1}^{n-1} x_i + [x_n, x_{n+1}] = \sum_{i=1}^{n-1} x_i + X.$$

Here, all $x_i$ are floating-point numbers. The lower bound $\underline{x}$ of $x$ is given by

$$\underline{x} := \sum_{i=1}^{n-1} x_i + x_n$$

and the upper bound $\overline{x}$ by

$$\overline{x} := \sum_{i=1}^{n-1} x_i + x_{n+1}.$$

Thus, for $n = 1$, the staggered interval $x$ collapses to the ordinary interval $X = [x_1, x_2]$. Because different staggered numbers usually have different numbers of floating point components, we indicate their individual lengths by $n_x$, $n_y$ and so on. For the staggered number $x$ from above, its length $n_x$ is defined to be equal to $n$. An extended real staggered interval (with length $n$) is given by

$$v = (e, x) = \left( e, \ \sum_{i=1}^{n-1} x_i + [x_n, x_{n+1}] \right) := 2^e \cdot \left( \sum_{i=1}^{n-1} x_i + [x_n, x_{n+1}] \right).$$

For clarity, we avoid the explicit use of this representation whenever possible. Instead we just give some hints, how (automatic) scalings are done.

In the following subsections we describe the realization of arithmetic operations for (extended) staggered numbers $x$ and $y$ [6,36]. The resulting (extended) staggered number is denoted by $z$. To simplify our presentation, we assume that both operands $x, y$

are already scaled properly. As far as possible, we omit the explicit use of the scaling factor introduced for the extended staggered data types [6]. Only in the case of division, we add some remarks on an appropriate scaling of numerator and/or denominator.

The operands of an arithmetic operation may have different staggered length $n_x$, $n_y$, respectively. The staggered length $n_z$ of the result $z$ can be prescribed by the user of the package using the global variable `stagprec`. The resulting staggered (interval) number $z$ has to be computed in such a way that it contains all corresponding point results for arbitrary point arguments taken from the (staggered interval) operands $x$ and $y$.

### 2.1   Addition/Subtraction and Multiplication

For addition, subtraction, and multiplication the (exact) result of these operations is always representable using two dotprecision variables (lower and upper bound are computable as exact scalar products of floating point vectors). Errors (overestimation) may only occur due to underflow situations when the content of the dotprecision variables is converted back to an array of floating point numbers (i.e. to a staggered interval number). Using an appropriate scaling allows more significant figures to be stored as (a set of) floating point numbers (these numbers must lie within the exponent range of IEEE double numbers).

Let us consider the multiplication $x * y$ of two real staggered numbers $x = \sum x_i$ and $y = \sum y_i$, $x_i, y_i$ being floating point numbers. We have to compute $x * y = \sum x_i * \sum y_i$. Thus, the exact result can be written in the equivalent form $\sum \sum x_i \cdot y_j$, i.e. as a dot product of length $n_x \cdot n_y$ of two vectors with floating point components $\in \{x_1, x_2, \ldots x_{n_x}, y_1, y_2, \ldots y_{n_y}\}$. This real number can be stored error free in a dotprecision variable. To get the final result, this intermediate (exact) result is to be stored as a sum of floating point values (i.e. as a staggered number). Please note that dotprecision values may or may not be representable as a sum of floating point numbers. This is due to the fact that a dotprecision value may have a much larger or much smaller exponent than ordinary floating point numbers allow. Thus, the resulting staggered representation $z$ of the product $x * y$ is in general only an approximation to the exact intermediate value stored during the computation of the dot product. The accuracy of $z$ is limited by the exponent range of the underlying floating point number system. Of course, when implementing staggered interval operations, the errors introduced when going from an exact intermediate result to a staggered representation have to be taken into account. This can be done easily using directed rounded conversions whenever the content of a dotprecision variable has to be converted to an ordinary floating point number.

### 2.2   Division

In the preceeding sections, we have described how to compute bounds for the results of our operations in two dotprecision variables and then round these to an interval staggered format. This can no longer be carried out conveniently in the case of the *division* of two staggered correction intervals $x = \sum_{i=1}^{n_x} x_i + X$ and $y = \sum_{i=1}^{n_y} y_i + Y$. Rather, we will apply an iterative algorithm computing successively the $n_z$ real components

$z_i$ of the quotient $x/y$. The algorithm corresponds to "manual" division as taught at elementary school.

In order to compute this approximation $\sum_{i=1}^{n_z} z_i$, we start with $z_1 = \Box m(x) \ \boxed{/}\ \Box$ $m(y)$; here $m(x)$ represents a point selected in the staggered interval $x$, e.g. the midpoint and $\Box$ is the rounding to the floating point screen $S$. Now, we proceed inductively: if we have an approximation $\sum_{i=1}^{k} z_i$, we can compute the next summand $z_{k+1}$ from

$$z_{k+1} = \Box \left( \sum_{i=1}^{n_x} x_i - \sum_{i=1}^{n_y} \sum_{j=1}^{k} y_i z_j \right) \ \boxed{/}\ \Box(m(y)), \tag{1}$$

where the numerator is computed exactly using a dotprecision variable and is rounded only once to $S$. The division is performed in ordinary floating point arithmetic.

As in the previous operations, this iteration guarantees that the $z_i$ do not overlap, since the defect (i.e. the numerator in (1)) of each approximation $\sum_{i=1}^{k} z_i$ is computed with only one rounding.

Now, the interval component $Z$ of the result $z$ may be computed as follows:

$$Z = \Diamond \left( \sum_{i=1}^{n_x} x_i - \sum_{i=1}^{n_y} \sum_{j=1}^{n_z} y_i z_j + X - \sum_{j=1}^{n_z} z_j Y \right) \ \boxed{/}\ \Diamond(y), \tag{2}$$

where $\Diamond$ is the rounding to an enclosing interval in the set $IS$ (set of intervals with ordinary floating point numbers as bounds).

It is not difficult to see that $z = \sum_{i=1}^{n_z} z_i + Z$ as computed from (1) and (2) is a superset of the exact range $\{\xi/\eta \mid \xi \in x, \eta \in y\}$; in fact, for all $\alpha \in X, \beta \in Y$ we have the identity:

$$\frac{\sum_{i=1}^{n_x} x_i + \alpha}{\sum_{i=1}^{n_y} y_i + \beta} = \sum_{j=1}^{n_z} z_i + \frac{\sum_{i=1}^{n_x} x_i + \alpha - \sum_{i=1}^{n_y} \sum_{j=1}^{n_z} y_i z_j - \sum_{j=1}^{n_z} z_j \beta}{\sum_{i=1}^{n_y} y_i + \beta}.$$

An interval evaluation of this expression for $\alpha \in X$ and $\beta \in Y$ shows immediately that the exact range of $x/y$ is contained in $\sum_{j=1}^{n_z} z_j + Z$, which is computed using (1) and (2).

Now it is clear how to get the result $z$ for the division of two staggered interval variables $x/y$ by the following three computation steps:

1. $z_1 := m(x) \ \boxed{/}\ m(y)$
2. compute real parts $z_{k+1}$ from (1) for $k = 0, \ldots, n_z - 1$
3. compute interval part $Z$ according to (2)    (3)

At this point we will discuss a proper scaling of the numerator $x$ and/or denominator $y$ (see [6] for more details). Let us assume for a moment that $x$ and $y$ are both very close to the overflow threshold (about 1e300 for double numbers). Then the result $z$ of the division would be close to 1. Thus, the exponent of the leading term of the staggered number $z$ would be zero. In this case only about the first 300 decimal digits of the exact result can be stored in an array of floating point numbers. Digits to the right of this leading part can not be accessed by floating point numbers due to underflow. Thus, even if numerator and denominator are point intervals we can not expect more than about 320 correct digits of the staggered result.

But we can do better. The general procedure is: Scale the numerator to be close to the overflow threshold maxreal and scale the denominator to be close to the square root of maxreal (about 1E150 for double numbers). Denote the scaled numbers by $x$ and $y$, respectively. If so, the quotient of the scaled numbers will also be close to the square root of maxreal, i.e. its exponent will be close to 150. In this way we obviously can convert about 300 + 150, i.e. about 450 leading digits to floating point numbers. The correct scale factor of the result can be computed easily by integer addition/subtraction from the scale factors used to scale the numerator and denominator.

An algorithm for the *square root* can be obtained analogously as in the case of the division. We compute iteratively as follows the $z_i, i = 1, \ldots, n_z$ of the approximation part:

$$
\begin{aligned}
z_1 &= \sqrt{\square(x)} \\
z_{k+1} &= \square\left( \sum_{i=1}^{n_x} x_i - \sum_{i,j=1}^{k} z_i z_j \right) \oslash (2z_1).
\end{aligned}
\tag{4}
$$

This guarantees again that the $z_i$ do not overlap significantly since in the numerator of (4) the defect of the approximation $\sum_{i=1}^{k} z_i$ is computed with one rounding only. Now, the interval part $Z$ is computed by use of

$$
Z = \frac{\diamond\left( \sum_{i=1}^{n_x} x_i - \sum_{i,j=1}^{n_z} z_i z_j + X \right)}{\sqrt{\diamond(x)} + \diamond\left( \sum_{i=1}^{n_z} z_i \right)}.
\tag{5}
$$

As in the case of the division, it is easy to see that $\sum_{i=1}^{n_z} z_i + Z$ as computed from (4) and (5) is a superset of the exact range $\{\sqrt{\xi} \mid \xi \in x\}$; in fact, for all $\gamma \in X$ we have the identity:

$$
\sqrt{\sum_{i=1}^{n_x} x_i + \gamma} = \sum_{j=1}^{n_z} z_j + \frac{\sum_{i=1}^{n_x} x_i + \gamma - \sum_{i,j=1}^{n_z} z_i z_j}{\sqrt{\sum_{i=1}^{n_x} x_i + \gamma} + \sum_{j=1}^{n_z} z_j}.
$$

Now, we see that the square root $z$ of a staggered interval $x$ can be computed by the following three steps very similar to the case of division:

$$
\begin{aligned}
&1. \; z_1 := \sqrt{\square x} \\
&2. \; \text{compute real parts } z_{k+1} \text{ from (4) for } k = 0, \ldots, n_z - 1 \\
&3. \; \text{compute interval part } Z \text{ according to (5)}
\end{aligned}
\tag{6}
$$

Before computing the square root as described above, the argument is scaled in the following way: Multiply the original argument by an even power of two, say by $2^{2n}$, such that the scaled argument $x$ comes close to maxreal. The correct scaling factor of the computed result then is $2^n$. For a point interval argument we may expect up to about 450 correct digits.

## 3   Some Transcendental Elementary Functions

In this section we first give an overview to the implementation of the exponential function $\exp(x)$. The implementation of the natural logaritm $\ln(x)$ is described in more detail.

### 3.1   Exponential Function

We only give an overview how the exponential function is realized [46,48]. The reader may refer to the source code to see the details.

The domain of the exponential using ordinary staggered intervals is only $|x| < 709.7$, whereas in case of the extended staggered interval data type it is $|x| < 1488521882.0$.

To implement the exponential we use the relation $e^x \equiv \left(e^{x \cdot 2^{-n}}\right)^{2^n}$. More precisely we do the following:

- Choose $n$ such that   $|x| \cdot 2^{-n} \sim 10^{-9}$
- Perform a Taylor approximation:   $e^{x \cdot 2^{-n}} \approx T_N(x \cdot 2^{-n})$
- Take into account absolute approximation error:   $e^{x \cdot 2^{-n}} \subset U(x, N)$

- Perform a result adaptation:   $e^x \subset U(x, N)^{2^n}$:
  ```
  for (int k=1; k<=n; k++) U = sqr(U);
  ```

### 3.2   The Natural Logarithm

Let us now present the implementation of the natural logarithm $\ln(x)$ in more details.

There are two cases to be considered: $x$ is close to the zero $x_0 = 1$ of the logarithm or $x$ is sufficiently far away from this zero.

By calculating the logarithm function near the zero $x_0 = 1$, the problem arises that due to cancellation effects the rather small function values can only be included with a few correct decimal digits. To avoid this problem, we introduce the auxiliary function $ln1p(t) := ln(1 + t)$ .

$$\texttt{lx\_interval Ln1p(const lx\_interval\& x)}$$

is implemented in order to include the function values $\ln(1 + x)$, $x \approx 0$, of type $\texttt{lx\_interval}$ with sufficient accuracy. The algorithm is based on the well-known series expansion

$$\ln(1 + x) = \zeta \cdot \sum_{k=0}^{\infty} \frac{2}{2k+1} \cdot (\zeta^2)^k, \quad \zeta := \frac{x}{2+x}, \quad x > -1, \quad |\zeta| < 1. \quad (7)$$

With the definitions   $P(\zeta) := \sum_{k=0}^{\infty} \frac{2}{2k+1} \cdot (\zeta^2)^k, \ P_N(\zeta) := \sum_{k=0}^{N} \frac{2}{2k+1} \cdot (\zeta^2)^k, N \geq 0$

$\ln(1 + x)$ is approximated by

$$\ln(1 + x) \approx \zeta \cdot P_N(\zeta), \ N \geq 0. \quad (8)$$

The absolute error $|P(\zeta) - P_N(\zeta)| =: \delta$ it holds

$$\delta = \sum_{k=N+1}^{\infty} \frac{2}{2k+1} \cdot (\zeta^2)^k = \sum_{n=0}^{\infty} \frac{2}{2n+2N+3} \cdot (\zeta^2)^{n+N+1}$$

$$= (\zeta^2)^{N+1} \cdot \sum_{n=0}^{\infty} \frac{2}{2n+2N+3} \cdot (\zeta^2)^n \leq (\zeta^2)^{N+1} \cdot \frac{2}{2N+3} \cdot \frac{1}{1-\zeta^2}$$

and the last upper bound can further be estimated by

$$\delta := |P(\zeta) - P_N(\zeta)| \leq \frac{(\zeta^2)^{N+1}}{N+1}, \tag{9}$$

using the following inequalities:

$$\frac{2}{2N+3} \cdot \frac{1}{1-\zeta^2} < \frac{1}{N+1} \quad \Longleftrightarrow \quad \zeta^2 < \frac{1}{2N+3}.$$

The last one is guaranteed in all practical cases, because with e.g., $|x| \sim 10^{-7}$ also $|\zeta| \sim 10^{-7}$ is valid. As we shall see, the maximum polynomial degree is about $N_{max} = 42$, so that the upper bound $1/(2N+3)$ cannot become smaller than $1/(2N_{max}+3) = 1.14 \ldots \cdot 10^{-2}$, i.e. $1/(2N+3)$ is surely greater than $\zeta^2 \sim 10^{-14}$.

We now consider an interval $x$ with[1] $|x| \ll 1$. Using $R := |x/(2+x)| = |\zeta|$, the absolute error $\delta$ is bounded by $\Delta$

$$\delta = |P(\zeta) - P_N(\zeta)| \leq \frac{R^{2N+2}}{N+1} =: \Delta, \quad \forall \zeta \in \zeta := \frac{x}{2+x}. \tag{10}$$

Concerning the approximation in (8), the next step is to determine an appropriate polynomial degree $N$. For $|\zeta| \ll 1$ it holds $P(\zeta) \approx P_N(\zeta) \approx 2$ and with a given precision $p := $ stagprec the absolute approximation error should be of order $2^{1-53 \cdot p}$. Thus, together with (10) we require

$$\frac{R^{2N+2}}{N+1} = 2^{1-53 \cdot p} \quad \Longleftrightarrow \quad R^{2N+2} = (N+1) \cdot 2^{1-53 \cdot p}. \tag{11}$$

For a facile calculation of $N$, the right-hand side in (11) must be simplified futhermore. Together with xi = li_part(x); ex = expo_gr(xi) (i.e. $ex$ denotes the exponent with respect to base 2 of leading part of the extended staggered number x) we have

$$|x| \approx 2^{ex+expo(x)} = 2^m, \quad \text{with} \quad m := ex + expo(x).$$

Furthermore it holds: $R \approx |x|/2 = 2^{m-1}$ with the consequence

$$2^{(m-1) \cdot (2N+2)} = (N+1) \cdot 2^{1-53 \cdot p},$$

---

[1] $|x| := \max\limits_{r \in x} \{|r|\}$.

and due to $(N + 1) = 2^{\log_2(N+1)}$ it follows

$$(m - 1) \cdot (2N + 2) = \log_2(N + 1) + 1 - 53 \cdot p$$

$$2N + 2 = \frac{53 \cdot p - 1 - \log_2(N + 1)}{1 - m}, \quad m \neq 1.$$

The requirement $|x| \ll 1$ implies that the condition $m \neq 1$ is surely satisfied. For the range $0 \leq N \leq 42$ it holds $0 \leq \log_2(N + 1) < 5.43$, so that, with $p \geq 2$,

$$53 \cdot p - 1 - \log_2(N + 1) \approx 53 \cdot p - 4$$

is a good approximation for calculating $N$. So we get

$$2N + 2 = \frac{53 \cdot p - 4}{1 - m} \quad \Longleftrightarrow \quad N = \frac{53 \cdot p - 4}{2 \cdot (1 - m)} - 1.$$

To ensure $N \geq 0$, the polynomial degree $N$ is additionally increased by 1, and thus, for calculating $N$, we get the quite simple formula:

$$N = \frac{53 \cdot p - 4}{2 \cdot (1 - m)}, \quad m := ex + \texttt{expo}(x), \quad N \geq 0. \tag{12}$$

The C-XSC function $\texttt{expo}(x)$ returns the exponent of the scaling factor of the extended staggered quantity of type $\texttt{lx\_interval}$.

With a sufficient small $|x|$ resp. with a sufficient great value $-m$ the evaluation of $2 \cdot (1 - m)$ in (12) will generate an overflow, which in case of $2 \cdot (1 - m) > 53 \cdot p - 4$ can be avoided by setting $N = 0$.

Since the evaluation of $2 \cdot (1 - m)$ can possibly produce an overflow, the last condition $2 \cdot (1 - m) > 53 \cdot p - 4$ must further be transformed. It holds

$$2 \cdot (1 - m) > 53 \cdot p - 4 \quad \Longleftrightarrow \quad 2m < 6 - 53 \cdot p \quad \text{resp.}$$

$$2 \cdot (ex + \texttt{expo}(x)) < 6 - 53 \cdot p \quad \Longleftrightarrow \quad \texttt{expo}(x) < 3 - \frac{53 \cdot p}{2} - ex.$$

The last inequality is valid if

$$\texttt{expo}(x) < 3 - 27 \cdot p - ex. \tag{13}$$

Thus, if (13) is realized, $N$ is set to zero, and otherwise $N$ is calculated by (12). In either case an overflow is avoided.

The next step is to calculate the upper bound $\Delta$ of the absolute approximation error in (10), where $\Delta$ is defined as follows

$$\Delta = \begin{cases} R^2, & N = 0, \\ \dfrac{R^{2N+2}}{N + 1}, & N \geq 1. \end{cases} \tag{14}$$

With all these quantities being so determined, the function $\texttt{Ln1p}(\ldots)$ ist implemented by:

```
lx_interval Ln1p(const lx_interval &x) throw()
// Calculating an inclusion of ln(1+x) for
// not too wide intervals,      |x| <= 1e-7;
{
    lx_interval res(0),z2,zeta,Ri,Two;
    l_interval xli;
    int N,ex,p;
    real m,expox;

    p = stagprec;
    xli = li_part(x);
    ex = expo_gr(xli); //exponent of leading part
    if (ex>-100000)    // x <> 0
    {
        expox = expo(x);
        if (expox < 3-27*p-ex) N = 0;
        else
        {
            m = ex + expox;    // m = ex + expo(x);
            N = (int) _double( (53*p-4)/(2*(1-m)) );
        }
        // N: Polynomial degree, 0<=N<=42;
        zeta = x / (2+x);
        Two = lx_interval(2); // exact, type cast
        Ri = lx_interval( Sup(abs(zeta)) );
        Ri = sqr(Ri);
        if (N==0)
            res = Two;
        else // N >= 1:
        {
            z2 = sqr(zeta); // z2 = zeta^2
            // Evaluating the polynomial (Horner's scheme):
            res = Two / (2*N+1);  // res = a_(N)
            for (int i=N-1; i>=0; --i)
                res = res*z2 + Two/(2*i+1);
            // Calculating the absolute approximation error:
            Ri = power(Ri,N+1)/(N+1);
        }
        // Implementing the approximation error:
        res += lx_interval(lx_real(0),Sup(Ri));
        res *= zeta;
    } // x <> 0;

    return res;
} // Ln1p(...)
```

**Remarks:**

1. Please note that due to the definition of the absolute approximation error $\delta$ in (9), the addition of its upper bound[2] $\Delta$ has to be done *before* the multiplication with $\zeta$.
2. Due to $P_N(\zeta) < P(\zeta)$ the absolute approximation error is not included by `lx_interval(-Sup(Ri),+Sup(Ri))`, but, coupled with a much smaller interval inflation, by `lx_interval(lx_real(0),Sup(Ri))` instead.

With the help of the `Ln1p` function, the logarithm function

$$\texttt{lx\_interval ln(const lx\_interval \&x);}$$

can now be implemented. In case of $x \approx 1$, i.e. $|x - 1| \leq 10^{-7}$, $\ln(x)$ is included by $\ln(x) \subseteq \texttt{Lnp1}(x \diamond 1)$ and in case of $|x - 1| > 10^{-7}$ the following identity is used

$$\ln(x) = \ln\left((x \cdot 2^{-n}) \cdot 2^n\right), \quad x \in \mathbb{R},\ n \in \mathbb{Z},$$
$$= \ln(t) + n \cdot \ln(2); \quad t := x \cdot 2^{-n} \in \mathbb{R}.$$

Concerning the first reduced argument $t := x \cdot 2^{-n}, n \in \mathbb{Z}$ is calculated to realize $t \approx 1$ as well as possible, in order to evaluate $\ln(t)$ with an accuracy as high as possible by using function `Lnp1()`: $\ln(t) = \texttt{Lnp1}(t - 1)$. Please keep in mind that the multiplication in $t = x \cdot 2^{-n}$ can be calculated error-free and quite effectively in the class `lx_interval`.

For a further improvement of $t \approx 1$ we use [46]

$$\ln(t) = 2^k \cdot \ln\left(\sqrt[2^k]{t}\right), \quad \text{with} \quad \lim_{k \to \infty} \sqrt[2^k]{t} = 1.$$

Thus, for a sufficient large $k \in \mathbb{N}$, the 2nd reduced argument $u := \sqrt[2^k]{t}$ lies sufficiently close to 1. However, for e.g. $k = 22$, the calculation of $u$, using the $2^k$-th root function, is quite expensive. A much more efficient method is to evaluate the loop

```
u = t;
for (int j=1; j<=k; j++)
    u = sqrt(u);
```

where the last value u is a quite good approximation of $\sqrt[2^k]{t} \approx u$. For the calculation of $k$, the exponent $m$ of $x = M \cdot 2^m$, $0.5 \leq M < 1$ has to be specified first.

Now choosing $n := m$, we get $t = M$, and, defining $t := 1 - \varepsilon$, it holds $0 < \varepsilon \leq 0.5$ and we get the quite good approximation

$$u = \sqrt[2^k]{t} = \sqrt[2^k]{1 - \varepsilon} \approx 1 - \frac{\varepsilon}{2^k}.$$

For an effective evaluation of $\ln(u) \approx \ln(1 - \varepsilon/2^k)$ we require

$$\frac{\varepsilon}{2^k} \leq 10^{-6} \quad \Longleftrightarrow \quad \varepsilon \leq 2^k \cdot 10^{-6}$$

$$\Longleftrightarrow \quad k \geq \frac{\ln(\varepsilon) + 6 \cdot \ln(10)}{\ln(2)}.$$

---

[2] in the source code: $\Delta := \texttt{Sup(Ri)}$.

In case of $\varepsilon \ll 1$, the above fraction becomes negative and $k = 0$ is set, i.e., the second argument reduction fail. In case of $k \geq 1$ it holds

$$\ln(x) = n \cdot \ln(2) + 2^k \cdot \ln(u), \quad t = x \cdot 2^{-n}, \quad u = \sqrt[2^k]{t}, \quad k = 1, 2, 3, \ldots \quad (15)$$

and $\ln(u) = \ln(1 + (u - 1))$. In order to enclose $\ln(x)$, the right-hand side of (15) has to be evaluated using intervals:

$$\ln(x) \in n \diamond < \ln(2) > \oplus 2^k \diamond \text{Lnp1}(u \ominus 1), \quad \forall x \in \text{x}.$$

$< \ln(2) >$ denotes a guaranteed enclosure of $\ln(2)$ in high accuracy. It is predefined as a C-XSC staggered interval constant `Ln2_lx_interval()`. The quantity u is the result of the above `for` loop performed by an interval evaluation, and before this loop $t \in \mathbb{R}$ has to be substituted by $x \diamond 2^{-n}$. The multiplication with $2^k$ can be realized effectively and error-free by use of the function `times2pown(...)`.

# 4   Complex Staggered (Interval) Operations and Complex Elementary Transcendental Functions

Extended complex staggered (interval) numbers are formed as pairs of two real extended staggered (interval) numbers in an obvious way (real and imaginary part, respectively). Such an extended complex staggered interval represents a rectangle in the complex plane with sides parallel to the axes (we have not implemented a center-radius representation). All basic operations as well as a large set of elementary transcendental functions are available for the new extended complex staggered interval data type [6]. More about complex interval functions may be found in [5,7,12,11,40].

## 4.1   Remark on Complex Division

By considering complex division we demonstrate the gain in accuracy when replacing the ordinary staggered arithmetic by the new extended staggered arithmeic. We restrict ourselves to the evaluation of the real part formula of a complex division. With

```
x= Rex + i Imx
y= Rey + i Imy
```

we have to compute

```
Re(x/y)= (Rex*Rey+Imx*Imy)/(Rey*Rey + Imy*Imy).
```

We perform this computation using ordinary staggered intervals and using extended staggered intervals.

In the following code snippet `l_interval` variables are ordinary staggered interval numbers:

```
stagprec= 30;

l_interval  Rex, Imx, Rey, Imy, q; //ordinary!
```

```
Rex= 1e150;   Imx= 1e150;   //x= 1e150  + 1e150 i
Rey= 1e-150; Imy=1e-150;   //y= 1e-150 + 1e-150 i

q= (Rex*Rey + Imx*Imy) / (Rey*Rey+Imy*Imy); //Re(x/y)

cout << "Re(x/y) ) = " << q << endl;
cout << RelDiam(q) << endl;

Output:
Re(x/y) ) = [9.9999999999999999745402366E+299,
               9.9999999999999999745402415E+299]
RelDiam(q): 4.94...e-24
```

Let us now perform the same computation using extended staggered intervals:

```
lx_interval  Rex, Imx, Rey, Imy, q; //extended!
Rex= 1e150;   Imx= 1e150;
Rey= 1e-150; Imy= 1e-150;

q= (Rex*Rey + Imx*Imy) / (Rey*Rey+Imy*Imy);

cout << RelDiam(q) << endl;

Output:
RelDiam(q): {-487, [ 1.1491393399, 1.1491393400]}
More than 480 correct decimal digits!
```

This gives more than 480 correct decimal digits.

We see that in the first case only about 24 digits are correct, whereas in the second case (using the new data type `lx_interval`) we get more than 480 correct decimals. This very strong improvement is due to new operations performing optimal scalings automatically.

### 4.2  Complex Transcendental Functions

Available functions for extended complex staggered arguments and extended complex staggered interval arguments are the root function, exp fuctions, logarithms, the trigono-metric functions, the inverse trigonometric functions, the hyperbolic functions and the inverse hyperbolic functions, the power function (and some additional functions). For multivalued functions the principal branch is realized [7,12,11,40]. For more details and a complete list of all functions provided by the new package, see [6] or updates of this documentation, respectively. To our knowledge there is no other package available providing elementary functions for any kind of multiple precision intervals.

## 5  Applications

In this section we demonstrate the ease of use and the power of staggered intervals delivering a special kind of a multiple precision arithmetic.

## 5.1   Dynamical System

Let us consider the simple dynamical system as given by the logistic equation:

$$x_{n+1} = a \cdot x_n \cdot (1 - x_n), \quad n \geq 0 \tag{16}$$

for some $a \in [0, 4]$ and $x_0 \in (0, 1)$.

Its Mean Value Form [36] (capital characters denote interval quantities) is:

$$X_{n+1} = a \cdot \left( y_n(1 - y_n) + (1 - 2X_n) \cdot (X_n - y_n) \right)$$

$$\text{with} \quad y_n \approx \text{midpoint of } X_n.$$

For parameter $a$ close to 4, this system exhibits chaotic behavior. Ordinary floating point computations will deliver quantitatively wrong results, when compared with the true trajectory.

The naive interval approach results in the following source code:

```
//Logistic equation using naive interval evaluations.
//The program works for
//  - ordinary intervals:            data type    interval
//  - ordinary staggered intervals:  data type  l_interval
//  - new scaled staggered intervals: data type lx_interval
//Please change line (*) below accordingly.

#include "simple_output.hpp"
#include <interval.hpp>      //ordinary intervals
#include <l_interval.hpp>    //ordinary staggered intervals
#include "lx_interval.hpp" //scaled staggered intervals (new)
using namespace std;
using namespace cxsc;

int main() {
  stagprec= 35;
  int iter;

  interval a(3.75);
  lx_interval x(0.5), y; //interval, l_interval, or lx_interval (*)

  cout << "Parameter a: " << out(a, 10, 2);
  cout << "x_0: " << out(x, 10, 2);

  for (iter=1; ; iter++) {
    x= a*x*(1-x);
    if ( diam(x) > 1/64.0) break; //accuracy lost
    if (iter%25 == 0)

      cout << "x_" << iter << ": " << out(x,30,2) << endl;
  }
  cout << "x_" << iter << ": " << out(x,15,2) << endl;
```

```
cout << "diam(x_" << iter << "): "
     << out(diam(x),5,2) << endl;

cout << "stagprec for l_interval or lx_interval: "
     << stagprec << endl;
} //end main
```

Depending on the data type used in the source code line marked by ( * ) we get using ordinary floating point intervals (C-XSC data type `interval`):

```
x_0:
[0.5000000000E00,
 0.5000000000E00]
x_25:
[0.81492020622606475832583281560E00,
 0.814968494495680428890693747235E00]

x_30:
[0.700265238773841E00,
 0.736074716058462E00]

diam(x_30): 0.35810E-1
```

Using ordinary staggered intervals (C-XSC data type `l_interval`) results in:

```
x_525:
[0.928090224814844289179247260075E00,
 0.928090224814844289179500794739E00]

x_550:
[0.648603399290149318368037256732E00,
 0.648603515173498124113393714652E00]

x_559:
[0.229605106308041E00,
 0.246599373683800E00]

diam(x_559): 0.16995E-1

stagprec for l_interval or lx_interval: 35
```

And using our new extended staggered intervals (new data type `lx_interval`) we find:

```
x_750:
[0.772410635893338359233942006639E00,
 0.772410635893338359233942006640E00]
```

```
x_775:
[0.65944712494111867648353695482E00,
 0.65944712494111867648353695489E00]

x_800:
[0.43447661328996839413818520370lE00,
 0.434476613289973057074888629359E00]

x_822:
[0.804358248382084E00,
 0.824700497605603E00]
```

```
diam(x_822): 0.20343E-1
```

```
stagprec for l_interval or lx_interval: 35
```

Using intervals with IEEE double numbers as bounds we can perform 30 time steps. Using ordinary staggered intervals allow 559, and using the new extended staggered intervals even allow 822 time steps to be performed.

The code snipped for the more sophisticated Mean Value Form [36] is as follows:

```
//Logistic equation using the mean value form.
for (iter=1; ;iter++) {
  y= mid(x);
  x= a*( y*(1-y) + (1-2*x)*(x-y) ); //mean value form
  if ( diam(x) > 1/64.0) break;      //accuracy lost
  if (iter%25 == 0)
    cout << "x_" << iter << ": " << out(x,30,2) << endl;
}

cout << "x_" << iter << ": " << out(x,15,2) << endl;

cout << "diam(x_" << iter << "): "
     << out(diam(x),5,2) << endl;

cout << "stagprec for l_interval or lx_interval: "
     << stagprec << endl;
} //end main
```

Again, depending on the data type used (interval, l_interval, or lx_interval) we get (output manually shortened) the following.

Output when using ordinary intervals:

```
x_77:
[0.373154693174543E00,
 0.412753336460682E00]
```

Output when using ordinary staggered intervals:

```
x_1815:
[0.846085793958738E00,
 0.863148620031332E00]

diam(x_1815): 0.17063E-1

stagprec for l_interval or lx_interval: 35
```

Output when using our new scaled staggered intervals:

```
x_2790:
[0.269878320807725E00,
 0.292405387978198E00]

diam(x_2790): 0.22528E-1

stagprec for l_interval or lx_interval: 35
```

These computations show that using the (extended) staggered operations, the number of time steps can be increased considerably (from 77 to 1815 to 2790).

Replacing the naive interval computations by computations using the Mean Value Form increases the number of time steps (in case of data type lx_interval) from 822 to 2790.

We have checked our computations against corresponding high precision computations using Maple and intpakX [30] successfully.

## 5.2 Straightforward Limit Calculations, Powers with Very High Exponents

To test our package let us try to compute some approximation to the Euler number $e$ in a straightforard way (there are much better methods to compute $e$). More precisely, let us compute an enclosure of the approximation

$$r = \left(1 + \frac{1}{10^{600,000,000}}\right)^{10^{600,000,000}}$$

Note that the exponent $n$, written as a decimal number, has sixhundred million and one digits.

```
#include <iostream>
#include "../../lx_interval.hpp" //extended staggered intervals
#include "../logistic/simple_output.hpp" //out function
using namespace std;
using namespace cxsc;

int main() {
    stagprec= 3; //about 3-fold IEEE double precision
```

```
cout << "Precision about " << stagprec*15
     << " digits ..." << endl;

int sixHundredMillion(600000000);
lx_interval n, r;
n= lx_interval(sixHundredMillion,"[1,1]");
//n now equals to 10^600,000,000

//xp1_pow_y(x,y) computes (1+x)^y;
//useful if 1+x is very close to 1
r= xp1_pow_y(1/n,n);
cout << "(1+1/n)^n with n=10^600,000,000: "
     << out(r,50,2) << endl;
return 0;
}
```

The output of the program is as follows:

```
Precision about 45 digits ...
(1+1/n)^n with n=10^600,000,000:
[2.7182818284590452353602874713526624977572470936840 7E00,
 2.7182818284590452353602874713526624977572470937223 9E00]
```

Thus, using stagprec = 3 gives an enclosure of the result accurate to about 45 decimal digits. The function xp1Pow(x, n) computes $(x+1)^n$. It should be used if $x+1$ is very close to 1 (i.e. if $|x|$ is very small). Increasing the length of the staggered numbers involved (i.e. simply increasing the value of the variable stagprec) increases the accuracy of the enclosure to several hundred correct digits. Note that a corresponding calculation cannot be done using the computer algebra systems Mathematica or Maple 12. Both systems will fail. We do not mention this fact to blame the Computer Algebra packages. We just want to emphasize the computational power of our new extended staggered interval data type.

Let us now see, how far

$$(1 + \frac{1}{n})^n \text{ with } n = 300$$

is apart from the limit

$$e = \lim_{n \to \infty} (1 + \frac{1}{n})^n.$$

The following source code snippet does the job:

```
stagprec= 20;   //about 20-fold IEEE double precision
cout << "Precision about " << stagprec*15
     << " digits ..." << endl;
//use predefined constant E_lx_interval() for e
lx_interval Euler(E_lx_interval()); //enclosure of exp(1)
```

```
n= lx_interval(300, "[1,1]");    //10^300
r= pow(1+1/n, n);                //r= (1+1/10^300)^(10^300)
cout << "Enclosure of displacement e-((1+1/10^300)^(10^300):"
     << out(Euler-r);
```

The output produced by this C-XSC program is

```
Precision about 300 digits ...
Enclosure of displacement e-((1+1/10^300)^(10^300):
[0.135914091181860E-299,
 0.135914091464271E-299]
```

We see, that

$$r = \left(1 + \frac{1}{10^{300}}\right)^{10^{300}}$$

is (as expected) smaller than the Euler number $e$. The difference $e - r$ is 0.1359... $E - 299$. This shows that $r$ approximates $e$ with 300 decimal digits.

### 5.3   Verified Root Enclosures of Complex Functions

We consider a nonlinear complex (interval) function. Finding its roots is a non trivial problem in numerical mathematics. Most algorithms deliver only an approximation to one of the exact zeroes without or with only a weak statement concerning its accuracy.

In this section, we describe an algorithm which allows the computation of verified enclosures of a root starting from an appropriate approximation. The algorithm used is based on the following Theorem 1 [9,26], where $\underline{\cup}$ denotes the convex hull of two complex sets, $A \overset{\circ}{\subset} B$ means that $A$ is fully contained in the interior of $B$, and $[S]$ is the interval hull of a bounded complex set $S$.

**Theorem 1.** *Let $Z$ be a complex interval, $z \in \mathbb{C}$, $0 \neq c \in \mathbb{C}$, and let $f : \mathbb{C} \to \mathbb{C}$ be an analytic function in the convex region $R \supset z \underline{\cup} (z + Z)$. If*

$$-c \cdot f(z) + [(1 - c \cdot f'(z \underline{\cup} (z + Z))) \cdot Z] \overset{\circ}{\subset} Z \qquad (17)$$

*holds true, then there exists a unique zero $z_0$ of $f(z)$, with $z_0 \in z + Z$.*
The proof of this theorem is given in the appendix on page 65 (see also [26]). In practice, the constant $c \neq 0$ is often set to $c = 1/f'(z)$.

In the following example we have calculated $f'(Z)$ by symbolic differentiation. This sometimes tedious procedure can be replaced by using automatic differentiation, which delivers enclosures $f(Z)$ as well as $f'(Z)$ simultaneously (see [18,20]).
The following numerical example is taken from [26]. We consider the function

$$f(z) = \arctan\left((z - a) \cdot \ln(z^2 - 5 \cdot z + 8 + i)\right) \text{ with first derivative}$$

$$f'(z) = \frac{\ln(z^2 - 5 \cdot z + 8 + i) + \dfrac{(z - a) \cdot (2 \cdot z - 5)}{z^2 - 5 \cdot z + 8 + i}}{1 + (z - a)^2 \cdot (\ln(z^2 - 5 \cdot z + 8 + i))^2}.$$

Then setting $a = 4i$, the zeros of $f(z)$ are

$$z_0 = 2+i, \qquad z_1 = 3-i, \qquad z_2 = 4i.$$

With a sufficiently close approximation to $z_0$ the following C-XSC program calculates guaranteed enclosures of the root $z_0$. The source code for the function $f$ and its derivative $df$ is as follows:

```
static const lx_cinterval c(8,1); //constant value 8+i
static const lx_cinterval a(0,4); //parameter value a = 4*i

//Complex function f(z) to be considered;
//its zeros are a, 2+i, and 3-i:
lx_cinterval f(const lx_cinterval &z) {
   return atan( (z-a)*ln(sqr(z)-5*z+c) );
}

//Derivative df(z) of the function f(z):
lx_cinterval df(const lx_cinterval &z) {
   lx_cinterval y, w;
   y= ln(sqr(z)-5*z+c);
   w= y + (z-a)*(2*z-5)/( sqr(z)-5*z+c );
   w= w/( 1 + sqr(z-a)*sqr(y) );
   return w;
}

lx_cinterval blow(const lx_cinterval &z) {
   lx_cinterval res;   //We use an epsilon inflation with
                       //fixed epsilon equal to 10^(-30):
   res= z*(1 - interval(-1e-30, 1e-30));
   return res; //Routine should be improved to be more useful
}
```

Now we show the computational part:

```
int main() {
   stagprec= 3; //We use only medium precision (about 45 digits)

   lx_cinterval xTilde, R, C, Z, X, Xnew;

   //Take as complex starting point an approximation to the root 2+i:
   xTilde= lx_cinterval(1.999, 0.999); //complex point interval
   cout << "Initial approximation to the root:" << out(xTilde);

   //Perform 3 (point) Newton steps to improve initial approximation:
   cout << "Improving initial approximation ..." << endl;
   X= xTilde;
   for (int i=1; i<4; i++) {
     Xnew= mid(X) - f(mid(X)) / df(mid(X));
     X= Xnew;
```

```
   }
   xTilde= mid(Xnew); //Hopefully improved approximation
   cout << "Improved approximation: " << out(xTilde,40,2);

   //Interval Newton steps could be performed. Instead we
   //use Theorem 1 to get a verification of the enclosure Xnew
   //of the error of our improved approximation xTilde.
   //(We do not include the zero itself but the difference
   //to the approximate solution xTilde.)
   //Thus, xTilde + Xnew is (hopefully) an accurate enclosure
   //of the zero:
   R= lx_cinterval( 1/Sup(df(xTilde)) );
   Z= -R*f(xTilde);
   X= blow(Z);
   bool verified;
   int iMax(10);
   cout << "Try to improve even more and to verify ..." << endl;
   for (int i=1; i<iMax; i++) {
      C= 1-R*df( xTilde | (xTilde+X) ); //interval hull
      Xnew= Z + C*X;
      verified= (Xnew < X); //Xnew in the interior of X?
      cout << "(Assumed) enclosure of root: "
           << out(xTilde+Xnew,40,2);
      cout << boolalpha << "Enclosure verified using Theorem 1: "
           << verified << endl;
      if (verified) break;
      X= blow(Xnew); //Perform another verification step after
                     //inflating Xnew (epsilon inflation)
   } //end for
   return 0;
} //end main
```

Executing the program produces the following output:

```
Initial approximation to the root:
Real part:
[1.999000000000000E00,
 1.999000000000001E00]
Imaginary part:
[0.998999999999999E00,
 0.999000000000000E00]

Improving initial approximation ...
Improved approximation:
Real part:
[1.999999999999999999999954685975568225289 9E00,
 1.999999999999999999999954685975568225290 0E00]
Imaginary part:
[0.99999999999999999999999473457220024265114E00,
```

```
0.9999999999999999999999473457220024265115E00]
```

```
Try to improve even more and to verify ...
(Assumed) enclosure of root:
Real part:
[1.9999999999999999999999999999999999999999E00,
 2.0000000000000000000000000000000000000001E00]
Imaginary part:
[0.9999999999999999999999999999999999999999E00,
 1.0000000000000000000000000000000000000001E00]
```

```
Enclosure verified using Theorem 1: true
```

The algorithm works well with a sufficiently good approximation to the root. Thus, it is advisable to perform some point Newton steps before (as we have done) to get an approximation even closer to the zero. Note that the verification step using Theorem 1 gives an enclosure with the number of correct digits doubled compared to the approximation.

In the code above we do not additionally implement $f$ and $df$ as functions with point arguments (or as template functions). Instead some type conversions from point to interval quantities and vice versa are used. See e.g. the code line to compute the quantity R at the beginning of the verification step. This leads to some (unnecessary) interval calculations which should be replaced by point computations for efficiency reasons.

## 6  Conclusion and Future Work

Extended staggered (interval) arithmetics are very useful tools for reliable numerical computations far beyond IEEE double computations and/or interval computations using ordinary interval data types. We have realized such extended arithmetics for real and for complex (staggered interval) computations. A complete set of transcendental elementary functions is available for the new extended staggered data types. The scaling factor introduced in the extended data types allows a very wide exponent range. Additionally, as our numerical examples show, the accuracy of numerical computations is improved significantly compared to ordinary staggered interval computations. This improvement resulted mainly from our automatic scalings introduced by the implementation of the basic arithmetical extended staggered operations.

The new arithmetics would be very fast if an exact dot product for vectors with floating point components were supported by hardware. Exact dot products are a key feature to get numerical results with high accuracy. We want the manufacturers of processors to incorporate an exact dot product facility on their microchips! The (little) additional amount of hardware [32,33] would be (very) valuable for scientists/engineers interested in fast and highly accurate reliable numerical computations.

Our work, concerned with extended staggered numbers, is still in progress [6]. Up to now the main focus has been on point computations or computations with very narrow intervals (with respect to the staggered level stagprec in use). In the future, we will support also wide interval computations. Additionally, we will replace the integer scaling factor (32 bit) by a scaling factor of type double (53 mantissa bit). Thus, the exponent range of our extended staggered numbers will be further increased. Last but not least, the input/output facilities of extended staggered quantities should be improved and automatic differentiation [8] should be provided.

# References

1. Alefeld, G., Herzberger, J.: Introduction to Interval Computations. Academic Press, New York (1983)
2. American National Standards Institute/Institute of Electrical and Electronics Engineers: IEEE Standard for Binary Floating-Point Arithmetic; ANSI/IEEE Std 754–1985, New York (1985)
3. Auzinger, W., Stetter, H.J.: Accurate Arithmetic Results for Decimal Data on Non-Decimal Computers. Computing 35, 141–151 (1985)
4. Blomquist, F., Hofschuster, W., Krämer, W.: Realisierung der hyperbolischen Cotangens-Funktion in einer Staggered-Correction-Intervallarithmetik in C-XSC. Preprint 2004/3, Scientific Computing/Software Engineering, University of Wuppertal (2004)
5. Blomquist, F.: Verbesserungen im Bereich komplexer Standardfunktionen, interne Mitteilung. Scientific Computing/Software Engineering, University of Wuppertal (2005)
6. Blomquist, F., Hofschuster, W., Krämer, W.: Real and Complex Staggered (Interval) Arithmetics with Wide Exponent Range (in German). Preprint 2008/1, Scientific Computing/Software Engineering, University of Wuppertal (2008)
7. Blomquist, F., Hofschuster, W., Krämer, W., Neher, M.: Complex Interval Functions in C-XSC, Preprint BUW-WRSWT 2005/2, Scientific Computing/Software Engineering, University of Wuppertal, pp. 1–48 (2005)
8. Blomquist, F., Hofschuster, W., Krämer, W.: Real and Complex Taylor Arithmetic in C-XSC. Preprint BUW-WRSWT 2005/4, Scientific Computing/Software Engineering, University of Wuppertal (2005)
9. Böhm, H.: Berechnung von Polynomnullstellen und Auswertung arithmetischer Ausdrücke mit garantierter maximaler Genauigkeit. Dissertation, Universität Karlsruhe (1983)
10. Bohlender, G.: What Do We Need Beyond IEEE Arithmetic? In: Ullrich, C. (ed.) Computer Arithmetic and Self-Validating Numerical Methods. Academic Press, London (1990)
11. Braune, K., Krämer, W.: High Accuracy Standard Functions for Real and Complex Intervals. In: Kaucher, E., Kulisch, U., Ullrich, C. (eds.) Computerarithmetic: Scientific Computation and Programming Languages, pp. 81–114. Teubner, Stuttgart (1987)
12. Braune, K.: Standard Functions for Real and Complex Point and Interval Arguments with Dynamic Accuracy. Computing Supplementum 6, 159–184 (1988)
13. Brent, R.P.: A Fortran Multiple-Precision Arithmetic Package. ACM Transactions on Mathematical Software (TOMS) 4(1), 57–70 (1978)
14. Cuyt, A., Kuterna, P., Verdonk, B., Vervloet, J.: Arithmos: a reliable integrated computational environment (2001),
   http://www.cant.ua.ac.be/arithmos/index.html
15. Cuyt, A., Petersen, V.B., Verdonk, B., Waadeland, H., Jones, W.B.: Handbook of Continued Fractions for Special Functions. Springer, Heidelberg (2008)
16. Dekker, T.J.: A Floating-Point Technique for Extending the Available Precision. Num. Math. 18, 224–242 (1971)
17. Fousse, L., Hanrot, G., Lefèvre, V., Pélissier, P., Zimmermann, P.: MPFR: A multiple-precision binary floating-point library with correct rounding. Transactions on Mathematical Software (TOMS) 33(2) (2007)

18. Griewank, A., Corliss, G. (eds.): Automatic Differentiation of Algorithms: Theory, Implementation, and Applications. SIAM, Philadelphia (1991)
19. Grimmer, M., Petras, K., Revol, N.: Multiple Precision Interval Packages. In: Alt, R., Frommer, A., Kearfott, R.B., Luther, W. (eds.) Numerical Software with Result Verification (Dagstuhl Seminar 2003). LNCS, vol. 2991, pp. 64–90. Springer, Heidelberg (2004)
20. Hammer, R., Hocks, M., Kulisch, U., Ratz, D.: C++ Toolbox for Verified Computing: Basic Numerical Problems. Springer, Heidelberg (1995)
21. Herzberger, J. (ed.): Topics in Validated Computations. Proceedings of IMACS-GAMM International Workshop on Validated Numerics, Oldenburg, 1993. North Holland, Amsterdam (1994)
22. Hofschuster, W., Krämer, W.: C-XSC – A C++ Class Library for Extended Scientific Computing. In: Alt, R., Frommer, A., Kearfott, R.B., Luther, W. (eds.) Numerical Software with Result Verification (Dagstuhl Seminar 2003). LNCS, vol. 2991, pp. 15–35. Springer, Heidelberg (2004)
23. Hofschuster, W., Krämer, W., Neher, M.: C-XSC and closely related software packages. In: Cuyt, A., et al. (eds.) Numerical Validation in Current Hardware Architectures (Dagstuhl Seminar 2008). LNCS, vol. 5492, pp. 68–102. Springer, Heidelberg (2009)
24. Klatte, R., Kulisch, U., Lawo, C., Rauch, M., Wiethoff, A.: C-XSC, A C++ Class Library for Extended Scientific Computing. Springer, Heidelberg (1993)
25. Klotz, G.: Faktorisierung von Matrizen mit maximaler Genauigkeit. Dissertation, Universität Karlsruhe (1987)
26. Krämer, W.: Inverse Standardfunktionen für reelle und komplexe Intervallargumente mit a priori Fehlerabschätzungen für beliebige Datenformate, Dissertation, Universität Karlsruhe (1987)
27. Krämer, W.: Mehrfachgenaue reelle und intervallmäßige Staggered-Correction Arithmetik mit zugehörigen Standardfunktionen, Bericht des Instituts für Angewandte Mathematik, Universität Karlsruhe, pp. S.1–80 (1988)
28. Krämer, W., Walter, W.: FORTRAN-SC: A FORTRAN Extension for Engineering/Scientific Computation with Access to ACRITH, General Information Notes and Sample Programs. IBM Deutschland GmbH (1989)
29. Krämer W., Kulisch U., Lohner, R.: Numerical Toolbox for Verified Computing II. Springer. Draft tb2.ps.gz (1994),
    http://www.rz.uni-karlsruhe.de/~Rudolf.Lohner/papers/
30. Krämer, W.: Introduction to the Maple Power Tool intpakX. Serdica Journal of Computing, Bulgarian Academy of Sciences 1(4), 467–504 (2007)
31. Kulisch, U.: The Fifth Floating-Point Operation for Top-Performance Computers or Accumulation of Floating-Point Numbers and Products in Fixed-Point Arithmetic. Bericht 4/1997 des Forschungsschwerpunkts Computerarithmetik, Intervallrechnung und Numerische Algorithmen mit Ergebnisverifikation, Universität Karlsruhe (1997)
32. Kulisch, U.: Advanced Arithmetic for the Digital Computer. Design of Arithmetic Units. Springer, Wien (2002)
33. Kulisch, U.: Computer Arithmetic and Validity – Theory. Implementation and Application. de Gruyter Studies in Mathematics 33 (2008)
34. Lohner, R.: Einschließung der Lösung gewöhnlicher Anfangs- und Randwertaufgaben mit Anwendungen. Dissertation, Universität Karlsruhe (1988)
35. Lohner, R.: Enclosing all Eigenvalues of Symmetric Matrices. In: Ullrich, C., Wolff von Gudenberg, J. (eds.) Accurate Numerical Algorithms, Research Reports ESPRIT. Springer, Heidelberg (1989)
36. Lohner, R.: Interval arithmetic in staggered correction format. In: Adams, E., Kulisch, U. (eds.) Scientific Computing with Automatic Result Verification, pp. 301–321. Academic Press, San Diego (1993)

37. Lozier, D.W.: The NIST Digital Library of Mathematical Functions Project. Annals of Mathematics and Artificial Intelligence 38 (2003)
38. Markstein, P.: IA-64 and Elementary Functions: Speed and Precision. Hewlett-Packard Professional Books
39. Muller, J.-M.: Elementary Functions Algorithms and Implementation, 2nd edn (2006) ISBN: 978-0-8176-4372-0
40. Neher, M.: Complex Standard Functions and Their Implementation in the CoStLy Library. ACM Transactions on Mathematical Software 33(1), 27 pages (2007)
41. Ogita, T., Rump, S.M., Oishi, S.: Accurate Sum and Dot Product. SIAM Journal on Scientific Computing (SISC) 26(6), 195520131988 (2005)
42. Overton, M.L.: Numerical Computing with IEEE Floating Point Arithmetic. SIAM, Philadelphia (2001)
43. Priest, D.: Algorithms for arbitrary precision floating point arithmetic. In: 10th IEEE Symposium on Computer Arithmetic, pp. 132–143 (1991)
44. Revol, N.: Motivation for an Arbitrary Precision Interval Arithmetic and the MPFI Library (2002),
    http://www.cs.utep.edu/interval-comp/interval.02/revo.pdf
45. Revol, N., Rouillier, F.: MPFI, a multiple precision interval arithmetic library based on MPFR (2005), http://mpfi.gforge.inria.fr/
46. Rotmaier, B.: Die Berechnung der elementaren Funktionen mit beliebiger Genauigkeit. Dissertation, Universität Karlsruhe (1971)
47. Rump, S.M.: Kleine Fehlerschranken bei Matrixproblemen. Dissertation, Universität Karlsruhe (1980)
48. Smith, D.M.: Algorithm 693; a FORTRAN package for floating-point multiple-precision arithmetic. ACM Transactions on Mathematical Software (TOMS) 17(2), 273–283 (1991)
49. Stetter, H.J.: Staggered Correction Representation, a Feasible Approach to Dynamic Precision. In: Cai, Fosdick, Huang (eds.) Proceedings of the Symposium on Scientific Software. China University of Science and Technology Press, Beijing (1989)
50. Temme, N.M.: Special Functions: An Introduction to the Classical Functions of Mathematical Physics. John Wiley & Sons Inc., Chichester (1996)
51. Toussaint, F.: Implementierung reeller und intervallmäßiger Standardfunktionen für eine staggered-correction Langzahlarithmetik in C-XSC. Diplomarbeit, Institut für Angewandte Mathematik, Universität Karlsruhe (1993)
52. XSC website on programming languages for scientific computing with validation, http://www.xsc.de

# A    Proof of Theorem 1

First some notations/definitions:

- $z = x + i \cdot y \in \mathbb{C}$.
  In this appendix we use $|z| := |x| + |y|$, with $|z| \geq \sqrt{x^2 + y^2}$.
- $S \subset \mathbb{C}$ denotes an arbitrary bounded subset of $\mathbb{C}$.
  We define $|S| := \max_{z \in S}\{|z|\}$.
  $[\,S\,]$ denotes the interval hull of $S$.
- With $S_1 \subset \mathbb{C}$ and $S_2 \subset \mathbb{C}$ the convex hull is denoted by $S_1 \cup S_2$.
- The diameter of a real interval $X = [\underline{x}, \overline{x}]$ is defined by $\mathrm{d}(X) := \overline{x} - \underline{x}$.

- The diameter of a complex interval $Z = X + i \cdot Y$ is defined by $d(Z) := d(X) + d(Y)$. It can easily be shown that $d(z + Z) = d(Z)$.
- $S \cdot Z := \{w \mid w = s \cdot z; \ s \in S, z \in Z\}$.

With the above notations it holds[3]

$$d([S \cdot Z]) \geq |S| \cdot d(Z). \tag{18}$$

**Theorem 1.** As formulated on page 59: *Let $Z$ be a complex interval, $z \in \mathbb{C}, 0 \neq c \in \mathbb{C}$, and let $f : \mathbb{C} \to \mathbb{C}$ be an analytic function in the convex region $R \supset z \underline{\cup} (z + Z)$. Then if*

$$-c \cdot f(z) + [(1 - c \cdot f'(z \underline{\cup} (z + Z))), \cdot Z] \overset{\circ}{\subset} Z \tag{19}$$

*there exists a unique zero $z_0$ of $f(z)$, with $z_0 \in z + Z$.*

**Proof.** (See also [26])

Let $f : \mathbb{C} \to \mathbb{C}$ be an analytic function in $R$. For the range $h(z + Z)$ of the analytic auxiliary function

$$h(z) := z - c \cdot f(z) \tag{20}$$

the following inclusion relation holds, [9, Theorem 5, page 35]

$$h(z + Z) \subset h(z) + [h'(z \underline{\cup} (z + Z)) \cdot Z]. \tag{21}$$

With the definition of $h(z)$ we find

$$h(z + Z) \subset z - c \cdot f(z) + [(1 - c \cdot f'(z \underline{\cup} (z + Z))) \cdot Z], \tag{22}$$

and together with (19) we get the inclusion relation

$$h(z + Z) \overset{\circ}{\subset} z + Z. \tag{23}$$

Thus, Brouwer's fixed-point theorem shows that the auxiliary (nonlinear) function $h(z)$ has at least one fixed-point $z_0 \in z + Z$, i.e. $h(z_0) = z_0$, and with the definition of $h(z)$ it follows that $f(z)$ has at least one zero $z_0 \in z + Z$.

We now show that this zero $z_0 \in z + Z$ is unique. The inclusion relation (19) implies

$$z - c \cdot f(z) + [(1 - c \cdot f'(z \underline{\cup} (z + Z))) \cdot Z] \overset{\circ}{\subset} Z + z,$$

and for the diameter d we get the estimations

$$\begin{aligned}
d(z + Z) &> d(z - c \cdot f(z) + [(1 - c \cdot f'(z \underline{\cup} (z + Z))) \cdot Z]) \\
&= d([(1 - c \cdot f'(z \underline{\cup} (z + Z))) \cdot Z]) \\
&\geq |1 - c \cdot f'(z \underline{\cup} (z + Z))| \cdot d(Z).
\end{aligned}$$

---

[3] It should be noted that (18) is a generalization of $d(A \cdot B) \geq |A| \cdot d(B)$, where $A$ and $B$ are complex intervals, [1, (15), page 72].

The equal sign follows from a displacement in the $z$-plane, generated by $z - c \cdot f(z)$, and the last line follows from (18). If condition (19) is fulfilled in Theorem 1, $Z$ cannot be a point interval and so $d(Z)$ has to be positive. Hence $d(z + Z) = d(Z) > 0$, and, with the above estimation, we get

$$|1 - c \cdot f'(z \underline{\cup} (z + Z))| < 1, \quad \text{resp.} \quad |h'(z \underline{\cup} (z + Z))| < 1. \tag{24}$$

This demonstrates that the function $h(z)$ is a contractive mapping in $z + Z \subset z \underline{\cup} (z + Z)$. According to Banach's fixed-point theorem exactly one fixed-point $z_0$ exists. Hence

$$z_0 \in z + Z, \quad \text{and} \quad h(z_0) = z_0.$$

With (24) we see

$$c \neq 0 \quad \text{and} \quad 0 \notin f'(z \underline{\cup} (z + Z)).$$

Hence, from the definition of $h(z)$ it follows that the unique fixed-point $z_0$ of $h(z)$ is a unique simple root of $f(z)$ ∎

# C-XSC and Closely Related Software Packages

Werner Hofschuster[1], Walter Krämer[1], and Markus Neher[2]

[1] Scientific Computing/Software Engineering, Bergische Universität Wuppertal
D-42097 Wuppertal, Gaußstraße 20, Germany
{hofschuster,kraemer}@math.uni-wuppertal.de
[2] Institut für Angewandte und Numerische Mathematik, Universität Karlsruhe (TH)
D-76128 Karlsruhe, Germany
markus.neher@math.uni-karlsruhe.de

**Abstract.** C-XSC is an extensive and sophisticated C++ class library for the development and implementation of self-validating numerical software. Many numerical data types of distinct precision as well as operators and functions for these data types are provided by the library. Moreover, a large number of self-verifying numerical routines are integrated, and many additional packages for the reliable solution of numerical problems have been built on the C-XSC library. An MPI extension for C-XSC data types is available, enabling the efficient implementation of C-XSC software on parallel computers.

In this paper, we present the basic features of C-XSC and we show by code examples that the development of sophisticated mathematical software delivering verified numerical results is considerably simplified when using C-XSC. Some features concerning complex interval arithmetic and complex interval functions (C-XSC, CoStLy, ACETAF) are discussed in more detail.

All sample codes listed in this paper are available on the web page
http://www.math.uni-wuppertal.de/~xsc/cxsc/examples

**Keywords:** Mathematical software, reliable computing, C-XSC.

**AMS subject classification:** 68N30, 68N19, 65F99, 65G20, 65G30.

## 1 Introduction

The numerical solution of any continuous mathematical problem is concerned with obtaining an approximate solution while maintaining reasonable bounds on errors. The practical computation of approximate solutions usually suffers from two kinds of errors: discretization and truncation errors, which depend on the respective problem and on the numerical algorithm that is employed, and accumulated roundoff errors, which depend on the implementation of the numerical algorithm on a computer and on the arithmetic that is installed on this computer. Validated error bounds for the approximate solution of a given problem can be computed if rigorous bounds for errors of the first kind are obtained by analytic reasoning and also if some guaranteed bound on the accumulated roundoff errors in the computation is available.

A. Cuyt et al. (Eds.): Numerical Validation, LNCS 5492, pp. 68–102, 2009.

However, the mere number of floating-point operations in a practical computation these days usually prohibits the determination of realistic error bounds with methods from traditional numerical analysis. For restoring validity in numerical computations, interval arithmetic as described in [1,20,32,37] has been developed. In interval arithmetic, basic arithmetic operations between real numbers are replaced by basic arithmetic operations between intervals. When interval arithmetic is implemented on a digital computer, the real numbers appearing in some given practical problem are enclosed by floating-point intervals (that is, intervals with floating-point upper and lower bounds). Rigor of the computation is then achieved by performing all calculations with directed rounding according to the rules of interval arithmetic [26]. Thus, it is indeed possible to calculate guaranteed bounds for continuous problems with a finite number of basic arithmetic operations between floating-point numbers.

This paper is concerned with software packages that have been designed for solving many basic mathematical problems rigorously, and providing guaranteed and sharp error bounds. The core of these packages is C-XSC [17,22], a C++ class library for verified computations. C-XSC has been developed and maintained for almost twenty years to enable and facilitate the implementation of reliable numerical methods on computers. Today, it is one of the most sophisticated software libraries available for this purpose (most wide-spread alternatives include INTLAB [41], filib++ [27], or the boost interval arithmetic library [8]).

C-XSC is published under the terms of the GNU Library General Public License. The software and its source code are distributed on the website for XSC-languages,

`http://www.xsc.de`

C-XSC is available for all major platforms of today: Linux, MS Windows, Mac OS and Sun Solaris. It provides all features indispensable for modern numerical software development, such as allow programming of user-defined operators, overloading of operators and functions, dynamic arrays, which are allocated at runtime, or controlled rounding modes.

Apart from the usual numerical data types (integers, reals, etc.), C-XSC provides advanced data types for verified computation. First, there are data types for real and complex intervals, interval vectors and interval matrices. These data types have the same precision as the real number data type. Second, C-XSC contains multiple precision data types in the staggered correction format [43]. The respective level of precision can be defined by the user for each variable. Third, so-called dotprecision data types are provided for real and complex intervals, interval vectors and interval matrices. These data types enable the evaluation of sums or scalar products of vectors with 1 ulp accuracy. Internally, this is achieved by some long accumulator [25,26], into which intermediate results of scalar products are stored without roundoff errors.

An extensive set of elementary mathematical functions for real and complex interval arguments of high accuracy is implemented in C-XSC, both for the basic interval types and for the multiple precision formats [17,22].

## 2    C-XSC Toolbox for Verified Computing and Related Software

Procedures for the verified solution of many basic problems in scientific computing have been collected in the C-XSC toolbox [16]. This toolbox contains subroutines for the extended interval division, for the accurate evaluation of polynomials, for automatic differentiation (including the computation of gradients, Jacobians and Hessians), for the numerical solution of linear systems, nonlinear equations, and nonlinear systems of equations, for the accurate evaluation of arithmetic expressions, for the computation of zeros of complex polynomials, and for verified multivariate global optimization.

In the following, we present sample procedures and selected code snippets. The purpose of our presentation is to illustrate the power and diversity of the C-XSC library.

### 2.1    Verified Multiple Precision Computations

C-XSC contains packages for multiple precision interval computations. These number formats are based on the exact dot product facility of C-XSC (long accumulator, dotprecision data type). The corresponding multiple precision data types are called staggered data types. The four basic arithmetic operations as well as the elementary mathematical functions are available for real and complex multiple precision intervals (staggered intervals). The staggered data types provide a very wide exponent range, by storing the exponent of such a number separately as a double floating point number [3].

The following code example demonstrates the ease of use of the multiple precision packages. The (global integer) variable stagprec is used to control the precision of the staggered numbers. For example, stagprec= 5 is approximately equivalent to 5-fold double precision.

```
#include "lx_imath.hpp"   //extended staggered intervals
using namespace std;
using namespace cxsc;

int main() {
    stagprec= 5;                            //5-fold double precision
    int sixHundredMillion(600000000);
    lx_interval n, r;
    n= lx_interval(sixHundredMillion,"[1,1]");
    //n now equals 10^600.000.000

    r= xp1_pow_y(1/n,n);                    //(*)
    cout << "(1+1/n)^n: " << r << endl;
    cout << "with Relative diameter: " << RelDiam(r) << endl;

    stagprec= 20;                           //20-fold double precision
    //use predefined constant E_lx_interval() for exp(1)
    lx_interval Euler(E_lx_interval()); //enclosure of exp(1)
```

```
n= lx_interval(300, "[1,1]");          //10^300
r= pow(1+1/n, n);                      //r= (1+1/10^300)^(10^300)
cout << "Enclosure of displacement e-r: ";
cout << Euler-r << endl;
cout << "with relative diameter: " << RelDiam(Euler-r) << endl;
return 0;
}
/*
(1+1/n)^n: { 10**(-306)*[2.7182818284E+0306,2.7182818285E+0306] }
with Relative diameter: { 10**(-386)*3.4128669415E+0306 }
Enclosure of displacement e-r:
{ 10**(-607)*[1.3591409118E+0307,1.3591409147E+0307] }
with relative diameter: { 10**(-315)*2.0778584011E+0306 }
*/
```

Please note that the output has been modified by hand to get better readability. The source code in the line indicated by (*) computes the expression (more precisely: an enclosure of)

$$r = \left( 1 + \frac{1}{10^{600000000}} \right)^{10^{600000000}} .$$

If you try to compute this expression using a computer algebra package like Maple or Mathematica you will most probably get an error message (something‍ like out of range).

The last line of the output says that if we use

$$r = \left( 1 + \frac{1}{10^{300}} \right)^{10^{300}}$$

as an approximation to the true value of $e$, about 300 decimal digits of this approximation are correct.

## 3   Problem Solving with C-XSC

In this section, we illustrate how some basic mathematical problems are solved using C-XSC. In the following, the set of compact real intervals is denoted by

$$\mathbb{IR} = \{ \, \boldsymbol{x} = [\underline{x}, \overline{x}] \mid \underline{x}, \overline{x} \in \mathbb{R}, \ \underline{x} \le \overline{x} \, \}.$$

A real number $x$ is identified with a point interval $\boldsymbol{x} = [x, x]$. Throughout this paper, intervals are denoted by boldface.

A rectangular complex interval $\boldsymbol{z}$ is defined by a pair of two real intervals $\boldsymbol{x}$ and $\boldsymbol{y}$:

$$\boldsymbol{z} = \boldsymbol{x} + i\boldsymbol{y}, \quad \boldsymbol{z} = \{ z = x + iy \mid x \in \boldsymbol{x}, \ y \in \boldsymbol{y} \}.$$

The set of all complex rectangular intervals is denoted by $\mathbb{IC}$. For a bounded subset $M$ of $\mathbb{C}$, the *interval hull* $\square M$ of $M$ is the smallest rectangular interval that contains $M$. We have

$$\square M = [\inf_{z \in M} \operatorname{Re} z, \sup_{z \in M} \operatorname{Re} z] + i[\inf_{z \in M} \operatorname{Im} z, \sup_{z \in M} \operatorname{Im} z].$$

The definition of the basic arithmetic operations between rectangular complex intervals is given in [1, Definition 5.3].

For $D \subseteq \mathbb{C}$, the range $\{f(z) : z \in D\}$ of a function $f : D \longrightarrow \mathbb{C}$ is denoted by $\operatorname{Rg}(f, D)$. An *inclusion function* $F$ of a given function $f : \mathbb{C} \to \mathbb{C}$ is an interval function $F : \mathbb{IC} \to \mathbb{IC}$ that encloses the range of $f$ on all intervals $z \subseteq D$:

$$F(z) \supseteq \operatorname{Rg}(f, z) \quad \text{for all} \ \ z \subseteq D.$$

The concepts of interval hull and inclusion functions carry over to sets and function ranges in $\mathbb{R}^n$ or $\mathbb{C}^n$.

## 3.1    Example 1: Complex Interval Newton Method

The interval Newton method for the determination of a zero of a given complex-valued function $f$ consists of the iteration

$$z_{k+1} := N(z_k) \cap z_k, \quad k = 0, 1, \ldots, \tag{1}$$

where

$$N(z) := m(z) - F(m(z))/dF(z)$$

is the interval Newton operator and $z_0$ is some complex interval which is tested for containing a zero of $f$. Here, $m(z)$ is any particular point in $z$ (e.g. the midpoint of $z$), $F(z)$ is an inclusion function for $f(z)$ and $dF(z)$ is an inclusion function for its first derivative $f'(z)$.

Provided that $0 \notin dF(z_k)$ holds for all $k$, the iteration (1) has the following properties [1, Chap. 7]:

a) If $N(z_k) \cap z_k = \emptyset$ for some $k$ then $f$ has no root in $z_0$.
b) If $N(z_k) \subset \operatorname{interior}(z_k)$ then $f$ has exactly one simple root in $z_0$ and this root is also contained in $N(z_k)$.

Usually, the verification of a zero $\zeta$ of $f$ is done in two stages. First, an approximate zero $\tilde{z}$ of $f$ is computed by some numerical method. Then some interval $z_0$ that is suspected to contain $\zeta$ is constructed and the interval Newton operation is applied on $z_0$.

In the following source code, the determination of a simple zero of

$$f(z) = \operatorname{atan}\big((z - 4i) \log(z^2 - 5z + 8 + i)\big)$$

within $z_0 = [1.997, 2.007] + i[0.996, 1.0091]$ is illustrated. Since C-XSC contains procedures for inclusion functions and for the computation of derivative values, the implementation of the interval Newton method is straightforward. It suffices to supply an expression for the function $f$ and some initial guess $z_0$ for a zero of $f$.

```cpp
// interval Newton method for verified computation of zeros

#include <iostream>
using namespace std;

#include <cinterval.hpp>  // complex intervals
#include "citaylor.hpp"   // automatic differentiation is used
                          // for evaluating f'(z)

using namespace cxsc;
using namespace taylor;   // automatic differentiation

// definition of f for computing Taylor coefficients
citaylor f(citaylor z) {
   const cinterval c(interval(8),interval(1));  // c:=8+i
   const cinterval a(interval(0),interval(4));  // a:=4*i
   return atan( (z-a)*ln(sqr(z)-5*z+c) );
}

// inclusion function for f via citaylor
cinterval f(const cinterval &w)
{
   citaylor z(0,w); // Taylor coefficients up to order 0
   return get_j_derivative(f(z), 0);
}

// inclusion function for f' via citaylor,
// using automatic differentiation
cinterval df(const cinterval &w)
{
   citaylor z(1,w); // Taylor coefficients up to order 1
   return get_j_derivative(f(z), 1);
}

// main procedure: interval Newton method
int main()
{
  cout << boolalpha << SetPrecision(20,15);
  cinterval m, dfxk, Nxk, xkp1;
  bool verified = false;


// starting interval
cinterval xk = cinterval(interval(1.997,2.007),interval(0.996,1.0091));
cout << "Iterate " << 0 << ": " << xk << endl;
```

```
// iteration
for (int k=1; k<5; k++) {
    m = mid(xk);            // midpoint
    dfxk = df(xk);          // enclosure of f'
    Nxk  = m - f(m)/dfxk;   // interval Newton operator
    xkp1 = Nxk & xk;        // next iterate
    cout << "Iterate " << k << ": " << xkp1 << endl;


    verified |= (Nxk < xk);  //check for proper inclusion
    cout << "Verification successful: " << verified << endl;


    if (xk == xkp1) break; // no further improvement possible


    xk = xkp1; // replace old iterate by new iterate, continue
}
return 0;
}
```

This program computes some highly accurate enclosure of the zero $2 + i$ of $f$ within four steps:

```
Iterate 4: ([   1.999999999999999,   2.000000000000001],
           [   0.999999999999999,   1.000000000000001])
Verification successful: true
```

## 3.2   Example 2: Accurate Linear Interval Iterations

Enclosure methods aim at computing a set in $\mathbb{R}^n$ or $\mathbb{C}^n$ that is guaranteed to contain the result of a particular numerical problem. In a general framework, it is not required that the set be an interval. For practical calculations, however, it may be necessary to extend the set to its interval hull. This process is called wrapping. Depending on the shape of the set, a significant amount of overestimation may be introduced by wrapping. In particular, wrapping becomes a problem when numerous intermediate results are enclosed into intervals.

The wrapping effect was first observed by Moore in 1965 [31], in connection with the verified solution of ordinary initial value problems. A recent analysis of wrapping has been given by Lohner [30].

In Moore's original example, a square is rotated in the plane by some angle $\phi$ and the rotated square is again wrapped into an interval. Repeated transformations show exponential growth of the diameter of the iterated set, even though the diameter of a square is not affected by rotation. The first stage is shown in Figure 1 for the set $x_0 = \epsilon \begin{pmatrix} [-1,1] \\ [-1,1] \end{pmatrix}$, $\epsilon > 0$.

The image of $x_0$ after rotation consists of the square $\{A_\phi x \mid x \in x_0\}$, where

$$A_\phi := \begin{pmatrix} \cos \phi & \sin \phi \\ -\sin \phi & \cos \phi \end{pmatrix}.$$

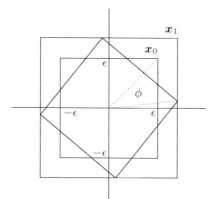

**Fig. 1.** Wrapping after rotation

The image of $x_0$ after $n$ such rotations is the square $x_n = \{A_\phi^n x \mid x \in x_0\}$, where

$$A_\phi^n = \begin{pmatrix} \cos(n\phi) & \sin(n\phi) \\ -\sin(n\phi) & \cos(n\phi) \end{pmatrix}.$$

Now suppose that $A_\phi^n$ is not available. This assumption may look strange in the above linear algebra setting, but it is natural in the context of ODEs, where this problem comes from. Under this condition, the image of the $x_0$ after repeated rotations can be described by the set $S_n = \{x_n = f_n(x_0) \mid x_0 \in x_0\}$, where $f_n(x_0)$ consists of $n$ steps of the iteration

$$x_{k+1} = A_\phi x_k, \quad k = 1, \ldots. \tag{2}$$

An enclosure of $S_n$ is readily computed by performing (2) in interval arithmetic. The interval vector iteration

$$x_{k+1} = A_\phi x_k, \quad k = 1, \ldots \tag{3}$$

yields the following iterates:

$$x_1 = \begin{pmatrix} [-\epsilon, \epsilon] \cos \phi + [-\epsilon, \epsilon] \sin \phi \\ [-\epsilon, \epsilon] \sin \phi + [-\epsilon, \epsilon] \cos \phi \end{pmatrix} = \epsilon(|\sin \phi| + |\cos \phi|) \begin{pmatrix} [-1, 1] \\ [-1, 1] \end{pmatrix}$$

$$x_2 = \epsilon(|\sin \phi| + |\cos \phi|)^2 \begin{pmatrix} [-1, 1] \\ [-1, 1] \end{pmatrix}$$

$$\vdots$$

$$x_n = \epsilon(|\sin \phi| + |\cos \phi|)^n \begin{pmatrix} [-1, 1] \\ [-1, 1] \end{pmatrix}.$$

The diameter of $x_n$ grows exponentially with factor $|\sin \phi| + |\cos \phi| > 1$.

Letting $y = (x_0^T, x_1^T, \ldots, x_n^T)^T$, $y = (x_0^T, [0, 0], \ldots, [0, 0])^T$, the iterates in (3) form the solution of a linear system

$$Ly = b$$

with a lower triangular matrix $L$. Solving this system by forward substitution in interval arithmetic is equivalent to the computation of the iteration in (3). Hence, forward substitution in an interval setting is also subject to wrapping and can produce large overestimations.

Moore [31] considered local coordinate transformations to reduce wrapping. In the above example, rotating the coordinate system with the square would leave the interval representation fixed, so that wrapping would be eliminated. Krückeberg proposed using parallelepipeds [24] instead of intervals as enclosure sets. Lohner [28,29] introduced the QR algorithm, which has been found to be the most successful approach for fighting the wrapping effect in the interval evaluation of matrix vector products.

We illustrate these concepts for the first order difference equation

$$y_{i+1} = A_i y_i + d_i, \quad i \geq 0, \quad \text{with} \quad y_0 \text{ given.} \tag{4}$$

Here, the $y_i$ and $d_i$ are $m$-vectors and the $A_i$ are $m \times m$-matrices $(i \geq 0)$.

As has been pointed out, performing the iteration (4) in interval arithmetic is likely to produce exponential overestimation of the result due to repeated wrapping. In the parallelepiped method, intermediate results are contained in parallelepipeds, which are represented by products of real matrices and interval vectors. For $B \in \mathbb{R}^n$, $x \in \mathbb{IR}^n$, the set

$$P := P(B, x) := \{Bx \mid x \in x\}$$

defines a parallelepiped with edges parallel to the column vectors of $B$.

The basic idea of the parallelepiped method is to replace the iterate $y_i$ in (4) by a sum of a floating-point approximation $\tilde{y}_i$ and an error term $\hat{y}_i$ which will be enclosed in a parallelepiped:

$$y_i = \tilde{y}_i + \hat{y}_i, \quad \hat{y}_i \in P(B_i, z_i). \tag{5}$$

The iteration is started with a floating point approximation $\tilde{y}_0$ to $y_0$, an interval vector $z_0$, which contains the defect $y_0 - \tilde{y}_0$, and $B_0 = I$, where $I$ denotes the identity matrix. If $y_0$ is a vector of floating point numbers, $\tilde{y}_0 = y_0$, $z = 0$ is used.

In the $i$-th iteration step, a floating point approximation $\tilde{y}_{i+1}$ to $A_i y_i + d_i$ is computed. Letting $\hat{d}_i := A_i \tilde{y}_i + d_i - \tilde{y}_{i+1}$, we have

$$y_{i+1} = A_i y_i + d_i = A_i \tilde{y}_i + d_i + A_i \hat{y}_i = \tilde{y}_{i+1} + A_i \hat{y}_i + (A_i \tilde{y}_i + d_i - \tilde{y}_{i+1})$$

$$= \tilde{y}_{i+1} + A_i \hat{y}_i + \hat{d}_i \in \tilde{y}_{i+1} + A_i B_i z_i + \hat{d}_i \subseteq \tilde{y}_{i+1} + B_{i+1} z_{i+1},$$

where $B_{i+1}$ is any nonsingular matrix and $z_{i+1}$ is given by

$$z_{i+1} = (B_{i+1}^{-1} A_i B_i) z_i + B_{i+1}^{-1} \hat{d}_i. \tag{6}$$

The choice $B_i = I$ for all $i \geq 0$ corresponds to the direct interval evaluation of (4). The classical parallelepiped method uses $B_{i+1} = A_i B_i$. For this choice, the global error $z_i$ is not transformed in the $i$-th iteration step. Only the local error $B_{i+1}^{-1}\hat{d}_i$ is added to $z_i$. However, these matrices $B_{i+1}$ tend to become ill-conditioned very soon, and the method breaks down early. To maintain well-conditioned matrices $B_i$, Lohner [28,29] proposed to compute the QR-factorization

$$A_i B_i = Q_i R_i$$

and use $B_{i+1} = Q_i$. The resulting iteration is called the QR method.

In practical computations, $Q_i$ is computed using traditional floating point arithmetic. Then $Q_i$ is only almost orthogonal. However, this does not affect the validity of (5) provided that an interval matrix that contains $Q_i^{-1}$ is used for $B_{i+1}^{-1}$ in (6). Such a matrix is easily computed using the Neumann series. For an almost orthogonal matrix $Q$, it holds that

$$\left\| Q^{-1} - Q^T \right\| \leq \left\| Q^T \right\| \frac{\left\| I - Q^T Q \right\|}{1 - \left\| I - Q^T Q \right\|} =: q,$$

which yields [29]

$$Q_i^{-1} \in Q^T + [-q, q] \begin{pmatrix} 1 & \cdots & 1 \\ \vdots & & \vdots \\ 1 & \cdots & 1 \end{pmatrix}.$$

In practical computations, $q$ is usually the size of the relative machine accuracy eps.

In the same way, the QR method is applied for computing enclosures of powers $A^k$, $k \in \mathbb{N}$, of an interval matrix $A$. The improvement with respect to the direct $k$-fold multiplication of $A$ is shown in our next example. For better readability of the presentation, we only display some code snippets. The source code of the missing procedures maxNorm (for computing the maximum norm of vectors and matrices) and QfromQR (for computing an approximate QR factorization) is straightforward.

```
/*************************************************************************/
// Powers of a square interval matrix A.
//
// Computation of A^k, k= 1,2,... using two different approaches:
//   a) using naive interval computations
//   b) using QR factorizations
//
// File: matwrap.cpp
/*************************************************************************/

#include <iostream>
using namespace std;
#include <mvi_util.hpp> //interval matrices/vectors
#include <imath.hpp>    //elementary interval functions
using namespace cxsc;
```

```
const int InvFailed= 1;
const int NoError= 0;
const int n= 2;

bool in(const imatrix& A, const imatrix &B)
//checks whether each component of A is
//contained in the corresponding component of B
{
   bool r(true);
   for (int i=Lb(A,1); i<=Ub(A,1); i++)
     for (int j=Lb(A,2); j<=Ub(A,2); j++)
        r&= in(A[i][j], B[i][j]);
   return r;
}


real maxNorm(const rvector& x)
{...}
real maxNorm(const rmatrix& a)
{...}
real maxNorm(const ivector& x)
{...}
real maxNorm(const imatrix& a)
{...}
rmatrix QfromQR(const rmatrix& A) //approximate QR factorization
{...}


void nearOrthoInv(const rmatrix& Q, imatrix& QInv)
//Compute inverse QInv of a nearly orthogonal matrix Q
{
   int ErrCode= NoError;
   real norm;
   interval q;
   rmatrix Qt( Lb(Q,1),Ub(Q,1),Lb(Q,2),Ub(Q,2) );

   ErrCode= NoError;
   Qt= transp(Q);
   norm= maxNorm( Id(Q)-Qt*imatrix(Q) );
   if (norm < 1.0)
   {
     norm= Sup( maxNorm(Qt)*interval(norm)/(interval(1) - norm) );
     q= interval(-norm, norm);
     for (int i=Lb(Q,1); i<=Ub(Q,1); i++)
       for (int j=Lb(Q,2); j<=Ub(Q,2); j++)
          QInv[i][j]= Qt[i][j] + q;
   }
   else
   {
     ErrCode= InvFailed;
     cout << "*** inversion failed! ***" << endl;
     exit(1);
```

```
    //QInv= Qt;
  }
}

int main()
{
  cout << boolalpha;
  imatrix A(n,n);
  imatrix Anp1;           //naive iteration
  imatrix QRnp1(n,n);   //improved version using QR
  imatrix Bnp1Inv(n,n);
  rmatrix Bn(n,n), Bnp1(n,n);
  imatrix Yn(n,n), Ynp1(n,n);
  interval phi;

  //numerical example for n=2: rotation matrix
  phi= atan(interval(1)); //enclosure of pi/4
  A[1][1]= cos(phi);    A[1][2]= sin(phi);
  A[2][1]=-sin(phi);    A[2][2]= cos(phi);
  cout << "Matrix A: " << endl;
  cout << A << endl;

  //prepare iteration:
  Anp1= A;
  Yn= A;
  Bn= Id(mid(A)); //identity matrix of appropriate dimension
  for (int n=1; n<=125; n++)
  {
    Anp1= A*Anp1; //n==1, then Anp1 == A^2

    Bnp1= QfromQR( mid(A*Bn) );
    nearOrthoInv( Bnp1, Bnp1Inv );
    Ynp1= (Bnp1Inv*A*Bn)*Yn;
    QRnp1= Bnp1*Ynp1; //contains A^(n+1)
    //prepare next step
    Bn= Bnp1;
    Yn= Ynp1;
    if (n%25 == 0)
    {
      cout << "A^" << n+1 << ":" << endl;
      cout << "Result using naive interval computations:";
      cout << endl << SetPrecision(0,9);
      cout << Anp1;
      cout << "Improved result using QR factorizations:" << endl;
      cout << QRnp1;
    }
  }
  return 0;
}
```

This program delivers the following results:

```
Matrix A:
[  0.707106,  0.707107] [  0.707106,  0.707107]
[ -0.707107, -0.707106] [  0.707106,  0.707107]


A^26:
Result using naive interval computations:
[-0.000000001,0.000000001] [0.999999999,1.000000001]
[-1.000000001,-0.999999999] [-0.000000001,0.000000001]
Improved result using QR factorizations:
[-0.000000001,0.000000001] [0.999999999,1.000000001] '
[-1.000000001,-0.999999999] [-0.000000001,0.000000001]
A^51:
Result using naive interval computations:
[-0.707107031,-0.707106531] [0.707106531,0.707107031]
[-0.707107031,-0.707106531] [-0.707107031,-0.707106531]
Improved result using QR factorizations:
[-0.707106782,-0.707106781] [0.707106781,0.707106782]
[-0.707106782,-0.707106781] [-0.707106782,-0.707106781]
A^76:
Result using naive interval computations:
[-1.001445763,-0.998554237] [-0.001445763,0.001445763]
[-0.001445763,0.001445763] [-1.001445763,-0.998554237]
Improved result using QR factorizations:
[-1.000000001,-0.999999999] [-0.000000001,0.000000001]
[-0.000000001,0.000000001] [-1.000000001,-0.999999999]
A^101:
Result using naive interval computations:
[-9.081858848,7.667645285] [-9.081858848,7.667645285]
[-7.667645285,9.081858848] [-9.081858848,7.667645285]
Improved result using QR factorizations:
[-0.707106782,-0.707106781] [-0.707106782,-0.707106781]
[0.707106781,0.707106782] [-0.707106782,-0.707106781]
A^126:
Result using naive interval computations:
[-48511.745857146,48511.745857146] [-48512.745857146,48510.745857146]
[-48510.745857146,48512.745857146] [-48511.745857146,48511.745857146]
Improved result using QR factorizations:
[-0.000000001,0.000000001] [-1.000000001,-0.999999999]
[0.999999999,1.000000001] [-0.000000001,0.000000001]
```

Naive multiplication exhibits huge overestimation, which is effectively reduced by the QR factorization.

## 3.3 Example 3: Verified Integration Using Simpson's Rule

For a sufficiently smooth function $f$ on the interval $[a, b]$, Simpson's rule of integration is given by the following formula:

$$\int_a^b f(x)\, dx = \frac{b-a}{6}\left(f(a) + 4f(\frac{a+b}{2}) + f(b)\right) - \frac{(b-a)^5}{90}f^{(4)}(\xi), \quad (7)$$

where $\xi$ is some unknown value in $[a, b]$. A validated enclosure for the integral is readily obtained by evaluating (7) using interval arithmetic. To bound the error term rigorously, it suffices to replace $\xi$ by $[a, b]$ and evaluate the fourth derivative of $f$ using automatic differentiation. High accuracy of the result can be achieved by splitting the domain $[a, b]$ into parts and applying the composite Simpson rule of integration. Depending on $f$, it may also be necessary to evaluate intermediate expressions with multiple precision. In particular, when $f$ has a zero in $[a, b]$, a long accumulator can absorb potential cancellation in the weighted sum of function values of $f$ at the grid points.

Thus, an enclosure for $\int_a^b f(x)dx$ consists of two sums of interval values. The diameter of the interval sum of the function values of $f$ is the size of machine precision, if a long accumulator is used. The diameter of the sum of the ranges of $f^{(4)}$ is at least as large as the discretization error of the composite Simpson rule. Hence, the latter sum is used for determining the fineness of the grid used in the composite Simpson rule.

As a numerical example, we present the computation of

$$\int_0^2 2xe^{x^2} \sin(e^{x^2})dx \ .$$

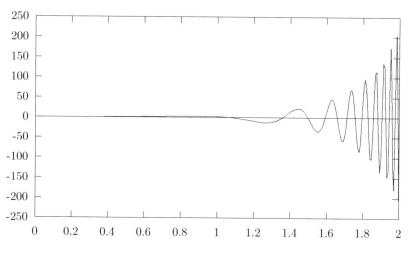

**Fig. 2.** $f(x) = 2xe^{x^2} \sin(e^{x^2})$

Figure 2 shows the graph of this integrand. The following C-XSC source code has been used for the computation:

```
#include <iostream>
#include <interval.hpp>
#include "itaylor.hpp"    // interval taylor arithmetic
using namespace std;
using namespace cxsc;
using namespace taylor;

typedef itaylor (*itayl_FctPtr)(const itaylor&);    // function pointer

// ------------------------------------------------------------------

interval integral (itayl_FctPtr f, const real &a, const real &b,
                                    const real &abs_err, bool error)
{
    int       p = 5;      // Order of expansion for taylor arithmetic
    interval z(a,b);      // Interval to include the point of expansion
    int       n = 2,j;
    interval h;           // length of each subinterval
    itaylor  x(p,z);      // function variables
    interval sum(0.0);    // Summation of the 4th derivatives (error bound)

    // initial step: error bound for ordinary Simpson rule
    h = (interval(b)-interval(a))/n;
    interval R     = get_j_derivative(f(x),4)*4.0*h*sqr(sqr(h))/15.0;
    interval R_old = R;

    while( ( diam(R) > abs_err ) && (diam(R) <= diam(R_old) ) )
    // iterative refinement of the grid
    // compute error bound for composite Simpson rule
    {
        n *= 2;
        h = (interval(b)-interval(a))/n;
        real x2i_minus_2, x2i;   // for f[x_2i-2,x_2i]

        R_old = R;

        for (int i=1;i<=n/2;i++)
        {
            j = 2*(i-1);
            itaylor x( p , interval(a) + h*interval(j,j+2));
            sum += get_j_derivative(f(x),4);
        }

        R = 4.0*h*sqr(sqr(h))*sum/15.0; // computation of the remainder term
    }
```

```
    // compute sum of function values
    interval J;
    interval xk;              // means x[k]
    real si;                       // weight of the Simpsons sum
    idotprecision accu(0.0);  // accurate dot product

    for (int k=0;k<=n;k++)
    {
        xk = a+k*h;
        if ( (k==0) || (k==n) )
            si = 1.0;
        else if ( k%2 == 0 )
            si = 2.0;
        else
            si = 4.0;
        // accurate summation
        accumulate(accu, si, get_j_derivative(f(var_itaylor(5,xk)),0) );
    }

    J = h * rnd(accu) / 3.0;

    interval res = R + J;

    // test if result meets required accuracy
    if ( diam(res) <= abs_err )
        error = 0;
    else
        error = 1;

    return res;
}

// ----------------------------------------------------------------------

itaylor f ( const itaylor &X )    // sample function
{
    return 2 * X * exp(sqr(X)) * sin(exp(sqr(X))) ;
}

// ----------------------------------------------------------------------

int main (void)
{
    real a = 0, b = 2.0;          // a, b integration bounds
    real abs_err = 1e-10;         // upper bound for absolute error
    bool error;                   // error indicator

    interval res;
    res = integral( f, a, b, abs_err, error);
    cout << SetPrecision(17,10) << Scientific << endl;
```

```
cout << "Integration of f(x) = 2 * X * exp(sqr(X)) * sin(exp(sqr(X)))"
     << endl;
cout << "Simpson Rule: " << res << endl;
if (error == 1) cout << "Warning: Insufficient accuracy." << endl;
return 0;
}
```

This program outputs the following result:

```
Integration of f(x) = 2 * X * exp(sqr(X)) * sin( exp(sqr(X)))
Simpson Rule: [9.1096403927E-001,9.1096403929E-001].
```

Alternatively, the CLAVIS (Classes for Verified Integration over Singularities) package by Stefan Wedner [44] can be used for verified integration. Since the above integrand has no singularities, the computation with CLAVIS may be more involved than necessary. On the other hand, using CLAVIS it suffices to supply the function expression of the integrand for obtaining verified values of definite integrals within a few lines of code.

```
#include "quadrature.h"  // from the CLAVIS package

int main() {

  real eps = 1e-10;
  integrand f;
  f = 2 * x * exp(sqr(x)) * sin( exp(sqr(x)) );
  integral b(f);
  b.integrate(0,2,eps);
  cout << b << endl;
  return 0;
}
```

The output of this code example is:

```
number of intervals : 12
#f                   : 171
approximationsum     : [9.109640E-001,9.109641E-001]
d(approximationsum)  : 2.519096E-012
remainder            : [-2.705889E-011,2.786000E-011]
d(remainder)         : 5.491889E-011
enclosure            : [9.109640E-001,9.109641E-001]
d(enclosure)         : 5.743805E-011
```

## 4  Selected Additional Packages

There is a growing collection of additional software for verified computation, which has been based on the C-XSC library. The following list is not exhaustive.

- Elementary functions of high accuracy (see www.xsc.de),
- self-verifying solvers for dense systems of linear equations [18],
- FastILSS (fast verified solvers for dense linear (interval-)systems) [45],
- one- and multidimensional interval Taylor arithmetic [2],
- one- and multidimensional (interval) slope arithmetic [5],
- ParLinSys (solving parametric interval linear systems) [38],
- CoStLy (complex interval standard functions library) [36],
- ACETAF (automatic computation of estimates for Taylor coefficients of analytic functions) [10],
- CLAVIS (classes for verified integration over singularities) [44],
- MPI extension for the use of C-XSC in parallel environments [15], and
- VFIS, a parallel solver for (Systems of) Linear Fredholm Integral Equations of the second kind.

In this section, we report on the MPI extension of C-XSC and on the highly developed packages CoStLy, ACETAF, and VFIS.

## 4.1   MPI Extension for the Use of C-XSC in Parallel Environments

There are several program packages based on C-XSC implementing parallelized versions of self-validating numerical methods. Solving large linear interval equations, solving problems in the field of global optimization, and solving integral equations are probably the most popular. All these implementations are based on an MPI extension for the use of C-XSC in parallel environments. This extension provides predefined functions to send and receive C-XSC objects like intervals, interval matrices, exact scalar products (dotprecision variables) and so on. The package is described in more detail in [15].

As an example for the usage of our MPI extension, we present the main routine for calling the parallelized solver for Fredholm integral equations of the second kind on the parallel computer ALiCEnext from the University of Wuppertal.

```
/*  Verified Fredholm Integral Equation Solver (parallel version)
 *
 *  this program is designed for the parallel computer ALiCEnext;
 *  on other machines, the handling of input parameters and output files
 *  may require adjustments  */

#include <mpi.h>
#include <string>
#include <iostream>
#include <fstream>
#include <sstream>
#include <cstdlib>

#include "IntegralEquation.hpp"  // Fredholm IE solver

// the following file is supposed to contain the kernel function
// and the right hand side of the Fredholm IE
```

```
#include "functions.in"

// typedef for kernel function pointer
typedef dim2taylor (*KFkt)(dim2taylor_vector&);

// typedef for right hand side function pointer
typedef itaylor (*ReFkt)(itaylor&);

// ----------------------------------------------------------------------

int executetest(int ord, int sysord,
                KFkt K, interval KS, interval KT,
                ReFkt ReS, interval GS, int procs, int mypid,
                int& commerrc)
/*
 *   execute a test run
 *
 *   @param[in] ord        Taylor order
 *   @param[in] sysord     system order
 *   @param[in] K          kernel function
 *   @param[in] KS         domain of first variable of kernel function
 *   @param[in] KT         domain of second variable of kernel function
 *   @param[in] ReS        right hand side function
 *   @param[in] GS         domain of right hand side
 *   @param[in] procs      number of parallel processes
 *   @param[in] mypid      process ID
 *   @param[out] commerrc  error code   */

{           *
  // parameters
  int width=23, digits=18;

  // output files
  ofstream outpot;
  string resfile="VFIS.res", plotfile="VFIS.plt";

  // define Fredholm IE
  IntegralEquation IGLSys;

  int root=0;
  if (mypid==root)
    IGLSys=IntegralEquation(K,KS,KT,ReS,GS,sysord,ord,outpot,resfile);
  else
    IGLSys.PartInitIntegralEquation(K,KS,KT,ReS,GS,
                                    sysord,ord,outpot,resfile);

  if (commerrc=IGLSys.DistributeValues(root)!=MPI_SUCCESS)
    MPI_err(commerrc,"MPI_Bcast",
            "IntegralEquation::DistributeValues",mypid);
```

```
  // compute enclosure
  IGLSys.ComputeEnclosure(outpot,resfile,procs,mypid,commerrc);

  outpot.open(resfile.c_str(),ios_base::app);

  // error message, if matrix inversion failed
  if (commerrc!=0)
    MPI_err(commerrc,"(MATINV Communication)", "MatInv",-1);

  // export result to Maple
  if (mypid==root)
  {
    IGLSys.ExportPlot("Maple",plotfile,8);
  }

  outpot.close();
  return 0;
}

// ------------------------------------------------------------------------

int main(int argc, char *argv[])
/*
 * main function processing the command line parameters, initializing the
 * parallel environment and calling the test execution function.
 *
 * @param[in] argc Argument count
 * @param[in] argv Argument vector  */
{
  // MPI communication initialization

  int procs,  mypid, commerrc;
  MPI_Status status;

  if ((commerrc=MPI_Init(&argc, &argv)) != MPI_SUCCESS)
    MPI_err(commerrc,"MPI_Init", "main",-1);
  if ((commerrc=MPI_Comm_rank(MPI_COMM_WORLD, &mypid)) != MPI_SUCCESS)
    MPI_err(commerrc,"MPI_Comm_rank", "main",mypid);
  if ((commerrc=MPI_Comm_size(MPI_COMM_WORLD, &procs)) != MPI_SUCCESS)
    MPI_err(commerrc,"MPI_Comm_size", "main",procs);

  // define MPI-CXSC data types
  MPI_Define_CXSC_Types();

  int arg_ord=atoi(argv[1]);
  int arg_sysord=atoi(argv[2]);

  executetest("Example",arg_ord,arg_sysord,
              K,KDefS,KDefT,ReSeite,ReSeiteDef,procs,mypid,commerrc);
```

```
if ((commerrc=MPI_Finalize()))
    MPI_err(commerrc,"MPI_Finalize","main",mypid);

return 0;
}
```

The MPI package is intended to stimulate C-XSC users to realize parallelized versions of self-validating algorithms. This will allow to attack not only academic problems but also more challenging real life problems. Based on this package and based on BLAS and error free transformations a very efficient linear system solver for dense interval matrices has been implemented and tested successfully with matrices up to more than 100 000 unknowns [46].

## 4.2   Inclusion Functions for Complex Standard Functions and Their Implementation in the CoStLy and C-XSC Libraries

CoStLy (Complex Standard Functions Library) has been developed as a C++ class library for the validated computation of function values and of ranges of the complex standard functions in

$$S_F = \{\exp, \ln, \arg, \mathrm{sqr}, \mathrm{sqrt}, \mathrm{power}, \mathrm{pow}, \mathrm{root}, \cos, \sin, \tan, \cot, \cosh, \\ \sinh, \tanh, \coth, \mathrm{acos}, \mathrm{asin}, \mathrm{atan}, \mathrm{acot}, \mathrm{acosh}, \mathrm{asinh}, \mathrm{atanh}, \mathrm{acoth}\},$$

where $\mathrm{power}(z, n)$ is the power function for integer exponents, $\mathrm{pow}(z, p)$ is the power function for real or complex exponents, and $\mathrm{root}(z, n)$ denotes the $n$th root function.

An interval library for the real standard functions in $S_F$ is required by CoStLy, for evaluating the compositions of real functions that make up the real and imaginary parts of the complex functions in $S_F$. CoStLy has been programmed such that either C-XSC or filib++ [27] can be used for this purpose. Today, CoStLy is also integrated in the C-XSC library.

CoStLy is distributed under the terms of the GNU General Public License. The software is currently available at the following sites:

```
http://www.xsc.de
http://iamlasun8.mathematik.uni-karlsruhe.de/~ae16/CoStLy.html
```

**Inclusion Functions.** $F$ is called *inclusion isotone*, if

$$z_1 \subseteq z_2 \;\Rightarrow\; F(z_1) \subseteq F(z_2)$$

holds for all $z_1, z_2 \subseteq D$. If $F(z) = \Box\mathrm{Rg}(f, z)$ holds for all $z \subseteq D$, then $F$ is called *inclusion optimal* or simply *optimal*.

The real and imaginary parts of any function in $S_F$ can be expressed as compositions of real standard functions. Optimal inclusion functions are obtained by determining the extremal values of these compositions [6,7,23,36].

**Earlier Implementations of Complex Inclusion Functions.** The inclusion functions described in the theses of Braune [6] and Krämer [23] were first realized in the ACRITH library by IBM [19]. Bühler [9] implemented the same algorithms in Pascal-XSC procedures, which were later extended to a Pascal-XSC interval library of complex standard functions by Krämer and Westphal. INTLAB [41] includes subroutines for complex standard functions using circular arithmetic, based on work by Börsken [4]. IntpakX [13] also contains procedures for circular complex interval arithmetic, but apart from the evaluation of complex polynomials, only the exponential function is implemented. To the authors' knowledge, no other packages currently supply complex inclusion function. As ACRITH was withdrawn from marketing in 1994, Pascal-XSC is no longer in wide use, and intpakX offers only the exponential function, the lack of available software was one of the motives for developing CoStLy.

**The CoStLy Library Functions.** The design of inclusion functions for the functions in $S_F$ has been guided by the paradigm that range bounds must be valid in any circumstance. For a single-valued complex function $f$, its inclusion function $F : \mathbb{IC} \to \mathbb{IC}$, and some given rectangular complex interval $z$, validity means only that $F(z)$ must contain the set $\{f(z)|z \in z\}$. The functions exp, sqr, power, cos, sin, tan, cot, cosh, sinh, tanh, and coth are single-valued and analytic on their respective domain. CoStLy contains optimal inclusion functions for these functions (where optimal refers to the accuracy of the implemented algorithms, if performed in exact arithmetic).

The meaning of a valid enclosure is less obvious for a multi-valued function. For example, the definition of $\sqrt{-1}$ depends very much on the context of the computation. Possible values include $+i$, $-i$, $\{+i, -i\}$, $i \cdot [-1, 1]$, or the empty set. Three types of inclusion functions have been implemented in CoStLy to accommodate varied demands.

Each multi-valued function $f$ in $S_F$ has analytic branches on appropriate subsets of the complex plane. The CoStLy library contains an inclusion function $F_p$ for the single-valued principal branch of $f$. Usually, $F_p$ is defined on a subset of $\mathbb{IC}$. If $z$ is not in the domain of definition of $f$, the computation is aborted throwing an exception and issuing a warning message.

Inclusion functions that are defined for all $z \in \mathbb{IC}$, for which at least one branch of $f$ is bounded on $z$, are denoted by $F_c$. Depending on the location of $z$ in the complex plane, $F_c(z)$ returns function values belonging to different branches of $f$. As an immediate consequence, there are regions in $\mathbb{C}$ where inclusion isotonicity is lost.

Where applicable, an inclusion function $F_a$ enclosing all function values of $f$ has also been implemented. For example, it is available for roots. For some multi-valued complex functions, however, the set of all function values is unbounded in general. In this case, no such inclusion function is available.

Before presenting numerical results, we exemplify the different types of inclusion functions. We refer to [36] for a detailed description of all inclusion functions contained in CoStLy. The implementation is also extensively commented in the CoStLy source code.

**Argument Functions.** In the following, let $\mathbb{C}^-$ denote the set $\mathbb{C} - (-\infty, 0]$ and let $\mathbb{C}_0^-$ denote the set $\mathbb{C} - (-\infty, 0)$. For $z \in \mathbb{C}^-$, the principal value of the argument function is the unique polar angle Arg $z \in (-\pi, \pi)$ in the polar representation of $z$. While a unique argument function can only be defined on some slit complex plane, it is possible to include the origin into the domain. By letting

$$\text{Arg } \boldsymbol{z} = \begin{cases} 0, & z = 0, \\ \square\{\text{Arg } z : 0 \neq z \in \boldsymbol{z}\}, \boldsymbol{z} \subset \mathbb{C}_0^-, & \boldsymbol{z} \neq 0, \\ \text{undefined}, & \text{otherwise}, \end{cases}$$

a unique interval argument function is defined for intervals that contain the origin, but do not intersect the negative real axis. If $0 \neq \boldsymbol{z}_1 \subseteq \boldsymbol{z}_2 \subseteq \mathbb{C}_0^-$ holds then we have Arg $\boldsymbol{z}_1 \subseteq$ Arg $\boldsymbol{z}_2$, so that both optimality of the range enclosure and inclusion isotonicity are maintained for all intervals in the domain of Arg $\boldsymbol{z}$, save for $\boldsymbol{z} = 0$.

An inclusion function of type $F_c$, denoted by arg $\boldsymbol{z}$, is also implemented for the argument function. It is defined for all $\boldsymbol{z} \in \mathbb{IC}$, with arg $\boldsymbol{z} \subseteq [-\pi, \frac{3\pi}{2}]$ and width $w(\text{arg } \boldsymbol{z}) \leq 2\pi$. If Arg $\boldsymbol{z}$ is defined then arg $\boldsymbol{z} = $ Arg $\boldsymbol{z}$ holds. If $\boldsymbol{z}$ intersects the negative real axis then arg $\boldsymbol{z}$ is not inclusion isotone (Figure 3). For example, for

$$\boldsymbol{z}_1 = [-\sqrt{3}, -1] + i[1, \sqrt{3}], \qquad \boldsymbol{z}_2 = [-\sqrt{3}, -1] + i[-\sqrt{3}, -1],$$

$$\boldsymbol{z}_3 = [-\sqrt{3}, -1] + i[-\sqrt{3}, \sqrt{3}], \boldsymbol{z}_4 = [-2, 2] + i[-2, -2],$$

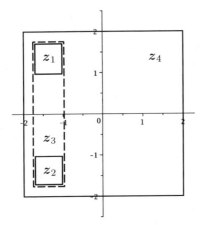

we have

$$\arg(\boldsymbol{z}_1) = [\frac{2\pi}{3}, \frac{5\pi}{6}],$$

$$\arg(\boldsymbol{z}_2) = [-\frac{5\pi}{6}, -\frac{2\pi}{3}],$$

$$\arg(\boldsymbol{z}_3) = [\frac{2\pi}{3}, \frac{4\pi}{3}] \not\supseteq \arg(\boldsymbol{z}_2),$$

$$\arg(\boldsymbol{z}_4) = [-\pi, \pi] \not\supseteq \arg(\boldsymbol{z}_3).$$

**Fig. 3.** Argument function in CoStLy

**Natural Logarithm.** The principal branch of the natural logarithm is given by

$$\text{Ln } z = \ln_{\mathbb{R}} |z| + i\text{Arg } z, \quad z \in \mathbb{C}^-.$$

Here, $\ln_{\mathbb{R}}$ denotes the real natural logarithm. For $\boldsymbol{z} \subset \mathbb{C}^-$, we define

$$\text{Ln } \boldsymbol{z} = \ln(\text{abs}(\boldsymbol{z})) + i\text{Arg } \boldsymbol{z} = \square\{\text{Ln } z : z \in \boldsymbol{z}\},$$

where
$$\mathrm{abs}(z) = \{\,|z| \,:\, z \in z\,\}.$$
The corresponding CoStLy procedure throws an exception when it is called with an argument $z$ that intersects the negative real axis.

An inclusion function for the logarithm that is also defined for negative reals is implemented in CoStLy as
$$\ln z = \ln(\mathrm{abs}(z)) + i\arg z.$$

**Root Functions.** The principal branch of the square root function $\sqrt{z}$ is defined as
$$\mathrm{Sqrt}\ z = e^{\frac{1}{2}\mathrm{Ln}\ z}, \quad z \in \mathbb{C}^-.$$
As for the argument function, it is desirable to include the origin into the domain of the square root. Letting $\mathrm{Sqrt}\ 0 = 0$, the interval function $\mathrm{Sqrt}\ z$ is defined as follows:
$$\mathrm{Sqrt}\ z = \begin{cases} \square\{\mathrm{Sqrt}\ z : z \in z\}, \, z \subset \mathbb{C}_0^-, \\ \text{undefined}, \qquad\qquad \text{otherwise.} \end{cases}$$
$\mathrm{Root}(z, n)$, $n \geq 2$, the inclusion function for the principal branch of the $n$-th root function,
$$\mathrm{Root}(z, n) = e^{\frac{1}{n}\mathrm{Ln}\ z}, \quad n \in \mathbb{N}, \quad z \in \mathbb{C}^-,$$
is defined in the same manner.

The CoStLy procedure for $\mathrm{Root}(z, n)$ throws an exception when it is called with an argument $z$ that intersects the negative real axis. For applications involving complex roots of negative real numbers, an inclusion function of type $F_a$ is included in CoStLy. It is implemented as a set function $\mathrm{root\_all}(z, n)$, which computes a list of $n$ intervals that contain all $n$-th roots of $z$:
$$\mathrm{root\_all}(z, n) \supseteq \{w : w^n = z, z \in z\}.$$

For some interval $z \subset \mathbb{C} - \{0\}$ with sufficiently small width, the optimal interval enclosure for all $n$-th roots consists of $n$ distinct intervals. While these could be computed (in exact arithmetic), such a procedure would be computationally expensive, especially for large values of $n$. We use the following strategy instead: $z$ is enclosed in the polar interval $(r, \phi) = ([\underline{r}, \overline{r}], [\underline{\varphi}, \overline{\varphi}]) = (\mathrm{abs}(z), \arg z)$. All $n$-th roots of $z$ are then contained in the union $\cup_{k=0}^{n-1}(r_k, \phi_k)$, where
$$r_k = [\underline{r}^{(1/n)}, \overline{r}^{(1/n)}], \quad \phi_k = (\phi + 2k\pi)/n, \quad k = 0, 1, \ldots, n - 1.$$
Finally, $(r_k, \phi_k)$ is enclosed in a rectangular interval $w_k$, such that $\mathrm{root\_all}(z, n) = \cup_{k=0}^{n-1} w_k$ (Figure 4).

**Inverse Trigonometric and Inverse Hyperbolic Functions.** If $f$ is any trigonometric or hyperbolic standard function in $S_F$ and $z$ a complex number in the range of $f$, then the set $\{w : f(w) = z\}$ is unbounded. Hence, it is impossible to enclose all values $f^{-1}(z)$ inside a compact interval. For this reason, the inverse trigonometric or inverse hyperbolic functions are only implemented as

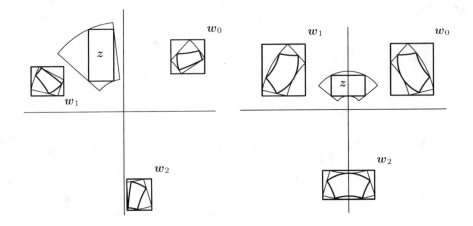

**Fig. 4.** Inclusion sets for root_all$(z, 3)$ for two different intervals $z$

single-valued principal values on proper subsets of $\mathbb{C}$. The details of the implementation are given in [36].

**Numerical Examples.** If performed in exact arithmetic, the inclusion functions of type $F_p$ compute optimal range bounds. For the sake of accuracy, a major effort has been made in the implementation of the algorithms in floating point arithmetic to eliminate all intermediate expressions subject to numerical overflow, underflow, or cancellation. The CoStLy library has been extensively tested for arguments with absolute values ranging from 1.0E-300 to 1.0E+300. For most arguments, the computed bounds for function values are highly accurate. In many test cases, the observed precision of the result was about 50 correct bits (out of the 53 bits available in IEEE 754 floating point arithmetic) for point arguments.

**Example 1: Function Values for Point Intervals.** In Table 1, we list results for point intervals for selected library functions. The following arguments were chosen:
$$z_1 = 1.0^{-300} + i\ 1.0^{-300}, \quad z_2 = 1.0^{300} + i\ 1.0.$$

Here and in the following, a short notation for numbers is used. $a.b^c$ means $a.b \times 10^c$.

In the execution of CoStLy, the arguments were entered as real constants, so that their IEEE 754 best approximations were actually used in the computation. In the second and the fourth column of Table 1, the approximate principal value of each function at the respective argument is given. In columns three and five, a pair of positive numbers denotes the number of correct bits for the real/imaginary part of the computed function value bounds. % is used if the IEEE 754 best approximation of the function value is zero. In this case, the relative accuracy of the function value enclosure is undefined.

**Table 1.** Function values for selected inclusion functions for point intervals

| $f$ | $f(z_1)$ | CoStLy 2.0 | $f(z_2)$ | CoStLy 2.0 |
|---|---|---|---|---|
| sqrt | $1.1^{-150} + i\, 4.6^{-151}$ | 50.0 / 50.0 | $1.0^{150} + i\, 5.0^{-151}$ | 50.7 / 50.7 |
| ln | $-6.9^2 + i\, 7.9^{-1}$ | 49.6 / 48.0 | $6.9^2 + i\, 1.0^{-300}$ | 49.6 / 51.4 |
| asin | $1.0^{-300} + i\, 1.0^{-300}$ | 50.1 / 49.3 | $1.6 + i\, 6.9^2$ | 51.6 / 47.9 |
| acos | $1.6 - i\, 1.0^{-300}$ | 51.6 / 49.3 | $1.0^{-300} - i\, 6.9^2$ | 50.0 / 47.9 |
| atan | $1.0^{-300} + i\, 1.0^{-300}$ | 50.4 / 48.8 | $1.6 + i\, 0.0$ | 51.6 / % |
| acot | $1.6 - i\, 1.0^{-300}$ | 51.6 / 48.8 | $1.0^{-300} + i\, 0.0$ | 49.8 / % |

**Table 2.** Range bounds for interval arguments

| $f$ | $F(z_3)$ | $F(z_4)$ |
|---|---|---|
| sqrt | $[3.4^{-1}, 1.6] + i\, [3.4^{-2}, 1.1]$ | $[1.0^{10}, 3.3^{10}] + i\, [1.6^9, 2.1^{10}]$ |
| tan | $[-5.0, 5.0] + i\, [\,1.0^{-1}, 1.1^1]$ | $[-1.2^{-308}, 1.2^{-308}] + i\, [9.9^{-1}, 1.1]$ |
| cot | $[-5.8^{-1}, 5.0] + i\, [-5.1, -1.0^{-1}]$ | $[-1.2^{-308}, 1.2^{-308}] + i\, [-1.1, -9.9^{-1}]$ |
| ln | $[-2.0, 1.1] + i\, [\,4.7^{-2}, 1.6]$ | $[4.6^1, 4.9^1] + i\, [1.1^{-1}, 1.5]$ |
| asin | $[\,4.2^{-2}, 1.6] + i\, [\,1.0^{-1}, 1.8]$ | $[1.1^{-1}, 1.5] + i\, [4.7^1, 5.0^1]$ |
| acos | $[\,5.4^{-2}, 1.6] + i\, [-1.8, -1.0^{-1}]$ | $[1.1^{-1}, 1.5] + i\, [-5.0^1, -4.7^1]$ |
| atan | $[\,1.0^{-1}, 1.6] + i\, [\,1.8^{-2}, 1.6]$ | $[1.5, 1.6] + i\, [1.2^{-22}, 5.1^{-21}]$ |

For brevity, we show only results for one argument with a very small absolute value and one argument with a very large absolute value. For arguments with absolute values in between, similar accuracy of the computed function values was observed in many test cases.

**Example 2: Range Bounds for Interval Arguments.** Range bounds for

$$z_3 = [0.1, 2.1] + i[0.1, 2.1], \quad z_4 = [1.0^{20}, 9.0^{20}] + i\, [1.0^{20}, 9.0^{20}].$$

are shown in Table 2 for selected inclusion functions. For clarity, the range bounds are displayed rounded. As in Example 1, the observed accuracy of the computed bounds was about 50 bits with respect to the optimal bounds in exact arithmetic.

## 4.3   Bounds for Taylor Coefficients: The ACETAF Package

The software package ACETAF has been developed by the third author and Ingo Eble. It is a C++ program for the accurate computation of error bounds for Taylor coefficients of analytic functions. For a user-defined complex function

$f$, the following problems are solved with ACETAF (we list the problems in the order in which they rely on each other).

- Rigorous computation of leading Taylor coefficients,
- check of analyticity in a user-defined disc,
- rigorous computation of bounds for Taylor coefficients of arbitrary order,
- rigorous computation of bounds for Taylor remainder series.

The CoStLy library is used for computing the necessary function values and ranges in the computation of these bounds.

ACETAF is distributed under the terms of the GNU General Public License. The software is currently available at the following sites:

`http://www.xsc.de`

`http://iamlasun8.mathematik.uni-karlsruhe.de/~ae16/acetaf.html`

**Admissible Functions.** For all features of the program, the user may enter an expression for a function $f$, which must be a finite composition of polynomials, rational functions, and the functions in $S_F$ (see Section 4.2). Loops and branches are not allowed in the expression for $f$. For multi-valued functions, principal branches are always assumed by the program.

Furthermore, the underlying mathematical theory of the algorithms in ACETAF requires that $f$ be analytic in a user-defined disc in the complex plane. For this reason, only inclusion functions of type $F_p$ are called from the CoStLy library. On request of the user, the program checks whether the user-defined function $f$ is analytic on the given disc.

**Computation of Complex Taylor Coefficients.** ACETAF offers the computation of some leading Taylor coefficients of a user-defined function. These Taylor coefficients are computed via automatic differentiation [12,40]. The real and imaginary parts of admissible functions can be expressed as compositions of real standard functions. These decompositions are used for computing complex derivatives from real derivatives. In general, if $f(z) = u(x, y) + iv(x, y)$ then we have $f'(z) = u_x(x, y) + iv_x(x, y)$. Similarly, specific Taylor coefficients of $f$ are calculated by applying the well known formulas of automatic differentiation to the real and the imaginary parts of $f$, respectively.

**Check of Analyticity.** The error bounds on the Taylor coefficients that are presented in the next subsection require that $f$ be analytic on the disc $B$. Multivalued analytic standard functions are all interpreted as being principal values with strict domain restrictions.

The analyticity of $f$ can be checked by the program before computation of the bounds. If the proof of analyticity fails on the user-defined disc then ACETAF computes a validated lower bound of the maximum radius $r$ to the given midpoint, such that $f$ is analytic on the full disc. This is done by a heuristic algorithm which uses bisection of the radius of the given disc.

**Bounds for Taylor Coefficients with Arbitrary Order.** The rigorous computation of bounds for Taylor coefficients with arbitrary order is the main feature of ACETAF. Such bounds are used for error analyses in numerical computations [33,42]. In ACETAF, four methods for calculating such bounds are implemented. Method I is Cauchy's estimate(8). For a function

$$f(z) = \sum_{j=0}^{\infty} a_j z^j, \quad |z| \leq r$$

that is analytic on a disc $B = \{z : |z| < r\}$ with positive radius $r$ and bounded on the circle $C = \{z : |z| = r\}$, it holds that

$$|a_j| \leq \frac{M(r)}{r^j}, \quad j \in \mathbb{N}_0, \tag{8}$$

where $M(r) = \max_{|z|=r} |f(z)|$. A branch and bound algorithm is employed in ACETAF to compute a validated upper bound for Cauchy's estimate $M(r)$ for an analytic function $f$ and a given circle $C$ with radius $r$ [11].

The three other methods that are implemented in ACETAF are variants of Cauchy's estimate, which have been developed in [34]. In method II, Cauchy's estimate is applied to the defect of some Taylor polynomial approximation of $f$; in method III, Cauchy's estimate is applied to some derivative of $f$. The most general method IV is a generalization of the other three methods. Instead of $M(r)$, the number

$$V(r, m, l) = \max_{|z|=r} |f^{(m)}(z) - s_l(z)|$$

is used in the estimation of the Taylor coefficients of $f$, where $m$ and $l$ are integers, $f^{(m)}$ is the $m$th derivative of $f$, and $s_l$ is the $l$th Taylor polynomial (expanded at the origin) of $f^{(m)}$. Instead of (8), we obtain [34,35]

$$|a_j| \leq \frac{(j-m)! \, V(r, m, l)}{j! \, r^{j-m}} \quad \text{for } j > m + l. \tag{9}$$

For $m > 0$ in (9), the remainder series of $f$ is bounded by a series that converges faster than any geometric series, for all $z \in B$. Thus, the estimate (9) is a considerable improvement over Cauchy's estimate.

**Bounds for Taylor Remainder Series.** In addition to bounds for the Taylor coefficients of $f$, ACETAF also computes bounds for the Taylor remainder series $R_p(z) = \sum_{j=p+1}^{\infty} a_j z^j$ of $f$, for some $z$ with $|z| < r$. Bounds for $R_p$ are obtained from summing up the respective estimates for the Taylor coefficients in the remainder series [35].

## 4.4   ACETAF Features

**Graphical User Interface.** All input data (such as the function $f$, the radius $r$ of the disk, etc.) can be entered via a self-explanatory graphical user interface

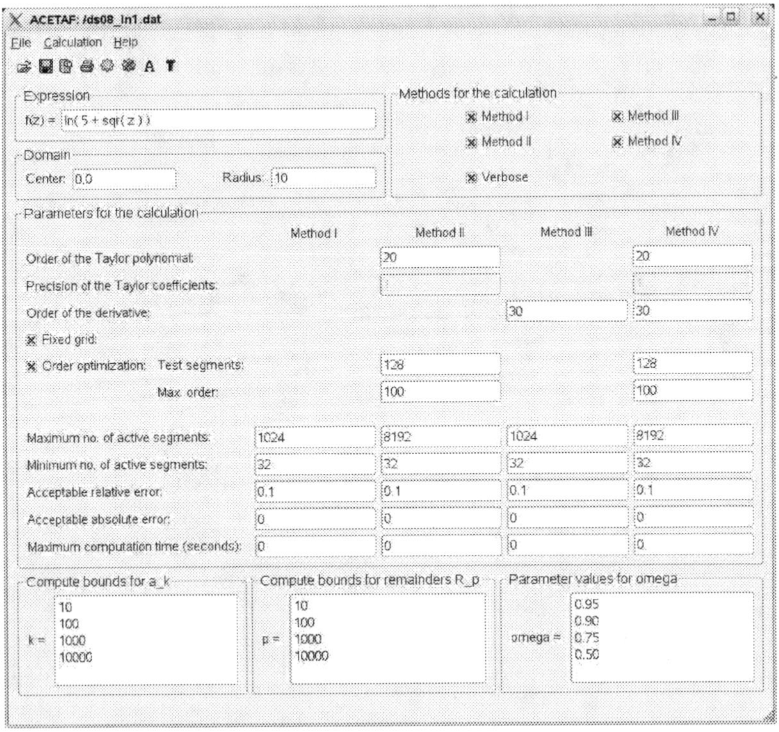

**Fig. 5.** ACETAF GUI

which has been designed with the QT3 library. The values are stored in an output file of the computation, and this file can be reused in other calculations. The user of the program may also enter several parameter values, which control the accuracy and the required time of the computation [11].

**Symbolic Expression Handler.** ACETAF includes a symbolic expression handler for arbitrary user-defined compositions of the supported library functions. The functions may be defined on arbitrary discs in the complex plane. Functions are entered as strings in the usual mathematical notation. The independent complex variable is represented by the literal "z". The literal "i" is used for complex unity. A function expression may contain constants in the scientific number format (such as 1.234E-05), the arithmetic operators $+$, $-$, $*$, $/$, the functions sqr, sqrt, exp, ln, sin, cos, tan, cot, asin, acos, atan, acot, sinh, cosh, tanh, coth, asinh, acoth, atanh, acoth, and the following functions with two arguments: power (integer powers), pow (real powers), and root (integer roots).

**Numerical Example.** In our numerical example, we are looking for bounds on the Taylor coefficients $a_k$ and on some Taylor remainder series $R_p$ for the function

$$f(z) = \ln(5 + z^2),$$

**Table 3.** Bounds for $f(z) = \ln(5 + z^2)$

| $l$ | $m$ | $M/V$ | $a_{100}$ | $a_{1000}$ | $R_{100}(0.75\,r)$ | $R_{1000}(0.75\,r)$ |
|---|---|---|---|---|---|---|
| 0 | 0 | $M = 2.3$ | $1.8^{-30}$ | $2.1^{-301}$ | $2.2^{-12}$ | $7.8^{-125}$ |
| 52 | 0 | $V = 4.3^{-4}$ | $3.4^{-34}$ | $4.0^{-305}$ | $4.1^{-16}$ | $1.5^{-128}$ |
| 0 | 30 | $V = 7.5^{58}$ | $7.6^{-30}$ | $1.1^{-332}$ | $3.5^{-12}$ | $3.6^{-156}$ |

the development point being the origin. The Taylor remainder series is estimated for some point $z$ with $|z| = \omega r$, $\omega \in (0,1)$, where $r$ is the user-defined radius of a disc around the development point. Since the bound on $\sum_{k=p+1}^{\infty} a_k z^k$ only depends on the absolute value of $z$, it is denoted by $R_p(\omega r)$.

Assuming no knowledge on singularities, the user may try an initial circle with $r = 10$, centered at the origin (cf. Figure 5). When the calculation is started with these values, ACETAF returns the error message "$f$ is not analytic on the complete domain given." Invoking the analyticity check, the program confirms that $f$ is analytic on the disc with radius 2.235782 (which is a good lower bound on $\sqrt{5}$, the maximum radius of analyticity of $f$). Since $f$ has a pole at $\pm i\sqrt{5}$, a slightly smaller radius should be used in the computation of $M(r)$ and $V(r, m, l)$. For $r = 2$, ACETAF calculates the bounds in Table 3.

## 4.5  VFIS: A C-XSC Package for Solving Integral Equations

The package VFIS (Verified Fredholm Integral Solver) by M. Grimmer is used for computing verified enclosures for Fredholm integral equations of the second kind. As a numerical example, we consider the Fredholm integral equation

$$y(s) - \int_{-1}^{1} (s\,t^2 - s^3\,t)\,y(t)dt = f(s), \quad -1 \le s \le 1,$$

with continuous forcing term

$$f(s) = (1 + \text{erf}(s))\,(s - 0.5)\,\log(1.5 - \sin(14s))$$

and continuous kernel function

$$K(s, t) = s\,t^2 - s^3\,t, \quad -1 \le s, t \le 1.$$

We are looking for the solution $y(s)$ on $[-1, 1]$.

The C-XSC source code (using the additional package VFIS) for this problem is as follows:

```
//-------------------------------------------------------------------
// Verified Fredholm Integral Equation Solver for linear
// Fredholm Integral Equations of the second kind
//-------------------------------------------------------------------
```

```
#include "interval.hpp"    //interval data types
#include "itaylor.hpp"     //automatic Taylor series computation
#include "dim2taylor.hpp"  //bivariate automatic differentiation
#include <fstream>

//Integral equation solver (system version) M. Grimmer
#include "IntegralEquation.hpp"

using namespace std;
using namespace cxsc;
using namespace taylor; //Taylor series

//Kernel function K of the integral equation
dim2taylor K(dim2taylor_vector& x)
{
  dim2taylor s=x[1];
  dim2taylor t=x[2];
  dim2taylor erg;

  erg=s*(sqr(t) - sqr(s)*t);   //s*t^2-s^3*t
  return erg;
}

//Right hand side of the integral equation
itaylor RS(itaylor& s)
{
  return (1+erf(s))*(s-real(0.5))*ln(real(1.5)-sin(14*s));
}

//Domain of the first kernel variable
const interval KDefS= interval(-1,1);

//Domain of the second kernel variable
const interval KDefT= interval(-1,1);

//Domain of the right hand side
const interval RSDef= interval(-1,1);


//Main function of the application
int main()
{
  int ord= 3;       //Taylor order
  int sysOrd= 10;   //Number of subintervals to create system

  //Output file used as logfile to monitor solution process
  ofstream logfile("IESolve.out");

  //Create integral equation object
  IntegralEquation IE(
```

```
  K,      //kernel function K(S,T)
  KDefS, //domain of first kernel variable S
  KDefT, //domain of second kernel variable T
  RS,     //right hand side function
  RSDef, //domain of right hand side function RS
  sysOrd,//order of subdivision of domain
  ord,    //Taylor order used to generate degenerate kernel approximation
  logfile //report on enclosure process and log timings
);

  //Solve integral equation
  IE.ComputeEnclosure(logfile);

  //Export results to the intpakX package & Maple
  IE.ExportPlot("Maple", "IE3_10_1.plot.mpl", 1);
  return 0;
}
```

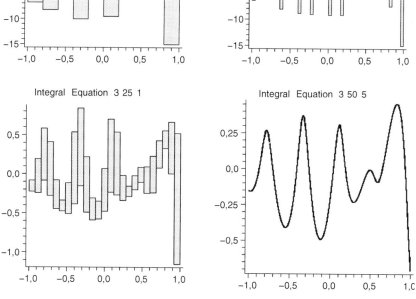

**Fig. 6.** Function enclosures for different discretization levels

The functions K and RS implement the bivariate kernel function and the right hand side $f(s)$, respectively. The scalar integral equation is first transformed into an equivalent system of integral equations. The order of this system is denoted by sysord. The parameter ord is used for approximating the kernel function K, using a bivariate Taylor approximation of order ord. The third integer parameter supplied to the function controls the number of subintervals used for plotting each part of the solution enclosure. For further details of the method and of the VFIS package we refer to [14].

The plotting information for a function tube containing the graph of the exact solution $y(s)$ in $-1 \leq s \leq 1$ is stored in the files IESolve.out and IE3_10_1.plot.mpl. The graphs in Figure 6 have been produced with the Maple power tool intpakX [13]. They nicely show the improvement of the computed enclosures of the solution, as discretization is refined.

## 5    Remarks on the Future Development of C-XSC

The development of the C-XSC library is being continued. Possible future extensions include the implementation of containment sets [39], parallel solvers for sparse matrices, simplified output procedures, extended sets of numerical test cases, etc.

Finally, C-XSC could benefit from hardware support for interval arithmetic, which would make the computations much faster than in the current implementation. It has been pointed out frequently [21,25] that the increase of complexity in current processors would only be moderate. Hence, the authors hope that hardware support for interval arithmetic will be included in the future development of floating-point standards.

## Acknowledgment

We wish to thank all friends and colleagues (see http://www.math.uni-wuppertal. de/~xsc/xsc/history.html) who have been contributing to the development of C-XSC.

## References

1. Alefeld, G., Herzberger, J.: Introduction to Interval Computations. Academic Press, New York (1983)
2. Blomquist, F., Hofschuster, W., Krämer, W.: Real and complex Taylor arithmetic in C-XSC. Preprint 2005/4, Universität Wuppertal (2005)
3. Blomquist, F., Hofschuster, W., Krämer, W.: Real and complex staggered (interval) arithmetic with wide exponent range (in German). Preprint 2008/1, Universität Wuppertal (2008)
4. Börsken, N.C.: Komplexe Kreis-Standardfunktionen. Freiburger Intervall-berichte 78/2 (1978)

5. Bräuer, M., Hofschuster, W., Krämer, W.: Steigungsarithmetiken in C-XSC. Preprint 2001/3, Universität Wuppertal (2001)
6. Braune, K.: Hochgenaue Standardfunktionen für reelle und komplexe Punkte und Intervalle in beliebigen Gleitpunktrastern. Ph.D thesis, Universität Karlsruhe (1987)
7. Braune, K., Krämer, W.: High-accuracy standard functions for real and complex intervals. In: Kaucher, E., Kulisch, U., Ullrich, C. (eds.) Computerarithmetic: Scientific Computation and Programming Languages, pp. 81–114. Teubner, Stuttgart (1987)
8. Brönnimann, H., Melquiond, G., Pion, S.: The design of the boost interval arithmetic library. Theor. Comput. Sci. 351, 111–118 (2006)
9. Bühler, G.: Standardfunktionen für komplexe Intervalle im 64 Bit IEEE Datenformat. Diploma thesis, Universität Karlsruhe (1993)
10. Eble, I., Neher, M.: CoStLy: Complex standard functions library (2002), http://www.uni-karlsruhe.de/~Markus.Neher/CoStLy.html
11. Eble, I., Neher, M.: ACETAF: A software package for computing validated bounds for Taylor coefficients of analytic functions. ACM TOMS 29, 263–286 (2003)
12. Griewank, A.: Evaluating Derivatives: Principles and Techniques of Algorithmic Differentiation. SIAM, Philadelphia (2000)
13. Grimmer, M.: Interval arithmetic in Maple with intpakX. Proc. Appl. Math. Mech. 2, 442–443 (2003)
14. Grimmer, M.: Selbstverifizierende mathematische Softwarewerkzeuge im High Performance Computing. Dissertation, Universität Wuppertal (2007)
15. Grimmer, M., Krämer, W.: An MPI extension for the use of C-XSC in parallel environments. In: Arabnia, et al. (eds.) Int. Conf. on Scientific Computing (CSC 2007, Worldcomp 2007), Proceedings, Las Vegas, pp. 111–117 (2007)
16. Hammer, R., Hocks, M., Kulisch, U., Ratz, D.: C++ Toolbox for Verified Computing – Basic Numerical Problems. Springer, Heidelberg (1995)
17. Hofschuster, W., Krämer, W.: C-XSC 2.0: A C++ library for extended scientific computing. In: Alt, R., Frommer, A., Kearfott, R.B., Luther, W. (eds.) Numerical Software with Result Verification (Dagstuhl Seminar 2003). LNCS, vol. 2991, pp. 15–35. Springer, Heidelberg (2004)
18. Hölbig, C.A., Krämer, W., Diverio, T.A.: An accurate and efficient self-verifying solver for systems with banded coefficient matrix. In: Parallel Computing: Software Technology, Algorithms, Architectures & Applications, pp. 283–290. Elsevier Science B.V., Amsterdam (2004)
19. IBM. High-accuracy arithmetic subroutine library (ACRITH). Program Description and User's Guide, 3rd ed. SC 33-6164-02, IBM (1986)
20. Jaulin, L., Kieffer, M., Didrit, O., Walter, E.: Applied Interval Analysis. Springer, London (2001)
21. Kirchner, R., Kulisch, U.: Hardware support for interval arithmetic. Reliable Computing 12, 225–237 (2006)
22. Klatte, R., Kulisch, U., Lawo, C., Rauch, M., Wiethoff, A.: C-XSC: A C++ Class Library for Extended Scientific Computing. Springer, Berlin (1993)
23. Krämer, W.: Inverse Standardfunktionen für reelle und komplexe Intervallargumente mit a priori Fehlerabschätzungen für beliebige Datenformate. Ph.D thesis, Universität Karlsruhe (1987)
24. Krückeberg, F.: Ordinary differential equations. In: Hansen, E. (ed.) Topics in Interval Analysis, pp. 91–97. Clarendon Press, Oxford (1969)
25. Kulisch, U.: Computer Arithmetic and Validity – Theory, Implementation. de Gruyter, Berlin (2008)

26. Kulisch, U., Miranker, W.L.: Computer Arithmetic in Theory and Practice. Academic Press, New York (1981)
27. Lerch, M., Tischler, G., Wolff von Gudenberg, J., Hofschuster, W., Krämer, W.: filib++, a fast interval library supporting containment computations. ACM TOMS 32, 299–324 (2006)
28. Lohner, R.: Enclosing the solutions of ordinary initial- and boundary-value problems. In: Kaucher, E., Kulisch, U., Ullrich, C. (eds.) Computerarithmetic: Scientific Computation and Programming Languages, pp. 255–286. Teubner, Stuttgart (1987)
29. Lohner, R.: Einschließung der Lösung gewöhnlicher Anfangs- und Randwertaufgaben und Anwendungen. Ph.D thesis, Universität Karlsruhe (1988)
30. Lohner, R.: On the ubiquity of the wrapping effect in the computation of error bounds. In: Kulisch, U., Lohner, R., Facius, A. (eds.) Perspectives of Enclosure Methods, pp. 201–217. Springer, Wien (2001)
31. Moore, R.E.: Automatic local coordinate transformations to reduce the growth of error bounds in interval computation of solutions of ordinary differential equations. In: Rall, L.B. (ed.) Error in Digital Computation, vol. II, pp. 103–140. John Wiley and Sons, New York (1965)
32. Moore, R.E.: Interval Analysis. Prentice Hall, Englewood Cliffs (1966)
33. Neher, M.: Geometric series bounds for the local errors of Taylor methods for linear $n$th order ODEs. In: Alefeld, G., Rohn, J., Rump, S., Yamamoto, T. (eds.) Symbolic Algebraic Methods and Verification Methods, pp. 183–193. Springer, Wien (2001)
34. Neher, M.: Validated bounds for Taylor coefficients of analytic functions. Reliable Computing 7, 307–319 (2001)
35. Neher, M.: Improved validated bounds for Taylor coefficients and for Taylor remainder series. J. Comput. Appl. Math. 152, 393–404 (2003)
36. Neher, M.: Complex standard functions and their implementation in the CoStLy library. ACM TOMS 33, 20–46 (2007)
37. Neumaier, A.: Interval Methods for Systems of Equations. Cambridge University Press, Cambridge (1990)
38. Popova, E., Krämer, W.: Inner and outer bounds for the solution set of parametric linear systems. J. Comp. Appl. Math. 199, 310–316 (2007)
39. Pryce, J.: Interval arithmetic with containment sets. Computing 78, 251–276 (2006)
40. Rall, L.B.: Automatic Differentiation: Techniques and Applications. LNCS, vol. 120. Springer, Heidelberg (1981)
41. Rump, S.: INTLAB – INTerval LABoratory. In: Csendes, T. (ed.) Developments in Reliable Computing, pp. 77–104. Kluwer, Dordrecht (1999)
42. Sakurai, T., Sugiura, H.: On factorization of analytic functions and its verification. Reliable Computing 6, 459–470 (2000)
43. Stetter, J.: Sequential defect correction for high-accuracy floating-point arithmetic. In: Numerical Analysis (Proceedings, Dundee 1983). Lecture Notes in Mathematics, vol. 1066, pp. 186–202 (1984)
44. Wedner, S.: Verifizierte Bestimmung singulärer Integrale – Quadratur und Kubatur. Dissertation, Universität Karlsruhe (2000)
45. Zimmer, M.: Laufzeiteffiziente, parallele Löser für lineare Intervallgleichungssysteme in C-XSC. Master thesis, Bergische Universität Wuppertal (2007)
46. Krämer, W., Zimmer, M.: Fast (parallel) dense linear interval systems solvers in C-XSC using error free transformations and BLAS. In: Cuyt, A., Krämer, W., Luther, W., Markstein, P. (eds.) Numerical Validation in Current Hardware Architectures (Dagtuhl Seminar 2008). LNCS, vol. 5492, pp. 230–249. Springer, Heidelberg (2009)

# Extending the Range of C-XSC: Some Tools and Applications for the Use in Parallel and Other Environments

Markus Grimmer

CETEQ GmbH & Co. KG
42119 Wuppertal, Lise-Meitner-Str. 5-9, Germany
`markus.grimmer@ceteq.de`,
`markus.grimmer@math.uni-wuppertal.de`

**Abstract.** We present some examples of extensions for C-XSC that have been developed lately. Among these are extensions that give access to further hardware and software environments as well as application software using the new possibilities.

The first area of extension is C-XSC usage in parallel environments. An MPI package for C-XSC data types allows to easily use C-XSC in parallel software without bothering about the internal structure of data types. Different versions of parallel verified linear system solvers based on the package are now available. An application making use of these solvers and further extensions is a parallel verified Fredholm integral equation system solver. Some results are given to demonstrate the reduction of computation time and the accuracy gain that can be obtained.

Another possibility to extend the range of C-XSC is to export results to different software environments as, for example, computer algebra packages. An example of this is presented for the Maple interval package intpakX.

**Keywords:** C-XSC, Integral Equations, Interval Arithmetic, Maple, MPI, Parallel Environment, Verified Linear System Solver.

## 1 Introduction

C-XSC is a well-known C++ class library for scientific computation. It is one important member of the family of XSC languages, libraries and compilers that cover a wide range of computational tools and methods. It is thus of special value not only to maintain and update all these, but also to extend the range towards new areas where XSC languages offered no support in the past.

One of these areas is parallel computation. Using C-XSC class objects in parallel communication in a straightforward way hasn't been possible in the past.

In this article, we present an extension for C-XSC that makes it possible to use C-XSC classes in parallel environments with the parallel communication interface MPI, together with some parallel applications that make use of it.

A. Cuyt et al. (Eds.): Numerical Validation, LNCS 5492, pp. 103–116, 2009.

Besides the usage of C-XSC in special environments it is also helpful to be able to export results from C-XSC programs to other computing environments as, for example, Computer Algebra packages. An example for this is presented as well.

## 1.1   C-XSC: A Short Overview

First of all, we want to give an overview of C-XSC and some of its existing older and lately developed extensions and applications.

The C-XSC library [1] [2] itself consists of the following elements:

*Interval Data Types.* First of all and most importantly, C-XSC offers a range of data types for interval computation:

- Basic Data Types: `real`, `interval`, `complex`, `cinterval`
- Vector and Matrix Types: Types for vector and matrix computation for either of the basic types
- Staggered Multiple Precision Arithmetic: Multiple precision arithmetic types allow for the use of n-fold precision using a vector of basic type elements to represent a staggered number.
- Dotprecision Types: These allow for the exact representation of scalar product expressions, i.e. sums of products of basic type numbers.

*Arithmetic.* For the mentioned data types, not only basic arithmetic operations are available, C-XSC also offers one of the most extensive sets of standard functions: Among these are also less well-known functions as the Gaussian error function or compound functions as $\sqrt{1 - x^2}$ and more.

*Toolbox.* The formerly separate C-XSC Toolbox [3] is now an integrated part of the library. It contains a number of numerical algorithms with result verification, among these

- Serial Linear System Solvers
- Global Optimization Algorithms

and more.

*Extensions.* Extensions for C-XSC can be divided into different categories:

- Arithmetic Extensions
- C-XSC Applications
- Technical Extensions

*Arithmetic Extensions.* Examples of arithmetic extensions are *Taylor Arithmetic* and *Hansen Arithmetic.* The C-XSC *Taylor Arithmetic* [4] [5] offers

- One- and multidimensional Interval Taylor Arithmetic types and functions
- Real and complex Interval Taylor Arithmetic types and functions
- Real staggered (multiple precision) Interval Taylor Arithmetic
- A complete set of standard functions

Lately added have been

- Improved function implementations for special expressions (as $\sqrt{1-x^2}$)
- Algorithms for Gaussian error function *erf* and complementary error function *erfc*

An example for the use of the C-XSC Taylor Arithmetic in an application will be given in the next sections.

The C-XSC *Hansen Arithmetic* which represents a generalized interval arithmetic has also been developed lately in the course of the development of a parametric interval linear system solver [6] and is a further useful arithmetic extension of C-XSC.

In addition, an improved staggered correction arithmetic with enhanced accuracy and very wide exponent range is now available [7].

*C-XSC Applications and Technical Extensions.* But there are not only arithmetic extensions of C-XSC. On the one hand, there are C-XSC applications beyond the Toolbox algorithms, as, for example,

- New and especially Parallel Linear System Solvers
- Linear Fredholm Integral Equation Solvers
- Parametric Linear System Solvers [6]

We will have a look at the first two of these below.

On the other hand, it is technical extensions that allow for the development of applications in the first place. An example of this kind is the MPI extension for C-XSC data types that is presented in the following section.

## 2   C-XSC in Parallel Environments

In this section, we present a package for C-XSC computation in parallel environments.

In distributed memory parallel environments it is necessary to communicate data between processes. MPI [8] is the most common interface for this kind of task. It offers a variety of functions for message passing and related tasks. Since MPI implementations operate on basic data types only, it is not possible to communicate class objects in a straightforward way. For a class library like C-XSC, additional packages for integration of MPI and the class library are necessary.

MPI communication with user defined data types can be done in different ways:

- Direct application of existing routines, applied to single data elements of objects
- Usage of the MPI data packing/unpacking mechanism
- Definition of MPI data types with the type definition mechanism

These approaches have advantages and disadvantages.

Direct application of existing routines, naturally, is quite always possible. Unfortunately, MPI routines cannot be applied to the data object in question since MPI only knows to handle elements or arrays of elements of a number of basic types. This is inconvenient, and it leaves the handling of class internal structures to the user or application developer. Moreover, communication will be time consuming, since all data elements are handled in separate communication calls.

MPI offers two strategies to make communication of data more convenient. The first of these is the *packing/unpacking* mechanism. It is the more versatile of the two since it allows to pack, then send, receive and finally unpack every kind of data you like.

The second strategy is the definition of new MPI data types. There is a collection of routines for data type definition in MPI making it possible to virtually assemble data by defining a so called *type map* and giving it a name, but unfortunately, there are limitations. Namely, no dynamically allocated data can be incorporated into the new type, and lengths of any data structures of variable size have to be known in advance to develop the new type, which is not the case in C-XSC and typically not useful for the definition of a general interface.

Hence, the package implemented for C-XSC data types uses the first of the two strategies for types that incorporate dynamic memory allocation and/or array-like structures like vector and matrix types.

It uses data type definition for the basic C-XSC data types `real`, `interval`, `complex` and `cinterval`, and includes packing/unpacking routines and communication routines as template functions for the types derived from these. All C-XSC types are included in the package:

- Basic types: `real`, `interval`, `complex`, `cinterval`
- Vector and Matrix data types for the basic types
- Staggered (= multiple precision) data types
- Dotprecision ("accumulator") data types

Regarding MPI communication, the following routines are covered:

- `MPI_Pack`, `MPI_Unpack`
- Point-to-point communication:
  - `MPI_Send`, `MPI_Bsend`, `MPI_Ssend`, `MPI_Rsend`
  - `MPI_Isend`, `MPI_Ibsend`, `MPI_Irsend`, `MPI_Issend`
  - `MPI_Recv`
- Collective Communication:
  - `MPI_Bcast`

A number of additional features is included as well:

- Communication functions for submatrices, i.e. rows, columns and proper submatrices; submatrices can also be used as full matrices on either communication node, i.e. a submatrix from a sending node can be stored as a full matrix on the receiving side.

- Communication functions for one and two-dimensional real C-XSC Taylor Arithmetic Types (see above)
- Communication functions for the STL vector type

In a general interface or package, it is not possible to offer general versions of further collective communication routines, since data subdivision for gather/scatter processes can be done in various ways, and the decision how to subdivide and distribute data has to be left to the author of the application.

To analyze the performance of the newly developed functions, tests have been done, and we want to give the following diagrams for illustration.

The tests were carried out in the parallel test environment ALiCEnext [9] in Wuppertal:

- 1024 1.8 GHz AMD Opteron 64 Bit Processors on 512 nodes
- LINPACK max. performance 2083 GFlops

The first diagram (see fig. 1) shows communication times for the circulation of C-XSC matrices of different sizes through 32 nodes. The test was carried out on randomly chosen nodes, so that the given times are only example times. The depicted ratio between the three methods, however, was found to be rather independent of the choice of nodes.

We secondly tested two different node topologies: In one case, the nodes were connected as a tree network, in the other case a crossbar switch was activated on the same machine. In order to find out if a typical example problem would be influenced by the different choice of topology, we computed the solution for different problem sizes and found that there was no significant change in the measured times (see fig. 2).

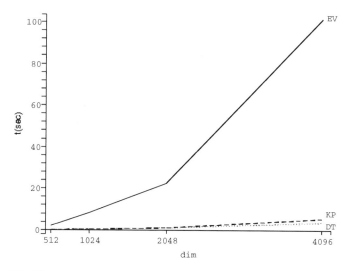

**Fig. 1.** EV: Element wise communication; KP: Communication package; DT: Data type definition for different fixed dimensions

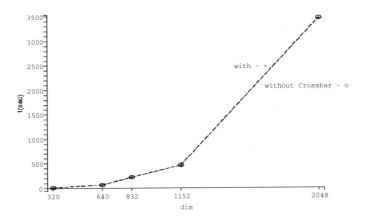

**Fig. 2.** Tree vs. Crossbar network (sample problem)

# 3    Applications Using C-XSC and MPI

In this section, we present a few applications that make use of the communication package described in the previous section.

An important type of application to use a parallel communication package are parallel linear system solvers.

In C-XSC, different interval linear system solvers are available now, building upon each other:

1. The base is the C-XSC Toolbox interval linear system solver, which is a serial solver for real input data
2. On stage 2, there is the serial interval linear system solver by Hölbig [10] including the second verification step with double precision computation of the approximate inverse as proposed by Rump [11]
3. The first parallel interval linear system solver developed in [12] builds upon the serial solver by Hölbig and allows for interval input data
4. Just recently developed there is now a fast interval linear system solver package by Zimmer [13] including fast serial and parallel solvers for various input formats using BLAS and LAPACK and the error free transformation dot product proposed by Rump, Oishi et al. [14]

Linear system solvers are applications of their own, but typically, they can also be found as subparts of more complex applications. As a C-XSC application using the parallel interval linear system solver 3 from above a verified integral equation system solver for linear Fredholm integral equation systems of the second kind is presented in the following paragraphs.

We will shortly describe the solver first and then give some results from the actual C-XSC implementation in a high performance computing environment.

A system of Fredholm Integral Equations of the second kind is given by

$$y^i(s) - \lambda \sum_{j=1}^{N} \int_{\alpha_j}^{\beta_j} k^{ij}(s,t) y^j(t) \, dt = g^i(s) \tag{1}$$

for $i = 1...N$ with continuous kernel functions $k^{ij}$ on $[\alpha_i, \beta_i] \times [\alpha_j, \beta_j]$ with

$$\alpha_i := a + \frac{i-1}{N}(b-a), \quad \beta_i := a + \frac{i}{N}(b-a), i, j = 1...N.$$

as well as continuous $g^i$ on $[\alpha_i, \beta_i]$ and unknown result functions $y^i$, $i = 1...N$.
With

$$\mathcal{Y} := (y^1, ..., y^N)^T$$
$$\mathcal{G} := (g^1, ..., g^N)^T$$
$$\mathcal{K} := (k^{ij})_{i,j=1...N}$$

we get

$$\mathcal{Y}(s) - \lambda \int_a^b \mathcal{K}(s,t)\mathcal{Y}(t) \, dt = \mathcal{G}(s). \tag{2}$$

The system of integral equations can thus be written in the same way as a single integral equation. For this reason, a solution method for systems of integral equations can be derived from a corresponding solution method for single equations.

If a kernel $\kappa$ has a representation

$$\kappa(s,t) = \sum_{m=1}^{T} a_m(s) b_m(t)$$

with continuous functions $a_m, b_m, m = 1...T$, it is called *degenerate kernel of order $T$*, so that matrices $\mathcal{A}_m, \mathcal{B}_m, m = 0..T$ (with some suitable $T \in I\!N$) for degenerate kernels can be additionally introduced for the above matrix notation.

The kernel of a linear Fredholm integral equation of the second kind can be represented as

$$K = K_{\mathfrak{E}} + K_{\mathfrak{N}}$$

with a degenerate part $K_{\mathfrak{E}}$ and a non-degenerate part $K_{\mathfrak{N}}$ (see, e.g., [15]). According matrix denotations $\mathcal{K}_{\mathfrak{E}}, \mathcal{K}_{\mathfrak{N}}$ can be introduced component wise.

The solution methods are described in detail in [12], [16] and [17] and shall not be discussed here. We only want to give the solution algorithm to indicate that the most relevant parts of the algorithm can be efficiently parallelized (see method 1).

The highlighted parts of the algorithm were parallelized, the remaining parts being of minor importance since they only have a small share of the method's overall complexity. We can see that one of the parallel parts is given by the application of a parallel interval linear system solver.

---

**Method 1:  Integral Equation System Solution Method**

---

For $j := 1...N, n := 1...2T$:

    Compute integrals of basic monomials $(t - t_0^j)^n$.

Carry out the iteration

    $\mathcal{F}^0 := \mathcal{G}; \quad \mathcal{F}^{i+1} := \mathcal{G} + \mathcal{K}_{\mathfrak{R}}\mathcal{F}^i, \quad i := 0, 1, ...$

until $\mathcal{F} := \mathcal{F}^{i+1} \subseteq \mathcal{F}^i$ (or abort).

---

For $m := 0...T$:                                                                    (PAR)

    For $j := 1...N$:

        Carry out the iteration

            $C_m^{j,0} := \mathcal{A}_m^j; \quad C_m^{j,i+1} := \mathcal{A}_m^j + \mathcal{K}_{\mathfrak{R}} C_m^{j,i}$

            $i := 0, 1, ...$

            until $C_m^j := C_m^{j,i+1} \subseteq C_m^{j,i}$ (or abort).

---

Compute the entries                                                                   (PAR)

  $- \mathcal{M} := (\mathcal{M}_{ij})_{i,j=0...T}, \mathcal{M}_{ij} := \int_a^b \mathcal{B}_i(t) C_j(t) dt$

  $- \mathcal{R} := (\mathcal{R}_i)_{i=0...T}, \mathcal{R}_i := \int_a^b \mathcal{B}_i(t) \mathcal{F}(t) dt$

of the interval linear system for the final application of the method for degenerate kernels.

---

Solve the interval linear system                                                      (PAR)

    $(I - \lambda \mathcal{M}) X = \mathcal{R}.$

---

Compute the solution function $\mathcal{Y} := \mathcal{G} + \lambda \sum_{m=0}^T C_m X_m.$

---

    The actual implementation of the solver was designed to solve single integral equations by splitting them up into integral equation systems as indicated above.

    Let us point out which elements of the solver make it a relevant example for a parallel C-XSC application using the presented extensions:

- We solve a functional problem with functions in one and two variables which are represented in interval Taylor arithmetic
- As a matrix problem with possibly high matrix dimensions, the method is time consuming and thus a good candidate to be parallelized for increased efficiency.
- The solution reduces to an interval linear system so that an interval linear system solver can be applied.

We now want to give some results for this integral equation system solver, taking into account time/parallelization and accuracy issues.

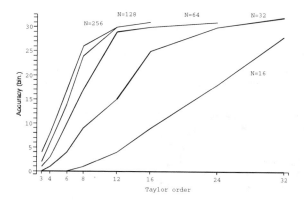

**Fig. 3.** Accuracy Gain for growing Taylor order and different system sizes

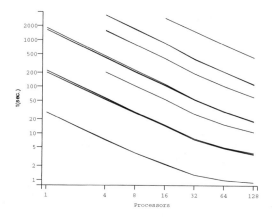

**Fig. 4.** Computation time for increasing number of processors (different parameter values for a sample problem)

In figure 3 result accuracy is plotted against Taylor order for different dimensions of the example integral equation system derived by splitting up the integral equation

$$y(s) - \int_{-1}^{1} st^2 - s^2t \ y(t) \ dt = (s - \frac{1}{2}) \cdot erf(sin(9s)).$$

It is clearly visible that solutions become more accurate with increasing dimension of the integral equation system, especially in cases where low system size does not yet yield reasonable results.

Parallelization is considered in figure 4, giving example timings for different parameter combinations and up to 128 processors. Linear speedup could be achieved for most of the relevant parameter combinations.

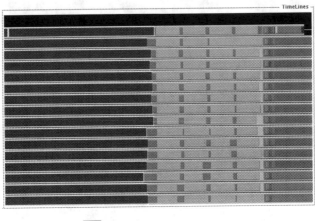

Phase 1:  ▓ Fixed Point Iterations
Phase 2:  ▓ LS Computation
Phase 3:  ▓ LSS
Gaps:     ▓ Comm.+Idle

**Fig. 5.** Example: Taylor order 3, System order 128, 16 procs., computation time $\sim 2$ min. - Time shares

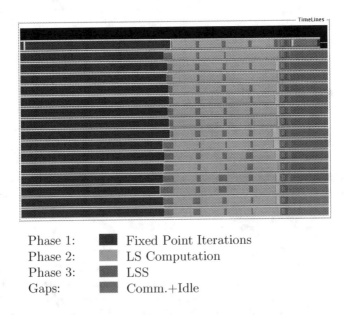

Phase 1:  ▓ Fixed Point Iterations
Phase 2:  ▓ LS Computation
Phase 3:  ▓ LSS
Gaps:     ▓ Comm.+Idle

**Fig. 6.** Example: Taylor order 12, System order 32, 16 procs., computation time $\sim 2$ min. - Time shares

We also analyzed time shares of different parts of the program:

- Iteration phase
- Computation of the entries of the linear system
- Linear system solution (including approximate matrix inversion and further matrix operations, e.g. matrix multiplications)

Figures 5 and 6 show the time shares of the different parts of the algorithm for different (medium sized) parameter combinations.

It is observable that time shares differ significantly for different parameter values due to the complexity of the parts of the algorithm. The greatest time share is used by either the iteration part or the linear system assembly, but not by linear system solution. In general, computation time is evenly distributed over the processors and idle times are kept within bounds.

## 4    Exporting C-XSC Results to Other Environments

It is not only important to extend the range of a library like C-XSC. It is also valuable to be able to export results to other environments since those typically offer further possibilities. For example, Computer Algebra Packages (with suitable interval facilities) allow for symbolical computation with result functions from a C-XSC integral equation solver, and they also allow for visualization of results.

As an example for C-XSC and Maple, a Maple interface has been included in the above integral equation application. It exports solution functions as Maple code and range enclosures of the solution functions for visualization in Maple.

Interval arithmetic in Maple is provided by the Maple package intpakX [18]. The package includes not only interval operators and functions, but also allows to visualize interval enclosures (2D and 3D).

*Example:* Consider the integral equation

$$y(s) - \frac{1}{2} \int_0^1 (s+1)e^{-st}y(t)\, dt$$
$$= e^{-x} - \frac{1}{2} + \frac{1}{2}e^{-x+1}, \qquad s, t \in [0,1]$$

which, according to Kress [19], has the analytic solution

$$y : s \to e^{-s}.$$

The verified Taylor coefficients of the first component of the solution can be computed as

```
[ 0.969232610773108516,  0.969235565177278713]
[-0.969233189716268040,-0.969233131674795078]
[ 0.484616598544399534,  0.484616637435440978]
[-0.161554269639638399,-0.161550720767527217]
[ 0.038892044738204872,  0.041956101920650240]
```

The function output in Maple code is

```
IGLSys_Lsg[0]  := x ->
[ 0.969232610773108516,   0.969235565177278713]
&+ ( [-0.969233189716268040,-0.969233131674795078]
&* ( ( x
&- [ 0.031250000000000000, 0.031250000000000000] )
   &intpower 1 ) )
&+ ( [ 0.484616598544399534, 0.484616637435440978]
&* ( ( x
&- [ 0.031250000000000000, 0.031250000000000000] )
   &intpower 2 ) )
&+ ( [-0.161554269639638399,-0.161550720767527217]
&* ( ( x
&- [ 0.031250000000000000, 0.031250000000000000] )
   &intpower 3 ) )
&+ ( [ 0.038892044738204872, 0.041956101920650240]
&* ( ( x
&- [ 0.031250000000000000, 0.031250000000000000] )
   &intpower 4 ) ) ;
```

The solution can be visualized in Maple as shown in figures 7 and 8.

Integral Equation System Solution Enclosure

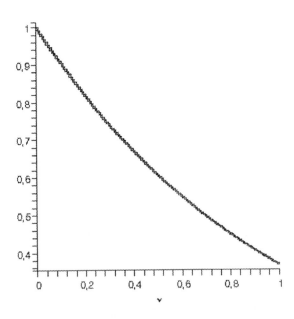

**Fig. 7.** Maple visualization of verified integral equation solution (note the enclosing rectangles)

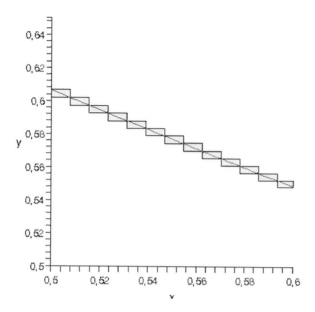

**Fig. 8.** Maple visualization of verified integral equation solution (detail)

## 5 Conclusions

The extensions presented in the above sections allow for the successful implementation of parallel applications using C-XSC and MPI, so that parallel environments as important computing environments for solving time consuming problems can be easily accessed with C-XSC. They contribute to making the XSC languages a valuable and still growing framework for scientific computing. Moreover, examples show how C-XSC can be connected to other environments with different focus. Work is going on to provide further efficient C-XSC problem solution applications and further arithmetical and technical C-XSC extensions to give access to further computing environments.

## References

1. C-XSC: C-XSC Download,
   http://www.math.uni-wuppertal.de/wrswt/xsc/cxsc_new.html
2. Hofschuster, W., Krämer, W.: C-XSC 2.0 – a C++ class library for extended scientific computing. In: Alt, R., Frommer, A., Kearfott, B., Luther, W. (eds.) Numerical Software with Result Verification (Dagstuhl Seminar 2003). LNCS, vol. 2991, pp. 15–35. Springer, Heidelberg (2004)
3. Hammer, R., Hocks, M., Kulisch, U., Ratz, D.: C++ Toolbox for Verified Computing: Basic Numerical Problems. Springer, Heidelberg (1995)

4. Blomquist, F., Hofschuster, W., Krämer, W.: Real and complex Taylor Arithmetic in C-XSC. Preprint BUW-WRSWT 2005/4, University of Wuppertal (2005), http://www.math.uni-wuppertal.de/wrswt/literatur/lit_wrswt.html
5. Bräuer, M.C.: Berechnungsmethoden für Ableitungen und Steigungen und deren Realisierung in C-XSC. Master's thesis, University of Karlsruhe (1999)
6. El-Owny, H.: Verified Solution of Parametric Interval Linear Systems. Ph.D thesis, University of Wuppertal (2007)
7. Blomquist, F., Hofschuster, W., Krämer, W.: Real and Complex Staggered (Interval) Arithmetics with Wide Exponent Range (in German). Preprint BUW-WRSWT 2008/1, University of Wuppertal (2008), http://www.math.uni-wuppertal.de/wrswt/literatur/lit_wrswt.html
8. Message Passing Interface Forum: MPI: A message passing interface standard. Library specification, University of Tennessee (1993-1995)
9. ALiCEnext: Alicenext information, http://www.alicenext.uni-wuppertal.de
10. Hölbig, C., Krämer, W.: Selfverifying solvers for dense systems of linear equations realized in C-XSC. Preprint BUW-WRSWT 2003/1, University of Wuppertal (2003), http://www.math.uni-wuppertal.de/wrswt/literatur/lit_wrswt.html
11. Rump, S.: Kleine Fehlerschranken bei Matrixproblemen. Ph.D thesis, University of Karlsruhe (1980)
12. Grimmer, M.: Selbstverifizierende mathematische Softwarewerkzeuge im High Performance Computing. Ph.D thesis, University of Wuppertal (2007)
13. Zimmer, M.: Laufzeiteffiziente, parallele Löser für lineare Intervallgleichungssysteme in C-XSC. Master's thesis, University of Wuppertal (2007)
14. Ogita, T., Rump, S., Oishi, S.: Accurate sum and dot product. SIAM Journal on Scientific Computing 26(6), 1955–1988 (2005)
15. Heuser, H.: Funktionalanalysis. Teubner, Stuttgart (1975)
16. Klein, W.: Zur Einschließung der Lösung von linearen und nichtlinearen Fredholmschen Integralgleichungssystemen zweiter Art. Ph.D thesis, University of Karlsruhe (1990)
17. Klein, W.: Enclosure methods for linear and nonlinear systems of Fredholm integral equations of the second kind. In: Adams, E., Kulisch, U. (eds.) Scientific computing with automatic result verification, Boston. Academic Press, London (1993)
18. Grimmer, M.: Interval Arithmetic in Maple with intpakX. PAMM - Proceedings in Applied Mathematics and Mechanics 2(1), 442–443 (2003)
19. Kress, R.: Linear Integral Equations. Springer, Heidelberg (1989)

# *Mathematica* Connectivity to Interval Libraries filib++ and C-XSC*

Evgenija D. Popova

Institute of Mathematics and Informatics
Bulgarian Academy of Sciences
Acad. G. Bonchev str., block 8, 1113 Sofia, Bulgaria
epopova@bio.bas.bg

**Abstract.** Building interval software interoperability can be a good solution when re-using high-quality legacy code or when accessing func-
tionalities unavailable natively in one of the software packages. In this
work we present the integration of programs based on the interval libraries filib++ and C-XSC into *Mathematica* via *MathLink* communication protocol. On some small easily readable programs we demonstrate:
i) some details of *MathLink* technology, ii) the transparency of numerical data communication without any conversion, iii) the advantage of
symbolic manipulation interfaces — the access to the external compiled
language functionality from within *Mathematica* is often even more convenient than from its own native environment.

**Keywords:** Software interoperability, interfacing, interval software,
C-XSC, filib++, *MathLink*, *Mathematica*, external programs.

## 1 Introduction

As the numerical methods based on interval analysis expand in their range and
applications, the number and diversity of interval software increase rapidly. The
existing interval software ranges from libraries for application development to
fully interactive software systems [8]. However there are only a few interval
software comparing studies. They were hampered by the diversity in the implementation supporting environments and in the interval data representations
(see e.g. [2] and the references given therein). The provided functionality also
varies from fairly basic and general to highly specialized. Although some specialized methods are brought to reliable, high-quality and fast implementations,
they remain isolated software systems. Some specific software tools are built on
the top of other more general interval libraries but there is no single environment supporting all (or most) of the available interval methods. Many problem
solving routines require symbolic or structured input data and building corresponding application programming interfaces would facilitate their usage. On the
other hand, most recent interval applications require a combination of diverse

---

* This work was partially supported by the Bulgarian National Science Fund.

A. Cuyt et al. (Eds.): Numerical Validation, LNCS 5492, pp. 117–132, 2009.

methods. It is difficult for the end-users to combine and manage the diversity of interval software tools, packages, and research codes, even the latter being accessible. Two recent initiatives: [3], directed toward developing of a comprehensive full-featured library of validated routines, and [11], intending to provide a general service framework for validated computing in heterogeneous environment, reflect the realized necessity for an integration of the available methods and software tools.

It is commonly understood that quality comprehensive libraries are not compiled by a single person or small group of people over a short time [3]. Therefore, in this paper we present an alternative approach based on interval software interoperability. In Section 2 we discuss some aspects concerning this approach and outline its advantages. Since on the one hand the general-purpose environments for scientific/technical computing like Matlab, *Mathematica*, Maple, etc. possess several features not attributable to the compiled languages and on the other hand most of the interval software is developed in some compiled language for efficiency reasons, it is interesting to study the possibilities for interoperability between these two kinds of interval supporting environments. In this paper we focus on the interaction between *Mathematica* [17] and two external C++ libraries for interval computations, filib++ [9], [10] and C-XSC [4], [7] via *MathLink* communication protocol [5], [15]. In particular, we present how to call external programs based on either of these two interval libraries from within a *Mathematica* session, thus exchanging data without using intermediate files but under dynamics and interactivity in the communication. The goal is to demonstrate some advantages of interval software interoperability. Namely, expanded functionality for both environments, symbolic manipulation interfaces for the compiled language interval software which often make access to the external functionality from within *Mathematica* more convenient even than from its own native environment. Section 3 presents some basics from *MathLink* technology for building external *MathLink* -compatible programs. The technology will be further demonstrated in more details in the next sections on some small and easily readable sample programs. This work does not intend to provide a complete *Mathematica* interface for the C-XSC and filib++ interval libraries but to demonstrate the connectivity technology and some important specific aspects of the interaction between *Mathematica* and filib++ in Section 4, or C-XSC in Section 5. The electronic supplementary archives that accompany this paper give: i) more insight into *MathLink* technology, ii) a framework for its expansion on other problems, and iii) more illustrations of the presented connectivity.

## 2   Some Aspects of Interval Software Interoperability

Compiling a library of full-featured, high quality, portable and uniform interval-based tools, as presented in [3], is an ambitious goal, requiring the work of many people over many years. In contrast to this approach, providing interoperability between the existing interval software may achieve similar goals at a considerably lower price and development time. The following advantages could be achieved with respect to the development process.

- When building software interoperability the usual tedious and error-prone work is removed providing in the same time a safeguard against the re-implementation bugs.
- Since we are usually interested to connect software which is already brought to a high quality and efficiency, only the connectivity and interoperability need to be tested but not the connected software components. The team can concentrate on the overall concept and the new implementations.
- Thus, in some cases providing interval software connectivity and interoperability would require considerably less development time than building everything from scratch. Software interoperability, instead of re-implementation, is especially suitable for complicated methods and large software systems which are already brought to a high quality and efficiency.

In the same time, a connectivity between two (or more) interval software environments would provide: expanded functionality, compatibility of interval representations, increased possibility for comparison and testing, accessibility by a wider range of users, performance improvement when a compiled code is integrated into an interpretative environment. A possible drawback is that each of the software ingredients should be maintained and ported to different platforms separately. In general, the problems that may arise in providing interoperability depend on the software that is to be connected and the purpose of the interaction. For example, the details in connecting C and Fortran programs will depend on the particular Fortran and C compilers (their calling conventions) and the types of the parameters to pass.

It is well-known that the general-purpose and multi-platform computing environments like Matlab, *Mathematica*, Maple, etc. possess several features not attributable to the compiled languages: dynamics and interactivity of the environment, symbolic and algebraic computations, numerics on all data types, powerful graphics programming, interfaces and connectivity, etc. The killer applications of these also called computer algebra environments are symbolic manipulation, education and prototyping. Thus, the interoperability between a computer algebra system and external compiled language software would bring additional benefits. The former will get expanded functionality and increased performance, while the external software could benefit from symbolic manipulations, powerful graphics capabilities, suitable interfaces, etc. Although all Matlab, *Mathematica* and Maple support interval computations, due to efficiency reasons most of the interval software is implemented in some compiled language. Therefore, it is interesting to study the interoperability between these general-purpose environments and the interval software developed in compiled languages.

There are two basic forms of communication between two software systems: structured and unstructured. Unstructured communication is based on file reading and writing operations to exchange ordinary text. This simplest form of communication between two software systems has some important drawbacks with respect to interval software systems. Namely, the necessity of avoiding inevitable input/output roundoff errors. For an example of such unstructured communication and the problems that have to be solved refer to [2]. Here we explore and demonstrate interval software interoperability via communication protocols. The idea of structured communication is to transfer data without using intermediate files, communicating with external programs on a higher level and exchanging more structured data or complete expressions with the external programs which are specially set up to handle such objects.

## 3    *MathLink* Basics

Extensively used within the *Mathematica* system itself, *MathLink* is *Mathematica*'s unique high-level symbolic interface standard for interprogram communication [5], [15]–[17]. With convenient bindings for a variety of languages, *MathLink* allows arbitrary symbolic objects — representing data, programs, or any other construct — to be efficiently exchanged between programs, on one computer or across a heterogeneous network. In this work we demonstrate one of the most common uses of *MathLink*: to allow external functions written in some compiled language to be called from within the *Mathematica* environment.

Given a function defined in an external program, then what is necessary to do in order to make it possible to call the function from within *Mathematica* is to add appropriate *MathLink* code that passes arguments to the function, and takes back the results it produces. The overall process consists of four steps:

1. Create an appropriate *MathLink* template for each external function;
2. Combine the template with the external source code into a communication module;
3. Process the *MathLink* template information and compile all the source code;
4. Install the binary in the current *Mathematica* session.

The intention is that the developers take pre-existing routines and with as little effort as possible (ideally with no source code changes to the routines themselves), package them so they can be called from *Mathematica*.

A *MathLink* template involves the following mandatory elements:

| | |
|---|---|
| :Begin: | begin the template for a particular function |
| :Function: | the name of the function in the external program |
| :Pattern: | the *Mathematica* pattern to be defined to call the function |
| :Arguments: | the arguments to the function |
| :ArgumentTypes: | the types of the arguments to the function |
| :ReturnType: | the type of the value returned by the function |
| :End: | end the template for a particular function |

*MathLink* templates are conventionally put in files with names of the form `file.tm`. Such files can also contain C source code, interspersed between the templates for different functions. When a *MathLink* template file is processed, two basic things are done. First, the `:Pattern:` and `:Arguments:` specifications are used to generate a *Mathematica* definition that calls an external function via *MathLink*. Second, the :`Function:`, :`ArgumentTypes:` and :`ReturnType:` specifications are used to generate C source code that calls the desired function within the external program. Both the :`Pattern:` and :`Arguments:` specifications in a *MathLink* template can be any *Mathematica* expressions. Whatever is given as the :`Arguments:` specification will be evaluated every time the external function is called. The result of the evaluation will be used as the list of arguments to pass to the function.

Sometimes it may be necessary to set up *Mathematica* expressions that should be evaluated not when an external function is called, but instead only when the external function is first installed. This can be done by inserting :`Evaluate:` specifications in the corresponding *MathLink* template. Usually, an usage message and/or error messages for the *Mathematica* functions are defined after :`Evaluate:`. When an external program is installed, the specifications in its *MathLink* template file are used in the order they were given. This means that any expressions given in :`Evaluate:` specifications that appear before :`Begin:` will have been evaluated before definitions for the external function are set up.

Once a *MathLink* template for a particular external function is constructed, this template has to be combined with the actual source code for the function. By the *MathLink* communication protocol the external programs send and receive *Mathematica* expressions using the fundamental C data types. Therefore, if the source code is written in the C programming language, all that should be done is just adding a line to include the standard *MathLink* header file, and then inserting a small main program. The form of main required on different systems may be slightly different, the appropriate form is given in the *MathLink* Developer Kit [17] for every particular computer system.

Once the couple of appropriate template file and C/C++ source files that make *MathLink* function calls is set up, they should be processed to build a *MathLink*-compatible program. The template file must first be processed into a C source file using a program named `mprep` included in the *MathLink* Developer Kit. `mprep` converts template entries into C functions, passes other text through unmodified, and writes out additional C functions that implement a remote procedure call mechanism using *MathLink*. The result is a C source file `file.tm.c` that is ready for compilation. All source files must be compiled and then the resulting object code must be linked with the `libML.a` library and any of the other standard libraries required by the applications. `mcc` is a script that preprocesses and compiles *MathLink* source files. For more information on how to compile and run *MathLink* programs written in C on Unix systems see [16].

Finally, the `Install` function is used to launch a *MathLink*-compatible program and to make its functions available in a *Mathematica* session.

# 4    *MathLink* Connection to `filib++`

The library `filib++` is known as an efficient portable C++ library supporting interval arithmetic and fast computation of guaranteed bounds for interval versions of a comprehensive set of elementary functions [9], [10]. There are two specific features of the library regarding the representation of real intervals. The standard input/output operators are overloaded for intervals but without appropriate directed rounding from/to the external decimal string format. Analogously, the interval constructors do not provide enclosure for not exactly representable data. This feature requires special considerations and data handling if the conversion errors have to be bounded. In this section we show that this problem can be transparently solved by calling the filib++ functions from *Mathematica* via the *MathLink* communication protocol. The second feature of filib++ is that the library can be used in two modes: normal and extended. In the normal mode, when an interval evaluation is not defined, an exception handling is activated which terminates the program with an error message. In the extended mode, intervals are defined over the set of floating-point numbers extended by $\{-\infty, +\infty\}$. To cope with the closed set of real numbers and to allow exception free computations, the designers of filib++ have accepted the IEEE representation of $-\infty$ and $+\infty$, allowing the latter to be used as left or right bound of an extended interval. The empty interval is represented as [NaN, NaN].

Let us consider a small *MathLink*-compatible external program which uses the extended interval data type of the library filib++ to perform containment computations. Below is the source file filibStdF.cpp involving the C function filibStdF() evaluating a standard mathematical function over an interval.

```cpp
#include "mathlink.h"          // MathLink include
#include <interval/interval.hpp> // filib include
typedef filib::interval<double,         /* simplify instantiation */
    filib::native_switched, filib::i_mode_extended> interval;
using namespace std;

void filibStdF(int fcode, double *data, long len)
{
  interval  x(data[0], data[1]), res;
  switch(fcode)
  { case  1: { res = acos(x); break; }
    case  2: { res = acosh(x); break; }
..........       not presenting all cases for simplicity
    case 28: { res = tanh(x); break; }
  }
// Initializing C variables passing the computed result to Mathematica
  double res_data[4];
  res_data[0] = x.inf();      // showing that the interval constructor
  res_data[1] = x.sup();      // does not perform any rounding
  res_data[2] = res.inf();
  res_data[3] = res.sup();

  MLPutRealList(stdlink, res_data, 4); //Send result back to Mathematica
  return ;
}
int main(int argc, char* argv[ ]) // Standard MathLink main function
{   return MLMain(argc, argv);  }
```

Here is the corresponding template file `filibStdF.tm` which must have the same name as the source file:

```
:Evaluate: filibStdF::usage = "filibStdF[fun, arg] uses the external
interval library filib++ to evaluate a standard mathematical function
'fun' of one argument over a specified real interval 'arg'."
:Begin:
:Function:          filibStdF
:Pattern:           filibStdF[fun_Symbol, arg_Interval]
:Arguments:         {fun/.{ArcCos->1, ArcCosh->2, ArcCot->3, ArcCoth->4,
                    ..... Tan->27, Tanh->28}, arg[[1]]}
:ArgumentTypes:     {Integer, RealList}
:ReturnType:        Manual
:End:
```

The `:Function:` line specifies the name of the C routine. The `:Pattern:` line shows how the routine will be called from within *Mathematica*. The names of the two routines do not have to be identical as in this case. Note that the arguments in the *Mathematica* function pattern are restricted: the first one to be a symbolic name and the second to be the *Mathematica* object `Interval`. The `:Arguments:` line specifies the expressions to be passed to the external program. In our case these expressions are not the same as the variable names on the `:Pattern:` line. The `:Arguments:` specification will be evaluated every time the external function is called. During the evaluation the first argument `fun` of the calling *Mathematica* function will be transformed into an integer number[1] and from the second argument `arg` only the first part, presenting a list of the interval end-points, will be taken. The result of the evaluation will be used as the list of arguments to pass to the C function. The `:ArgumentTypes:` and `:ReturnType:` lines contain special keywords used by `mprep` to create the appropriate *MathLink* function calls that transfer data across the link. There are six keywords (`Integer`, `Real`, `IntegerList`, `RealList`, `String`, `Symbol`) for some more common types of data. For example, the keyword `Integer` on the `:ArgumentTypes:` causes `mprep` to create a call to *MathLink* function `MLGetInteger` which transfers C ints. Using keywords `IntegerList` or `RealList`, however, an extra argument has to be included in the corresponding C function to represent the length of the list, see the declaration of `filibStdF()` above. If the external function needs to receive or return expression types that are not among the set handled automatically by `mprep`, or if the function returns different types of results (such as an integer or the symbol `$Failed`) in different situations, then the keyword `Manual` can be included on the `:ArgumentTypes:` lines to inform `mprep` that we will write our own calls to get the arguments or (as in our case) on the `:ReturnType:` line to put the results ourselves.

The external programs should not modify the arrays generated by the *Math-Link* functions `MLGetRealList()`, `MLGetRealArray()`, etc. Since the external libraries we connect to *Mathematica* use special data types for representing intervals, **the main purpose of the communication modules that have**

---

[1] For simplicity, not all elements of the transformation rule are presented.

to be developed is to initialize new variables having the corresponding specific data types with the incoming data, and after the actual computations to transform the computed results into variables of fundamental C data types that will be passed back to *Mathematica*.

Once the filibStdF.tm and filibStdF.cpp files have been processed and compiled to produce an executable file called filibStdF, we can install it into a *Mathematica* session. The *Mathematica* commands, presented below, illustrate its usage.

```
In[1] := lnk = Install["filibStdF"]
Out[1] = LinkObject[./filibStdF, 2, 2]
```

The Install function launches the program and opens a link through which the external function can be called. The program sends to *Mathematica* the definitions for its functions specified in the template file along with whatever code is given on the :Evaluate: lines. Let us see our external function in action and request the evaluation of $\cos(x)$ over the interval $[-1, 3]$. The output wrapper function InputForm is used to show all the digits of the results.

```
In[2] := filibRes= filibStdF[Cos, Interval[{-1, 3}]]
         filibRes // InputForm
Out[2] = {-1., 3., -0.989992, 1.}
Out[3]//InputForm = {-1., 3., -0.9899924966004472, 1.}
```

In order that the user can monitor the input/output communication of the data, our external function is designed to send a list of four numbers back to *Mathematica*. The first two components are the input interval end-points and the next two components are the end-points of the result. Another reason for designing the communication so that it does not pass back the *Mathematica* Interval object but lists of interval end-points is that we want to avoid an extra outward rounding introduced by the *Mathematica* function Interval as below. *Mathematica*'s Take function is used below to get the last two components of a list.

```
In[4] := Interval[Take[filibRes, -2]] // InputForm
Out[4]//InputForm = Interval[{-0.9899924966004473, 1.0000000000000002}]
```

Since both the machine-precision numbers in *Mathematica* and the arithmetic of filib++ are based on the same C data type double and because the underlying architecture is IEEE-compliant, the communication is transparent without any data conversion. Furthermore, *MathLink* is efficient and will send data in a binary format when communicating with external programs that run on the same computer or when the computers are sufficiently compatible.

Interfacing filib++ by *Mathematica*, we can overcome the difficulties in using the interval constructors in filib++ for a correct enclosure of real data. Namely, *Mathematica*'s function Interval provides a correct enclosure of intervals involving inexact real data at the end-points.

```
In[5] := Interval[{-1, 2.7}] // InputForm
Out[5]//InputForm = Interval[{-1, 2.7000000000000006}]
```

Then these outwardly rounded end-points are transparently passed to the external program which constructs the filib++ intervals without rounding.

```
In[6] := filibStdF[Cos, Interval[{-1, 2.7}]] // InputForm
Out[6]//InputForm = {-1., 2.7000000000000006, -0.904072142017063, 1.}
```

While cos() is defined over the whole real line, log() function is not. Let us see what is the result produced by filib++.

```
In[7] := filibRes = Take[filibStdF[Log, Interval[{-1, 2.7}]] , -2];
         filibRes // InputForm
Out[8]/InputForm = {-Infinity, 0.9932517730102848}
```

The transparency of floating-point communication between *Mathematica* and filib++, explained above, is the reason for obtaining straightforward the *Mathematica* symbol Infinity at the corresponding end-point of the result.

Since Indeterminate is *Mathematica*'s symbol for the IEEE Not-a-Number and the interval [NaN, NaN] is adopted by filib++ to represent the empty set, the following result is not surprising.

```
In[9] := filibStdF[Log, Interval[{-2, -1}]]
Out[9] = {-2., -1., Indeterminate, Indeterminate}
```

Another example demonstrates again the transparency of the communication and a property of the extended arithmetic of filib++. By definition, the point interval [+infinity] is represented in filib++ by the interval [M, +infinity], where M is the overflow threshold [10]. Since $\operatorname{acoth}(1) = +\infty$, we have

```
In[10] := Take[filibStdF[ArcCoth, Interval[1]], -2]// InputForm
Out[10]//InputForm = {1.7976931348623157*^308, Infinity}
```

Compare this result to the value of *Mathematica*'s global variable $MaxMachine Number representing the largest machine-precision number.

```
In[11] := $MaxMachineNumber //InputForm
Out[11]//InputForm = 1.7976931348623157*^308
```

We should mention that passing the symbolic objects $\infty$ and Not-a-Number of the IEEE floating-point formats from *Mathematica* to filib++ is not straightforward because the communication requires numerical data, while Infinity and Indeterminate are symbols in *Mathematica*. Therefore, a special design (possibly by catching and handling the exceptions) is required for that purpose.

At the end of using an external program, Uninstall[link] should be used to terminate the program represented by the corresponding link object and to remove the *Mathematica* definitions set up by it.

More examples demonstrating *MathLink* connectivity to the library filib++ can be found in an electronic supplement accessible at
        http://www.math.bas.bg/~epopova/papers/filibMathLink.zip
The archive contains the source couples filibStdF.tm/cpp and horner.tm/cpp necessary for building the corresponding *MathLink*-compatible programs under Linux together with a sample Makefile and a *Mathematica* notebook demonstrating the execution of these programs from within *Mathematica*. A printable version filibML.pdf of the notebook is provided for non-*Mathematica* users.

The *MathLink*-compatible program horner is designed to demonstrate the advantage of software interoperability for symbolic preprocessing and checking the consistency of input data. A filib++ function `horner()` implements Horner's rule for interval evaluation of a polynomial in one variable when the latter varies within a given interval. This function requires numerical input data: the coefficients of the polynomial and the interval on which the polynomial is evaluated. A communication module is designed and compiled together with the filib++ function `horner` into a *MathLink* -compatible program allowing the filib++ function to be called from within a *Mathematica* session. For more details of the implementation see the template file `horner.tm` and the source file `horner.cpp` which we will not comment here since the code is relatively straightforward. For the end-users it is more convenient to introduce a polynomial symbolically. That is why, in the environment of *Mathematica* we have expanded the function `hornerML`, which is named in the template file and maps the external function communicating with the filib++ function `horner`, by defining a function with the same name `hornerML` but having different type of arguments. The latter function transforms any symbolic-numeric polynomial into a list of its coefficients, does a preliminary check of the user input for consistency, then calls the external function. Thus, *MathLink* connectivity between *Mathematica* and filib++ allows the latter to exploit all the symbolic-algebraic power of the former. For example, for the *Mathematica* function `hornerML` it does not matter whether or not the polynomial is explicitly given in an expanded form.

```
In[16]  := hornerML[(3 - 2x) (x - 1)^2, Interval[{-1., 1.}]]
Out[16] = {-14.000000000000014, 20.000000000000014}
```

It is not only more convenient but also more efficient to check the consistency of the input data within the environment of *Mathematica*. Therefore all argument processing and data-checking is done by the *Mathematica* code, as well as issuing all error messages.

```
In[17]  := hornerML[x*y - 2, Interval[{-1, 2}]]
  hornerML::pol: Polynomial of one variable is expected.
Out[17] = hornerML[-2 + x y, Interval[{-1, 2}]]
```

Since the above functionality is achieved entirely by *Mathematica* programming we refer to the electronic supplement for more details and illustrations.

# 5    Integrating C-XSC Programs into *Mathematica*

C-XSC is another open source C++ class library which facilitates the implementation of reliable numerical methods [4], [6], [7]. Beside a lot of predefined numeric data types and the corresponding arithmetic of maximum accuracy for computations in most traditional numerical spaces, the C-XSC environment provides also dotprecision types and several multiple precision data types. A lot of problem-solving numerical routines providing validated results are involved in the distribution of C-XSC (e.g. the former C++ Toolbox for Verified Computing) or provided as external modules or additional software systems [4], [6]. To demonstrate the interoperability between *Mathematica* and C-XSC functions, we have chosen the C-XSC module `parlinsys.cpp` for solving parametric interval linear systems [14]. The same *MathLink* technology can be applied to other C-XSC functions, e.g. for solving non-parametric (interval) linear systems. The parametric solver was chosen to illustrate the benefit of the *Mathematica* interface for symbolic preprocessing of input data.

The function `ParLinSolve()` from the C-XSC module `parlinsys.cpp` computes guaranteed outer (and inner) inclusions for the exact hull of the united solution set of a parametric linear system involving affine-linear dependencies between interval parameters. Although solving parametric systems, the function requires only numerical input data, namely corresponding sequences of numerical matrices/vectors representing the coefficients for each of the parameters involved, for more details see [14]. We assume that C-XSC module `parlinsys` was successfully compiled and is part of the corresponding include directory of the C-XSC environment. Following *MathLink* technology presented in previous sections, building a *MathLink*- and C-XSC-compatible program, say `ParLinSys`, we first develop a C++ program which includes both libraries and several functions. The details of the implementation code can be found in

http://www.math.bas.bg/~epopova/papers/cxscMathLink.zip

Below we present only those aspects of *MathLink* technology that have not been applied and discussed so far.

`ParLinSolveML()` is the function which reads input data from *Mathematica* via variables of fundamental C data types, initializes new variables having the specific C-XSC data types with the incoming data, then calls the C-XSC function `ParLinSolve()` and transforms the computed results into variables of fundamental C data types that will be passed back to *Mathematica*. Since our external function will need to receive expression types that are not among the set handled automatically by `mprep`, we write our own calls (using `MLGet` functions) to get the arguments. For example, by the following code we get an array of floating-point numbers.

```
MLGetDoubleArray(stdlink, &data, &dimensions, &heads, &depth)
...... // Allocation C-XSC data types & filling up the parametric matrix
MLDisownDoubleArray(stdlink, data, dimensions, heads, depth);
```

When an external program gets data from *Mathematica*, it must set up a place to store the data. The first `ML` function above will automatically do this allocation, storing the array in (`double* data`), its dimensions in (`long* dimensions`) and its depth in (`long depth`). After processing these data in the second line above, the memory used to store the array must be released, as in the third code line above. All the input and output data for the external function `ParLinSolveML()` are processed this way. Therefore the `:ArgumentTypes:` and `:ReturnType:` lines in the corresponding template file `ParLinSys.tm` involve the keyword `Manual`. Here is a part of the template file

```
:Function:      ParLinSolveML
:Pattern:       ParLinSolveTB[p_Integer, flag_Integer, ap_?MatrixQ,
                              bp_?MatrixQ, ip_?MatrixQ ]
:Arguments:     {p, flag, ap, bp, ip}
:ArgumentTypes: {Manual}
:ReturnType:    Manual
```

Note, in this case the name of the *Mathematica* calling function `ParLinSolveTB` is different from the name of the external function `ParLinSolveML`. The template file establishes a correspondence between these functions, see Fig. 1.

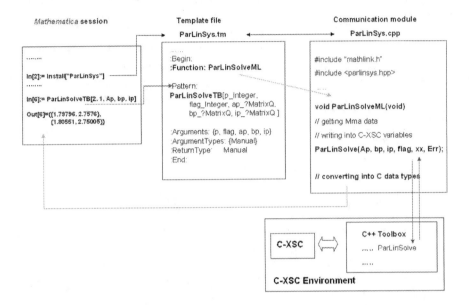

**Fig. 1.** Interaction between *Mathematica* and an external C-XSC program via *Math-Link* technology

After developing and compiling the external *MathLink* -compatible program, it can be installed in any *Mathematica* session and the function, defined in the communication module, can be called with appropriate input data.

```
In[1] := lnk = Install["ParLinSys"]
Out[1]= LinkObject["./ParLinSys", 2, 2]
```

Although solving parametric systems, the function requires only numerical input data. For the end-users, it is usually more convenient to define parametric matrices and parametric vectors symbolically as below.

```
In[3] := mat = {{3, p1}, {p1, 3}}; vec = {p2, p2};
```

Therefore, the *Mathematica* interface will be used for symbolically preprocessing the parametric system data. To this end, a new function `parToNumMLData` is defined in the *Mathematica* notebook `cxscML.nb`. This function transforms a parametric matrix, or a parametric vector, whose elements depend affine-linearly on given parameters into a numeric matrix suitable for input for the C-XSC function `ParLinSolve()`, respectively for the external function called by `ParLinSolveTB`. Transforming our symbolic data we get the required numerical input form of the parametric matrix/vector.

```
In[4] := Ap = parToNumMLData[mat, {p1, p2}];
         bp = parToNumMLData[vec, {p1, p2}];
In[6] := pVals = {{1, 2}, {10, 10.5}};
```

For the parameter interval values `pVals`, we just specify a list of interval end-points in the same parameter order {p1, p2} as specified by the second argument of `parToNumMLData`. This is because the interval constructors in C-XSC provide directed outward rounding for the interval end-points and the *Mathematica* function `Interval`, if applied, would introduce extra rounding.

Now, we are ready to call our external function.

```
In[7] := ParLinSolveTB[2, 1, Ap, bp, pVals] //InputForm
Out[7] = {{1.792638317329675, 2.762917238225881},
          {1.8018848752730778, 2.753670680282478}}
```

The result of `ParLinSolveTB` is a list involving just the interval end-points, corresponding to the interval vector generated by the C-XSC function. The goal is the same as for the input intervals: to avoid an extra outward rounding introduced by the *Mathematica* function `Interval`.

## Communicating Error Messages

Most of the error-checking for the function `hornerML`, discussed at the end of Section 4, is done by, as well as most of the error messages for this function are issued by, the *Mathematica* code. Some errors, however, can only be detected inside the external functions. Such errors include out-of-memory situations, failed *MathLink* calls, and so on. The external program also can issue some errors that are informative for and should be communicated to the user. *MathLink* can transmit out-of-band data such as exceptions [5], [15]–[17]. Here we demonstrate this extremely important aspect of *MathLink* programming.

Most *MathLink* functions return 0 to indicate an error has occurred, and it is possible to check their return values. If *MathLink* calls are issued after an error has occurred, without clearing the error, the link will probably die. Checking for `MLGet` errors is handled automatically by the code that `mprep` writes for the arguments that are read automatically. This effect can be illustrated by the functions in Section 4.

The code of `ParLinSolveML()` contains calls of `MLGet` functions in order to transmit data types that are not among those handled automatically. If an `MLGet` call fails, the easiest thing to do is simply to abandon the external function call completely and return the symbol `$Failed`. However, it would be more informative to trigger some kind of diagnostic message. The *MathLink* function `MLErrorMessage` returns a string describing the current error and this string is a good candidate for use in an error message to be seen by the user. The following fragment from the communication module `ParLinSys.cpp` detects an error

```
if(!MLGetInteger(stdlink, &p)) PrintMLErrorMessage();
```

and calls the function `PrintMLErrorMessage()` which issues an useful message, then safely bails out of the function call.

```
void PrintMLErrorMessage(void)
{ char err_msg[100];
  sprintf(err_msg, "%s\"%.76s\"%s",
          "Message[ParLinSolveTB::mlink,", MLErrorMessage(stdlink), "]");
  MLClearError(stdlink);   MLNewPacket(stdlink);
  MLEvaluate(stdlink, err_msg);
  MLNextPacket(stdlink);   MLNewPacket(stdlink);
  MLPutSymbol(stdlink, "$Failed");
}
```

Upon detecting the error, the first thing we do in the above function is calling MLClearError to attempt to remove the error condition, and then MLNewPacket to abandon the rest of the packet containing the original inputs to the function (in case it hasn't been completely read yet). The sprintf is used to construct a string of the form:

`"Message[ParLinSolveTB::mlink, "the text returned by MLErrorMessage"]"`

which is what is sent to MLEvaluate. The message triggered here, ParLinSolveTB::mlink, needs to be defined in an :Evaluate: line in the template file ParLinSys.tm as follows:

`:Evaluate: ParLinSolveTB::mlink = "Low-level MathLink error: `1`."`

After the call to MLEvaluate, *Mathematica* will send back a ReturnPacket containing the return value of the Message function (which is the symbol Null). To drain this packet off the link we call MLNextPacket and then MLNewPacket to discard the contents. Since we have several MLGet calls in our external code, the collection of the above actions is implemented as a separate function PrintMLErrorMessage() transferring the communication error messages.

We demonstrate triggering *MathLink* communication error messages, by calling the function ParLinSolveTB with a big value for the first integer argument.

```
In[7] := ParLinSolveTB[2^100, 1, Ap, bp, pVals]
 ParLinSolveTB::mlink: Low-level MathLink error: machine number overflow.
 Out[7]= $Failed
```

Any subsequent call of the external function, even with correct data, returns a communication error until the external program is installed again. The same external program can be installed arbitrary many times within a *Mathematica* session. Each installation creates a separate LinkObject.

Looking at the code of the external function ParLinSolveML(), the extensive check of the input data for consistency should be noticed, e.g.

```
if(dimensions[1] != n) PrintErrorMessage(1);
.............
   if(int_arr[0] > int_arr[1]) PrintErrorMessage(5);
```

Most important is, however, that the C-XSC function ParLinSolve() returns also an integer error code. All messages for inconsistent data and computational error messages are passed to *Mathematica* in the same way as the communication error messages but by another function `PrintErrorMessage()`. The different message strings are defined in separate `:Evaluate:` lines in the template file.

In order to demonstrate the computational error messages in action, we call the function `ParLinSolveTB` with a large interval for the first interval parameter.

```
In[7] := ParLinSolveTB[2, 1, Ap, bp, {{1, 20}, {10, 10.5}}]
   ParLinSolveTB::cond: Verification failed, system is probably ill cond.
Out[7]= $Failed
```

The `ParLinSolveTB::cond` error is triggered whenever the verification iteration is not convergent and the fixed-point parametric iteration fails.

# 6   Conclusion

It is a relatively simple matter to incorporate C-XSC or `filib++` routines into *Mathematica* without any change in the original external code. A communication C/C++ module is necessary to be developed, where *MathLink* functions transmit to and back *Mathematica* expressions via fundamental C data types, the incoming data should initialize new variables of data types specific for the particular external interval environment, and after calling the actual computations to transform the computed results into variables of fundamental C data types that will be passed back to *Mathematica*. *MathLink* protocol allows transparent communication of numerical data without conversion on the same computer. Furthermore, the extended intervals involving $\pm\infty$ at the interval end-points, as well as the empty interval supported in the extended mode of `filib++`, are passed back to *Mathematica* in the same transparent way. By *MathLink* we use the external functions in a way completely integrated into *Mathematica* taking advantage of the good properties of both environments, as demonstrated above. The variety of numerical data types provided in C-XSC, e.g. complex interval arithmetic or dotprecision computations, could be also integrated into *Mathematica* under an appropriate design.

Once provided, *Mathematica* connectivity to external interval software opens up an array on new possibilities for the latter. web*Mathematica* technology, that integrates *Mathematica* into a web server, can be utilized for providing dynamic web access to the external software [12], [13]. The important consequences and benefits from a dynamic web interface concern the development of framework and platforms for distant interval learning and/or remote problem solving.

While the present work demonstrates mainly the interactive and dynamic interfaces for the C-XSC and `filib++` libraries via *MathLink* communication protocol, our further efforts will be directed towards providing interval software interoperability that not only expands the functionality but also improves the performance of the interval tools in solving some practical problems. A current work on communicating symbolic functional expressions between *Mathematica* and C-XSC/`filib++` will allow *interactive* execution of more problem-solving routines that are part of or based on these libraries.

# References

1. Alt, R., Frommer, A., Kearfott, R.B., Luther, W. (eds.): Numerical Software with Result Verification (Dagstuhl Seminar 2003). LNCS, vol. 2991. Springer, Heidelberg (2004)
2. Corliss, G.F., Yu, J.: Interval Testing Strategies Applied to COSY's Interval and Taylor Model Arithmetic. In: [1], pp. 91–106
3. Corliss, G.F., Kearfott, R.B., Nedialkov, N., Pryce, J.D., Smith, S.: Interval subroutine library mission. In: Hertling, P., Hoffmann, C.M., Luther, W., Revol, N. (eds.) Reliable Implementation of Real Number Algorithms: Theory and Practice. Dagstuhl Seminar Proceedings, Number 06021, Internationales Begegnungs- und Forschungszentrum für Informatik, Schloss Dagstuhl, Germany (2006)
4. C-XSC library: http://www.math.uni-wuppertal.de/~xsc/xsc/cxsc_new.html, solvers: http://www.math.uni-wuppertal.de/~xsc/xsc/cxsc_software.html
5. Gayley, T.: A MathLink Tutorial. Wolfram Research (2002)
6. Hofschuster, W., Krämer, W., Neher, M.: C-XSC and Closely Related Software Packages. In: Cuyt, A., et al. (eds.) Numerical Validation in Current Hardware Architectures (Dagstuhl Seminar 2008). LNCS, vol. 5492, pp. 68–102. Springer, Heidelberg (2009)
7. Hofschuster, W., Krämer, W.: C-XSC 2.0: A C++ Library for Extended Scientific Computing. In: [1], pp. 15–35
8. Kreinovich, V.: Interval Computations website, Interval and Related Software, http://www.cs.utep.edu/interval-comp/intsoft.html
9. Lerch, M., Tischler, G., Wolff von Gudenberg, J., Hofschuster, W., Krämer, W.: The Interval Library filib++ 2.0 — Design, Features and Sample Programs. Preprint 2001/4, Universität Wuppertal (2001), Library download: http://www.math.uni-wuppertal.de/org/WRST/software/filib.html
10. Lerch, M., Tischler, G., Wolff von Gudenberg, J., Hofschuster, W., Krämer, W.: filib++, a Fast Interval Library Supporting Containment Computations. ACM TOMS 32(2), 299–324 (2006)
11. Luther, W., Krämer, W.: Accurate Grid Computing. In: Luther, W., Krämer, W. (eds.) 12th GAMM-IMACS Int. Symposium on Scientific Computing, Computer Arithmetic and Validated Numerics (SCAN 2006), Duisburg, September 26-29 (2006)
12. Popova, E.: Web-Accessible Tools for Interval Linear Systems. Proceedings in Applied Mathematics & Mechanics (PAMM) 5(1), 713–714 (2005)
13. Popova, E.: WebComputing Service Framework. Int. Journal Information Theories & Applications 13(3), 246–254 (2006)
14. Popova, E.D., Krämer, W.: Parametric Fixed-Point Iteration Implemented in C-XSC. Preprint BUW-WRSWT 2003/3, Universität Wuppertal (2003), Software download: http://www.math.uni-wuppertal.de/~xsc/xsc/cxsc_software.html#plss
15. Wolfram Research, Inc.: MathLink Reference Guide, Version 2.2., Wolfram Research Inc., Champaign, IL (2003)
16. Wolfram Research, Inc.: MathLink for UNIX Developer Guide, Version 4, Revision 14, Wolfram Research Inc., Champaign, IL, December 15 (2004)
17. Wolfram Research Inc.: Mathematica, Version 5.2, Champaign, IL (2005)

# Some Applications of Interval Arithmetic in Hierarchical Solid Modeling

Eva Dyllong

University of Duisburg-Essen, Department of Computer Science and Applied
Cognitive Science
D-47057 Duisburg, Lotharstrasse 65, Germany
dyllong@inf.uni-due.de

**Abstract.** Reliable computing techniques, like interval arithmetic, can be used to guarantee reliable solutions even in the presence of numerical round-off errors. The use of such techniques can eliminate the need to trace bounds for the error function separately.

In this paper, we show how the techniques and algorithms of reliable computing can be applied to the construction and further processing of hierarchical solid representations, using the octree model as an example.

**Keywords:** Reliable solid modeling, hierarchical data structure, interval arithmetic.

## 1 Introduction

Accurate and reliable computations are important demands made on many applications. Reliable computing techniques, like interval arithmetic, can solve problems, guaranteeing correct results even when the computation has been done using floating point operations with finite precision. In the field of solid modeling, using these techniques ensures that all points of the modeled object are included in its interval-based representation or that a computed path among obstacles is collision-free. Nevertheless, until now, interval methods have been applied only to a limited class of problems in solid modeling.

Duff [1] proposes an interval-based approach to performing collision detection between constructive solid geometry objects using binary subdivisions of space along each axis. Snyder [2] uses an interval Newton method to solve the system of equations that specifies the tangency constraints at the touching points to detect collisions between curved surfaces. How interval analysis can be used to solve a wide variety of problems in computer graphics is discussed in [2]. In [3] several interval linear solvers are tested with respect to their ability to build higher-dimensional convex hulls, even in close-to-pathological situations. In [4] Huber shows how the intersection curve for objects defined by general parametric surfaces can be computed with guaranteed results by applying automatic differentiation and by cutting off dispensable regions using interval methods and divide-and-conquer techniques. Patrikalakis et al. [5] deal with interval-based

A. Cuyt et al. (Eds.): Numerical Validation, LNCS 5492, pp. 133–144, 2009.

manifold and non-manifold solid models based on interval geometric representations and graph data structures. The use of affine arithmetic and other improved techniques of reliable computing in the field of modeling is discussed in [6,7]. For moving multibody models, Zhang et al. [8] propose using a continuous collision detection algorithm that relies on Taylor models to compute dynamic bounding volumes (AABB hierarchies).

In this paper, we show how the techniques and algorithms of reliable computing can be applied to the construction and further processing of hierarchical solid representations, using a novel generalization of the octree model created from a constructive solid geometry object as an example. The octree model was chosen because it is particularly suitable for accurate and reliable computation. On the one hand, an octree node belonging to an arbitrary hierarchy level geometrically defines an axis-aligned box. All boxes have as vertices machine numbers that are multiples of powers of two. In the case of an axis-aligned octree, accurate algorithms for proximity queries are feasible [7]. On the other hand, interval-based evaluation of the structure allows us to apply the tests for classifying points in space as inside the object, on the boundary or outside the object, simultaneously to whole sections of the space.

## 2     Construction of Reliable Hierarchical Solid Modeling

Constructive solid geometry models (CSG models), boundary representation models (B-Rep models) and tessellations (for example, octrees) are the most widely used representations of geometric objects on the computer. An octree is a common hierarchical data structure with which to represent 3D geometrical objects in solid modeling systems or to reconstruct a real scene. In this section, we propose a possible approach for applying techniques and algorithms of reliable computing to the construction of hierarchical solid representations using the octree model as an example.

### 2.1     The Octree Data Structure

The idea of the octree data structure is to recursively subdivide a box including objects in a three-dimensional space into eight disjoint boxes until the required closeness to the objects is reached [9]. Each box is checked to see whether it is full of solid material (*a black tree node*), partially empty (*a gray tree node*) or empty (*a white tree node*). If the boxes are empty or full, they do not need to be subdivided any further. If they are partially empty, the boxes need to be subdivided to improve the approximation of the object. The subdivision process is repeated until all tree nodes are either black or white or until the maximum resolution level has been achieved. To obtain an outer approximation of the object, the partially occupied boxes at the maximum level of the tree are considered full. In a common octree, a parent node stores pointers to all child nodes.

This object representation yields relatively high visual quality – particularly when extensions of the data structure are used [10] –, and features stable numerical computations. The underlying testing or computing is, for the most part,

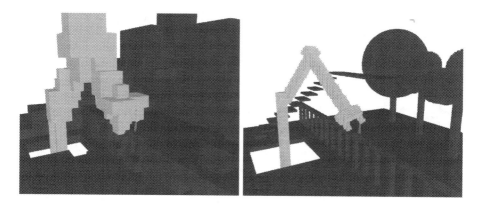

**Fig. 1.** An octree-encoded robot and its environment: different approximation levels

reduced to operations between boxes. A further advantage is the adaptive control of the approximation level that can be used in such applications as robotic simulations to speed up geometrical computation (see Figure 1).

## 2.2 Interval-Based Octrees

In contrast to the CSG or B-Rep model, the octree-encoded object representation is particularly suitable for use with interval arithmetic. An axis-aligned box as the underlying basic entity of the tree can be directly stored as an interval vector. If the geometry of the primary object is known, for example, if its surface is described by a union or intersection of implicit functions, we can perform the test for classifying points in space as inside, on the boundary or outside the object, simultaneously on the whole axis-aligned box using interval arithmetic.

Let's consider a case in which the implicit functions describe CSG primitives, such as spheres, cubes or cylinders. The characteristic function of a primitive $P$ can be defined with the aid of the corresponding implicit function $F_P(x, y, z) = 0$, which describes the shape of the primitive $P$. It is

$$P = \{(x, y, z) \mid x, y, z \in \mathbb{R}, F_P(x, y, z) \leq 0\}.$$

For example, the following holds for the unit sphere, cube and cylinder respectively:

$$F_{sphere}(x, y, z) = x^2 + y^2 + z^2 - 1,$$
$$F_{cube}(x, y, z) = \max\{x^2, y^2, z^2\} - 1,$$
$$F_{cylinder}(x, y, z) = \max\{x^2, y^2 + z^2\} - 1.$$

We define the characteristic function of a primitive $P$ with the implicit function $F_P$ as

$$\mathcal{X}_P(x, y, z) = \begin{cases} 1, & \text{if } F_P(x, y, z) \leq 0, \\ 0, & \text{if } F_P(x, y, z) > 0. \end{cases}$$

We extend the result set of the characteristic function to $\{0, 1, 2\}$ to permit three possible answers: a box is guaranteed to be inside or to be outside the primitive, or its location is indeterminate with respect to the primitive. Using this extended set, we define the interval extension of the characteristic function $\mathcal{X}_P$ as follows:

$$\mathcal{X}_P(X, Y, Z) := \begin{cases} 0, & \text{if } \underline{F_P(X, Y, Z)} > 0, \\ 1, & \text{if } 0 \in F_P(X, Y, Z), \\ 2, & \text{if } \overline{F_P(X, Y, Z)} < 0. \end{cases}$$

The underscore denotes the lower bound and the overscore the upper bound of the interval values. If we extend an implicit function on real numbers to an implicit function on intervals and solve it for an interval $I$, we acquire an interval $J$. If the interval $I$ intersects the surface of the implicit object, the interval $J$ includes zero und the interval extension of the characteristic function results in 1. On the other hand, if $J$ does not include zero, $I$ does not intersect the surface of the object, and we can reliably decide whether $I$ is contained within the implicit object or not. One should note that, since interval arithmetic does not always yield tight bounds, we cannot guarantee that all gray tree nodes include parts of the surface of the implicit object. Still, we can guarantee that white and black nodes do not intersect the surface of the object. Thus, the gray nodes yield both a reliable enclosure of the surface, and the union of the black and gray nodes a reliable enclosure of the whole CSG primitive.

The characteristic functions of the set-theoretic operations of a CSG object are realized with Boolean operations. Let $A, B$ be CSG objects, and $\mathcal{X}_A, \mathcal{X}_B$ their characteristic functions. Then the characteristic functions of the set-theoretic operations are defined as follows [1]:

$$\mathcal{X}_{A \cup B} = \mathcal{X}_A \vee \mathcal{X}_B,$$
$$\mathcal{X}_{A \cap B} = \mathcal{X}_A \wedge \mathcal{X}_B,$$
$$\mathcal{X}_{A \setminus B} = \mathcal{X}_A \wedge \neg \mathcal{X}_B.$$

In case of interval extension, we replace the Boolean operations $\vee, \wedge$ with the functions min and max, and the operation $\neg x$ with $(2 - x)$:

$$\mathcal{X}_{A \cup B} = \max(\mathcal{X}_A, \mathcal{X}_B)$$
$$\mathcal{X}_{A \cap B} = \min(\mathcal{X}_A, \mathcal{X}_B)$$
$$\mathcal{X}_{A \setminus B} = \min(\mathcal{X}_A, 2 - \mathcal{X}_B)$$

Thus, we are able to construct an octree which approximates the object described by a union or intersection of implicit functions. If we consider all gray tree nodes at the highest level as solid, the construction provides a guaranteed superset of the primary object.

### Illustrative Example

We use the all-purpose markup language XML (Extensible Markup Language) as a file format to store the CSG tree of an object. The XML format is easy to

**Fig. 2.** An example of an interval-based octree data structure at levels 6 and 8

design and to process. It provides appropriate text-based means to describe tree-based structures like CSG trees. Furthermore, the XML format is well-suited for data transfer. Transformations of the primitives can simply be mapped to the XML syntax. For example, a sphere translated by the vector $(-2.5, 2.0, 0.0)$ with radius 0.2 can be described as

```
<sphere scale="0.2" translate="-2.5 2 0"/>
```

The CSG object associated with the constructed interval-based octree shown in Figure 2 can be described using this XML description:

```
<csg scale="0.05 0.05 0.05" translate="0.5 0.5 0.5">
<union><union>
<cylinder scale="3 1 1" translate="3 2 0"/>
<cylinder scale="0.1 0.8 0.8" rotate="0 1 0 90" translate="1 0.8 1.3"/>
<cylinder scale="0.1 0.8 0.8" rotate="0 1 0 90" translate="1 0.8 -1.3"/>
<cylinder scale="0.1 0.8 0.8" rotate="0 1 0 90" translate="3 0.8 1.3"/>
<cylinder scale="0.1 0.8 0.8" rotate="0 1 0 90" translate="3 0.8 -1.3"/>
<cylinder scale="0.1 0.8 0.8" rotate="0 1 0 90" translate="5 0.8 1.3"/>
<cylinder scale="0.1 0.8 0.8" rotate="0 1 0 90" translate="5 0.8 -1.3"/>
<cube scale="1 1.5 1" translate="1 2.5 0"/>
<cube scale="1.2 0.2 1.2" translate="1 4 0"/>
<cylinder scale="0.5 0.25 0.25" rotate="0 0 1 90" translate="4.5 3.5 0"/>
</union>
<cylinder scale="0.6 0.1 0.1" translate="-0.5 1 0"/>
<union>
<difference>
<cube scale="1.5 0.5 1" translate="-2.5 1 0"/>
<cube scale="1.3 0.5 1" translate="-2.5 1.2 0"/>
</difference>
<cylinder scale="0.1 0.4 0.4" rotate="0 1 0 90"
          translate="-1.7 0.4 1.3"/>
<cylinder scale="0.1 0.4 0.4" rotate="0 1 0 90"
          translate="-1.7 0.4 -1.3"/>
<cylinder scale="0.1 0.4 0.4" rotate="0 1 0 90"
          translate="-3.3 0.4 1.3"/>
<cylinder scale="0.1 0.4 0.4" rotate="0 1 0 90"
          translate="-3.3 0.4 -1.3"/>
```

```
<sphere translate="-2.5 2 0"/>
</union></union>
</csg>
```

The interval-based data structure for solid modeling has been implemented in an object-oriented style in the C++ programming language. We used the C++ library for scientific computing, C-XSC [11] for interval representations and calculations, and the OpenGL library for visualizations [12].

## 2.3  Interval-Based Extended Octrees

Unfortunately, the classical octree data structure may require a large amount of memory if it uses a set of very small boxes to approximate a solid. In recent years several generalizations (polytrees, integrated polytrees, extended octrees) have been developed to reduce the depth of required subdivisions by including additional information about the relevant parts of an object. Brunet et al. [10] suggested an efficient way to handle a boundary representation hierarchically. Using this data structure, the space is divided recursively as for an octree, but the leaf nodes of the tree are also allowed to represent boxes that contain a plane, edge or vertex of the boundary of the object. Another schema that includes geometry data from a boundary representation is independently proposed by Carlbom [13]. The main difference between polytrees [13] and extended octrees [10] is the way they represent faces, edges and vertices in the terminal nodes. In the context of ray tracing, Wyvill et al. [14] propose the use of octree representations to deal with CSG objects. The subdivision process of an octree is continued either until each cell contains fewer than two primitive objects of a suitably reduced version of the original CSG structure or until the cell is small enough to be ignored. The authors called the process adaptive space division.

We refine these strategies and construct in [12] an interval-based octree model that maintains not only additional information about relevant parts of the CSG object within a node but also contains two types of gray nodes: *terminal* and *nonterminal* gray nodes. Terminal gray nodes are nodes that contain only parts of the surface that result from exactly one primitive of the CSG object and thus are not further divided. All other gray nodes are nonterminal gray and have to be subdivided if a higher octree level is required.

A CSG object is represented as a binary tree with leaf nodes that correspond to the CSG primitives. The tree is called a CSG tree. Set operations, such as union, difference or intersection, describe in the interior nodes of the CSG tree how the object represented by the two child nodes is combined. Following Duff [1], we simplify the CSG object for each octree node to a CSG object that is equivalent to the original object within that octree node. If the octree has sufficient subdivision depth, the CSG tree can be reduced to only one primitive for most octree nodes.

The following algorithm 1 determines a simplified CSG tree within the interval $X$ that defines the same set of points as the given CSG object $C$ with respect to $X$. The set $U$ denotes the complement of the empty set $\emptyset$ and $S$ an arbitrary child element of the CSG tree.

---

**Algorithm 1.** Simplification of the CSG object $C$ with respect to the interval vector $X$

---

**Input.** CSG object $C$ and interval vector $X$
**Output.** A simplified CSG tree
1 **while** *The following rules can be applied* **do**
2      Replace all leaf nodes of $C$ fulfilling $\mathcal{X}(X) = 0$ with $\emptyset$;
3      Replace all leaf nodes of $C$ fulfilling $\mathcal{X}(X) = 2$ with $U$;
4      Replace all union nodes of the form $\emptyset \cup S$ and all intersection nodes of the form $U \cap S$ with $S$;
5      Replace all union nodes of the form $U \cup S$ with $U$;
6      Replace all intersection nodes of the form $\emptyset \cap S$ with $\emptyset$;
7 **end**

---

Each extended octree node consists of an interval vector that describes the location and extension of the node, a color attribute and a reference to the relevant part of the primary CSG object. The evaluation of the relevant part yields the range of the implicit function of the CSG object within the given octree node. With the aid of interval arithmetic, the evaluation is not complicated and provides verified results. Subsequent to the evaluation, the CSG object is simplified with respect to the interval vector $X$ describing the octree node.

---

**Algorithm 2.** Construction of an octree representation of the CSG object $C$

---

**Input.** CSG object $C$ and the root node $X$
**Output.** The interval-based extended octree of the maximum depth $k$
1 Evaluate the characteristic function $\mathcal{X}_C$ of $C$ on $X$;
2 **if** *X is inside C* **then**
3      mark $X$ as *black* node and stop;
4 **end**
5 **if** *X is outside C* **then**
6      mark $X$ as *white* node and stop;
7 **else**
8      mark $X$ as *gray* node;
9      attach to the node $X$ the simplified version of $C$ with respect to $X$;
10      **if** *the CSG tree of X consists of exactly one CSG primitive* **then**
11          mark $X$ as *terminal* gray node and stop;
12      **else**
13          mark $X$ as *nonterminal* gray node;
14      **end**
15      **if** *the maximum recursion depth k is not reached* **then**
16          subdivide $X$ into eight equal child nodes $X_i, 0 \leq i \leq 7$ and start the algorithm recursively for each $X_i$;
17      **else**
18          stop the algorithm;
19      **end**
20 **end**

---

The following algorithm 2 sketches the construction of an interval-based extended octree. The algorithm is initialized with the root node $X = [0, 1]^3$.

The subdivision process can be restarted for the nonterminal gray nodes in any part of postprocessing if a more detailed hierarchical approximation model of the CSG object is required.

The subdivision process is enhanced by the new leaf nodes. The number of nonterminal gray nodes at each level of the new structure is, in general, much smaller than the number of gray nodes in the case of the classical octree structure. This is due to the fact that the number of CSG primitives per tree node approaches zero or one asymptotically as the resolution increases. From a certain subdivision level, all nonterminal gray nodes are located along the intersection points of the CSG primitives as shown in Figure 3 (depicted in red or dark gray). The example illustrates the common and the extended octree of the CSG object constructed by the intersection of the unit sphere and a cube.

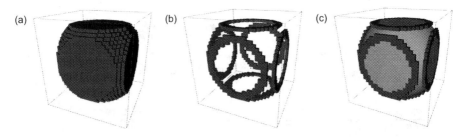

**Fig. 3.** The common octree of depth 5 in (a) has 9,304 nodes; the extended octree in (b) and (c) has only 5,160 nodes

In the example given, there are just 912 nonterminal gray nodes at level 5, 1,824 at level 6, and 15,072 at level 9. The number of gray nodes in the corresponding common octree is 3,680 at level 5, 15,200 at level 6 and 975,920 at level 9 (see Figure 4). The transparent boxes in Figure 4 display the nonterminal gray nodes, and the green or gray boxes the terminal gray nodes in the extended octree at level 5, 6 and 9.

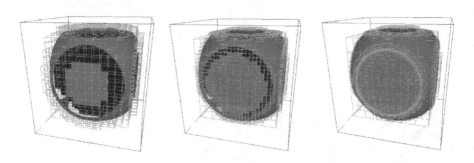

**Fig. 4.** An example of an extended octree at levels 5, 6 and 9

## 3    Further Processing

Even in further processing, we can benefit from applying interval arithmetic. We take as an example the proximity query, which is an important part of many applications. The octree data structure provides the means for efficient distance calculations between complex (in the number of primitives) CSG objects because it enables us to quickly prune parts of the CSG object that do not minimize the distance between two objects, especially when the octree representation is reused for several consecutive coherent distance calculations.

The following algorithm 3 describes how the distance between two interval-based octrees $P$ and $Q$ can be computed (see [15] for further distance algorithms).

---

**Algorithm 3.** Reliable distance computation between interval-based octrees

---

**Input.** Interval-based octrees $P$ and $Q$
**Output.** Distance (lower bound) $d_{inf,L}$

 1  $L := (P, Q)$;
 2  $d_{sup,L} := \infty$; $d_{inf,L} := \infty$;
 3  **while** $L \neq \{\}$ **do**
 4  $\quad$ $(p, q) := head(L)$; remove $(p, q)$ from $L$;
 5  $\quad$ **if** $color(p) = gray \vee color(q) = gray$ **then**
 6  $\quad\quad$ **if** $color(q) \neq gray \vee$
 $\quad\quad\quad$ $(color(p) = gray \wedge diam(p) > diam(q))$ **then**
 7  $\quad\quad\quad$ $(p, q) := (q, p)$;
 8  $\quad\quad$ **end**
 9  $\quad\quad$ **foreach** $c \in children(q)$ **do**
 10 $\quad\quad\quad$ **if** $color(c) \neq white$ **then**
 11 $\quad\quad\quad\quad$ insert $(p, c)$ into $L$;
 12 $\quad\quad\quad\quad$ $d_{rough,sup,L} := \min\{d_{rough,sup,L}, \sup(d(p,c))\}$;
 13 $\quad\quad\quad$ **end**
 14 $\quad\quad$ **end**
 15 $\quad$ **else**
 16 $\quad\quad$ $d_{tight,inf,L} := \min\{d_{tight,inf,L}, \inf(d(p,q))\}$;
 17 $\quad$ **end**
 18 **end**

---

The main idea of the algorithm is to keep a list of pairs of octree nodes $(p, q)$ that potentially minimize the distance between the octrees. The list is initialized with a pair containing the root nodes of both octrees. The algorithm takes one pair from the list, splits one of the nodes into its child nodes and inserts the resulting eight pairs back into the list until only pairs with leaf nodes are left on the list.

A basic operation of the algorithm is the proximity query $d(p, q)$ between two octree nodes $p$ and $q$. It returns an interval inclusion of the distance of the nodes. The proximity query distinguishes among three cases:

(1) If at least one of the nodes is a white node, the distance is set to infinity since a white node will not minimize the distance between the octrees.

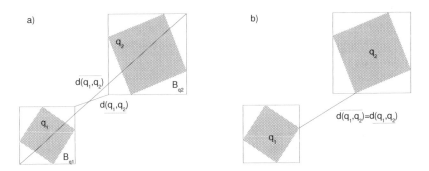

**Fig. 5.** (a) a rough enclosure $B_{q_1} - B_{q_2}$ and (b) a tight enclosure $d(q_1, q_2)$ of the distance between two rotated boxes $q_1$ and $q_2$ bounded by the axis-aligned boxes $B_{q_1}$ and $B_{q_2}$

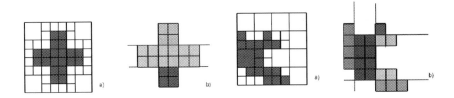

**Fig. 6.** Examples (a), (b) on the left: Reduction from 20 to 3 AABs (85 % compression); Examples (a), (b) on the right: Reduction from 17 to 6 AABs (65 % compression)

(2) If at least one of the nodes is a gray node, it calculates the interval inclusion of the distance of the axis-aligned bounding boxes of the nodes because we know nothing of the interior geometry of the gray nodes yet and the rough estimation of the distance between the nodes provides enough information to know whether the pair is likely to minimize the distance. This interval-based operation is fast and cheap in comparison with the next one.

(3) If both nodes are black nodes, a tight enclosure of the distance between the nodes is calculated. This operation is slow and expensive because the nodes' features that minimize the distance (vertices/edges/faces) have to be detected and then the distance between those features has to be calculated (see Figure 5).

The computation of the rough enclosure of the distance takes about $3\mu s$, while the tight estimation takes about $1000\mu s$ on the same machine. Applying the interval-based evaluation enhances the performance of the distance calculation. Furthermore, using interval arithmetic guarantees that the algorithm yields reliable results. A comparison with other distance algorithms, e.g. the branch-and-bound approach described in [16] yields an average computation time improvement by factor four.

Also, higher dimensional interval-based trees show efficiency in the field of geometric modeling and robotics, particularly in the process of path planning.

Within the scope of single-query path planning, several approaches for searching in high-dimensional spaces based on the presented data structure are being investigated. The method of Rapidly-exploring Random Trees (RRTs) is very promising and has been already researched in [17].

Interval methods can also be used for data compression. Convex decomposition of an octree yields as a result a union of axis-aligned rectangles (AABs) that can be stored as interval vectors. Figure 6 gives some examples of compression in the two-dimensional case.

## 4 Summary

The utilization of interval techniques in the context of geometric modeling guarantees that all points of the object are enclosed in its interval-based representation and that exact results of geometric operations executed on this object representation are always included in the result intervals. We have shown in this paper how interval techniques can be applied to the octree-encoded schema of object representation and made clear the advantages that result from their application.

## References

1. Duff, T.: Interval arithmetic and recursive subdivision for implicit functions and constructive solid geometry. In: SIGGRAPH 1992: Proceedings of the 19th annual conference on Computer graphics and interactive techniques, pp. 131–138. ACM Press, New York (1992)
2. Snyder, J.M.: Interval Analysis for Computer Graphics. Computer Graphics 26, 121–130 (1992)
3. Krivsky, S., Lang, B.: Using interval arithmetic for determining the structure of convex hulls. Numerical Algorithms 37, 233–240 (2004)
4. Huber, E., Barth, W.: Surface-to-surface intersection with complete and guaranteed results. Developments in Reliable Computing, 189–202 (1999)
5. Patrikalakis, N.M., Hu, C.Y., Ye, X.: Robust interval solid modelling. Part I: representations. Computer Aided Design 28, 807–817 (1996)
6. Ratschek, H., Rokne, J.: Geometric Computations with Interval and New Robust Methods. Horwood Publishing, Chichester (2003)
7. Bühler, K., Dyllong, E., Luther, W.: Reliable Distance and Intersection Computation Using Finite Precision Geometry. In: Alt, R., Frommer, A., Kearfott, R.B., Luther, W. (eds.) Numerical Software with Result Verification (Dagstuhl Seminar 2003). LNCS, vol. 2991, pp. 160–190. Springer, Heidelberg (2004)
8. Zhang, X., Redon, S., Lee, M., Kim, Y.J.: Continuous Collision Detection for Articulated Models Using Taylor Models and Temporal Culling. ACM Transactions on Graphics 26 (2007)
9. Samet, H.: The Design and Analysis of Spatial Data Structures, and Applications of Spatial Data Structures. Addison-Wesley, Reading (1990)
10. Brunet, P., Navazo, I.: Solid Representation and Operation Using Extended Octrees. ACM Transactions on Graphics 9, 170–197 (1990)

11. Hofschuster, W., Krämer, W.: C-XSC 2.0: A C++ Library for Extended Scientific Computing. In: Alt, R., Frommer, A., Kearfott, R.B., Luther, W. (eds.) Numerical Software with Result Verification (Dagstuhl Seminar 2003). LNCS, vol. 2991, pp. 15–35. Springer, Heidelberg (2004)
12. Dyllong, E., Grimm, C.: Verified Adaptive Octree Representations of Constructive Solid Geometry Objects. In: SimVis, pp. 223–236 (2007)
13. Carlbom, I., Chakravarty, I., Vanderschel, D.: A Hierarchical Data Structure for Representing the Spatial Decomposition of 3D Objects. IEEE Computer Graphics and Applications 5, 24–31 (1985)
14. Wyvill, G., Kunii, T., Shirai, Y.: Space division for ray tracing in CSG. IEEE Comp. Graphics Applic. 6, 28–34 (1986)
15. Dyllong, E., Grimm, C.: Proximity Queries between Interval-Based CSG Octrees. In: Proceedings of International Conference of Numerical Analysis and Applied Mathematics (ICNAAM 2007), Corfu, Greece, September 16-20, AIP Conference Proceedings, vol. 936, pp. 162–165 (2007)
16. Major, F., Malenfant, J., Stewart, N.F.: Distance between objects represented by octtrees defined in different coordinate systems. Computers and Graphics 13, 497–503 (1989)
17. Grimm, C.: Result Verification of RRT-based Single-Query Path Planning through Interval Analysis. In: GAMM 2008 (sent to publication) (2008)

# Numerical Verification Assessment in Computational Biomechanics

Ekaterina Auer and Wolfram Luther

Department of Computer Science and Applied Cognitive Science
University of Duisburg-Essen
{auer,luther}@inf.uni-due.de

**Abstract.** In this paper, we present several aspects of the recent project PROREOP developing a new prognosis system for optimizing patient-specific preoperative surgical planning for the human skeletal system. We address verification and validation assessment in PROREOP with special emphasis on numerical accuracy and performance. To assess numerical accuracy, we propose to employ graded instruments, including accuracy tests and error analysis. The use of such instruments is exemplified for the process of accurate femur reconstruction. Moreover, we show how to verify the simulation results and take into account measurement uncertainties for a part of this process using tools and techniques developed in the project TellHIM&S.

**Keywords:** Numerical verification assessment, validation, uncertainty, result verification.

## 1 Introduction

In the United States, there is a long tradition in the Computational Fluid Dynamics (CFD) community [1] and the American Society of Mechanical Engineers [2] of designing methodologies and of implementing and testing tools for the verification and validation (V&V) assessment. Recently, these efforts have been broadened to include application processes in biomechanics and biomedicine [3]. The authors of the overview papers cited define the terms verification and validation in the context of modeling and simulation, software engineering and numerical mathematics in engineering and physical applications. Moreover, they develop requirements for categorizations and classifications of processes as a result of precise assessment procedures. However, the known assessment methodologies do not provide a definitive step-by-step V&V procedure immediately applicable by the engineer. In the understanding of the key researchers in this field, all-encompassing procedures for obtaining proofs of correctness do not exist, and V&V activities can only assess the correctness or accuracy of specific (parts of) processes examined.

This voluntary limitation on a small part of the whole modeling, verification and validation cycle is not surprising. In CFD and solid mechanics, process models are based predominantly on continuous mathematics and the use of spatial

A. Cuyt et al. (Eds.): Numerical Validation, LNCS 5492, pp. 145–160, 2009.

and temporal discretization or iterative solution methods (possibly with insufficient convergence). In such models, huge equation systems or partial differential equations are solved or finite element methods applied. The usual verification methodology is to look for analytical solutions and theoretical proofs of existence and convergence, which are generally difficult to obtain in the above-mentioned cases. One possible solution to these problems is to use computer-aided proofs, real number algorithms or algorithms with result verification. A recent collection of papers [4] demonstrates further ways of developing robust and reliable numerical software. However, most of these methods do not occur in standard V&V methodologies to a noticeable degree, not even as interval data types in the discussion of the uncertainty concept as highlighted in [5]. Interval arithmetic and result verification are not addressed at all. In fact, the verification instrument proposed there focuses only on analytic or benchmark solutions, making it very limited.

This community is not aware that several environments for validated modeling and simulation of the kinematics and dynamics of various classes of mechanical systems (e.g., NiceMOBILE or SmartMOBILE) already exist [6]. This is confirmed by the astonishing fact that numerical verification using interval tools was not considered in Verisoft (http://www.verisoft.de/), a recent project funded by the German Federal Ministry of Education and Research, either — even though Verisoft focuses on verifying the design of integrated computer systems. The correct functionality of systems is to be proved in selected application scenarios by using mathematical formalisms, formal program verification and model checkers.

It is our conviction that verified computer-based modeling and formal verification of underlying hardware, operating systems and software programs should be treated in an integrated way by defining the common objectives, comparable standards and methods as well as balanced V&V taxonomies. It is particularly important to devise a set of requirements for the interfaces between software and hardware. A prominent example of such a requirement set is the IEEE 754 floating point standard and its revision. Similarly, the standardization of the interval arithmetic is long overdue and now worked upon. Other examples concern programming languages and operating systems, for example, the verified concurrent context switching or formal verification of device drivers (http://qpq.csl.sri.com/vsr/vstte-08).

First and foremost, the existing numerical verification methodologies deal with accuracy measured a posteriori in relation to benchmark solutions or model problems. Our suggestion is to perform elements of V&V assessment during the designing step. It should begin with the specification of the process and its subprocesses, the design of the building blocks and software modules, the definition of interfaces and data flows and, finally, the selection and adaptation of appropriate data types and algorithms. Furthermore, it is important to define the tolerances present within the input parameters to obtain a certain accuracy of computation.

The paper begins with a short introduction to the modeling, simulation and verification cycle and defines several concepts important for further considerations. Then it proposes a new numerical verification taxonomy and discusses accurate femur reconstruction as an example. We show how to employ recently developed methodologies to transfer this process into a higher verification class and how to use SMARTMOBILE to verify the results of one of its parts.

## 2    Verification Assessment in Mechanics

In this section we describe three major steps in the verification and validation assessment process (cf. Figure 1). The first step is to analyze the real world problem and to design a formal model of the system under consideration. The application domain is described, relevant parameters and their ranges defined and types of uncertainty in the model and its parameters identified.

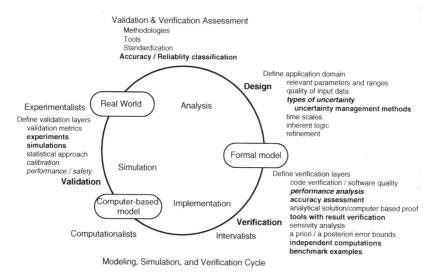

**Fig. 1.** Validation & Verification Assessment and Addressed Topics (in bold) [7]

The second step is verification, which pursues two major goals: code verification — that is, finding logical and programming errors in the code — followed by numerical verification. We are mainly interested in the latter. We are currently developing a four-tier hierarchy that specifies the degree of verification of a given numerical program. A selection of graded instruments helping to identify the class to which the program belongs consists of instruments for subsystem cases and benchmark problems, for independent computations checking the correctness of results and for the calculation of a priori or a posteriori error bounds. In addition, we use tools for sensitivity analysis to identify parameters that have a significant influence on the result as well as tools with result verification or computer-aided proofs of the existence of the solution.

For example, consider a dynamical process modeled by solving a differential equation with an initial condition. There are many algorithms based on floating point arithmetic such as Runge-Kutta's to solve this problem. Simultaneously, different kinds of verified solvers as described in [5] can be used to check the appropriateness of results provided by standard methods.

In some cases it is difficult to verify a process as a whole. So it may be necessary to divide it into several subprocesses which can be treated by appropriate methods. This makes sense especially if the process naturally consists of several interconnected parts as in our example from Section 4 or if parts of the process show different levels of reliability.

Benchmark and subsystem cases are also used in the third and final step, validation. This step addresses model fidelity, defines a validation metric and compares the outcomes of simulations and experiments.

Other techniques cannot be associated with only one step in the V&V assessment; for example, calibration, which concerns the identification and adjustment of the model parameters. Usually, calibration is carried out to achieve a high degree of correspondence between the model and the experimental outcome. Similarly, performance issues influence both the simulation and the numerical algorithms, and the uncertainty problem affects the parameters, the model and/or the experiments.

We would like to emphasize that the notion of reliability is not used only in verified numerics but also in mechatronic systems. In the latter case, reliability refers to the probability that the system will provide correct service within a certain time period. System reliability goes hand in hand with further issues, e.g., safety and availability. Often, dependability is used as a synonym for reliability. Kochs [8] explains mechatronic dependability as a "qualitative and quantitative assessment of performance with regard to reliability and safety and taking into consideration all relevant attributes and factors." System dependability describes the ability of the system to provide specified services to the user.

To obtain system reliability, the V&V assessment has to overcome uncertainty. There are two types of uncertainty. Experimental uncertainty depends on the precision of measurements and can be characterized by varying initial values or parameters following a probability distribution, which may be unknown. Model or epistemic uncertainty causes unpredictable system behavior as a consequence of missing knowledge about the system or the environment [9].

Figure 2 shows methods for propagating uncertainties throughout the system. The imprecision in the outcome can be measured by providing bounds enclosing all possible results or by using probability theory or, alternatively, Dempster-Shafer belief theory[5]. If the probabilities are unknown, Bayes theory can be used. In most cases, it is necessary to compute accurate enclosures of interval functions $f([a, b])$ where $f$ denotes a system function and $[a, b]$ is an arbitrary interval or interval vector built with machine numbers $a$ and $b$ to model the uncertainty on input parameters. This problem may be solved by using an interval optimization solver providing $\inf f([a, b])$ and $\sup f([a, b])$ or interval tools supporting the rounding to $\pm\infty$. Otherwise, Monte Carlo methods can be

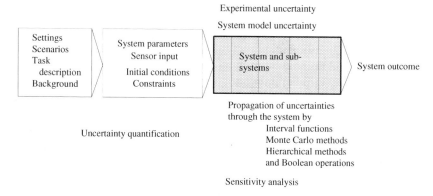

**Fig. 2.** Uncertainty analysis

applied; they yield no overestimation, but they are time-consuming and the bounds obtained are not guaranteed [10].

At first glance, numerical verification based on interval enclosures does not provide any information on the fidelity of the computational model since the relationship between model and experiment is not being investigated at this moment. However, in several applications, we observed that, if the result enclosures obtained were wide or the verification procedure was unsuccessful, the models were often poor for that parameter range. In [11] we studied the identification and simulation of a hydraulic differential cylinder with servo valve. As a controller, a Sugeno-Takagi fuzzy model was used. It was shown that numerical verification was possible in cases where conventional simulation also yielded good results. Therefore, failure to verify a simulation is usually an indicator of a need to improve the corresponding model.

On the other hand, numerical verification based on intervals can be of use also at the design stage. For example, interval based controllers for dynamical systems can be developed in such a way as to minimize their sensitivity to uncertainties in the corresponding system models [12].

# 3    A Taxonomy for Numerical Verification Assessment

In this section we propose a numerical verification taxonomy. Furthermore, we give some guidelines for performing a verification assessment analysis. These guidelines help to characterize a computational model and its implementation from the point of view of numerical verification.

We introduce four classes, from lowest to highest certification standard. The lowest class covers only the use of a standardized floating point arithmetic and a detailed documentation of the results. The remaining higher classes address the fidelity of the model translation into a programming language and examine whether the numerical model implementation accurately represents the conceptual description of the model.

**Class 4:** The process implementation uses standard floating-point or fixed-point arithmetic; results are not verified.

**Class 3:** The system is subdivided into subsystems. The numerical implementation of the process uses at least standardized IEEE (P)754 floating-point arithmetic. Furthermore,

- sensitivity analysis is carried out to overcome uncertainties; alternatively uncertainty is propagated throughout the subsystems using methods like Monte Carlo;
- a priori/posteriori error bounds are provided for important subprocesses; alternatively, self-correcting algorithms are used or numerical stability is proved; condition numbers are computed, and failure conditions identified.

**Class 2:** Relevant subsystems are implemented using tools with result verification or delivering reliable error bounds. The tools use language extensions for scientific computation with standardized floating-point, (enhanced) interval, multiple precision (multiword) or stochastic arithmetic; the actual precision is computed at run-time according to the needs of input data and the predicted outcome. The convergence of numerical algorithms is proved via existence theorems, analytical solutions, computer-aided proofs or fixed-point theorems.

**Class 1:** Uncertainty is quantified and propagated throughout the process using interval or ensemble computing. Model parameters are optimized by calibration. The whole system is verified using tools with result verification. Basic numeric algorithms and (special) functions are certified. Alternatively, real number algorithms, analytical solutions or computer-aided existence proofs are used. Performance issues are addressed. Numerical verification is accompanied by code verification. Software and hardware comply with the IEEE 754 and follow a proposed interval standard.

This taxonomy helps us to establish standardized descriptions of application and validation domains, data capture and visualization methods, software

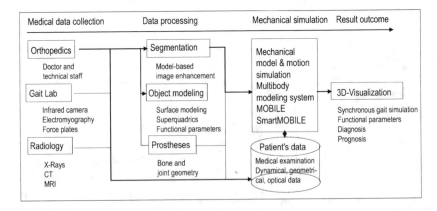

**Fig. 3.** Process flow in the PROREOP project

building-blocks, data flow through the system, standardized interfaces and model descriptions within a heterogeneous hardware and software environment. In parallel, assessment management tools for biomechanical applications have been developed and used within the modeling process of parts of the human skeletal system to support hip and lower-limb surgery. An overview of the complete process flow is provided in Figure 3.

## 4    A Case Study: Accurate Femur Reconstruction

Our goal in this section is to determine how a parameterized model for efficient and accurate femur reconstruction using model-based segmentation and superquadric shapes [13] fits into the proposed V&V taxonomy. Computational model verification starts with an analysis of the collected patient data coming from medical examination in the gait lab and the radiology department, which is subsequently used in the PROREOP process flow.

Using a recently developed questionnaire, accuracy aspects of the data flow and of important subprocesses and algorithms are identified and analyzed. The algorithms and data exchange types are described in a standardized manner: input and output values with their significant digits, types of uncertainties and characteristic parameters of the algorithms with an impact on the accuracy and reliability (numerical data types, conversions, precision loss, cancelation, discretization and truncation errors, error accumulation, stability and condition numbers, test cases) are calculated or estimated. This allows us to determine the level of V&V in the process according to the developed V&V taxonomy.

To quantify the quality of input data and the process uncertainty, the following questions have to be answered:

– Which data source(s) (raw data) is used to acquire the initial data? (MRI, CT, X-RAY, etc.)
– How is the initial data described, and are there any requirements for a generic data type definition in XML?
– Which kind of data selection/fusion was used? (Kind of sensor, camera, MRI, etc.)
– How accurate is this initial data? (Type of noise, one- or two-sided distribution, percentage of wrong or missing values, failure and redundancy, kind of pre-calculation by firmware program as used in MRI systems)
– How is the raw and initial data described? Is there a common global coordinate system?
– Is there a potential deficiency in the modeling process (model error), unknown data or a lack of knowledge concerning parameters or constraints?

Then, the ability of the conceptual model and its translation into a computer-based representation has to be judged and the computational strategy characterized. Typical questions here concern the type of algorithms used (iterative, recursive, stochastic, geometric).

Next, a detailed description of mathematical operations actually used in the algorithm is collected. Additionally, concise information about the initial and resulting data types for these mathematical operations is gathered. Finally, the outcome has to be analyzed: In which format is the resulting data described, and is there any need for a general format? Are there any known or anticipated failures in the resulting data or a systematic loss of precision?

This methodology was applied to study the process for segmenting, reconstructing and measuring a femur bone on the basis of a 3D MRI scan. The goal was to automatically extract important geometric bone features to support hip and lower limb surgery. (These features concerned geometrical measurements highlighted in Figure 4.)

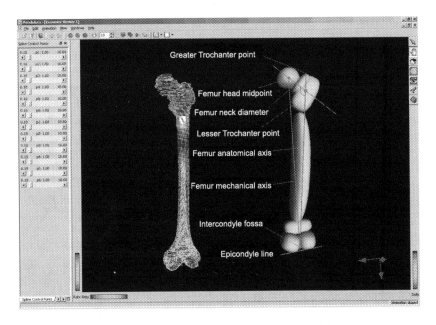

**Fig. 4.** Femur bone and SQ-model with typical features

The process was split into several building-blocks. First, a thresholding method to convert the original 3D MRI images to 3D binary images containing only bones and other tissues of the same intensity was used. The second step provided a region growing method to eliminate most tissues that were not bones. After region growing, the shaft of the femur was already sufficiently segmented, but the femur ball needed extra-processing. Therefore, in the third step, we used a VRML model of a standard femur to further refine the binary image.

Then, a patient-specific superquadric (SQ) bone model was built. The basic SQ type possesses only eleven parameters, the type with local deformations eighteen parameters. In both cases the optimization process that fits the SQ to the data cloud contained considerably fewer parameters than B-spline surfaces. To construct a kind of CSG-tree with SQ leaves, a split and merge approach was applied to reduce the number of SQs while maintaining the quality of the fit. Candidates for merging were chosen in such a way that the feature-oriented

SQ model of the femur was constructed (Figure 4). From this model, significant points and quantities, like the mechanical length or the center of the femur head, could easily be extracted by using the orientation of the SQ within a global coordinate system and basic operations on the parameters. Together with the SQ-based approach, a manual extraction of the visualized patient data and a parallel calculation based on the VRML model delivered three independent computations of the patient-specific bone features and justified the implementation to be classified into class three of the V&V taxonomy [13].

The reconstruction of the bones of the hip and lower limbs is then used together with marker data coming from a gait lab to build a patient-specific mechanical model and motion simulation. To this end, reasonable bounds for the knee and hip joint positions are needed.

One of the upcoming problems is the characterization of artifacts induced by skin motion that directly influences the position of markers with respect to the bones and joints during the experiments in the gait lab (see Figure 5). Initial results were obtained by applying the modeling and simulation tool SmartMO-BILE, to the identification of body segment motion. SMARTMOBILE provides results guaranteed to be correct within the constraints of the considered computational model of a mechanical system that fits into Class 2 of the numerical verification taxonomy.

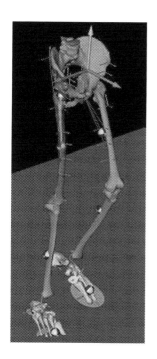
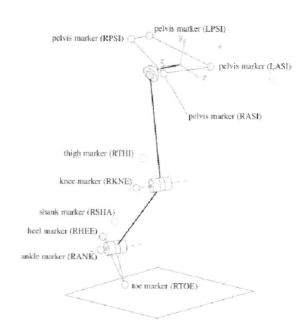

**Fig. 5.** Skeleton-hip prosthesis — relevant markers to identify body segment motion

# 5    Verification of Body Segment Motion in SMARTMOBILE

In this section, we give a short description of SMARTMOBILE and then turn to the problem of identification of body segment motion from marker trajectories. In conclusion, we mention the recent developments concerning validated sensitivity analysis.

SMARTMOBILE [6] is a C++ object-oriented software for verification of various classes of mechanical systems based on MOBILE [14] which employs usual numerics. Models in both tools are executable C++ programs built of the supplied classes for transmission elements such as rigid links for modeling of rigid bodies, scalar or spatial objects such as coordinate frames and solvers such as those for differential equations.

SMARTMOBILE is one of the first integrated environments providing result verification for kinematic and dynamic simulations of mechanical systems. The advantage of this environment is its flexibility due to the template structure: the user can choose the kind of (non)verified arithmetics according to his task. An overview of arithmetics available in SMARTMOBILE at this moment is given in Table 1. However, advanced users are not limited to them and are free to plug in their own implementations if they follow the general instructions from [15].

Although it is easy for MOBILE users to switch to SMARTMOBILE [15], this might involve a considerable amount of manual work depending on the problem. That is why they are assisted by several converters. The first type helps to transform newly developed MOBILE elements into SMARTMOBILE templates via series of automatically generated LINUX scripts. The second type converts already existing MOBILE models into the form defined by SMARTMOBILE. Elements generated by both converter types might require a heuristic improvement by the user, if they contain code fragments transformation of which cannot be automatized, for example, non-verified equation solvers.

For most kinematical problems, it is sufficient to use the basic data type from Column 3 of the Table 1 as the parameter of all the template classes used for a particular model. The main idea for dynamical and special kinematical tasks such as finding of system equilibria is to use pairs basic data type/corresponding solver (Columns 3 and 4). Our experience shows that the general tendency as to what kind of arithmetic to use is as follows. If only a reference solution is of interest, floating point arithmetics with `MoReal` and a usual numerical integrator such as Runge-Kutta's can be employed for dynamic simulations. If the user is interested in fast verification of a relatively simple system with little uncertainty, interval-based pairs are of use. Taylor arithmetics should be mostly chosen for offline simulations with considerable uncertainty [6].

Now we consider the problem of identification of body segment motion using marker trajectories. A subtask of this problem, for which a new algorithm has been developed recently [20], is the reconstruction of the hip joint position from positions of markers fastened to specified places on a patient's leg (Figure 5, right side). The corresponding model is purely kinematic. At first, the segment frame motion is obtained by orthogonalizing the bone and joint axes sequentially. In the second step, the model parameters and the motion of the model segments

**Table 1.** Arithmetics supplied with SMARTMOBILE

| Description | Arithmetic | Kinematic | Dynamics |
|---|---|---|---|
| reference | floating point | MoReal | MoRungeKutta,... |
| based on VNODE [16] | intervals | TMoInterval | TMoAWA |
| based on VALENCIA-IVP [17] | intervals | TMoFInterval | TMoValencia |
| based on RiOT [18] | Taylor | TMoTaylorModel | TMoRiOT |
| based on COSY [19] | Taylor | RDAInterval | — |
| equilibrium states | intervals | MoFInterval | MoIGradient |
| sensitivity with VALENCIA-IVP | intervals | MoSInterval | TMoValenciaS |

are adjusted to the marker trajectories using nonlinear optimization. For the purposes of verification, the fitting task of this second stage was simplified in such a way as to be explicitly solvable.

The data on marker positions contains uncertainties which appear, for example, due to various kinds of skin displacement during motion. The task of quantifying the influence of such uncertainties on the simulation result was to be solved in SMARTMOBILE. The uncertainties of interest were $\pm 10$ mm in knee and ankle widths. Besides, uncertainties due to skin displacements underneath markers were to be taken into account. The displacement tangential to skin could amount to up to $\pm 10$ mm, normal to skin up to $\pm 5$ mm, and marker displacement due to soft tissue movement was again $\pm 10$ mm. The nominal values of these parameters in the model were 120 mm for the knee width and 80 mm for the ankle width. It would be very space consuming to provide the positions of all markers, so we only mention the position of the first one: [105.682, $1.453 \cdot 10^3$,848.547] m. The femur length obtained with MOBILE for the certain system was 0.3863 m (rounded up to the fourth digit after the decimal point). We were interested in the influence of the uncertainties on the hip joint position and, consequently, the length of the femur bone. Only the right leg was considered; the algorithm works for the left leg analogously.

At first, we transformed the corresponding MOBILE package into SMART-MOBILE. After this semi-automatic procedure, we tried to use interval arithmetic on the model obtained in this way. These first results were discouraging: to begin with, we could not work with the above mentioned uncertainties. Already an uncertainty of $\pm 0.6$ mm in the knee width gave us the result interval of over 30 m (!) in diameter, which was of course meaningless in the context. This indicated, on the one hand, that the automatically generated classes had to be improved by an expert, and, on the other hand, that a different kind of verified arithmetic had to be used.

There were several code fragments which could be rewritten in such a way as to produce less overestimation. The main problem with the old code, however, was the routine which computed the solution of a linear system of equations $Ax = b$ directly by inverting the matrix $A$, $x = A^{-1}b$, which is a well-known source of overestimation in the interval case. It was not the task of our converter program to detect such code fragments, and, generally, this cannot be easily done. After having solved this system by a corresponding routine from PROFIL/BIAS for

**Table 2.** Verified identification of body segment motion under uncertainties: hip joint position and femur length in m

| Uncertainty | Position (x,y,z) | Femur length |
|---|---|---|
| Knee, ankle | ([-0.0805;-0.0697], [-0.0602;-0.0452], [0.0403; 0.0701]) | [0.3776; 0.3967] |
| Skin displacement | ([-0.3351;0.1939], [-0.3628; 0.2319], [-0.0066; 0.1158]) | [0.0000; 0.6214] |

intervals and having performed other smaller improvements, we could reduce diameter of the resulting interval to approximately 20 m for the initial uncertainty of $\pm 0.6$ mm in the knee width, which was still not good enough from the practical point of view.

Our next step was to use Taylor models instead of intervals for this simulation. However, we were confronted with limitations imposed by the Taylor arithmetic libraries RiOT and COSY. The former does not implement the inverse sine function $\arcsin x$ which was employed in the original algorithm; the parameters of the latter concerning memory management had to be thoroughly tuned to make it work with the big amount of measurement data. The results of simulations with COSY are shown in Table 2. (They are rounded to the fourth digit after the decimal point.) Taylor models were bound by the LDB algorithm from COSY to obtain upper and lower bounds on the overall uncertainty. Although this simulation took more CPU time than the interval one[1] and considerably more time than the non verified simulation in MOBILE, it was still presumed to be faster than the corresponding series of Monte Carlo simulations.

We see from Table 2 that the uncertainties in knee and ankle widths result in the uncertainty of approximately 20 mm in the femur length (Line 2). The overall uncertainty due to skin movement has a greater impact on the system: the diameter of the best possible enclosure of the femur length is approximately 622 mm. This result indicates the need to perform all corresponding measurements with great care if the proposed algorithm is to be used. Here, the displacement due to soft tissue movement has the biggest influence, the displacement normal to skin the smallest, as shown in Table 3. Here, the femur length was measured under $\pm 5$, $\pm 10$ and $\pm 20$ mm uncertainty individually for each kind of displacement.

The fact that Taylor arithmetic was so much more successful than the interval one is not astonishing since the proposed algorithm in MOBILE has a lot of cancelation in the sense described in [21]. However, since what we were interested in was essentially an enclosure of the range of a function, the actual final results were negatively influenced by the use of the LDB algorithm bounding the range of a Taylor model. Therefore, our future task will be to employ a (Taylor model based) optimizer instead. Another interesting direction will be to compute the overall uncertainty using differential sensitivity using a tool similar to the one described in the next paragraph for dynamic systems and in this way quantify the overestimation in the SMARTMOBILE simulation. The employment of result

---

[1] 36.1 s versus 0.4 s for a simulation with $\pm 10$ mm uncertainty in the knee width on Intel Xeon CPU 2GHz under Linux 2.6.23.14-115.fc8.

**Table 3.** Sensitivity of the model with respect to marker displacements (m) due to skin movements: femur length (m)

| Marker displacement | [-0.005;0.005] | [-0.010;0.010] | [-0.020;0.020] |
|---|---|---|---|
| tangential to skin | [0.3492;0.4203] | [0.3008;0.4576] | [0.1146;0.5468] |
| normal to skin | [0.3742;0.3985] | [0.3279;0.4413] | [0.3335;0.4427] |
| soft tissue | [0.3593;0.4125] | [0.3279;0.4413] | [0.0000;0.6330] |

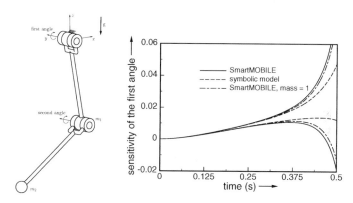

**Fig. 6.** Sensitivity of the double pendulum wrt. the first mass

verification for accurate femur reconstruction allows us to place it in Class 2 of the V&V taxonomy proposed in section 3.

A new development in SMARTMOBILE, important for V&V analysis of dynamic systems, is the class `TMoValenciaSIntegrator`, which provides validated sensitivities of all states with respect to parameters of interest. This class is based on the corresponding algorithm from VALENCIA-IVP. Sensitivity in this case is understood as the partial derivative of a given state with respect to a certain parameter. As an example, we consider the double pendulum from [17] with the uncertainty of ±1% in the first initial angle. In Figure 6, its sensitivity with respect to the first mass $m_1$ is shown. The dashed-dotted curves show results obtained with SMARTMOBILE for $m_1 = 1$ kg, the solid ones for $m_1 \in [0.99; 1.01]$ kg. For comparison, results for the corresponding symbolic equations with $m_1 \in [0.99; 1.01]$ kg from VALENCIA-IVP are represented by the dashed curves.

The enclosures obtained in VALENCIA-IVP are tighter, which is not very remarkable since the symbolic model contains less numerical operations and is therefore lass prone to overestimation. The sensitivity is increasing in the considered interval, but its values are small. It leads to the conclusion that the mass does not influence the simulation much. The enclosures for certain and uncertain masses do not differ much over this time interval (cf. Figure 7, where the difference between the angle enclosures obtained for the interval and point masses, respectively, is shown). Here, we enclose the difference using the sensitivity obtained for $m_1 \in [0.99; 1.01]$ based on the mean value theorem:

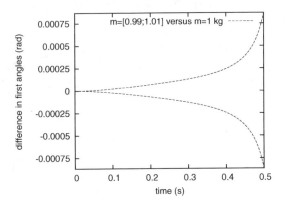

**Fig. 7.** Sensitivity-based enclosure of the difference $\Delta\varphi_1(t)$ for the first angle with uncertain and point mass $m_1$, respectively

$$\varphi_1(t, m_1) \in [\varphi_1(t, m_1 = 1)] + \left.\frac{\partial\varphi_1(t, m_1)}{\partial m_1}\right|_{m_1 \in [0.99;1.01]} \cdot ([0.99; 1.01] - 1).$$

That is, the difference in angles is proportional to the difference in masses with the sensitivity for the uncertain parameter as the coefficient. In Figure 7, it is illustrated that mass uncertainty does not contribute as much as the uncertainty in the initial conditions to the overall overestimation which shows itself in the continuous widening of enclosure widths over time.

## 6    Conclusion and Further Work

In this paper we proposed a new taxonomy of numerical verification and provided guidelines for performing a verification assessment analysis that allowed us to associate a computational model and its implementation with a certain V&V class. The methodology was demonstrated by the example of accurate bone motion reconstruction. A part of this process could be verified using SMARTMOBILE.

In the future, we plan to place this research in a more general context and work on an assessment framework in the form of step-by-step instructions for performing an assessment analysis to classify (bio)mechanical processes and their computational realizations.

## References

1. Oberkampf, W.L., Trucano, T.G., Hirsch, C.: Verification, validation, and predictive capability in computational engineering and physics. Technical Report SAND2003-3769, Sandia National Laboratories (2003)
2. ASME Committee (PT60) on Verification and Validation in Computational Solid Mechanics: Guide for verification and validation in computational solid mechanics (2006)

3. Anderson, A.E., Ellis, B.J., Weiss, J.A.: Verification, validation and sensitivity studies in computational biomechanics. Computer Methods in Biomechanics and Biomedical Engineering 10(3), 171–184 (2007)
4. Einarsson, B. (ed.): Accuracy And Reliability in Scientific Computing. Society for Industrial and Applied Mathematics, U.S. (2005)
5. Kreinovich, V., Beck, J., Ferregut, C., Sanchez, A., Keller, G.R., Averill, M., Starks, S.A.: Monte-Carlo-type techniques for processing interval uncertainty, and their engineering applications. In: Proceedings of the Workshop on Reliable Engineering Computing, Savannah, GA, September 2004, pp. 139–160 (2004)
6. Auer, E., Luther, W.: SMARTMOBILE — An environment for guaranteed multibody modeling and simulation. In: Proceedings of the Fourth International Conference on Informatics in Control, Automation and Robotics ICINCO (2007) ISBN: 978-972-8865-87-0
7. Schlesinger, S.: Terminology for model credibility. Simulation 32(3), 103–104 (1979)
8. Kochs, H.D.: Key factors of dependability of mechatronic units: Mechatronic dependability. In: 28th Annual International Computer Software and Application Conference (COMP-SAC 2004), Hong Kong, China, pp. 584–586. IEEE Computer Society, Los Alamitos (2004)
9. On Uncertainty Management, E.P.G.: Uncertainty in Industrial Practice — A guide to quantitative uncertainty management. Wiley, Chichester (to appear)
10. Hörsken, C., Traczinski, H.: Modeling of multibody systems with interval arithmetic. In: Krämer, W., van Gudenberg, J.W. (eds.) Scientific Computing, Validated Numerics, Interval Methods, pp. 317–328. Kluwer, Dordrecht (2001)
11. Luther, W., Dyllong, E., Fausten, D., Otten, W., Traczinski, H.: Numerical verification and validation of kinematics and dynamical models for flexible robots in complex environment. In: Kulisch, U., Lohner, R., Facius, A. (eds.) Perspectives on Enclosure Methods, pp. 181–199. Springer, Heidelberg (2001)
12. Rauh, A.: Theorie und Anwendung von Intervallmethoden für Analyse und Entwurf robuster und optimaler Regelungen dynamischer Systeme. Ph.D thesis, University of Ulm (2008)
13. Cuypers, R., Tang, Z., Luther, W., Pauli, J.: A parametrized model for efficient and accurate femur reconstruction using model-based segmentation and superquadric shapes. In: I-ASTED, Baltimore (April 2008)
14. Kecskeméthy, A.: Objektorientierte Modellierung der Dynamik von Mehrkörpersystemen mit Hilfe von Übertragungselementen. Ph.D thesis, Gerhard Mercator Universität Duisburg (1993)
15. Auer, E.: SmartMOBILE: A framework for reliable modeling and simulation of kinematics and dynamcis of mechanical systems. Ph.D thesis, Universität Duisburg-Essen. WiKu Verlag Dr. Stein (2007) ISBN: 978-3-86553-240-4
16. Nedialkov, N.S.: The design and implementation of an object-oriented validated ODE solver. Kluwer Academic Publishers, Dordrecht (2002)
17. Auer, E., Rauh, A., Hofer, E.P., Luther, W.: Validated Modeling of Mechanical Systems with SMARTMOBILE: Improvement of Performance by VALENCIA-IVP. In: Hertling, P., Hoffmann, C.M., Luther, W., Revol, N. (eds.) Real Number Algorithms. LNCS, vol. 5045, pp. 1–27. Springer, Heidelberg (2008)
18. Eble, I.: RiOT, http://iamlasun8.mathematik.uni-karlsruhe.de/~ae08/

19. Berz, M., Makino, K.: COSY INFINITY 9.0. Programmer's manual. Technical Report MSUHEP 060803, Michigan State University (2006)
20. Stark, T., Kecskeméthy, A., Tändl, M.: Application of MOBILE for an improved kinematical model using motion- and MRI measurements. In: The 15th European Conference on Mathematics for Industry, London, England, June 30 - July 4 (2008)
21. Neumaier, A.: Taylor forms — use and limits. Reliable Computing 9, 43–79 (2002)

# Robustness of Boolean Operations on Subdivision-Surface Models

Di Jiang and Neil F. Stewart*

Département IRO, Université de Montréal,
CP6128, Succ. CentreVille, H3C 3J7, Canada
{jiangdi,stewart}@iro.umontreal.ca

**Abstract.** This paper describes an algorithm to perform Boolean operations, based on the use of limit meshes, in the case when input objects are defined in terms of triangular meshes and Loop subdivision. The focus of the paper is on robustness, including error bounds and numerical methods for the *a posteriori* validation of topological form.

## 1 Introduction

Boolean operations on standard trimmed-NURBS geometric models [29] are still notoriously difficult problems, and the associated difficulties manifest themselves in the appearance of artifacts such as cracks and gaps [11]. The framework necessary to prove that algorithms work rigorously is available [3], but, so far at least, the required analyses appear to be intractable.

On the other hand, subdivision-surface models are more and more frequently being used in place of trimmed-NURBS representations due to their simplicity, generality, and efficiency for smooth surface construction [6]. In this paper we describe an algorithm for computing Boolean operations on objects defined by their boundaries, represented as subdivision surfaces. The algorithm is similar to the one described in [5], but uses what is called the limit mesh to perform the initial boundary intersection calculation rather than a refined version of the control mesh. The focus of the paper is on robustness: for example, we do not discuss fitting operations [5] in detail. We do, however, consider several robustness issues: integration of Fortune's $\alpha$-predicate into the code for triangle-triangle intersection [15], new error bounds for the limit surface, and, at least in the regular case, simple and rigorous methods to verify *a posteriori* that the polyhedral computed solution has the same topological form as its corresponding boundary surface. Finding such bounds, and performing such *a posteriori* validations, are essential steps in providing an *a posteriori* backward error analysis [19] for a Boolean-operation algorithm.

Previous work on robustness for Boolean operations on subdivision surfaces includes [22] and [28]. In [22], voxelization representations were used to calculate

---

* The research of the second author was supported in part by a grant from the Natural Sciences and Engineering Research Council of Canada.

A. Cuyt et al. (Eds.): Numerical Validation, LNCS 5492, pp. 161–174, 2009.

the Boolean intersection of sets defined by Catmull-Clark subdivision surfaces. In [28], symbolic perturbation methods were used to guarantee topological correctness of the computed result of a Boolean operation.

The algorithm presented here has been implemented, and to some extent we have been concerned with questions of efficiency and triangle count, as described below. In this paper, however, we restrict our attention for the most part to the robustness issues mentioned above.

We suppose that the reader has a general familiarity with subdivision-surface methods for the representation of solids [10].

Boolean operations on solids defined using a subdivision-surface representation are usually carried out on a piecewise polygonal mesh (the *control mesh*), rather than the *limit surface* that defines the true geometry of an input operand [23]. Such an approximation might not be accurate (nor, in the context of collision detection, safe) [32]. The accuracy can be improved, however, by using the *limit mesh*, a polyhedral approximation formed by driving each of the control points in the control mesh to its limit position [17,21]. This representation better approximates the limit surface while maintaining the same topological form as the control mesh.

The algorithm discussed in this paper is based on the use of the limit mesh. The discussion refers to the Loop subdivision scheme, but the ideas are more generally applicable. As already mentioned, we do not discuss fitting procedures, but we note here that the *a posteriori* validation is applicable both before and after such fitting procedures have been applied. Also, we often phrase the discussion in terms of regularized Boolean intersection [27] (there is no loss in generality in doing so: different Boolean operations merely change which segments of the original meshes should be retained). The input solids may be denoted $S$ and $S'$, and the operation studied is $S \cap^* S'$, where $\cap^*$ denotes regularized intersection. The input solids are represented by subdivision surfaces defining their boundaries.

The remainder of the paper is organized as follows. In Section 2 we discuss the representation of solids using subdivision surfaces. In Section 3 we describe the Boolean intersection algorithm. This is followed by the discussion of error bounds and validation of topological form in Section 4, and by a short concluding section.

## 2    Representations of Solids

A typical solid will be denoted $S$. It is defined by its boundary surface $\partial S$, a two-manifold without boundary embedded in $\mathbb{R}^3$, and a directed normal vector specifying which side of $\partial S$ corresponds to the inside of the object. The surface $\partial S$ is defined by a polyhedral mesh $(M, P)$, where $M$ is a (logical) locally-planar triangular mesh, $P^T$ is a $3 \times L$ matrix containing the control points $\mathbf{p}_i \in \mathbb{R}^3, i = 1, \ldots, L$, and the limit surface is defined implicitly by Loop subdivision. We call the polyhedral mesh a *control mesh*, and denote it $M$.

Loop subdivision was proposed in [24] and extended in [4,16,25]. Triangles are subdivided by splitting each edge, and joining the new vertices created by

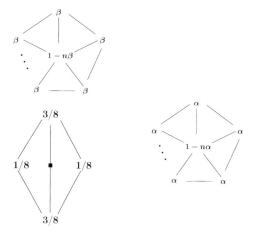

**Fig. 1.** Subdivision masks (left) and limit mask (right)

this split with an edge. The weight for a newly introduced edge point is given by the mask in Figure 1 (lower left), and existing vertices are modified using the mask in Figure 1 (upper left), with $\beta = \beta(n) = a(n)/n$, and $a(n) = 5/8 - (3 + 2\cos(2\pi/n))^2/64$ [16]. Since $\beta(6) = 1/16$, for regular triangular meshes (*i.e.*, meshes for which the valence $n$ of each vertex is equal to 6) we have $1 - n\beta = 5/8$. Figure 1 (right) is discussed below.

The limit surface defined by Loop subdivision is a box spline surface [9], and $\partial S$ can be expressed as

$$\partial S = \partial S(u, v) = \sum_i \mathbf{p}_i b_i(u, v) \tag{1}$$

where on regular parts of the mesh the basis functions[1] $b_i$ are piecewise polynomials.

The range of the index $i$ in (1) was left undefined. In the case of a box spline defined on all of $\mathbb{R}^2$, the range of $i$ could be taken to be the entire grid $\mathbb{Z}^2$. Both in this case and in the case of a finite locally-planar mesh without boundary, however, it is sufficient to consider only vertices in a one-ring neighbour of a triangular patch, as illustrated in Figure 2 (right), provided that at least one step of subdivision has been carried out, so that there are no adjacent non-regular vertices.

This can be seen as follows. If we consider the domain of the $b_i(u, v)$ to be all of $\mathbb{R}^2$, the functions $b_i(u, v)$ can be found by substituting a scalar control point with $p_i = 1$ for $i$ corresponding to a particular grid-point labelled $i$ in $h\mathbb{Z}^2 \subset \mathbb{R}^2$, and $p_j = 0$ for $j \neq i$, and then applying the subdivision process until convergence. If we do this by using the masks given in Figure 1 (left), it can be shown that the support of $b_i(u, v)$ lies in the convex hull of the set of

---

[1] In fact, in contrast to the tensor-product B-spline case, these functions do not form a basis for the spline space. A better name would be "nodal functions" [26].

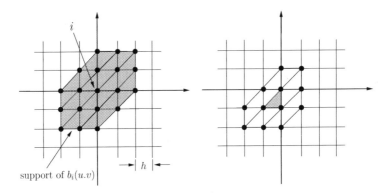

**Fig. 2.** Loop subdivision

vertices at distance 2 from $i$, where distance is measured as an integer quantity in the graph formed by the triangulated grid embedded in $\mathbb{R}^2$ (see Figure 2, left). Figure 2 (right) is the consequence of looking at this fact from the opposite point of view: the value of the surface on the patch corresponding to a single triangle is determined by the control points that are 1-ring neighbours of the patch. Similarly, if the local parametric domain is supposed to be embedded in $\mathbb{R}^2$ as shown in Figure 3 (left) [32], then the corresponding nodal function can be found in the same way. It is illustrated for the regular case in Figure 3 (right).

Finally, to deal with creases introduced due to design considerations, or due to Boolean operations, it is necessary to introduce additional subdivision rules for crease edges and corner vertices [4,16,25]. The implementation described below permits crease edges in the input objects, and produces crease edges along intersection curves.

By using the limit mask in Figure 1 (right) we can drive any control point to its position on the limit surface. If we take the set of such limit points, and

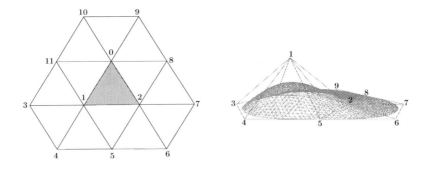

**Fig. 3.** Left: a base mesh used to generate the basis functions for the triangle 0-1-2 (regular case: vertex with valence $n = 6$) [32]; right: the resulting basis function at node 1 evaluated at subdivision level four

link them together into a polyhedral mesh with the same connectivity as $\check{M}$, we obtain the *limit mesh*, denoted $\bar{M}$. Both $\check{M}$ and $\bar{M}$ depend on the level of subdivision $\iota$, but since $\iota$ is the same for both meshes, and fixed, we do not show it explicitly.

## 3   The Boolean Algorithm

The goal of the Boolean-operation algorithm is to apply the operation to two subdivision-surface models, and to form the result, made up of the desired boundary segments. The algorithm takes the boundaries $\partial S$ and $\partial S'$ of two solids, as described in Section 2, and produces a single well-formed object boundary as output. The algorithm introduces modifications of ideas previously suggested by other authors, *e.g.*, the *triangle-triangle-intersection* procedure of [15] is modified by the $\alpha$-predicate [13] to ensure robustness. The overall idea of the algorithm is similar to [5], but we use the limit meshes $\bar{M}$ and $\bar{M}'$, rather than refined control meshes (which have more triangles), for the intersection-curve calculation. The limit mesh $\bar{M}$ is generally closer to the limit surface than the control mesh $\check{M}$, with fewer triangles than a refined control mesh of comparable accuracy, which makes the calculation less expensive. An example (in this case, a union operation) produced by the implemented algorithm is given in Figure 4.

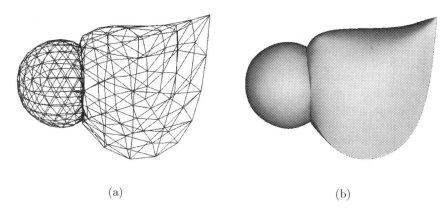

(a)                                         (b)

**Fig. 4.** (a) control mesh (b) union

Here is the overall description of the algorithm.

1. **Surface intersection.** This step computes the intersection curves of two limit meshes $\bar{M}$ and $\bar{M}'$ and maps them to the control meshes $\check{M}$ and $\check{M}'$. The computation uses a triangle-triangle-intersection test, and takes floating-point roundoff error into account.
2. **Cutting.** This step takes the mapped intersection curves as a reference to construct cutting curves, and separates the original control meshes into cut meshes.

3. **Merging.** This step combines the desired parts to form a well-formed object; the intersection curve is tagged as a crease.
4. **Fitting.** This is an optional procedure that aims to reduce the difference between the computed result and true solution [5].

The Boolean intersection algorithm involves two main procedures, *triangle-triangle intersection*, and *refinement*, which is used in the cutting and merging steps. A *snapping* procedure is also used in [5] (if a vertex in the mapped intersection curve is within a certain threshold of a vertex in the control mesh, the latter vertex is moved, and all segments of the intersection curve within a one-ring neighbourhood of the displaced control point are updated). Based on our observation in the context of an algorithm based on the limit mesh, such a procedure has little influence on the number of triangles in the computed result, but a large (negative) effect on the geometric form of the result. Consequently, we did not include it. This reduces both the amount of work and potential robustness problems.

Our first comments on robustness concern the *triangle-triangle-intersection* procedure. This procedure is largely based on the work of Guigue and Devillers [15]. For our implementation, we downloaded their source code (available online); modifications were made in order to introduce the equivalent of Fortune's $\alpha$-predicate, for robustness reasons. The hypothesis [15] that there are no degenerate triangles in the input will always be satisfied in practice if the input objects have been provided by means of a coarse control mesh. Otherwise this condition must be checked.

Similarly to [8,13], we define $\epsilon$ to be an upper bound $\epsilon > |\delta|$, for all $x, y$, where $x \hat{*} y = (x * y)(1 + \delta)$ and $\hat{*}$ is a set of operations $\hat{+}, \hat{-}, \hat{\times}, \hat{/}$ defined on the representable reals with relative error $\epsilon$.

The intersection computation relies exclusively on the sign of certain $4 \times 4$ determinants, where *sign* is a three-valued function taking values in $\{-1, 0, 1\}$. Consider first the *above-predicate*, which determines whether the point $t$ is above (positive), below (negative), or on (zero) the plane through $p, q$ and $r$:

**Definition 1.** *Given four three-dimensional points $p = (p_x, p_y, p_z)$, $q = (q_x, q_y, q_z)$, $r = (r_x, r_y, r_z)$, and $t = (t_x, t_y, t_z)$, we define the above-predicate*

$$ap[p, q, r, t] := - \begin{vmatrix} p_x & q_x & r_x & t_x \\ p_y & q_y & r_y & t_y \\ p_z & q_z & r_z & t_z \\ 1 & 1 & 1 & 1 \end{vmatrix} = (t - p) \cdot ((q - p) \times (r - p)). \quad (2)$$

The evaluation of this predicate is error-prone due to the use of finite precision arithmetic [5]. Consequently, a perturbation $\delta'$ is introduced similar to the $\alpha$-*predicate* in [13], and the classification of point positions is modified as follows:

$$ t \leftrightarrow \begin{cases} above\triangle & : & ap[\triangle, t] \in (\delta', \infty) & (sign(ap[\triangle, t]) = 1) \\ on\triangle & : & ap[\triangle, t] \in [-\delta', \delta'] & (sign(ap[\triangle, t]) \Leftarrow 0) \\ below\triangle & : & ap[\triangle, t] \in (-\infty, -\delta') & (sign(ap[\triangle, t]) = -1) \end{cases} \quad (3) $$

where $\Leftarrow$ means *considered* to be zero. With these modifications, the plane through $\triangle \boldsymbol{pqr}$ is thickened to contain an ambiguity zone with $\delta' = 160 M^3 \epsilon$, neglecting higher-order terms of $\epsilon$, and $M$ is a fixed upper bound for the absolute value of any coordinate of any point.

We assume that not all points are coplanar. If all the vertices of one triangle have sign equal to zero with respect to the other triangle, we are in the coplanar case, and we can ignore the potential intersection, since the edges of neighbouring triangles will produce the desired result. To eliminate ambiguities in the opposite case, the first step is to perturb the point having sign equal to 0 by an amount $\rho$, where $\rho > 2\tau$, in a direction away from the edge opposite the point [15]. The vertices of the two triangles $T_1$ and $T_2$ are then permuted to form the layout shown in Figure 5, where a simple comparison of intervals determines whether there is a non-empty intersection.

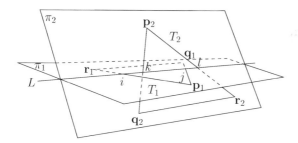

**Fig. 5.** Triangle-triangle intersection

Given two triangles $T_1 : (\boldsymbol{p}_1, \boldsymbol{q}_1, \boldsymbol{r}_1)$ and $T_2 : (\boldsymbol{p}_2, \boldsymbol{q}_2, \boldsymbol{r}_2)$, suppose that at least one of the vertices of $T_1$ has a non-zero sign for the *above-predicate*, say, $sign(ap[T_2, \boldsymbol{r}_1]) \neq 0$, and that at least one of the vertices of $T_1$ has different sign from vertex $\boldsymbol{r}_1$, e.g., $sign(ap[T_2, \boldsymbol{p}_1]) \neq sign(ap[T_2, \boldsymbol{r}_1])$. Thus, we are in the case where there is a potential intersection.

Without loss of generality, let $sign(ap[T_2, \boldsymbol{r}_1]) = 1$. Then there are two possibilities for the position of point $\boldsymbol{p}_1$ in the case of intersection:

1. $sign(ap[T_2, \boldsymbol{p}_1]) = -1$; in this case there is definitely an intersection, and we apply the original Guigue-Deveillers algorithm [15].
2. $sign(ap[T_2, \boldsymbol{p}_1]) = 0$; this means that the point $\boldsymbol{p}_1$ falls in the ambiguity zone, and an $\alpha$-*arithmetic* modification must be applied in order to remove this ambiguity. The $\rho$ perturbation is applied: let the perturbed point be $\boldsymbol{p}'_1 = \boldsymbol{p}_1 + \rho \boldsymbol{n}$, where $\boldsymbol{n}$ is the direction of perturbation, determined by the direction through $\boldsymbol{p}$ and orthogonal to the opposite edge of $T_1$. Here, $\|\boldsymbol{n}\| = 1$.

Our version of the algorithm described here fails safe, in the sense that if there is actually an intersection, it will be detected, but errors of the opposite type may occur. The maximum error in the case of errors of opposite type can be determined by applying the standard *a priori* bounds [8, p. 107] to the Guigue-Devillers algorithm [15].

The arguments presented here clearly do not constitute a proof of the correctness of the overall process: in particular, such a proof would have to involve consideration of multiple perturbations of a single vertex; the merging step, described below; and take into account the classical steps described in [30] to obtain a regularized result. Note also that, given the fail-safe nature of our algorithm, it might be decided to implement a postprocessing step to eliminate small thin sets (slivers) [28]. This, however, lies outside the domain of numerical analysis.

The goal of *refinement* is first to guarantee that the mesh remains valid (merging step), and secondly, that the cutting curves conform to the shape of the mapped intersection curves (cutting step). A triangle containing a part of the intersection curve is refined if it is detected as "bad", *i.e.* the curve intersects the triangle boundary more than twice, does not intersect at all (the curve is completely inside the triangle), or intersects the boundary twice but on the same side. The refinement is done using quadrisection (midpoint insertion on the triangle edges).

The steps just summarized make up a large part of the implemented Boolean operation algorithm, but since they are not directly concerned with the robustness questions we discuss, we omit the details (the main requirement, from the robustness point of view, is that the process should not modify the topological form of the meshes).

In order to improve the approximation to the true intersection result, an optional fitting step can be applied [5]. This step is applied after execution of the complete Boolean operation. We have used a modified fitting procedure which minimizes the functional formed by the sum, for the two objects, of the terms

$$\sum_{j} \|f(\tilde{\boldsymbol{p}}_j^\iota) - \mathcal{L}\boldsymbol{p}_j^\iota\|^2, \tag{4}$$

where $j$ indexes the vertices in the mesh at subdivision level $\iota$, $\boldsymbol{p}_j^\iota$ is one vertex in the mesh at level $\iota$, $\tilde{\boldsymbol{p}}_j^\iota$ is its corresponding position in the original coarse control mesh $\check{M}$, $f(\cdot)$ is the limit-surface evaluation function, and $\mathcal{L}$ is the limit matrix that determines the limit position of the vertex $\boldsymbol{p}_j^\iota$. Other constraints can be added to obtain better fitting.

## 4    Error Estimation and Verification of Well-Formedness

### 4.1    Error Estimation

Using the limit mesh as an approximation to the limit surface for the intersection calculation implies potential errors in the final result. In this section, we will give a bound on the possible error, based on the work of [21], followed by some possible improvements.

Bounds of this type were discussed in a preliminary way in [18]. Other work on this topic includes [17,32], as well as earlier work [12] on B-splines that used derivatives to bound the surface.

Each face $\bar{F}$ in the limit mesh $\bar{M}$ is defined by the corners $q_0$, $q_1$, and $q_2$, which can be obtained by limit-surface evaluation

$$q_j = \partial S(u_j, v_j) = \sum_{i=0}^{n+5} p_i \cdot b_i(u_j, v_j), \quad j = 0, 1, 2, \tag{5}$$

where the $p_i$ are the control points in the control mesh $\check{M}$ that affect the position of $q_j$, the $b_i$ are the nodal functions, and $(u_j, v_j)$ is the coordinate for $q_j$ in the parametric domain illustrated in Figure 3 (left).

Let $n$ denote the face normal of $\bar{F}$. An upper and lower bound at each of these three vertices can be obtained:

$$\ell_j \leq n^T q_j \leq \mu_j \tag{6}$$

where

$$\ell_j = \sum_{i=0}^{n+5} (n^T(p_i - q_j))^+ \, b_i^- + \sum_{i=0}^{n+5} (n^T(p_i - q_j))^- \, b_i^+$$

$$\mu_j = \sum_{i=0}^{n+5} (n^T(p_i - q_j))^+ \, b_i^+ + \sum_{i=0}^{n+5} (n^T(p_i - q_j))^- \, b_i^- \tag{7}$$

as illustrated in Figure 6 for a two-dimensional case, and

$$(n^T(p_i - q_j))^+ = \max\{n^T(p_i - q_j), 0\}$$
$$(n^T(p_i - q_j))^- = \min\{n^T(p_i - q_j), 0\}$$

(see [21]). It is necessary here to estimate the range $[b_i^-, b_i^+]$ of the basis function $b_i$, where

$$b_i^- = \min_{u,v} b_i(u, v), \qquad b_i^+ = \max_{u,v} b_i(u, v),$$

and the minimum and maximum are taken over the triangle 0-1-2 in Figure 3 (left). As suggested in [21], this can be done by estimating the basis function by

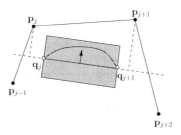

**Fig. 6.** A 2D illustration for the upper and lower bound construction

applying the subdivision process to the Dirac polygon described above ($p_i = 1$, $p_j = 0$ if $j \neq i$). Since this only gives an estimate, however, it is necessary to iterate the process [21], beginning with the coarse estimate of the range $[-1, 1]$. In this way we get a bounding volume $\mathcal{V}$ defined by the offsets of limit-mesh vertices (see Figure 7):

$$q_j + \frac{\ell_j}{n^T \tilde{n}_j} \tilde{n}_j, \qquad q_j + \frac{\mu_j}{n^T \tilde{n}_j} \tilde{n}_j \tag{8}$$

where $\tilde{n}_j$ is the normal vector at each vertex $q_j$.

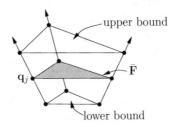

**Fig. 7.** Upper and lower bounds for a single face in the limit mesh

Possible improvements on the bounding volume can be obtained by using the fact that the limit mesh is a down-sampling of the limit surface, which means that all of its vertices lie on the limit surface (except for floating-point error). We will modify the bound above for a tighter enclosure of the limit mesh by exploring this idea.

Using the tangent mask, a tangent plane $\mathcal{P}_j, j = 0, 1, 2$, at the three vertices of each limit face can be obtained as:

$$\mathcal{P}_j = (q_j, \tilde{n}_j) \tag{9}$$

where $q_j$ is vertex of the limit face that lies in the plane, and $\tilde{n}_j$ is its vertex normal, given as

$$\tilde{n}_j = u_1 \times u_2 \tag{10}$$

$$u_1 = c_1 p_1 + c_2 p_2 + \ldots + c_n p_n$$
$$u_2 = c_2 p_1 + c_3 p_2 + \ldots + c_1 p_n,$$

where $p_1, p_2, \ldots, p_n$ are the neighbours of vertex $q_j$, and $c_i = \cos(2\pi i/n)$ are the limit-mask coefficients. Let

$$\theta_j = \frac{n^T \tilde{n}_j}{||n|| ||\tilde{n}_j||}, j = 0, 1, 2, \tag{11}$$

and

$$\theta = \min\{\theta_j, j = 0, 1, 2\}. \tag{12}$$

We can adjust each vertex normal $\tilde{\boldsymbol{n}}_j$ outward from the center of the limit face, by rotating the vector $\boldsymbol{c} - \boldsymbol{q}_j$ around the axis formed by $\tilde{\boldsymbol{n}}_j \times (\boldsymbol{c} - \boldsymbol{q}_j)$ where $\boldsymbol{c}$ is the center of the limit face, until the new vertex normal $\tilde{\boldsymbol{n}}'_j$ satisfies

$$\frac{\boldsymbol{n}^T \tilde{\boldsymbol{n}}'_j}{||\boldsymbol{n}|| ||\tilde{\boldsymbol{n}}'_j||} = \theta, \ j = 0, 1, 2. \tag{13}$$

Then for each vertex $\boldsymbol{q}_j$ we get a new plane

$$\mathcal{P}_j = (\boldsymbol{q}_j, \tilde{\boldsymbol{n}}'_j). \tag{14}$$

By reflecting each of these three planes with respect to the limit face $\bar{\boldsymbol{F}}$, we get three other planes $\mathcal{P}'$. Intersecting each of these planes with the bounding volume $\mathcal{V}$ previously calculated, $\mathcal{P}_j$ with the upper bound, and $\mathcal{P}'$ with the lower bounds (see Figure 8), we can get a tighter enclosure for each face in the limit mesh.

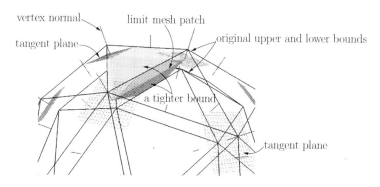

**Fig. 8.** Illustration for tighter bound construction

For now, these modifications provide only approximate bounds, and more work is required to transform them into provable bounds that are guaranteed to enclose the limit surface.

## 4.2  A Posteriori Verification of Well-Formedness

It is of interest to be able to confirm that the limit mesh $\bar{M}$ (respectively $\bar{M}'$) has the same topological form as the corresponding input set, represented by its boundary $\partial S$ (respectively $\partial S'$). Similarly, suppose that $M^c$ is the mesh corresponding to the computed approximation of the result of the Boolean operation, i.e., $M^c$ is intended to approximate the boundary of $S_I = S \cap^* S'$. (The mesh $M^c$ is obtained from refined control meshes corresponding to each input operand.) Again, it may be of interest to confirm that $M^c$ has the same topological form as $\partial S_I^c$, the actual surface associated with the computed mesh. We will phrase the discussion of these questions in terms of the first of the examples just given.

Given the limit mesh $\bar{M}$, the fact that two of its faces are disjoint does not imply that the corresponding faces of $\partial S$ are disjoint. Similarly, it may happen that

$\bar{F}_1$ and $\bar{F}_2$ are adjacent faces sharing an edge or vertex, but that the corresponding faces $F_1$ and $F_2$ of $\partial S$ have extraneous intersections, *i.e.*, intersections other than those along the designated edge or at the designated vertex. A completely robust algorithm should be able to perform *a posteriori* validations of computed results that exclude the possibility of inconsistencies of this kind. (Note that there is no practical inconvenience in assuming that faces in a well-formed mesh do not share more than a single edge or vertex.)

Detection of intersection between patches $F_1$ and $F_2$ that are supposed to be disjoint can be detected on a fail-safe basis by comparison of convex hulls (*i.e.*, non-intersection of convex hulls is a sufficient condition for non-intersection of patches). Excluding the possibility of self-intersection of a patch $F_1$, and of extraneous intersections of adjacent patches $F_1$ and $F_2$, was discussed in [14], where the method of [31] was used. We extend that work as follows. First of all, we conclude that in the regular case, it is not necessary to compute the projection direction required in [31]. This means, in particular, that in the regular case there is no need to omit verification of the second condition in [31], which was suggested as a possible approach in [14]. Secondly, [14] detects extraneous intersections by applying the criterion of [31] to the union of adjacent patches. It was shown in [2], however, that there is a supplementary condition to be satisfied if this method is used, and we show how to verify this supplementary condition in the regular case.

The details for the following extensions can be found in [1]. The first extension follows from the fact that if the corners of $\bar{F}_1$ and $\bar{F}_2$ all have valence 6 (the regular case), then the corresponding patches $F_1$ and $F_2$ can be expressed as Bézier surfaces, and the Bézier coefficients are explicitly available [7,20]. This means that extraneous intersections can be detected by the convex-hull criterion [1, Crit. 3.2.1*] (common edge) and [1, Crit. 3.2.2*] (common vertex). Furthermore, it is easy to extend this approach to work in a fail-safe manner, once the separation plane specified in these criteria has been found, by applying the standard *a priori* bounds for floating-point arithmetic to the calculation of the inner products defining the separation planes. Similar remarks apply to the case of self-intersection of a patch, say $F_1$, using [1, Crit. 3.1*].

The second extension, mentioned above, concerns the fact that application of the criterion of [31] to the union $F_1 \cup F_2$ of adjacent patches requires verification of a supplementary condition along the common boundary, namely that the mapping defining the combined patch must be locally one-to-one along the common boundary [2, Prop. 2.2]. This is true in both the regular and non-regular case. In the regular case the condition can be verified, using the fact that the common boundary is a Bézier curve, and using [1, Crit. 2.1*]. Again, this result can be made fail-safe when ordinary floating-point arithmetic is used.

## 5    Conclusion

We have given a summary description of an implemented algorithm that computes Boolean operations on objects represented by their subdivision-surface boundaries. The algorithm is based on the use of the limit mesh, rather than a refined control mesh, for the computation of the intersection between the surfaces defining the two operands. Most of the discussion in the paper was concerned with three robustness issues of interest in the context of this algorithm, namely the robustness of triangle-triangle intersection, approximation of the limit surface by the limit mesh, and *a posteriori* verification of well-formedness. While the nature of the mathematical arguments necessary to resolve these issues was described, the paper did not give proofs. Thus, future work should include integration of the analysis outlined above into a combined whole, to produce a unified robustness result for Boolean intersection, including validation results in the non-regular case. Such a result would include, in particular, procedures permitting the *a posteriori* validation of topological form.

# References

1. Andersson, L.-E., et al.: Self-intersection of composite curves and surfaces. CAGD 15(5), 507–527 (1998)
2. Andersson, L.-E., et al.: Conditions for use of a non-selfintersection conjecture. CAGD (23), 599–611 (2006)
3. Andersson, L.-E., et al.: Error analysis for operations in solid modeling in the presence of uncertainty. Sc. J. Sci. Comput. 29(2), 811–826 (2007)
4. Biermann, H., et al.: Piecewise smooth subdivision surfaces with normal control. In: Proc. ACM SIGGRAPH, pp. 113–120 (2000)
5. Biermann, H., et al.: Approximate Boolean operation on free-form solids. In: Proc. ACM SIGGRAPH (2001)
6. Bischoff, S., Kobbelt, L.: Teaching meshes, subdivision and multiresolution techniques. Computer-Aided Design 36(14), 1483–1500 (2004)
7. Boehm, W.: Triangular spline algorithms. CAGD (1), 61–67 (1985)
8. Dahlquist, G., Björk, A.: Numerical Methods in Scientific Computing, vol. I. Society for Industrial and Applied Mathematics, Philadelphia (2008)
9. de Boor, C., et al.: Box Splines. Springer, Heidelberg (1993)
10. DeRose, T., et al.: Subdivision for modeling and animation. SIGGRAPH course notes (2000)
11. Farouki, R.: Closing the gap between CAD model and downstream application. SIAM News 5(32) (1999)
12. Filip, D., et al.: Surface algorithms using bounds on derivatives. Computer Aided Geometric Design (3), 295–311 (1986)
13. Fortune, S.: Stable maintenance of point set triangulations in two dimensions. In: Proc. 30th annual IEEE Symp. Foundations of Computer Science, (30), pp. 494–499 (1989)
14. Grinspun, E., Schröder, P.: Normal bounds for subdivision-surface interference detection. In: IEEE Visualization (2001)
15. Guigue, P., Devillers, O.: Fast and robust triangle-triangle overlap test using orientation predicates. J. Graphics Tools 8(1), 25–32 (2003)
16. Hoppe, H., et al.: Piecewise smooth surface reconstruction. J. Computer Graphics, 295–302 (1994)
17. Huang, Z., Wang, G.: Distance between a Catmull-Clark subdivision surface and its limit surface. In: Proc. ACM Symp. Solid and Physical Modeling, pp. 233–240 (2007)

18. Jiang, D., Stewart, N.F.: Robustness of Boolean operations on subdivision-surface models. In: Dagstuhl seminar proceedings, Dagstuhl Research Online Publication Server, DROPS (2008), http://drops.dagstuhl.de/opus/volltexte/2008/1443

19. Jiang, D., Stewart, N.F.: Floating-point arithmetic for computational-geometry problems with uncertain data. In: IJCGA (2008) (to appear)

20. Kim, M., Peters, J.: Fast and stable evaluation of box-splines via the Bézier form. Technical Report, University of Florida, REP-2007-422 (2007)

21. Kobbelt, L.: Tight bounding volumes for subdivision surfaces. In: Werner, B. (ed.) Pacific Graphics, pp. 17–26 (1998)

22. Lai, S., Cheng, F.: Robust and error controllable Boolean operations on free-form solids represented by Catmull-Clark subdivision surfaces. Computer Aided Design and Applications 4(1-4), 487–496 (2007)

23. Linensen, L.: Netbased Modelling. In: Proc. SCCG, pp. 259–266 (2000)

24. Loop, C.T.: Smooth subdivision surfaces based on triangles. M.Sc thesis, Department of Mathematics, University of Utah (August 1987)

25. Ma, W., et al.: A direct approach for subdivision surface fitting from a dense triangle mesh. Computer-Aided Design 36(6), 525–536 (2004)

26. Peters, J., Reif, U.: Structure of Subdivision Surfaces (2007) (manuscript)

27. Requicha, A.A.G.: Representations for rigid solids: theory, methods and systems. Computing Surveys 12(4), 437–464 (1980)

28. Smith, J.M., Dodgson, N.A.: A topologically robust algorithm for Boolean operations on polyhedral shapes using approximate arithmetic. Computer-Aided Design (39), 149–163 (2007)

29. STEP International Standard. Industrial automation systems and integration—Product data representation and exchange—Part 42. ISO 10303-42 (1997)

30. Tilove, R.B.: Set membership classification: a unified approach to geometric intersection problems. IEEE trans. Computers 29(10), 874–883 (1980)

31. Volino, P., Thalmann, N.M.: Efficient self-collision detection on smoothly discretized surface animations using geometrical shape regularity. In: Eurographics (13), C155–C164 (1994)

32. Wu, X., Peters, J.: Interference detection for subdivision surfaces. In: Eurographics (2004)

# Towards the Development of an Interval Arithmetic Environment for Validated Computer-Aided Design and Verification of Systems in Control Engineering

Andreas Rauh[1,*], Johanna Minisini[2], and Eberhard P. Hofer[2]

[1] Chair of Mechatronics
University of Rostock, D-18059 Rostock, Germany
Andreas.Rauh@uni-rostock.de
[2] Institute of Measurement, Control, and Microtechnology
University of Ulm, D-89069 Ulm, Germany
Johanna.Minisini,Eberhard.Hofer@uni-ulm.de

**Abstract.** In this paper, an overview of the potential use of validated techniques for the analysis and design of controllers for linear and nonlinear dynamical systems with uncertainties is given. In addition to robust pole assignment for linear dynamical systems with parameter uncertainties, mathematical system models and computational techniques are considered in which constraints for both state and control variables are taken into account. For that purpose, the use of interval arithmetic routines for calculation of guaranteed enclosures of the solutions of sets of ordinary differential equations and for the calculation of validated sensitivity measures of state variables with respect to parameter variations are discussed. Simulation results as well as further steps towards the development of a general-purpose interval arithmetic framework for the design and verification of systems in control engineering are summarized.

## 1 Introduction

Modern techniques for the design and analysis of control strategies for nonlinear dynamical systems are often based on the simulation of the open-loop as well as the closed-loop behavior of suitable mathematical models described by continuous-time and discrete-time state-space representations. In addition to sets of ordinary differential equations (ODEs) and difference equations, sets of differential algebraic equations (DAEs) are commonly used in control engineering. Since we will focus on computational techniques which are applicable to the design and mathematical verification of controllers for lumped parameter systems, i.e., systems which do not contain elements with distributed parameters, partial differential equations will not be considered in this paper.

The prerequisite for the design and robustness analysis of each control system is the identification of mathematical models which describe the dynamics of the plant to be controlled as well as the available measurement devices with a sufficient accuracy.

---

* This work was performed while A. Rauh was with the Institute or Measurement, Control, and Microtechnology, University of Ulm.

A. Cuyt et al. (Eds.): Numerical Validation, LNCS 5492, pp. 175–188, 2009.

The model identification task comprises the derivation of physically motivated state equations, their parameterization based on measured data, the identification of uncertainties and their sources, as well as simplifications of the mathematical system models to apply specific approaches for controller design.

Since dynamical system models are subject to uncertain parameters and uncertain initial conditions in most practical applications, detailed mathematical specifications of the desired dynamics of the controlled system are necessary. These involve the definition of robustness with respect to uncertainties. For linear system representations, robustness is commonly specified in terms of regions in the complex domain containing all admissible poles of the closed-loop transfer functions ($\Gamma$-stability) or in terms of specifications of worst-case bounds for the frequency response ($\mathscr{B}$-stability) [1,2,3,4].

In addition, interval arithmetic techniques have been developed in recent years which allow to characterize the stability of dynamical systems and to parameterize robust control laws. Especially for linear dynamical systems with parameter uncertainties, robust Hurwitz stability can be proven using the procedure described in [5].

However, these approaches do not allow for inclusion of state constraints in the time-domain which are often available if controllers are designed for safety-critical applications. In general, pole assignment after linearization of the state equations is not sufficient for nonlinear systems since the asymptotic stability of the resulting closed-loop dynamics has to be proven regardless which eigenvalues are chosen.

In Section 2, an interval arithmetic framework for the design of robust controllers for linear systems with parameter uncertainties is introduced. This approach provides a guaranteed solution for $\Gamma$-stability-based robust controller design by calculating both inner and outer enclosures of the admissible parameters of controllers with a predefined structure. Using the time-domain approach summarized in Section 3, constraints for both state and control vectors can be mapped into the parameter space. In contrast to the $\Gamma$-stability approach, it is directly applicable to nonlinear systems. Possible combinations with routines for robust pole assignment and optimal control are highlighted. In Section 4, an extension of the validated initial value problem solver VALENCIA-IVP is introduced to compute differential sensitivities of the trajectories of all state variables with respect to system parameters. This information can be used to identify strategies for the adaptation of controller parameters to eliminate — or at least to reduce — the effects of uncertainties and disturbances on the state variables of controlled systems. This procedure for validated sensitivity analysis is used to analyze a feedforward control strategy for a simplified model of biological wastewater treatment plants in Section 5. Finally, conclusions and an outlook on future research are given in Section 6.

## 2   Robust Pole Assignment Using Interval Techniques

In this paper, the design of closed-loop controllers for dynamical systems described by sets of ODEs

$$\dot{x}(t) = f(x(t), p(t), u(t)) \quad \text{with} \quad x \in \mathbb{R}^{n_x}, \ p \in \mathbb{R}^{n_p}, \ u \in \mathbb{R}^{n_u} \tag{1}$$

is discussed. First, robust pole assignment for linear dynamical systems

$$\dot{x}(t) = A(p) \cdot x(t) + B(p) \cdot u(t) \tag{2}$$

will be addressed, where the control laws under consideration are given by

$$u(t) = -k \cdot x(t) \quad \text{with} \quad k \in \mathbb{R}^{n_u \times n_x} . \tag{3}$$

It is well known that for linear, fully state-controllable systems with exactly known parameters $p$, suitable feedback gain matrices $k$ can be determined such that the closed-loop system has any desired eigenvalues. For single-input-single-output systems, a closed-form expression for pole assignment has been derived by Ackermann [1]. However, for systems with multiple control inputs, this problem is underdetermined such that additional assumptions are necessary to find a unique parameterization of the control law (3). These additional assumptions are generally related to certain robustness or optimality criteria as well as decoupling properties.

For linear systems with bounded uncertainties of the parameters $p$, pole assignment can be generalized to the assignment of domains of admissible eigenvalues. In control engineering, such specifications are usually referred to as $\Gamma$-stability domains. Let the characteristic polynomial of the closed-loop control system be defined by

$$a(s,p,k) := \det(s \cdot I - A_R(p,k)) \quad \text{with} \quad A_R(p,k) := A(p) - B(p) \cdot k . \tag{4}$$

The roots of the family of polynomials

$$A(s,p,k) := \{ a(s,p,k) \mid p \in [p], \ k \in [K] \} \tag{5}$$

with

$$[K] := \{ k_{ij} \mid k_{ij} \in [\underline{k}_{ij} \, ; \, \overline{k}_{ij}], \ i = 1, \ldots, n_u, \ j = 1, \ldots, n_x \} \tag{6}$$

are denoted by

$$\text{Roots}[A(s,p,k)] := \{ v \in \mathbb{C} \mid a(v,p,k) = 0, \ a(s,p,k) \in A(s,p,k) \} . \tag{7}$$

A linear dynamical system is $\Gamma$-stable if all roots of its characteristic polynomial have strictly negative real parts and if they are completely included in a region $\Gamma \subset \mathbb{C}^-$ for all possible parameters $p \in [p]$ and at least one $k$, i.e., if $\text{Roots}[A(s,p,k)] \subseteq \Gamma \subset \mathbb{C}^-$ holds. Based on this definition, Ackermann and Kaesbauer developed an approach to determine the set of all controller parameters $k$ which are consistent with a prescribed region $\Gamma$, see e.g. [1]. This approach is based on mapping so-called *real root boundaries*, *complex root boundaries*, and *infinite root boundaries* into the parameter space, where all coefficients $a_i$, $i = 0, 1, \ldots, n_x$, of the characteristic polynomial $a(s,p,k)$ are real, non-negative, and continuously depending upon $p$ and $k$. Since this approach, as it is implemented in the MATLAB toolbox PARADISE [2], is mostly a graphical procedure which makes use of the boundary crossing theorem of Frazer and Duncan [6], due to which the roots of $a(s,p,k)$ depend continuously on continuous variations of $p$ and $k$, it is limited to a small number of controller parameters. For higher-dimensional problems, gridding of the parameter space is usually unavoidable.

To avoid this shortcoming and to make routines for robust pole assignment available for systems with coefficients $a_i$ which do not depend continuously upon the parameters $p$, an interval arithmetic routine has been developed to exclude intervals $[k] \subset [K]$ for the controller gains from an a-priori given enclosure $[K]$ if at least one eigenvalue is certainly not included in $\Gamma$ for at least one $p \in [p]$ and for every possible $k \in [k]$.

In Fig. 1, the interval algorithm for pole assignment which has been implemented in MATLAB using the interval arithmetic toolbox INTLAB [7,8] is summarized. In this algorithm, the roots of $a(s,p,k)$ are enclosed by the interval boxes $[\lambda_{R,i}(k)]$, $i = 1, \ldots, n_x$.

Its basic components are the calculation of guaranteed a-priori bounds of all eigenvalues of the closed-loop control systems using Gershgorin discs [9, 10]. These a-priori bounds for the eigenvalues are refined using a splitting procedure in which the INT-LAB routine verifyeig is used. Additionally, the characteristic polynomial of the corresponding interval matrix $[A_R(p,[k])]$ is evaluated with the help of a validated LU-decomposition to check whether all eigenvalues $\lambda_{R,i}$, $i = 1, \ldots, n_x$, are included in admissible regions $[\lambda_{R,i}] \subseteq \Gamma$. The LU-decomposition is applied if the routine verifyeig does not give any solution or if no decision about the admissibility of a controller parameterization is possible since the resulting eigenvalue enclosure is overlapping with the region $\Gamma$ and, thus, is neither completely inside or completely outside of $\Gamma$. To eliminate inadmissible regions of controller gains at the earliest possible stage, the tests for admissibility are not only performed for the complete parameter interval $[p]$. Instead, the set of possible solutions is first restricted by a parameterization of the control law (3) for the nominal system parameter $p_{nom}$ which is followed by the exclusion of controller gains which are inadmissible for further specific parameter values such as $\underline{p}$ and $\overline{p}$, resp.

For a subdivision of $[K]$ into several subintervals $[k] \subset [K]$ obtained by application of the criteria from Fig. 1, the inner interval enclosure of the set of admissible controller gains is given by

$$\mathscr{K}_{\Gamma,i} := \left\{ [k] \,\middle|\, [\lambda_{R,i}(k)] \subseteq \Gamma, \ \forall \, p \in [p], \ \forall \, k \in [k] \subset [K], i = 1, \ldots, n_x \right\} . \tag{8}$$

Its outer enclosure, for which $\mathscr{K}_{\Gamma,i} \subseteq \mathscr{K}_{\Gamma,o}$ holds, results from eigenvalues $[\lambda_{R,i}(k)]$ which are not completely outside of $\Gamma$ according to

$$\mathscr{K}_{\Gamma,o} := \left\{ [k] \,\middle|\, [\lambda_{R,i}(k)] \cap \Gamma \neq \emptyset, \ \forall \, p \in [p], \ \forall \, k \in [k] \subset [K], i = 1, \ldots, n_x \right\} . \tag{9}$$

*Example 1.* In the following, the double integrating plant

$$\dot{x}(t) = \begin{bmatrix} 0 & \alpha \\ 0 & 0 \end{bmatrix} x(t) + \begin{bmatrix} 0 \\ 1 \end{bmatrix} u(t) \quad \text{with} \quad \alpha \in [\alpha] := [0.9 \,;\, 1.1] \tag{10}$$

and $u := -k \cdot x = \begin{bmatrix} k_1 & k_2 \end{bmatrix} \cdot x, k \in [K] = \big[ [-10 \,;\, 10] \, [-10 \,;\, 10] \big]$ is considered as a simple application scenario to visualize the interval routine for robust pole assignment. Using this procedure, guaranteed interval enclosures of the regions of admissible controller gains have been determined for both the nominal system parameter $\alpha_{nom} = 1.0$ and the uncertain parameter $[\alpha]$. In Fig. 2, the inner and outer enclosures of the admissible controller gains defined in (8) and (9) are depicted together with the resulting eigenvalues for gain factors from the enclosures $\mathscr{K}_{\Gamma,i}$. The domain $\Gamma$ is defined as shown in the Figs. 2(c) and 2(d) to guarantee an absolute stability margin, a minimum damping, and a limitation of bandwidth. For illustration purposes, the eigenvalues have only been computed for the vertices of the interval boxes $[k]$ of the corresponding inner enclosures.

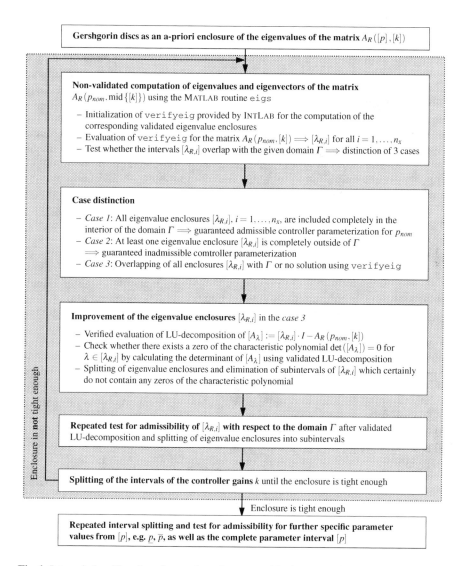

**Fig. 1.** Interval algorithm for robust pole assignment with given eigenvalue domains $\Gamma \subset \mathbb{C}^-$

As shown in this example, the controller parameterization is usually not unique, since arbitrary gain factors from the computed inner interval enclosures $\mathscr{K}_{\Gamma,i}$ are consistent with the robustness specifications. At the end of the following section, possible criteria are discussed which can be applied to further restrict the set of admissible parameterizations. Furthermore, it should be pointed out that the interval arithmetic routine presented in this section does not make any assumptions whether the eigenvalue domain $\Gamma$ consists of a single region or of the union of several disconnected domains.

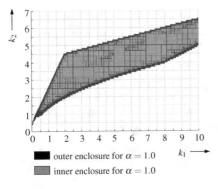

**(a)** Controller gains for $\alpha = \alpha_{nom}$.

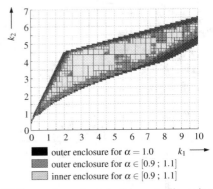

**(b)** Comparison of admissible controller gains for $\alpha = \alpha_{nom}$ and $\alpha \in [\alpha]$.

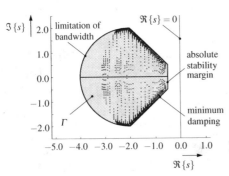

**(c)** Eigenvalues corresponding to the inner enclosure in Fig. 2(a), $\alpha = \alpha_{nom}$.

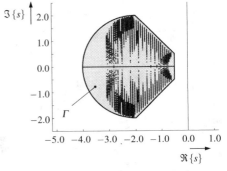

**(d)** Eigenvalues corresponding to the inner enclosure in Fig. 2(b), $\alpha \in [\alpha]$.

**Fig. 2.** Enclosures of the controller gains $k_1$ and $k_2$ which are consistent with the $\Gamma$-stability domain and visualization of the corresponding eigenvalues for $\alpha_{nom} = 1.0$ and $[\alpha] = [0.9 ; 1.1]$ with a limited number of subdivisions of the a-priori enclosure $[K]$

## 3    Time-Domain Approach for Robust Controller Design

In contrast to robust pole assignment, the time-domain approach presented in the following is also applicable to nonlinear systems without the necessity to linearize the state equations for parameterization of controllers with a given structure. As for the interval arithmetic approach for robust pole assignment, a-priori bounds $[K]$ for the feedback gain matrix in (3) are assumed to be given. In addition to linear controllers, any other parameterized control law can be considered. The time-domain approach relies on calculating guaranteed enclosures of the trajectories of the states of the control system

$$\dot{x}(t) = f\Big(x(t), p(t), u(x(t), w(t), k)\Big) \quad \text{with} \quad p \in [p], \ w(t) \in [w(t)], \ k \in [k] \quad (11)$$

over a finite time horizon $t \in [t_0 ; t_f]$. In (11), $w(t)$ denotes a given reference signal. To compute guaranteed enclosures of the state variables $x(t)$ with given initial conditions $x(t_0)$ over the time interval $[t_0 ; t_f]$, validated ODE solvers such as COSY VI, VALENCIA-IVP, VNODE, or VSPODE are applicable [11]. Starting from the complete a-priori enclosure $[K]$, the intervals for the controller gains are successively split into subintervals $[k]$. All subintervals which certainly lead to a violation of prescribed time-domain constraints $\mathscr{X}(t)$ according to

$$[x(t)] \cap \mathscr{X}(t) = \emptyset \quad \text{for at least one} \quad t \in [t_0 ; t_f] \tag{12}$$

are excluded. For all other subintervals $[k]$ two cases have to be distinguished. First, intervals $[k]$ belong to the desired inner enclosure of admissible controller gains if

$$\mathscr{K}_{T,i} := \left\{ [k] \,\middle|\, [x(t)] \subseteq \mathscr{X}(t) \text{ for all } t \in [t_0 ; t_f] \right\} \tag{13}$$

holds. Second, the corresponding outer interval enclosure is defined by

$$\mathscr{K}_{T,o} := \left\{ [k] \,\middle|\, [x(t)] \cap \mathscr{X}(t) \neq \emptyset \text{ for all } t \in [t_0 ; t_f] \right\} . \tag{14}$$

All subintervals which neither belong to the list of inadmissible intervals nor to the inner enclosure $\mathscr{K}_{T,i}$ have to be split further to assign them to one of these two lists.

Since this approach relies on pure time-domain specifications of robustness, it is applicable to arbitrary nonlinear systems which can be handled by the above-mentioned validated ODE solvers. Especially for control laws for linear systems, which can also be parameterized efficiently using the $\Gamma$-stability approach presented in Section 2 (resp. the $\mathscr{B}$-stability approach [3,4] which is not considered in this paper), a combination of these different types of restrictions for the gain factors is straightforward by intersecting the resulting interval enclosures $\mathscr{K}_\Gamma$ and $\mathscr{K}_T$.

*Example 2.* As a simple demonstration example, again the double integrating plant (10) with a linear state controller $u(x(t), w(t), k) = [k_1 \ k_2] \cdot (w(t) - x(t))$ and the reference signal $w(t) = [1 \ 0]^T = const$ is considered. The initial conditions are $x(t_0 = 0) = [0 \ 0]^T$. In Fig. 3(a), those subintervals from the a-priori bounds $[K_1] := [0 ; 5]$, $[K_2] := [0 ; 5]$ of the controller gains are depicted that are consistent with the time-domain constraints

$$\mathscr{X}(t) := \begin{cases} -1.0 \cdot 10^{-5} \leq x_1(t) \leq 1.2 \text{ for } 0 \leq t < 0.75 \\ 0.5 \leq x_1(t) \leq 1.2 \text{ for } 0.75 \leq t < 1.0 \\ 0.8 \leq x_1(t) \leq 1.2 \text{ for } t \geq 1.0 \\ x_2 = \text{unbounded for } t \geq 0 . \end{cases} \tag{15}$$

In this example, the underlying validated evaluation of the state equations has been performed using VALENCIA-IVP for both $\alpha = \alpha_{nom} = 1.0$ and $\alpha \in [\alpha] := [0.9 ; 1.1]$. The time-domain constraints $\mathscr{X}(t)$ are guaranteed to be fulfilled for arbitrary controller gains $k$ from the inner interval enclosure $\mathscr{K}_{T,i}$. In Fig. 3(b), the time response for $x_1(t)$ is shown for $k = k^* = [2.7340 \ 0.3125] \in \mathscr{K}_{T,i}$ for selected $\alpha \in [\alpha]$.

*Example 3.* Instead of choosing an arbitrary gain vector $k$ which is consistent with the constraints $\mathscr{X}(t)$, systematic approaches such as optimality criteria can be used. In the previous example, validated evaluation of the integral performance index

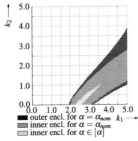
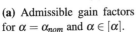

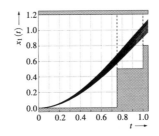
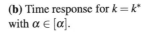

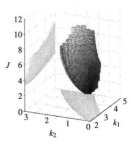

**(a)** Admissible gain factors for $\alpha = \alpha_{nom}$ and $\alpha \in [\alpha]$.

**(b)** Time response for $k = k^*$ with $\alpha \in [\alpha]$.

**(c)** Evaluation of the performance index $J$ for $\alpha = \alpha_{nom}$.

**Fig. 3.** Robust controller parameterization using time-domain constraints for $[t_0 \; ; \; t_f] := [0 \; ; \; 1]$

$$J = \int_{t_0}^{t_f} \left( \underbrace{(x_1(t) - 1)^2 + x_2(t)^2}_{=: \, f_{0,A}} + \underbrace{(k_1 \cdot (1 - x_1(t)) - k_2 \cdot x_2(t))^2}_{=: \, f_{0,B}} \right) dt \qquad (16)$$

for all $k \in \mathcal{K}_{T,i}$ using VALENCIA-IVP leads to the interval enclosures $[J]$ depicted in Fig. 3(c). The cost function (16), which has to be minimized by choosing a combination of admissible controller parameters $k_1$ and $k_2$, quantifies the deviation of the system states $x(t)$ from the desired final state $x_1 = 1$ and $x_2 = 0$ in the term $f_{0,A}$ as well as the required effort for the control action over the time horizon $[t_0 \; ; \; t_f]$ using the term $f_{0,B}$.

A general framework for interval arithmetic structure and parameter optimization for dynamical systems with both nominal and uncertain parameters has been presented in detail from an algorithmic and application-oriented point of view by the authors in [12, 13]. Using the definition of optimality for uncertain systems which has been introduced therein, a gain factor is *optimal* if it leads to the *smallest upper bound* of the performance index for all possible $p \in [p]$.

In Fig. 4, an algorithm for the calculation of both optimal control strategies in structure optimization problems as well as parameter optimization problems is summarized. In structure optimization, the optimal control sequence is approximated by a sequence of $m$ piecewise constant values for $u(t)$. In the case of parameter optimization, a control law $u(x)$ with free parameters $k$ is given. This control law is parameterized using admissible values for $k$ such that the performance index $J$ is minimized. Since the optimization algorithm relies on the validated integration of the set of state equations for different controller parameterizations, it can easily be parallelized. For that purpose, different independent tasks are defined. In the case of structure optimization, usually $m$ independent optimization problems are solved in the separate tasks which correspond to control strategies with different numbers $N_m$ of switchings between piecewise constant control inputs $u(t)$, where their number is denoted by $N_1, \ldots, N_m$. In the case of parameter optimization, which is discussed in this Section, the number of piecewise constant controls is $N_1 = \ldots = N_m = 1$ in all tasks. That means, the controller parameters $k$ to be determined are formally treated as time-invariant inputs which are calculated with

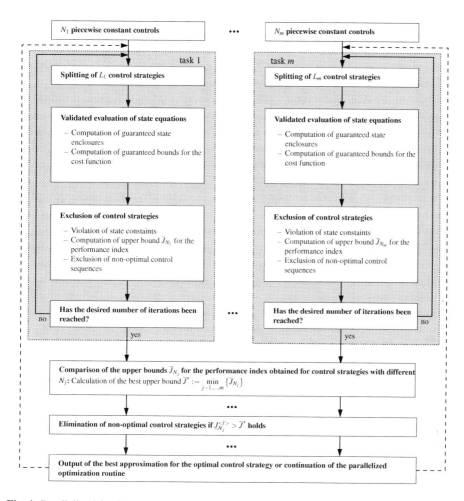

**Fig. 4.** Parallelized implementation of the interval arithmetic procedure for the calculation of optimal control strategies

exactly the same routine that is also used for structure optimization. However, the assignment of the subintervals $[k]$ to the different tasks, which is related to the number of switchings of the control input in the structure optimization problem, now has to be performed in a slightly different way. All candidates for controller parameterizations for which inadmissibility (due to violation of state constraints) or non-optimality (due to the existence of a control sequence with a smaller upper bound $\bar{J}^*$ of the performance index for all $p \in [p]$) has not yet been shown are distributed equally to the available processors using $m$ tasks.

In addition to optimality criteria, also sensitivity measures for the system states $x(t)$ and as well as the performance index $J$ with respect to the uncertain parameters can be taken into account to find a specific robust controller parameterization in a systematic way. In Section 4, an interval-based approach for calculation of guaranteed enclosures of such differential sensitivity measures is introduced using an extension of the validated ODE solver VALENCIA-IVP.

## 4   Validated Sensitivity Analysis Using VALENCIA-IVP

In the following, ODEs $\dot{x}(t) = f(x(t), p)$ are considered which describe both the open-loop and closed-loop system behavior, where the vector $p$ consists of all time-invariant system parameters as well as all controller parameters. The differential sensitivities of the solution $x(t)$ with respect to the parameters $p$ are defined by the state equations

$$\dot{s}_i(t) = \frac{\partial f(x(t), p)}{\partial x} \cdot s_i(t) + \frac{\partial f(x(t), p)}{\partial p_i} \quad \text{for all} \quad i = 1, \ldots, n_p \ . \tag{17}$$

The new state vectors $s_i(t)$ in (17) are given by

$$s_i(t) := \frac{\partial x(t)}{\partial p_i} \in \mathbb{R}^{n_x} \quad \text{with} \quad s_i(t_0) = \frac{\partial x(t_0, p)}{\partial p_i} \ . \tag{18}$$

For initial states $x(t_0)$ which are independent of $p$ the equality $s_i(t_0) = 0$ holds for the corresponding initial conditions of $s_i$. In VALENCIA-IVP, the ODEs (17) do not need to be derived symbolically, since all required partial derivatives with respect to the state variables $x$ and the system parameters $p$ are computed by algorithmic differentiation using FADBAD++ [14, 15, 16].

As for the case of solving an initial value problem for the ODEs $\dot{x}(t) = f(x(t), p)$, guaranteed state enclosures

$$[x(t)] := x_{app}(t) + [R_x(t)] \tag{19}$$

are determined in a first stage. In (19), $x_{app}(t)$ denotes an approximate solution for the initial value problem which is determined numerically using a non-validated ODE solver. The guaranteed error bounds $[R_x(t)]$ are calculated by an iterative procedure which can be derived using Banachs fixed-point theorem [17, 18]. In a second sta ge, additional enclosures

$$[s_i(t)] := s_{i,app}(t) + [R_{s,i}(t)] \quad \text{with} \quad s_{i,app}(t) \in \mathbb{R}^{n_x} \quad \text{and} \quad i = 1, \ldots, n_p \tag{20}$$

are determined for the sensitivities. Here, the approximate solutions $s_{i,app}(t)$ are again determined numerically with the help of a non-validated ODE solver. In principle, the differential equations for $\dot{x}(t)$ and $\dot{s}_i(t)$ could be combined to a single set of ODEs which does not have to be solved in a two-stage procedure as described above. However, for a computationally efficient implementation, the ODEs (17) are only evaluated after convergence of the iteration providing the enclosure $[x(t)]$ since the interval enclosures $[s_i(t)]$ of the sensitivities depend upon the enclosure $[x(t)]$ of all reachable states. Using this procedure, for both exactly known and uncertain values of the parameters $p$ and the initial states $x(t_0)$, the intervals $[s_i(t)]$ are determined such that the partial derivatives of all reachable states with respect to all possible $p_i$ are included. For time-varying parameters $p(t)$, the sensitivities $s_i(t)$ are computed w.r.t. time-invariant variables $\varepsilon_i \approx 0$

after substituting $p(t) + \varepsilon$ with $\varepsilon \in \mathbb{R}^{n_p}$ for $p(t)$. The variables $\varepsilon_i$ are either replaced by the value 0 or by time-invariant interval bounds containing the value 0.

The explicit calculation of the differential sensitivities $s_i(t)$ using a validated ODE solver without symbolic derivation of the corresponding ODEs (17) provides useful information for the design of controllers. For example, guaranteed bounds of the maximum possible sensitivities of the state variables can be obtained for uncertain system parameters $p \in [p]$ using a single evaluation of the state equations even in the case of a non-monotonic relation between the system parameters $p$ and the state variables $x$.

## 5   Sensitivity Analysis of a Wastewater Treatment Process

The procedure for validated sensitivity analysis is demonstrated for the subsystem model of biological wastewater treatment depicted in Fig 5 which is a simplification of the Activated Sludge Model No. 1 of the International Water Association [19]. In contrast to the complete system model, the reduction of nitrogen fractions from the wastewater is neglected in the following. The concentration $S$ of biodegradable organic substrate is reduced by heterotrophic bacteria with the concentration $X$ under external oxygen supply with the flow rate $u_{O2}$. The concentration of dissolved oxygen in the aeration tank is denoted by $S_O$. The bacteria concentration in the settler, which is modeled as a perfect separator of sludge and purified water, is denoted by $X_{Set}$. A portion of the activated sludge is fed back into the aeration tank with the flow rate $Q_{RS}$ of return sludge. The excess sludge $Q_{EX}$ is removed from the process.

According to [20, 18], this process is described by the nonlinear ODEs

$$\dot{S} = \frac{Q_W}{V_A}(S_W - S) - \hat{\mu}_H \frac{S}{S + K_S} \frac{S_O}{S_O + K_{OS}} \frac{1}{Y} X$$

$$\dot{X} = -\frac{Q_W}{V_A}X + \frac{Q_{RS}}{V_A}(X_{Set} - X) + \left(\hat{\mu}_H \frac{S}{S + K_S} \frac{S_O}{S_O + K_{OS}} - b\right)X$$

$$\dot{S}_O = \frac{Q_W}{V_A}(S_{OW} - S_O) - \hat{\mu}_H \frac{S}{S + K_S} \frac{S_O}{S_O + K_{OS}} \frac{1 - Y}{Y} X + \frac{\rho_{O2}}{V_A}\left(1 - \frac{S_O}{S_{O,sat}}\right)u_{O2} \tag{21}$$

$$\dot{X}_{Set} = \frac{Q_W + Q_{RS}}{V_{Set}}X - \frac{Q_{EX} + Q_{RS}}{V_{Set}}X_{Set} \ .$$

Assuming a constant oxygen concentration $S_O = \hat{S}_O = const$, i.e., $\dot{S}_O = 0$, the corresponding feedforward control for the oxygen input rate $u_{O2}$ is defined by

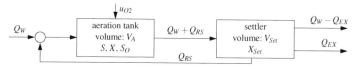

**Fig. 5.** Block diagram of a simplified biological wastewater treatment process

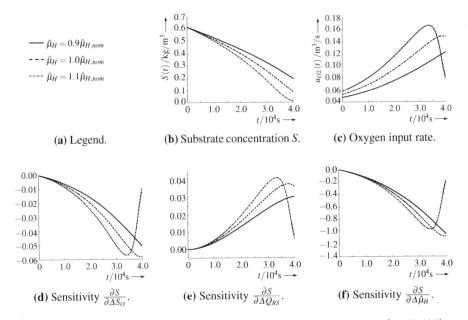

(a) Legend.    (b) Substrate concentration $S$.    (c) Oxygen input rate.

(d) Sensitivity $\frac{\partial S}{\partial \Delta S_O}$.    (e) Sensitivity $\frac{\partial S}{\partial \Delta Q_{RS}}$.    (f) Sensitivity $\frac{\partial S}{\partial \Delta \hat{\mu}_H}$.

**Fig. 6.** Sensitivity analysis of a biological wastewater treatment process for $t \in [0 \, ; \, 40,000]$ s

$$u_{O2} = \frac{V_A}{\rho_{O2}} \frac{S_{O,sat}}{S_{O,sat} - \hat{S}_O} \left( \hat{\mu}_H \frac{S}{S + K_S} \frac{\hat{S}_O}{\hat{S}_O + K_{OS}} \frac{1 - Y}{Y} X - \frac{Q_W}{V_A} \left( S_{OW} - \hat{S}_O \right) \right) \ . \quad (22)$$

The design and parameterization of controllers which compensate variations of states caused by parameter uncertainties relies on the adaptation of the available control variables. These are the oxygen input rate $u_{O2}$, related to the desired oxygen concentration $\hat{S}_O$ via (22), and the flow rate $Q_{RS}$ of return sludge. The differential sensitivities of the state variables $S, X$, and $X_{Set}$ with respect to variations $\Delta S_O$ and $\Delta Q_{RS}$ of the control variables and with respect to variations $\Delta \hat{\mu}_H$ with

$$\begin{aligned} S_O &:= \hat{S}_O \cdot (1 + \Delta S_O) & Q_{RS} &:= Q_{RS,nom} \cdot (1 + \Delta Q_{RS}) \\ \hat{\mu}_H &:= \hat{\mu}_{H,nom} \cdot (1 + \Delta \hat{\mu}_H) & Q_{EX} &:= Q_{EX,nom} - Q_{RS,nom} \cdot \Delta Q_{RS} \end{aligned} \quad (23)$$

provide the required information. For $\hat{S}_O = 3.5 \cdot 10^{-3} \frac{\text{kg}}{\text{m}^3}$, these sensitivities have been computed using VALENCIA-IVP for three different growth rates of substrate consuming bacteria. The results of these simulations are shown in Fig. 6, where each curve represents the guaranteed enclosure for one of the considered values of $\hat{\mu}_H$. Note that the diameters of the resulting enclosures are below the resolution of these graphs.

According to Fig. 6, a reduced rate of the reduction of the substrate concentration $S$ caused by smaller growth rates $\hat{\mu}_H$ of the bacteria (leading also to a smaller concentration $X$) can be compensated by increasing $\hat{S}_O$ and/ or reducing $Q_{RS}$ to meet legal performance requirements for wastewater treatment plants specified, e.g., in [21].

# 6   Conclusions and Outlook on Future Research

In this paper, basic interval routines for the design and analysis of controllers have been presented which are the prerequisite for nonlinear controller design. For nonlinear systems, often properties such as differential flatness [22] or exact input-output as well as input-to-state linearizability [23, 24] are exploited. To generalize design procedures and to account for uncertainties and modeling errors in these cases, further interval techniques for simulation and optimization of both ODE and DAE systems will be developed in future work. VALENCIA-IVP is currently being extended to DAE systems to determine open-loop control laws matching predefined output signals in spite of uncertainties.

This feature is of great practical importance since the previously mentioned calculation of control laws exploiting differential flatness is so far only being performed analytically for nominal system models. On the one hand, it is often not a trivial task to determine flat outputs of dynamical systems analytically. On the other hand, current design procedures often do not take into account uncertainties at early stages of controller design. These uncertainties are inherent in any real-world system since they are, e.g., caused by tolerances resulting from specific production processes or implementations as well as by model simplifications. A general-purpose interval arithmetic design tool for systems in control engineering will provide engineers with useful information about the realizability of control tasks if closed-form analytical solutions cannot be found. Additionally, it will help to incorporate uncertainties directly in the system design and to avoid tedious parameter tuning that becomes necessary to meet specifications for functionality and reliability if controllers are designed for idealized operating conditions only.

# References

1. Ackermann, J., Blue, P., Bünte, T., Güvenc, L., Kaesbauer, D., Kordt, M., Muhler, M., Odenthal, D.: Robust Control: The Parameter Space Approach, 2nd edn. Springer, London (2002)
2. Sienel, W., Bünte, T., Ackermann, J.: PARADISE – PArametric Robust Analysis and Design Interactive Software Environment: A MATLAB-Based Robust Control Toolbox. In: Proc. of the 1996 IEEE Intl. Symposium on Computer-Aided Control System Design, Dearborn, pp. 380–385 (1996)
3. Odenthal, D., Blue, P.: Mapping of Frequency Response Magnitude Specifications into Parameter Space. In: Proc. of the 3rd IFAC Symposium on Robust Control Design, Prague, Czech Republic (2000)
4. Bünte, T.: Mapping of Nyquist/ Popov Theta-Stability Margins into Parameter Space. In: Proc. of the 3rd IFAC Symposium on Robust Control Design, Prague, Czech Republic (2000)
5. Walter, É., Jaulin, L.: Guaranteed Characterization of Stability Domains Via Set Inversion. IEEE Transactions on Automatic Control 39(4), 886–889 (1994)
6. Frazer, R., Duncan, W.: On the Criteria for the Stability of Small Motions. Proc. of the Royal Society A 124, 642–654 (1929)
7. Rump, S.M.: INTLAB — INTerval LABoratory. In: Csendes, T. (ed.) Developments in Reliable Computing, pp. 77–104. Kluwer Academic Publishers, Dordrecht (1999)
8. Rump, S.M.: INTLAB, Version 5.4 (2007),
http://www.ti3.tu-harburg.de/~rump/intlab/

9. Golub, G.H., van Loan, C.F.: Matrix Computations, 3rd edn. Johns Hopkins University Press, Baltimore (1996)
10. Weinmann, A.: Uncertain Models and Robust Control. Springer, Wien (1991)
11. Nedialkov, N.S.: Interval Tools for ODEs and DAEs. In: CD-Proc. of the 12th GAMM-IMACS International Symposium on Scientific Computing, Computer Arithmetic, and Validated Numerics SCAN 2006, Duisburg, Germany. IEEE Computer Society, Los Alamitos (2007)
12. Rauh, A., Hofer, E.P.: Interval Methods for Optimal Control. In: Buttazzo, G., Frediani, A. (eds.) Proc. of the 47th Workshop on Variational Analysis and Aerospace Engineering, Erice, Italy. Springer, Heidelberg (2007) (in print)
13. Rauh, A., Minisini, J., Hofer, E.P.: Interval Techniques for Design of Optimal and Robust Control Strategies. In: CD-Proc. of the 12th GAMM-IMACS International Symposium on Scientific Computing, Computer Arithmetic, and Validated Numerics SCAN 2006, Duisburg, Germany. IEEE Computer Society, Los Alamitos (2007)
14. Bendsten, C., Stauning, O.: FADBAD++, Version 2.1 (2007),
    http://www.fadbad.com
15. Bendsten, C., Stauning, O.: FADBAD, a Flexible C++ Package for Automatic Differentiation Using the Forward and Backward Methods. Technical Report 1996-x5-94, Technical University of Denmark, Lyngby (1996)
16. Bendsten, C., Stauning, O.: TADIFF, a Flexible C++ Package for Automatic Differentiation Using Taylor Series. Technical Report 1997-x5-94, Technical University of Denmark, Lyngby (1997)
17. Auer, E., Rauh, A., Hofer, E.P., Luther, W.: Validated Modeling of Mechanical Systems with SMARTMOBILE: Improvement of Performance by VALENCIA-IVP. In: Hertling, P., Hoffmann, C.M., Luther, W., Revol, N. (eds.) Real Number Algorithms. LNCS, vol. 5045, pp. 1–27. Springer, Heidelberg (2008)
18. Rauh, A., Auer, E., Hofer, E.P.: VALENCIA-IVP: A Comparison with Other Initial Value Problem Solvers. In: CD-Proc. of the 12th GAMM-IMACS International Symposium on Scientific Computing, Computer Arithmetic, and Validated Numerics SCAN 2006, Duisburg, Germany. IEEE Computer Society, Los Alamitos (2007)
19. Henze, M., Harremoës, P., Arvin, E., la Cour Jansen, J.: Wastewater Treatment, 3rd edn. Springer, Berlin (2002)
20. Rauh, A., Kletting, M., Aschemann, H., Hofer, E.P.: Reduction of Overestimation in Interval Arithmetic Simulation of Biological Wastewater Treatment Processes. Journal of Computational and Applied Mathematics 199(2), 207–212 (2007)
21. Office for Official Publications of the European Communities: Council Directive of 21 May 1991 Concerning Urban Waste Water Treatment (91/271/EEC) (2003),
    http://ec.europa.eu/environment/water/water-urbanwaste/directiv.html
22. Fliess, M., Lévine, J., Martin, P., Rouchon, P.: Flatness and Defect of Nonlinear Systems: Introductory Theory and Examples. International Journal of Control 61, 1327–1361 (1995)
23. Marquez, H.J.: Nonlinear Control Systems. John Wiley & Sons, Inc., New Jersey (2003)
24. Khalil, H.K.: Nonlinear Systems, 3rd edn. Prentice-Hall, Upper Saddle River (2002)

# Distributed Bounded-Error
# Parameter and State Estimation
# in Networks of Sensors

Michel Kieffer⋆

LSS - CNRS - SUPELEC - Univ Paris-Sud,
3 rue Joliot-Curie, 91192 Gif-sur-Yvette, France
kieffer@lss.supelec.fr
http://michel.kieffer.lss.supelec.fr

**Abstract.** This paper presents distributed bounded-error parameter
and state estimation algorithms suited to measurement processing by
a network of sensors. Contrary to centralized estimation, where all data
are collected to a central processing unit, here, each data is processed locally by the sensor, the results are broadcasted to the network and taken
into account by the other sensors. A first analysis of the conditions under which distributed and centralized estimation provide the same results
has been presented. An application to the tracking of a moving source
using a network of sensors measuring the strength of the signal emitted
by the source is considered.

## 1 Introduction

A wireless sensor network (WSN) consists of spatially distributed autonomous
devices equipped with sensors and interconnected via wireless links. Sensors may
be designed for measuring pressure, temperature, sound, vibration, motion...
Initially WSN were developed for military applications (battlefield surveillance).
Now, many civilian applications (environment monitoring, home automation,
traffic control) may take advantage of WSN, see, *e.g.*, [1,2].

Applications suggest many research topics, such as the design of protocols for
communication between sensors, localization problems, data compression and
aggregation, security issues... All these problems are made more complicated by
the constraints imposed on each node of the WSN, which usually has limited
computing capabilities, communication capacity, and, to increase its autonomy,
has strong power consumption constraints.

The application considered here is WSN for source tracking, which may be
important when considering mobile phone localization and tracking, computer
localization in an ad-hoc network, co-localisation in a team of robots, speaker
localization... Figure 1 illustrates a typical localization problem: a source represented by a circle moves in a field of sensors, each of which is represented by a
cross.

⋆ This work has been partly supported by the NoE NEWCOM++.

A. Cuyt et al. (Eds.): Numerical Validation, LNCS 5492, pp. 189–202, 2009.
© Springer-Verlag Berlin Heidelberg 2009

**Fig. 1.** Source (o) and sensors (x )

The localization technique used depends on the type of information available to the sensor nodes. Time of arrival (TOA), time difference of arrival (TDOA) and angle of arrival (AOA) usually provide the best results [3], however, these quantities are difficult to obtain, as they require a good synchronization between timers (for TOA), exchanges between sensors (for TDOA) or multiple antennas (for AOA). Contrary to TOA, TDOA or AOA data, readings of signal strength (RSS) at a given sensor are easily obtained, as they only require low-cost sensors or are already available, as in IEEE 802.11 wireless networks, where these data are provided by the MAC layer [4].

This paper focuses on source localization and tracking from RSS data. Centralized approaches (see Figure 2, left) have been proposed to solve this problem for acoustic sources [5] and for sources emitting electromagnetic waves, see, *e.g.*, [6,7,8]. In the first case, some knowledge of the decay rate of the RSS (*path loss exponent*) is needed for efficient nonlinear least squares estimation. In the second case, an off-line training phase is required to allow maximum *a posteriori* localization. In both cases, a good initial guess of the location of the source facilitates convergence to the global minimum of the cost function. Distributed approaches (see Figure 2, right) have also been employed, *e.g.*, in [9], where a distributed version of a nonlinear least squares solver has been presented. When badly initialized, it suffers from the same convergence problems as the centralized approach, as illustrated in [10], which advocates projection on convex sets. Nevertheless, the latter requires an accurate knowledge of the source signal strength and of the path loss exponent.

The localization and tracking problems are considered as distributed discrete-time state estimation problems involving bounded state perturbations and

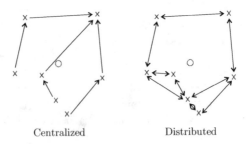

Centralized                    Distributed

**Fig. 2.** Centralized (left) and distributed (right) processing of measurements

measurement errors. This problem is addressed with the help of interval analysis [11,12], which will provide at each node of the network and at each time instant a set estimate guaranteed to contain the true location of a moving source, provided that the hypotheses on the model and measurement noise are satisfied. Section 2 describes an idealized and a practical distributed state estimation algorithm able to deal with bounded-error measurements. Section 3 presents the application of the preceding algorithm to source localization and tracking.

## 2   Distributed State Estimation

Consider a system described by a discrete-time state equation

$$\mathbf{x}_k = \mathbf{f}_k\left(\mathbf{x}_{k-1}, \mathbf{w}_k, \mathbf{u}_k\right), \tag{1}$$

where $\mathbf{x}_k$ is the state vector of the model at time instant $k$ (the sampling period is $T$). The state perturbation vector $\mathbf{w}_k$ accounts for unmodelled parts of the system and is assumed to remain in a known box $[\mathbf{w}]$. The input vector $\mathbf{u}_k$ is also assumed known. At $k = 0$, $\mathbf{x}_0$ is only assumed to belong to some (possibly large) known set $\mathbb{X}_0$.

Assume that at time $k$, each sensor $\ell = 1 \ldots L$ of a WSN has access to a noisy measurement vector $\mathbf{y}_k^\ell$. The measurement process is described by the observation equations

$$\mathbf{y}_k^\ell = \mathbf{g}_k^\ell\left(\mathbf{x}_k, \mathbf{v}_k^\ell\right), \tag{2}$$

where $\mathbf{v}_k^\ell$ is the measurement noise, assumed bounded in some known box $[\mathbf{v}]$. Usual observation equations are

$$\mathbf{g}_k^\ell\left(\mathbf{x}_k, \mathbf{v}_k^\ell\right) = \mathbf{h}_k^\ell\left(\mathbf{x}_k\right) + \mathbf{v}_k^\ell \tag{3}$$

or

$$\mathbf{g}_k^\ell\left(\mathbf{x}_k, v_k^\ell\right) = \mathbf{h}_k^\ell\left(\mathbf{x}_k\right) \cdot v_k^\ell, \tag{4}$$

depending on whether the measurement noise is additive or multiplicative.

### 2.1   Back to Centralized Discrete-Time State Estimation

Centralized state estimation is briefly summarized, since it constitutes the reference which distributed algorithms should reach.

When all measurements at time $k$ are available at a central processing unit, one gets

$$\begin{cases} \mathbf{x}_k = \mathbf{f}_k\left(\mathbf{x}_{k-1}, \mathbf{w}_k, \mathbf{u}_k\right), \\ \mathbf{y}_k = \mathbf{g}_k\left(\mathbf{x}_k, \mathbf{v}_k\right), \end{cases} \tag{5}$$

with $\mathbf{y}_k^{\mathrm{T}} = \left(\left(\mathbf{y}_k^1\right)^{\mathrm{T}}, \ldots, \left(\mathbf{y}_k^L\right)^{\mathrm{T}}\right)$ and $\mathbf{v}_k^{\mathrm{T}} = \left(\left(\mathbf{v}_k^1\right)^{\mathrm{T}}, \ldots, \left(\mathbf{v}_k^L\right)^{\mathrm{T}}\right)$. Determining an estimate for $\mathbf{x}_k$ from the measurement $\mathbf{y}_\ell$, $\ell = 0 \ldots k$ is a classical state estimation problem, the solution of which depends on the linearity of (1) and (2) and on the noise model. For a gaussian noise, with linear state and observation

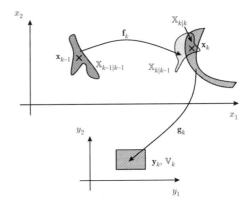

**Fig. 3.** Idealized recursive bounded-error state estimator

equations, the Kalman filter [13] is the natural solution. When the model is non-linear, one may use an extended Kalman filter [14], gridding techniques [15], or particle filters [16]. In a bounded-error context, with a linear model, the set of state vectors consistent with the model and noise on the measurements may be evaluated exactly using polytopes [17], or outer-approximated using ellipsoids [18]. With a nonlinear model, again, an outer-approximation of the state is possible using subpavings, *i.e.*, unions of non-overlapping boxes [19].

Summarizing the information available at time $k$, one gets

$$\mathcal{I}_k = \left\{ \mathbb{X}_0, \{[\mathbf{w}_j]\}_{j=1}^k, \{[\mathbf{v}_j]\}_{j=1}^k, \{[\mathbf{y}_j]\}_{j=1}^k \right\}. \tag{6}$$

Centralized bounded-error state estimation at time $k$ aims at characterizing the set $\mathbb{X}_{k|k}$ of all values of $\mathbf{x}_k$ that are consistent with (1), (2), and $\mathcal{I}_k$. One may propose an idealized algorithm [19], alternating, as the Kalman filter a prediction step involving (1)

$$\mathbb{X}_{k|k-1} = \left\{ \mathbf{f}_k\left(\mathbf{x}, \mathbf{w}, \mathbf{u}_k\right) \mid \mathbf{x} \in \mathbb{X}_{k-1|k-1}, \ \mathbf{w} \in [\mathbf{w}] \right\} \tag{7}$$

and a correction step accounting for the new measurement using (2)

$$\mathbb{X}_{k|k} = \left\{ \mathbf{x} \in \mathbb{X}_{k|k-1} \mid \mathbf{y}_k = \mathbf{g}_k\left(\mathbf{x}, \mathbf{v}\right), \ \mathbf{v} \in [\mathbf{v}]^L \right\}. \tag{8}$$

The two steps of the idealized algorithm are depicted in Figure 3.

This idealized algorithm requires the evaluation of the direct image of a set by a function in the prediction step (7) and the evaluation of the inverse image in the correction step (8).

Usually, state estimation starts with an observability study to determine whether there is a chance to get an satisfying state estimate [20,21]. With set estimators, this study is not required *a priori*. A lack of observability typically results in the increase of the size of the components of $\mathbb{X}_{k|k}$ which are not observable. Alternatively, $\mathbb{X}_{k|k}$ may also consist of several disconnected subsets. Lack of observability may thus be detected during the estimation process.

## 2.2    Distributed State Estimation

Distributed versions of the Kalman filter have been proposed in [22], assuming linear models, gaussian noise, and instantaneous communications. Application to distributed estimation in power systems have been addressed in [23] and to distributed estimation in WSN are considered in [24]. Nevertheless, to the best of our knowledge, no similar tools have been proposed in a bounded-error context.

Consider a network of $L$ sensors. Ideally, any sensor $\ell$, $\ell = 1 \ldots L$ of the WSN should provide

$$\mathbb{X}^\ell_{k|k} = \mathbb{X}_{k|k}. \tag{9}$$

To establish conditions under which (9) is satisfied, some notions of graph theory have to be recalled. For more details, the reader is referred to [25,26].

The network of $L$ sensors is represented by a *graph* $\mathcal{G} = (\mathcal{V}, \mathcal{E})$. $\mathcal{V}$ is the set of $L$ *vertices* of the graph, each vertex representing a sensor of the network and $\mathcal{E}$ is the set of *edges* of the graph. An edge $\{k, \ell\} \in \mathcal{E}$ connecting two vertices $k \in \mathcal{V}$ and $\ell \in \mathcal{V}$ indicates that the two corresponding sensors are able to directly exchange information; the graph is thus *undirected*. In what follows, it is assumed that $\mathcal{G}$ is *entirely connected*, i.e., that there is always a path from any vertex to any other vertex in $\mathcal{G}$ and that each vertex is connected to itself.

The *distance* between two vertices in $\mathcal{G}$ is the number of edges in a shortest path connecting them. Consider a vertex $\ell \in \mathcal{V}$, then

$$\mathcal{C}(\{\ell\}) = \{k \in \mathcal{V} \mid (k, \ell) \in \mathcal{E}\} \tag{10}$$

denotes the set of all vertices that are directly connected to $\ell$, i.e., that are at a distance not larger than one of $\ell$. More generally, for any $\mathcal{W} \subset \mathcal{V}$, $\mathcal{C}(\mathcal{W}) \subset \mathcal{V}$ is the set of all vertices which are at a distance not larger than one from a given vertex of $\mathcal{W}$. The set

$$\mathcal{C}(\mathcal{C}(\{\ell\})) = \mathcal{C}^2(\{\ell\}) \tag{11}$$

contains thus all vertices that are at a distance not larger than two of $\ell$. More generally, $\mathcal{C}^n(\{\ell\})$ contains all vertices that are at a distance not larger than $n$ of $\ell$. The *eccentricity* $\varepsilon$ of a vertex $\ell \in \mathcal{V}$ is the largest distance between $\ell$ and any other vertex in $\mathcal{G}$. Finally, the *diameter* $d$ of $\mathcal{G}$ is the maximum eccentricity of any vertex in $\mathcal{G}$.

**Hypotheses and idealized algorithm.** The following measurement processing and communication will be considered. At time $k$, each sensor processes its own measurement $\mathbf{y}^\ell_k$. Between time $k$ and $k+1$, a first round trip is considered ($r = 1$) in which each sensor $\ell$ broadcasts its own estimate $\mathbb{X}^{\ell,r}_{k|k}$ to all the sensors of the network (only those which are directly connected to $\ell$ receive the information). Then each sensor $\ell$ receives and processes $\mathbb{X}^{s,1}_{k|k}$, $s \in \mathcal{C}(\{\ell\})$. Depending on the sampling time $T$, more round trips ($r > 1$) may be considered. Just before time $k+1$, each sensor $\ell$ builds a final estimate $\mathbb{X}^\ell_{k|k}$.

This way of processing and transmitting information leads to the following idealized distributed algorithm.

For each sensor $\ell = 1 \ldots L$,

1. At time $k$:

$$\mathbb{X}_{k|k-1}^{\ell} = \left\{ \mathbf{f}_k \left( \mathbf{x}, \mathbf{w}, \mathbf{u}_k \right) \mid \mathbf{x} \in \mathbb{X}_{k-1|k-1}^{\ell}, \ \mathbf{w} \in [\mathbf{w}] \right\}. \tag{12}$$

$$\mathbb{X}_{k|k}^{\ell,0} = \left\{ \mathbf{x} \in \mathbb{X}_{k|k-1}^{\ell} \mid \mathbf{y}_k^{\ell} = \mathbf{g}_k^{\ell} \left( \mathbf{x}, \mathbf{v} \right), \ \mathbf{v} \in [\mathbf{v}] \right\}. \tag{13}$$

2. Between $k$ and $k+1$,
   for $r = 1$ to $R_{\max}$ (number of round trips)

$$\mathbb{X}_{k|k}^{\ell,r} = \bigcap_{s \in \mathcal{C}(\{\ell\})} \mathbb{X}_{k|k}^{s,,r-1} \tag{14}$$

3. Just before $k+1$

$$\mathbb{X}_{k|k}^{\ell} = \mathbb{X}_{k|k}^{\ell,R_{\max}}. \tag{15}$$

As for the centralized algorithm, the idealized distributed algorithm requires the evaluation of the direct and inverse images of a set by a function. Proposition 1 gives some conditions under which the distributed approach gives results similar to the centralized one.

**Proposition 1.** *Consider a WSN of L nodes represented by an entirely connected graph $\mathcal{G} = (\mathcal{V}, \mathcal{E})$ of diameter d. Assume that at time $k-1$, $\mathbb{X}_{k-1|k-1}^{\ell} = \mathbb{X}_{k-1|k-1}$ for all $\ell \in \mathcal{V}$. If the number of roundtrips $R_{\max}$ satisfies $R_{\max} \geqslant d$, then one has at time k*

$$\mathbb{X}_{k|k}^{\ell} = \mathbb{X}_{k|k} \tag{16}$$

*for all $\ell \in \mathcal{V}$.* ◇

*Proof.* Consider a vertex $\ell \in \mathcal{V}$. Since $\mathbb{X}_{k-1|k-1}^{\ell} = \mathbb{X}_{k-1|k-1}$, after the prediction step (12), $\mathbb{X}_{k|k-1}^{\ell} = \mathbb{X}_{k|k-1}$, where $\mathbb{X}_{k|k-1}$ is provided by (7). The first correction step done at $\ell$ involves only the measurement vector $\mathbf{y}_k^{\ell}$ to get $\mathbb{X}_{k|k}^{\ell,0}$. After the first roundtrip, the estimate at $\ell$ becomes

$$\begin{aligned}
\mathbb{X}_{k|k}^{\ell,1} &= \bigcap_{s \in \mathcal{C}(\{\ell\})} \mathbb{X}_{k|k}^{s,0} \\
&= \bigcap_{s \in \mathcal{C}(\{\ell\})} \left\{ \mathbf{x} \in \mathbb{X}_{k|k-1}^{s} \mid \mathbf{y}_k^{s} = \mathbf{g}_k^{s} \left( \mathbf{x}, \mathbf{v} \right), \ \mathbf{v} \in [\mathbf{v}] \right\} \\
&= \bigcap_{s \in \mathcal{C}(\{\ell\})} \left\{ \mathbf{x} \in \mathbb{X}_{k|k-1} \mid \mathbf{y}_k^{s} = \mathbf{g}_k^{s} \left( \mathbf{x}, \mathbf{v} \right), \ \mathbf{v} \in [\mathbf{v}] \right\} \\
&= \left\{ \mathbf{x} \in \mathbb{X}_{k|k-1} \mid \mathbf{y}_k^{\mathcal{C}(\{\ell\})} = \mathbf{g}_k^{\mathcal{C}(\{\ell\})} \left( \mathbf{x}, \mathbf{v} \right), \ \mathbf{v} \in [\mathbf{v}] \right\},
\end{aligned}$$

where $\mathbf{y}_k^{\mathcal{C}(\{\ell\})}$ and $\mathbf{g}_k^{\mathcal{C}(\{\ell\})} \left( \mathbf{x}, \mathbf{v} \right)$ are the vector and function consisting of the concatenation of all $\mathbf{y}_k^{s}$ and $\mathbf{g}_k^{s} \left( \mathbf{x}, \mathbf{v} \right)$, with $s \in \mathcal{C} \left( \{\ell\} \right)$.

After a second roundtrip, the estimate at $\ell$ becomes

$$\mathbb{X}_{k|k}^{\ell,2} = \bigcap_{s \in \mathcal{C}(\{\ell\})} \mathbb{X}_{k|k}^{s,1}$$

$$= \bigcap_{s \in \mathcal{C}(\{\ell\})} \left\{ \mathbf{x} \in \mathbb{X}_{k|k-1} \mid \mathbf{y}_k^{\mathcal{C}(\{s\})} = \mathbf{g}_k^{\mathcal{C}(\{s\})}(\mathbf{x}, \mathbf{v}), \ \mathbf{v} \in [\mathbf{v}] \right\}$$

$$= \left\{ \mathbf{x} \in \mathbb{X}_{k|k-1} \mid \mathbf{y}_k^{\mathcal{C}(\mathcal{C}(\{\ell\}))} = \mathbf{g}_k^{\mathcal{C}(\mathcal{C}(\{\ell\}))}(\mathbf{x}, \mathbf{v}), \ \mathbf{v} \in [\mathbf{v}] \right\}$$

$$= \left\{ \mathbf{x} \in \mathbb{X}_{k|k-1} \mid \mathbf{y}_k^{\mathcal{C}^2(\{\ell\})} = \mathbf{g}_k^{\mathcal{C}^2(\{\ell\})}(\mathbf{x}, \mathbf{v}), \ \mathbf{v} \in [\mathbf{v}] \right\}.$$

Similarly, after $R_{\max}$ roundtrips, one gets at $\ell$

$$\mathbb{X}_{k|k}^{\ell,R_{\max}} = \left\{ \mathbf{x} \in \mathbb{X}_{k|k-1} \mid \mathbf{y}_k^{\mathcal{C}^{R_{\max}}(\{\ell\})} = \mathbf{g}_k^{\mathcal{C}^{R_{\max}}(\{\ell\})}(\mathbf{x}, \mathbf{v}), \ \mathbf{v} \in [\mathbf{v}] \right\}.$$

It is now enough to show that $\mathcal{C}^{R_{\max}}(\{\ell\}) = \mathcal{V}$ in order to prove that $\mathbb{X}_{k|k}^{\ell,R_{\max}} = \mathbb{X}_{k|k}$. First, one has $\mathcal{C}^{R_{\max}}(\{\ell\}) \subset \mathcal{V}$. Assume now that there exists some $k \in \mathcal{V}$ such that $k \notin \mathcal{C}^{R_{\max}}(\{\ell\})$. This means that $k$ lies at a distance strictly larger than $R_{\max}$ from $\ell$. Since the diameter $d$ of $\mathcal{G}$ is lower than $R_{\max}$ the distance between two vertices is necessarily lower than $d$, which contradicts the initial assumption. Thus any $k \in \mathcal{V}$ satisfies $k \in \mathcal{C}^{R_{\max}}(\{\ell\})$ and $\mathcal{C}^{R_{\max}}(\{\ell\}) = \mathcal{V}$.

The result of Proposition 1 is not very surprising. It mainly states that when there are enough information exchanges between sensors, the distributed estimate converges at any sensor to the centralized estimate. What is more interesting is that the number of roundtrips needed for convergence depends only on the diameter of the graph associated with the WSN.

When $R_{\max} < d$, the situation is much more complex, since not all sensors will have access to all measurements (or to their contribution to the estimation of $\mathbf{x}_k$). For the first roundtrips at time $k+1$, sensor $\ell$ will have to broadcast information about $\mathbb{X}_{k+1|k+1}^{\ell,r}$, but also about $\mathbb{X}_{k|k}^{\ell,r}$, as long as $\mathbb{X}_{k|k}^{\ell,r}$ has not converged to $\mathbb{X}_{k|k}$. Again, the diameter of the graph plays a crucial role. Further analysis is still required.

**Practical algorithm.** The implementation of the proposed idealized algorithm is done in a way similar to that of the centralized algorithm presented in [19]. In a most basic version of the algorithm, sets are represented by boxes, basic interval evaluations are performed for the prediction step and interval constraint propagation is done for the correction step. The advantage of this version is that it may readily be implemented on chips with reduced computational capabilities [27]. A more sophisticated version could involve description of sets using subpavings, a prediction step implemented using IMAGESP [19] and SIVIA [28] combined with interval constraint propagation for the correction step.

## 3   Applications

For the application part, a static localization problem for a single source is considered first. Then, the source will be moving, and the localization problem is cast into a problem of state estimation.

## 3.1  Static Source Localization

The known location of the sensors is denoted by $\mathbf{r}_\ell \in \mathbb{R}^2$, $\ell = 1 \ldots L$. The unknown location of the source is $\theta = (\theta_1, \theta_2)^{\mathrm{T}} \in \mathbb{R}^2$. The mean power $\overline{P}_{\mathrm{dB}}(d_\ell)$ (in dBm) received by the $\ell$-th sensor is described by Okumura-Hata model [29]

$$\overline{P}_{\mathrm{dB}}(d_\ell) = P_0 - 10 n_{\mathrm{p}} \log \frac{d_\ell}{d_0}, \tag{17}$$

where $n_{\mathrm{p}}$ is the path-loss exponent (unknown, but constant), $d_\ell = |\mathbf{r}_\ell - \theta|$. The received power is assumed to lie within some bounds

$$P_{\mathrm{dB}}(d) \in \left[ P_0 - 10 n_{\mathrm{p}} \log \frac{d}{d_0} - e, P_0 - 10 n_{\mathrm{p}} \log \frac{d}{d_0} + e \right], \tag{18}$$

where $e$ is assumed known.

The RSS by sensor $\ell = 1 \ldots L$ may be rewritten as

$$y_\ell = h_\ell(\theta, A, n_{\mathrm{p}}) v_\ell, \tag{19}$$

with

$$h_\ell(\theta, A, n_{\mathrm{p}}) = \frac{A}{|\mathbf{r}_\ell - \theta|^{n_{\mathrm{p}}}}, \quad A = 10^{P_0/10} d_0^{n_{\mathrm{p}}}, \tag{20}$$

and $v_\ell \in [v] = \left[ 10^{-e/10}, 10^{e/10} \right]$. The noise is thus multiplicative in the normal domain. The parameter vector to be estimated is then $\mathbf{x} = (A, n_{\mathrm{p}}, \theta_1, \theta_2)^{\mathrm{T}}$.

**Distributed approach: interval constraint propagation.** At sensor $\ell$, $y_\ell \in [y_\ell]$ is measured. Some boxes $[\theta]$, $[A]$, and $[n_{\mathrm{p}}]$ are assumed to be available, *a priori*, or as results transmitted by the other sensors to sensor $\ell$. The parameter vector has to satisfy the constraint provided by the RSS model

$$y_\ell - \frac{A}{|\mathbf{r}_\ell - \theta|^{n_{\mathrm{p}}}} = 0. \tag{21}$$

Using interval constraint propagation, it is possible to reduce the domains for the variables using (21). The contracted domains may be written as

$$\begin{cases} [y_\ell'] = [y_\ell] \cap \dfrac{[A]}{|\mathbf{r}_\ell - [\theta]|^{[n_{\mathrm{p}}]}}, \\[2mm] [A'] = [A] \cap [y_\ell'] \, |\mathbf{r}_\ell - [\theta]|^{[n_{\mathrm{p}}]}, \\[2mm] [n_{\mathrm{p}}'] = [n_{\mathrm{p}}] \cap (\log([A']) - \log([y_\ell'])) / \log(|\mathbf{r}_\ell - [\theta]|), \\[2mm] [\theta_1'] = [\theta_1] \cap \left( r_{\ell,1} \pm \sqrt{([A']/[y_\ell'])^{2/[n_{\mathrm{p}}']} - (r_{\ell,2} - [\theta_2])^2} \right), \\[2mm] [\theta_2'] = [\theta_2] \cap \left( r_{\ell,2} \pm \sqrt{([A']/[y_\ell'])^{2/[n_{\mathrm{p}}']} - (r_{\ell,1} - [\theta_1])^2} \right). \end{cases} \tag{22}$$

**Simulation results.** A network of $L = 2000$ sensors randomly distributed over a field of $100 \text{ m} \times 100 \text{ m}$ is considered. The source is placed at $\theta^* = (50 \text{ m}, 50 \text{ m})$ and emits a wave with $P_0 = 20$ dBm, $d_0 = 1$ m. The path-loss exponent $n_{\mathrm{p}} = 2$ is assumed to be constant over the field. The measurement noise is such that

**Table 1.** Example of measurements (static localization)

| Sensor | 68 | 741 | 954 |
|---|---|---|---|
| Measurement | [9.303, 58.698] | [17.856, 112.664] | [18.644, 117.640] |

$e = 4$ dBm. Table 1 provides some examples of the measurements which are available to the sensors.

For 100 realizations of the sensor field, data have been simulated with (18). To limit computational load, only sensors such that $y_\ell > 10$ participate to localization. The initial search box for $\mathbf{p}$ is taken as $[0, 100] \times [0, 100] \times [50, 200] \times [2, 4]$ in a first scenario, where $A$ (or $P_0$) is assumed unknown. In a second scenario, $A$ is assumed perfectly known. For the distributed approach, five cycles in the sensor network are performed.

The two proposed techniques are compared to localization by a closest point approach (CPA), which searches for the index of the sensor with the largest RSS $\ell_{\text{CPA}} = \arg\max_\ell y_\ell$ and uses the location of this sensor $\widehat{\theta}_{\text{CPA}} = \mathbf{r}_{\ell_{\text{CPA}}}$ as an estimate for $\theta^*$. This technique, albeit it is not the most efficient [5], performs well for dense sensor networks, as here. Point estimates for $\theta^*$ are evaluated as $\widehat{\theta}_C = \text{mid}([\text{proj}_\theta \overline{\mathbb{P}}])$, the midpoint of the smallest box containing the projection of $\overline{\mathbb{P}}$ onto the $\theta$-plane in the centralized approach and as the center of the projection onto the $\theta$-plane of the solution box $[\mathbf{p}]$, $\widehat{\theta}_D = \text{mid}(\text{proj}_\theta [\mathbf{p}])$, in the distributed approach.

Figures 4 and 5 provide typical solutions obtained using a centralized and distributed localization algorithm. The centralized algorithm involves set description using subpavings, whereas the distributed one only uses boxes, to limit the amount of information exchanged between sensors.

Figure 6 presents the histogram of the $L_2$ norm of the difference between $\theta^*$ and its estimates ($\widehat{\theta}_{\text{CPA}}$, $\widehat{\theta}_D$, and $\widehat{\theta}_C$) provided by the three techniques previously described. The centralized approach performs better than the distributed

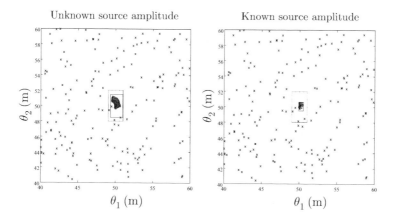

**Fig. 4.** Projection of the solution on the $(\theta_1, \theta_2)$-plane

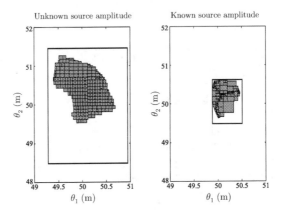

**Fig. 5.** Zoom of the projection of the solution on the $(\theta_1, \theta_2)$-plane

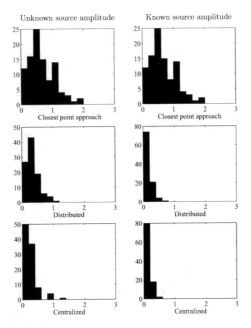

**Fig. 6.** Histograms of estimation error (in meters) for $\theta$ (100 realizations of the sensor field)

one, but the distributed approach provides a reasonable estimate at a much lower computation and transmission cost. Both techniques outperform CPA, the performances of which do not depend on whether $A$ is known.

## 3.2   Source Tracking

In this part, the source is assumed to be moving. $A$ and $n_\mathrm{p}$ are now known. The state vector is taken as

$$\mathbf{x}_k = (\theta_{1,k}, \theta_{2,k}, \phi_{1,k}, \phi_{2,k}, \theta_{1,k-1}, \theta_{2,k-1}, \phi_{1,k-1}, \phi_{2,k-1})^{\mathrm{T}} \tag{23}$$

where $(\phi_1, \phi_2)$ represents the speed of the source. This extended state vector is considered, as it allows to estimate $(\phi_{1,k}, \phi_{2,k})$.

**Model.** The following uncertain linear state equation is considered to determine the evolution with time of $\mathbf{x}_k$

$$\begin{pmatrix} \theta_{1,k} \\ \theta_{2,k} \\ \phi_{1,k} \\ \phi_{2,k} \end{pmatrix} = \begin{pmatrix} \theta_{1,k-1} + T\phi_{1,k-1} \\ \theta_{2,k-1} + T\phi_{2,k-1} \\ \phi_{1,k-1} \\ \phi_{2,k-1} \end{pmatrix} + T \cdot \begin{pmatrix} 0 \\ 0 \\ w_1 \\ w_2 \end{pmatrix} . \tag{24}$$

Since the inputs are unknown, they are considered as bounded state perturbations. Thus, $w_1 \in [w]$ and $w_2 \in [w]$.

**Interval constraint propagation.** Interval constraint propagation is used at the correction step. From (21) and (24), one gets the contracted domains at node $\ell$

$$\begin{cases} [y'_{\ell,k}] = [y_{\ell,k}] \cap \dfrac{A}{|\mathbf{r}_\ell - [\theta_k]|^{[n_{\mathrm{p}}]}}, \\[2ex] [\theta'_{1,k}] = [\theta_{1,k}] \cap \left( r_{\ell,1} \pm \sqrt{\left( A / [y'_{\ell,k}] \right)^{2/n_{\mathrm{p}}} - (r_{\ell,2} - [\theta_{2,k}])^2} \right), \\[2ex] [\theta'_{2,k}] = [\theta_{2,k}] \cap \left( r_{\ell,2} \pm \sqrt{\left( A / [y'_{\ell,k}] \right)^{2/n_{\mathrm{p}}} - (r_{\ell,1} - [\theta_{1,k}])^2} \right). \\[2ex] [\phi'_{1,k}] = [\phi_{1,k}] \cap \left( \dfrac{[\theta'_{1,k}] - [\theta'_{1,k-1}]}{T} + T[w] \right), \\[2ex] [\phi'_{2,k}] = [\phi_{2,k}] \cap \left( \dfrac{[\theta'_{2,k}] - [\theta'_{2,k-1}]}{T} + T[w] \right). \end{cases} \tag{25}$$

Each sensor will perform this constraint propagation before transmitting its updated estimate to its neighbours.

**Results.** Now, a field of 50 m×50 m is considered, with its origin at the center. A WSN of $L = 25$ sensors with communication range of 15 m is spread over this field. The source is placed at $\theta^* = (5 \text{ m}, 5 \text{ m})$, with characteristics $\overline{P}_0 = 20$ dBm, $d_0 = 1$ m. The measurement noise is such that $e = 4$ dBm. The path-loss exponent is $n_{\mathrm{p}} = 2$, assumed constant over the field. The sampling time is $T = 0.5$ s and $[\mathbf{w}] = [-0.5, 0.5]^2$ m·s$^{-2}$. Figure 7 illustrates the connectivity of the considered regular WSN and a typical trajectory followed by the source.

The simplest algorithm implementation presented in Section 2.2 has been considered: sets are represented by boxes, simple image evaluations using inclusion

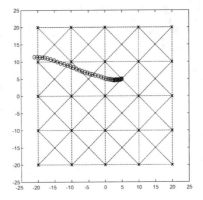

**Fig. 7.** Trajectory of the source (o); each sensor is represented by a cross (x), distances are in meters

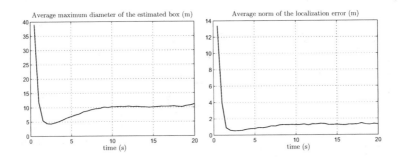

**Fig. 8.** Width of the box $[\theta_{1,k}] \times [\theta_{2,k}]$, and norm of the localization error when the estimate is taken as the center of the solution box (average over 100 random paths followed by the source)

functions are performed and correction is done by interval constraint propagation. This limits the amount of information to be exchanged between sensors and the computational effort. The localization performance using this algorithm is depicted in Figure 8 for 100 realizations of the source trajectory. The average width of the solution box (left part of Figure 8) provided at each time instant decreases very quickly before reaching a floor slightly higher than the minimum width and increases again after about 18 s. At the beginning, the source is close to the middle of the field and many sensors participate to the localization. When the sensor moves near the limits of the field, the number of involved sensors decreses and as a result the localization accuracy worsens. This effect is even more important when the source moves outside the field. A similar behavior is seen for the average norm of the localization error taking the center of the solution boxes at each time instant as estimate. The convergence is quite fast and the number of round trips has only a very limited impact on the convergence of the algorithm.

# 4   Conclusions

In this paper, we have considered distributed bounded-error state estimation applied to the problem of source tracking with a network of wireless sensors. Estimation is performed in a distributed context, *i.e.*, each sensor has only a limited amount of measurements available. A guaranteed set estimator is put at work.

There is still large space for improvements in the considered problem. First, convergence properties have to be more carefully studied. In particular, more general conditions under which the distributed solution coincides with the centralized one have to be determined. This type of problem is partly addressed in [30,31]. Robustness to outliers and network optimization for optimal estimation have also to be considered. Another challenging application would be the distributed estimation, *e.g.*, in a team of robots.

# References

1. Kay, R., Mattern, F.: The design space of wireless sensor networks. IEEE Wireless Communications 11(6), 54–61 (2004)
2. Haenselmann, T.: Sensornetworks. GFDL Wireless Sensor Network textbook (2006), http://www.informatik.uni-mannheim.de/~haensel/sn_book
3. Patwari, N., Ash, J.N., Kyperountas, S., Hero III, A.O., Moses, R.L., Correal, N.S.: Locating the nodes. IEEE Signal Processing Magazine 22(4), 54–69 (2005)
4. Sayed, A.H., Tarighat, A., Khajehnouri, N.: Network-based wireless location. IEEE Signal Processing Magazine 22(4), 24–40 (2005)
5. Sheng, X., Hu, Y.H.: Maximum likelihood multiple-source localization using acoustic energy measurements with wireless sensor networks. IEEE Transactions on Signal Processing 53(1), 44–53 (2005)
6. Kontkanen, P., Myllymäki, P., Roos, T., Tirri, H., Valtonen, K., Wettig, H.: Probabilistic methods for location estimation in wireless networks. In: Ganesh, R., Kota, S., Pahlavan, K., AgustÍ, R. (eds.) Emerging Location Aware Broadband Wireless Adhoc Networks. Kluwer Academic Publishers, Dordrecht (2004)
7. Gustafsson, F., Gunnarsson, F.: Mobile positioning using wireless networks. IEEE Signal Processing Magazine 22(4), 41–53 (2005)
8. Gezici, S., Tian, Z., Giannakis, G.B., Kobayashi, H., Molish, A.F., Poor, H.V., Sahinoglu, Z.: Localization via ultra-wideband radios. IEEE Signal Processing Magazine 22(4), 70–84 (2005)
9. Rabbat, M.G., Nowak, R.D.: Decentralized source localization and tracking. In: Proc. ICASSP (2004)
10. Hero III, A.O., Blatt, D.: Sensor network source localization via projection onto convex sets (POCS). In: Proceedings of ICASSP (2005)
11. Moore, R.E.: Interval Analysis. Prentice-Hall, Englewood Cliffs (1966)
12. Jaulin, L., Kieffer, M., Didrit, O., Walter, E.: Applied Interval Analysis. Springer, London (2001)
13. Kalman, R.E.: A new approach to linear filtering and prediction problems. Transactions of the AMSE, Part D, Journal of Basic Engineering 82, 35–45 (1960)
14. Gelb, A.: Applied Optimal Estimation. MIT Press, Cambridge (1974)

15. Terwiesch, P., Agarwal, M.: A discretized non-linear state estimator for batch processes. Computers and Chemical Engineering 19, 155–169 (1995)
16. Pitt, M., Shephard, N.: Filtering via simulation: Auxiliary particle filters. Journal of the American Statistical Association 94(446), 590–599 (1999)
17. Schweppe, F.C.: Recursive state estimation: unknown but bounded errors and system inputs 13(1), 22–28 (1968)
18. Maksarov, D., Norton, J.P.: State bounding with ellipsoidal set description of the uncertainty 65(5), 847–866 (1996)
19. Kieffer, M., Jaulin, L., Walter, E.: Guaranteed recursive nonlinear state bounding using interval analysis. International Journal of Adaptative Control and Signal Processing 6(3), 193–218 (2002)
20. Kwakernaak, H., Sivan, R.: Linear Optimal Control System. John Wiley-Interscience, Chichester (1974)
21. Hermann, R., Krener, A.J.: Nonlinear controllability and observability. IEEE trans. Automatic Control 22(5), 728–740 (1977)
22. Speyer, J.: Computation and transmission requirements for a decentralized linear-quadratic-gaussian control problem. IEEE Trans. Automatic Control 24(2), 266–269 (1979)
23. Lin, S.-S., Chang, H.: An efficient algorithm for solving distributed state estimator and laboratory implementation. In: ICPADS 2005: Proceedings of the 11th International Conference on Parallel and Distributed Systems (ICPADS 2005), Washington, DC, USA, pp. 689–694. IEEE Computer Society, Los Alamitos (2005)
24. Ribeiro, A., Giannakis, G.B., Roumeliotis, S.I.: SOI-KF: Distributed Kalman filtering with low-cost communications using the sign of innovations. IEEE Trans. Signal Processing 54(12), 4782–4795 (2006)
25. Harary, F.: Graph Theory. Addison-Wesley, Reading (1994)
26. Bollobás, B.: Modern Graph Theory. Springer, New-York (1998)
27. Piskorski, S., Lacassagne, L., Kieffer, M., Etiemble, D.: Efficient 16-bit floating-point interval processor for embedded systems and applications. In: Proc. 12th GAMM - IMACS Int. Symp. on Scientific Computing, Computer Arithmetic and Validated Numerics (SCAN 2006), September 26-29, p. 23 (2006)
28. Jaulin, L., Walter, E.: Set inversion via interval analysis for nonlinear bounded-error estimation. Automatica 29(4), 1053–1064 (1993)
29. Okumura, Y., Ohmori, E., Kawano, T., Fukuda, K.: Field strength ans its variability in VHF and UHF land-mobile radio service. Rev. Elec. Commun. Lab. 16, 9–10 (1968)
30. Yokoo, M.: Distributed Constraint Satisfaction: Foundations of Cooperation in Multi-Agent Systems. Springer, Berlin (2001)
31. Bejar, R., Fernandez, C., Valls, M., Domshlak, C., Gomes, C., Selman, B., Krishnamachari, B.: Sensor networks and distributed CSP: Communication, computation and complexity. Artificial Intelligence Journal 161(1-2), 117–148 (2005)

# Error Bounds for Lanczos Approximations of Rational Functions of Matrices

Andreas Frommer[1] and Valeria Simoncini[2]

[1] Fachbereich Mathematik und Naturwissenschaften, Bergische Universität
Wuppertal, D-42097 Wuppertal, Germany
`frommer@math.uni-wuppertal.de`
[2] Dipartimento di Matematica, Università di Bologna, Piazza di Porta S. Donato, 5,
I-40127 Bologna, Italy and CIRSA, Ravenna, Italy
`valeria@dm.unibo.it`

**Abstract.** Having good estimates or even bounds for the error in computing approximations to expressions of the form $f(A)v$ is very important in practical applications. In this paper we consider the case that $A$ is Hermitian and that $f$ is a rational function. We assume that the Lanczos method is used to compute approximations for $f(A)v$ and we show how to obtain a posteriori upper and lower bounds on the $\ell_2$-norm of the approximation error. These bounds are computed by minimizing and maximizing a rational function whose coefficients depend on the iteration step. We use global optimization based on interval arithmetic to obtain these bounds and include a number of experimental results illustrating the quality of the error estimates.

## 1 Introduction

Today, matrix functions are used in a large number of application problems, and the theoretical understanding of numerical methods for their computation is of topical interest. We refer to the recent book of Higham [12] as a survey reference. Usually, the function $f(A) \in \mathbb{R}^{n \times n}$ of a matrix $A \in \mathbb{R}^{n \times n}$ will be a full matrix even when $A$ is sparse. This prevents $f(A)$ to be computed directly when $n$ becomes large, as it is common in many applications. Fortunately, though, it is then usually sufficient to compute the action of the matrix function on a vector, i.e., $f(A)v$ for $v \in \mathbb{R}^n$, which is the task we are considering in this paper.

A prominent example where such computations arise is in exponential integrators. Here, the action of the matrix exponential $\exp(A)v$ or of $\varphi(A)v$ with $\varphi(t) = (\exp(t) - 1)/t$ must be computed. We refer to [8,13,28], e.g., for papers dealing with Krylov subspace approximations for the matrix exponential. Exponential integrators have recently emerged for numerically solving stiff or oscillatory systems of ordinary differential equations; see, e.g., [14], [10]. They can also be used for the integration of the time-dependent Schrödinger equation in quantum mechanics or for wave equations in which case one uses trigonometric functions rather than the exponential; see [9]. Another example arises in

A. Cuyt et al. (Eds.): Numerical Validation, LNCS 5492, pp. 203–216, 2009.

lattice gauge theory where so-called chiral overlap fermions are simulated using a Monte-Carlo approach. In each step one has to solve linear systems of the form $(P + \text{sign}(A))x = b$, where $P$ is a permutation matrix and $A$ is the Wilson fermion matrix; see [4]. When solving $(P + \text{sign}(A))x = b$ with an iterative method, each step will usually require the computation of $(P + \text{sign}(A))p$ and thus of $\text{sign}(A)p$ for a vector $p$ which changes at each iteration. Although neither the sign function nor the exponential are rational functions, they may be approximated by a rational function, and many numerical methods indeed rely on such approximations; see the discussion below.

In general, for any square matrix $A$, the matrix function $f(A)$ can be defined for a sufficiently smooth function $f$ by means of the Jordan canonical form of $A$; see, e.g., [16]. In this paper we are only concerned with the situation where the matrix $A$ is Hermitian. Then $f(A)$ is defined as soon as $f$ is defined on $\text{spec}(A)$, the set of all eigenvalues of $A$. Many equivalent definitions for $f(A)$ can be given. One is to take $f(A) = p(A)$ where $p$ is the polynomial that interpolates $f$ on $\text{spec}(A)$. Alternatively, let $A = V\Lambda V^*$ denote the spectral decomposition of $A$ where the columns of the orthogonal matrix $V$ represent eigenvectors of $A$ and the diagonal entries of the diagonal matrix $\Lambda$ the corresponding eigenvalues $\lambda_i$. Then we can put

$$f(A) = V f(\Lambda) V^* \text{ where } f(\Lambda) = \text{diag}(f(\lambda_1), \ldots, f(\lambda_n)).$$

In the case of many functions such as the exponential, the sign, the square-root and trigonometric functions, a particularly attractive approach for large matrices is to use a rational function approximation

$$f(t) \approx g(t) = \frac{p_{s_1}(t)}{p_s(t)},$$

where $p_i(t)$ are polynomials of degree $i$. See, for example, the books [3] and [24] for the general theory of such rational approximations and the papers [18] and [29] for their use in matrix functions. Note that the built-in Matlab ([19]) function for the matrix exponential uses a Padé rational approximation. A convenient way to use rational functions in a matrix context is by considering the partial fraction expansion. Assuming that there are no multiple poles, we then have

$$g(t) = \frac{p_{s_1}(t)}{p_s(t)} = p_{s_2}(t) + \sum_{i=1}^{s} \omega_i \frac{1}{t - \sigma_i}. \tag{1}$$

Since the computation of $p_{s_2}(A)b$ is trivial, we assume from now on that $p_{s_2} = 0$, and concentrate on the sum representing the fractional part. When applied to a matrix $A$, this gives

$$z = g(A)v = \sum_{i=1}^{s} \omega_i (A - \sigma_i I)^{-1} v = \sum_{i=1}^{s} \omega_i x_i. \tag{2}$$

Since we assume the problem dimension to be large, the solutions $x_i$ to the systems $(A - \sigma_i I)x_i = v$ must be approximated using an iterative technique.

The iterative method we consider here is the Lanczos method which will be described in detail in section 2. Denoting $x_i^{(k)}$ the $k$-th iterate for the system $(A - \sigma_i I)x_i = v$, we get an overall approximation to $z = g(A)v$ as

$$z^{(k)} = \sum_{i=1}^{s} \omega_i x_i^{(k)}. \tag{3}$$

The aim of this paper is to present a method which obtains lower and upper bounds for

$$\|g(A)v - z^{(k)}\|, \tag{4}$$

the Euclidean norm of the error of the Lanczos approximation. Such bounds are important in computational practice because they can be used as a stopping criterion for the Lanczos process. We obtain the bounds as global minima and maxima of certain (one-dimensional) rational functions. For their computation we use a global optimization algorithm based on interval arithmetic. Note that the cost of this method does not depend on the matrix dimension $n$, but only on the number $s$ of poles in the rational function and the width of the spectrum of $A$.

The rest of this paper is organized as follows: In section 2 we review some important facts for the Lanczos process and the Lanczos approximations to families of shifted linear systems as well as to rational matrix functions. Section 3 explains how to obtain a posteriori bounds on the error, and section 4 exposes the global optimization algorithm based on interval arithmetic that we use to compute these bounds. Finally, section 5 contains a full algorithmic description of the Lanczos method including the computation of the error bounds as well as several numerical results illustrating the quality of the error bounds.

## 2   The Lanczos Approximation

Given a vector $v$ such that $\|v\| = 1$ and a Hermitian matrix $A$, the Lanczos process generates a sequence of orthonormal vectors that span the Krylov subspace $\mathcal{K}_k(A, v) = \mathrm{span}\{v, Av, \ldots, A^{k-1}v\}$. As $k$ grows, the subspaces are nested, that is $\mathcal{K}_k(A, v) \subseteq \mathcal{K}_{k+1}(A, v)$. Therefore, by denoting with $\{v^{(0)}, \ldots, v^{(k-1)}\}$ the generated orthonormal basis of $\mathcal{K}_k(A, v)$, with $v^{(0)} = v$, the next vector $v^{(k)}$ such that $v^{(0)}, \ldots, v^{(k)}$ span $\mathcal{K}_{k+1}(A, v)$ is given as

$$v^{(k)}\beta_{k+1} = Av^{(k-1)} - \alpha_k v^{(k-1)} - \beta_k v^{(k-2)}.$$

The coefficients $\alpha_k, \beta_k$, $k = 1, 2, \ldots$ are computed so that $(v^{(j)})^* v^{(i)} = \delta_{j,i}$. Setting $V_k = [v^{(0)}, \ldots, v^{(k-1)}]$, the recurrence above can be written in compact form as

$$AV_k = V_k T_k + v^{(k)}\beta_{k+1}e_k^T, \qquad T_k = \begin{pmatrix} \alpha_1 & \beta_2 & & \\ \beta_2 & \alpha_2 & \ddots & \\ & \ddots & \ddots & \beta_k \\ & & \beta_k & \alpha_k \end{pmatrix}, \tag{5}$$

where $e_k$ is the $k$th column of the identity matrix whose dimension will be clear from the context. An approximation to the solution of the linear system $Ax = v$ may be obtained in $K_k(A, v)$ as $x_k = V_k y_k$, where $y_k$ is obtained by imposing that the residual $r_k = v - AV_k y_k$ be orthogonal to the space, namely $V_k^* r_k = 0$. Assuming that $T_k$ is nonsingular, explicitly writing this condition yields

$$y_k = T_k^{-1} e_1,$$

where $e_1 = (1, 0 \ldots, 0)^\mathsf{T} \in \mathbb{R}^k$.

In the context of solving shifted systems $(A - \sigma I)x = v$, we will need the following key features of the Lanczos procedure, see, e.g. [23],[29].

**Lemma 1.** *With the notation above, and $T_k(\sigma)$ the tridiagonal matrix from (5) with $A$ replaced by $A - \sigma I$*

1. *For any $\sigma \in \mathbb{C}$, $K_k(A, v) = K_k(A - \sigma I, v)$ and $T_k(\sigma) = T_k - \sigma I$.*
2. *For the residual $r^{(k)}(\sigma) = v - (A - \sigma I)V_k y_k(\sigma)$ it holds*

$$r^{(k)}(\sigma) = (-1)^k \rho^{(k)}(\sigma) v^{(k)}.$$

*Denoting $\theta_\nu^{(k)}, \nu = 1, \ldots, k$ the eigenvalues of $T_k$, we actually have*

$$\rho^{(k)}(\sigma) = \prod_{\nu=1}^{k} \frac{1}{1 - \sigma/\theta_\nu^{(k)}},$$

*as well as*

$$\rho^{(k)}(\sigma) = (e_k^T T_k(\sigma)^{-1} e_1) \cdot \beta_k.$$

The first result shows that when solving systems that only differ for the shifting parameter $\sigma$, approximations can be carried out in a single approximation space. The second result says that the residuals associated with the shifted systems are all collinear to the next basis vector. Note that the Ritz values $\theta_\nu$ are all real, since $T_k = V_k^* A V_k$ is Hermitian.

## 3    Error Bounds

The approach we propose here to bound the error between $z = g(A)v$ and its Lanczos approximation $z^{(k)}$ requires the a priori knowledge of an interval enclosing the spectrum of $A$, i.e. we assume that we know $\ell_1, \ell_2$ such that $\text{spec}(A) \subseteq [\ell_1, \ell_2]$. Our crucial observation starts from (3) which gives

$$g(A)v - z^{(k)} = \sum_{i=1}^{s} \omega_i \left( (A - \sigma_i I)^{-1} b - x_i^{(k)} \right) = \sum_{i=1}^{s} \omega_i (A - \sigma_i I)^{-1} r_i^{(k)}.$$

Since the $x_i^{(k)}$ arise from the Lanczos process, using Lemma 1 and the notation $\rho_i^{(k)} = \rho^{(k)}(\sigma_i)$, gives

$$g(A)v - z^{(k)} = \sum_{i=1}^{s} (-1)^k \rho_i^{(k)} \omega_i (A - \sigma_i I)^{-1} v^{(k)}. \tag{6}$$

Herein, $\|v^{(k)}\| = 1$. So the error can be expressed as the action of a rational matrix function $\mathcal{R}^{(k)}(A)$, namely

$$\mathcal{R}^{(k)}(A) = \sum_{i=1}^{s} (-1)^k \rho_i^{(k)} \omega_i (A - \sigma_i I)^{-1} \tag{7}$$

on the vector $v^{(k)}$. Some additional discussion of the partial fraction expansions used is in order here. We are interested in matrix functions $f(A)$ where $f$ is real on the real axis. It is thus natural that the rational function $g$ which we use to approximate $f$ is real on the real line, too. Its partial fraction expansion (1), however, might have complex poles which then come in complex conjugate pairs $\sigma, \bar{\sigma}$ and corresponding complex conjugate coefficients $\omega, \bar{\omega}$. This is the case for instance when $f$ is the exponential function and $g$ is a Padé or Chebyshev rational approximation. For computing our error bounds it will turn out useful to have a *real* partial fraction expansion for the rational functions $\mathcal{R}^{(k)}$ in these cases. Note that from Lemma 1 we see that for complex conjugate poles $\sigma$ the factors $\rho_i^{(k)}$ in $\mathcal{R}^{(k)}$ are complex conjugate, too. Putting the terms with real coefficients first we thus have

$$(-1)^k \cdot \mathcal{R}^{(k)}(t) = \sum_{i=1}^{s'} \frac{\rho_i^{(k)} \omega_i}{t - \sigma_i} + \sum_{i=s'+1}^{s''} \left( \frac{\rho_i^{(k)} \omega_i}{t - \sigma_i} + \frac{\overline{\rho_i^{(k)} \omega_i}}{t - \bar{\sigma}_i} \right)$$

$$= \sum_{i=1}^{s'} \frac{\rho_i^{(k)} \omega_i}{t - \sigma_i} + \sum_{i=s'+1}^{s''} \frac{\gamma_i^{(k)} t + \delta_i^{(k)}}{(t - \eta_i)^2 + \mu_i} \quad \text{with} \tag{8}$$

$$\gamma_i^{(k)} = 2\mathrm{Re}(\rho_i^{(k)} \omega_i), \delta_i^{(k)} = -2\mathrm{Re}(\rho_i^{(k)} \omega_i \bar{\sigma}_i),$$
$$\eta_i = \mathrm{Re}(\sigma_i), \mu_i = |\sigma_i|^2 - (\mathrm{Re}(\sigma_i))^2 > 0,$$

where the second line represents the real partial fraction expansion of $\mathcal{R}^{(k)}$. Note that we have $s'' = s'$ if the complex and the real partial fraction expansion coincide.

We now proceed by deriving bounds for the error using the rational functions $\mathcal{R}^{(k)}$. From standard norm estimates and using $\|v^{(k)}\| = 1$ we get from (6)

$$\|g(A)v - z^{(k)}\| \leq \|\mathcal{R}^{(k)}(A)\|$$

and, in case that $\mathcal{R}^{(k)}(A)$ is non-singular,

$$\|g(A)v - z^{(k)}\| \geq \|(\mathcal{R}^{(k)}(A))^{-1}\|^{-1}.$$

Since we assume $A$ to be Hermitian and since $\mathcal{R}^{(k)}$ is real, the matrix $\mathcal{R}^{(k)}(A)$ is Hermitian, too, so that

$$\|\mathcal{R}^{(k)}(A)\| = \max\{|\mu| : \mu \in \mathrm{spec}(\mathcal{R}^{(k)}(A))\} = \max\{|\mathcal{R}^{(k)}(\lambda)| : \lambda \in \mathrm{spec}(A)\}$$

and

$$\|\mathcal{R}^{(k)}(A)^{-1}\|^{-1} = \min\{|\mu| : \mu \in \mathrm{spec}(\mathcal{R}^{(k)}(A))\} = \min\{|\mathcal{R}^{(k)}(\lambda)| : \lambda \in \mathrm{spec}(A)\}.$$

In general, the quantities on the right hand side cannot be computed because the spectrum of $A$ is not known. However, assuming that we know bounds $\ell_1, \ell_2$ such that $\mathrm{spec}(A) \subset [\ell_1, \ell_2]$ we can use the maximum and minimum over the whole interval, a computable quantity, to get bounds for the error. We summarize this next.

**Theorem 1.** *For $k = 1, 2, \ldots$ define*

$$\varepsilon^{(k)} = \min\{|\mathcal{R}^{(k)}(\lambda)| : \lambda \in [\ell_1, \ell_2]\}, \quad \mathcal{E}^{(k)} = \max\{|\mathcal{R}^{(k)}(\lambda)| : \lambda \in [\ell_1, \ell_2]\}. \quad (9)$$

*Then $\varepsilon^{(k)} \leq \|g(A)v - z^{(k)}\| \leq \mathcal{E}^{(k)}$.*

To solve the global optimization problems defining $\varepsilon^{(k)}$ and $\mathcal{E}^{(k)}$ we suggest to use a simple branch and bound method based on interval arithmetic which will be described in detail in the following section.

## 4    A Branch and Bound Method Based on Interval Arithmetic

We start by introducing some additional notation. (Compact) intervals on the real line are denoted in boldface, as $\mathbf{x} = [\underline{\mathbf{x}}, \overline{\mathbf{x}}]$. The midpoint $(\underline{\mathbf{x}} + \overline{\mathbf{x}})/2$ of the interval $\mathbf{x}$ is denoted as $\mathrm{mid}(\mathbf{x})$, and $\mathrm{diam}(\mathbf{x}) = \overline{\mathbf{x}} - \underline{\mathbf{x}}$ is its diameter. The arithmetic operations $+, -, *, /$ on intervals are defined in a set theoretic manner as usually; their result is thus again a compact interval (see, e.g. [1], [17], [22]). The absolute value $|\mathbf{x}|$ is defined as the range of $|\cdot|$ over the interval. As with the arithmetic operations, it can be computed just from the endpoints of $\mathbf{x}$, since

$$|\mathbf{x}| = \begin{cases} [0, \max\{|\underline{\mathbf{x}}|, |\overline{\mathbf{x}}|\}] & \text{if } 0 \in \mathbf{x} \\ [\min\{|\underline{\mathbf{x}}|, |\overline{\mathbf{x}}|\}, \max\{|\underline{\mathbf{x}}|, |\overline{\mathbf{x}}|\}] & \text{otherwise} \end{cases}.$$

With these definitions, given the real partial fraction expansion of the rational function $\mathcal{R}^{(k)}$ from (8) and an interval $\mathbf{x} \subset \mathbb{R}$ which does not contain any real pole $\sigma_i$ of $\mathcal{R}^{(k)}$, the *interval arithmetic evaluation* of $|\mathcal{R}^{(k)}|$ is defined as

$$|\mathcal{R}^{(k)}(\mathbf{x})| = \left| \sum_{i=1}^{s'} \frac{\rho_i^{(k)} \omega_i}{\mathbf{x} - \sigma_i} + \sum_{i=s'+1}^{s''} \frac{\gamma_i^{(k)} \mathbf{x} + \delta_i^{(k)}}{(\mathbf{x} - \eta_i)^2 + \mu_i} \right|.$$

By the inclusion property of interval arithmetic, the interval $|\mathcal{R}^{(k)}(\mathbf{x})|$ contains the range of $|\mathcal{R}^{(k)}|$ over the interval $\mathbf{x}$ which we denote by $\mathrm{Range}(|\mathcal{R}^{(k)}|, \mathbf{x})$. Since $|\mathcal{R}^{(k)}|$ satisfies a Lipschitz condition, we have that the difference $\mathrm{diam}(|\mathcal{R}^{(k)}(\mathbf{x})|) - \mathrm{diam}(\mathrm{Range}(|\mathcal{R}^{(k)}|, \mathbf{x}))$ tends to zero when $\mathrm{diam}(\mathbf{x})$ tends to zero; see, e.g., [1] or [22]. Note also that interval arithmetic evaluations are inclusion isotone, i.e. $\mathbf{y} \subset \mathbf{x} \Rightarrow |\mathcal{R}^{(k)}(\mathbf{y})| \subseteq |\mathcal{R}^{(k)}(\mathbf{y})|$.

For simplicity, we now use the generic notation $f$ for the function $|\mathcal{R}^{(k)}|$. Given that we have an interval arithmetic evaluation of $f$ at hand, we use a simple standard branch-and-bound strategy to obtain the global maximum, see

[11], [17] ,[26]. It relies on three ideas. The first is that if we keep on subdividing into ever smaller intervals, the interval arithmetic evaluations will tend towards the range of $f$. The second is that a global maximizer cannot lie in a subinterval $\mathbf{x}$ of $[\ell_1, \ell_2]$ for which $\overline{f}(\mathbf{x})$, the right end point of the interval arithmetic evaluation of $f$ at $\mathbf{x}$, is less than the largest known value of $f$. The third is that lower and upper bounds for the global maximum of $f$ may be easily updated by using computed function values and the right end points of the interval arithmetic evaluations, respectively. Technically, we will maintain a set of subintervals as a heap $H$ containing pairs $(\mathbf{x}, \tilde{f})$. Here, each $\mathbf{x}$ is a subinterval of the initial interval $[\ell_1, \ell_2]$ and $\tilde{f} = \overline{f}(\mathbf{x})$, thus representing an upper bound for the maximum of $f$ over that interval. The heap $H$ is ordered with respect to the key $\tilde{f}$, so that if we retrieve the topmost element from the heap we always get the one with the largest value of $\tilde{f}$.

We keep track of two values $f^*$ and $\hat{f}$ representing the best known values for which $\hat{f} \le \mathcal{E} \le f^*$, where $\mathcal{E} = \max_{x \in [\ell_1, \ell_2]} f(x)$. In each step we remove the entry $(\mathbf{x}, \tilde{f})$ with largest $\tilde{f}$ from $H$. The value of $f^*$ is updated to be $\tilde{f}$. Then we bisect $\mathbf{x}$ into two intervals $\mathbf{x}_1$ and $\mathbf{x}_2$ and update $\hat{f}$ using the values of $f$ at the midpoints of $\mathbf{x}_1$ and $\mathbf{x}_2$. We also compute $f(\mathbf{x}_i)$ giving us $\tilde{f}$ for both intervals $\mathbf{x}_i$. Only if $\tilde{f}$ is larger than $\hat{f}$ will the corresponding pair be inserted into the heap $H$. This is because otherwise $\mathbf{x}_i$ does not contain a global maximizer, and, by inclusion isotonicity, any subinterval of $\mathbf{x}_i$ will not contribute to further improve $\hat{f}$ or $f^*$.

We stop the bisection process once the difference between $f^*$ and $\hat{f}$ is small enough. The following algorithm MAXIMIZE gives the details.

**Algorithm.** MAXIMIZE

    **Input:** expression for function $f : [\ell_1, \ell_2] \subset \mathbb{R} \to \mathbb{R}_0^+$, relative accuracy $\alpha$
    **Output:** upper bound $f^*$ for global maximum $\mathcal{E}$
    $\mathbf{x} = [\ell_1, \ell_2]$, $\mathbf{f} = f(\mathbf{x})$, $\tilde{f} = \overline{\mathbf{f}}$
    insert $([\ell_1, \ell_2], \tilde{f})$ into empty heap $H$
    $f^* = \tilde{f}$, $\hat{f} = f(\mathrm{mid}(\mathbf{x}))$
    **while** $|(f^* - \hat{f})/f^*| > \alpha$ **do**
        remove top element $(\mathbf{x}, \tilde{f})$ from heap $H$         {has largest $\tilde{f}$}
        $f^* = \tilde{f}$         {improved upper bound for maximum}
        bisect $\mathbf{x} = \mathbf{x}_1 \cup \mathbf{x}_2$
        **for** $i = 1, 2$ **do**
            $\mathbf{f} = f(\mathbf{x}_i)$, $\tilde{f} = \overline{\mathbf{f}}$
            **if** $\tilde{f} > \hat{f}$ **then** {$\mathbf{x}_i$ may contain maximizer}
                insert $(\mathbf{x}_i, \tilde{f})$ in heap $H$
                $\hat{f} = \max\{\hat{f}, f(\mathrm{mid}(\mathbf{x}_i))\}$         {update largest function value}
            **end if**
        **end for**
    **end while**

Upon termination, this algorithm will have determined $f^*$ as an upper bound for $\mathcal{E}$ with relative accuracy $\alpha$, since $|(f^* - \hat{f})/f^*| \leq \alpha$ and $\hat{f} \leq \mathcal{E} \leq f^*$ imply $|(f^* - \mathcal{E})/f^*| \leq \alpha$.

Algorithm MAXIMIZE can be modified in a straightforward manner to deliver a lower bound for the minimum of $f$ over the interval $[\ell_1, \ell_2]$.

# 5    The Lanczos Algorithm with Error Bounds

We are now in a position to describe the Lanczos method to approximate $g(A)v$ in full detail, including the convergence test based on the error bound from Theorem 1, and its computation using the global optimization algorithm just described. In exact arithmetic this algorithm is guaranteed to yield an approximation for $g(A)b$ with the chosen accuracy. In floating point arithmetic no such guarantee can be given since the crucial relation

$$(A - \sigma_i I)x_i^{(k)} = (-1)^k \rho_i^{(k)} v^{(k)}$$

will not be fulfilled exactly with the computed quantities. Nevertheless, we consider our approach to be highly useful also in the floating point context since it produces a cheaply computable and, as numerical experiments will show, quite accurate stopping criterion.

**Algorithm.** PFE-LANCZOS

> Choose tol, maxit                                                    {for stopping test}
> $\beta = 0, v_0 = b, v_{-1} = 0, \rho_i^{(0)} = 1$ for $i = 1, \ldots, s$
> **for** $k = 1, \ldots,$maxit **do** {iteration}
> $\quad q = Av_{k-1} - \beta v_{k-2}, \quad \alpha = v_{k-1}^* q, \quad t_{k,k} = \alpha$    {Lanczos coeff's and vectors}
> $\quad \tilde{v} = q - \alpha v_{k-1}$
> $\quad \beta = (\tilde{v}^* \tilde{v})^{1/2}, \quad v_k = \tilde{v}/\beta, \quad t_{k+1,k} = \beta, \quad t_{k,k+1} = \beta$
> $\quad y_i = (T_k - \sigma_i I_k)^{-1} e_1, \quad i = 1, \ldots, s$                    {get projected solutions}
> $\quad \rho_i^{(k)} = e_k^T y_i t_{k+1,k}, \quad i = 1, \ldots, s$                    {factors for residuals}
> $\quad$ Compute upper bound $\left(\mathcal{E}^{(k)}\right)^*$ for $\mathcal{E}^{(k)}$ with algorithm MAXIMIZE
> $\quad\quad\quad\quad\quad\quad\quad\quad\quad\quad\quad\quad\quad\quad\quad\quad\quad\quad$ {bounds from Theorem 1}
> $\quad$ **if** $\left(\mathcal{E}^{(k)}\right)^* < $ tol **then** {iteration converged}
> $\quad\quad z_k = \sum_{i=1}^{s} \omega_i y_i, \quad x_k = \sum_{i=0}^{k-1} (z_k)_{i+1} v_i,$ **stop**              {approximate solution}
> $\quad$ **end if**
> **end for**

We first remark that upon termination of the algorithm we could include the computation of a guaranteed *lower bound* for the error by using the modification of algorithm MAXIMIZE discussed at the end of section 4. In this manner, we are able to appreciate the accuracy of the computed solution in more detail. We also remark that underflow may occur for some of the numbers $\rho_i^{(k)}$ if the convergence for the corresponding systems is much faster than for others. It is therefore reasonable to incorporate a strategy to remove 'converged' systems from further computation and to set $\rho_i^{(k)} = 0$ for all subsequent iterations, see [7].

As already mentioned, in the presence of two complex conjugate poles, all quantities to be computed for the two poles are just complex conjugates of each other. Therefore, these computations have to be done for one of the poles only.

Finally, let us mention that there exists an alternative implementation of the Lanczos method which applies the conjugate gradient method to all $s$ shifts simultaneously. Its advantage over Algorithm PFE-LANCZOS is that it requires storage only proportional to $s$, the number of poles, but not to the number of iterations performed. We refer to [7] for details.

## 6  Numerical Experiments

In this section we report on the results of our numerical experiments. They were all programmed in Matlab with interval arithmetic provided through the Intlab toolbox; see [27]. In all experiments the accuracy parameter $\alpha$ in MAXIMIZE was taken to be 0.1. In our figures, we will also include two different *estimates* for the error—not necessarily upper bounds—known from the literature. The first one, referenced as 'estimate' in the sequel, is from [7], where an error estimate at iteration $k$ is obtained using the CG coefficients corresponding to iterations $k, k+1, \ldots, k+2d$. We took $d = 1$ in all our examples. The second error estimate, called 'simple', refers to a computationally very cheap estimate introduced in [28]: At iteration $k$, the estimate is simply computed from the individual residuals $r_i^{(k)}$ as $\| \sum \omega_i r_i^{(k)} \|$.

*Example 1.* We consider the Zolotarev rational function approximation to the inverse square root function on a positive interval $[a_1, a_2]$, namely $\tilde{g}(A)b \approx A^{-1/2}v$. We refer to [24, Chapter 4] for details on the Zolotarev approximation, which is a rational function with all simple poles lying on the negative real axis. We took $[a_1, a_2] = [1, 1000]$ and used the Zolotarev approximation with $s = 12$ poles. The matrix $A$ was taken to be a $200 \times 200$ diagonal matrix $A$ with diagonal entries equispaced in the interval $[1, 1000]$ so that $\ell_1 = 1, \ell_2 = 1000$; $v$ was taken as the normalized vector of all ones. With these parameters, the accuracy of the Zolotarev approximation turns out to be of the order of $10^{-7}$.

Numerical results are given in Figure 1. The dashed curve represents the norm of the error. This error can be computed easily for this example, since, $A$ being diagonal, the exact value of $g(A)v$ can be computed directly. The solid line represents the error bound. We see that the error bound very well captures the convergence behaviour of the Lanczos method, while being roughly two orders of magnitude too pessimistic during the whole iteration process. The estimate from [7] provably (see Theorem 5.4 in [7]) represents a lower bound in this example, and it comes very close to the true error. For the inverse square root, the 'simple' estimate – which is not known to be a bound – is very close to our bounds.

As a last comment to this example we note that if we base a stopping criterion upon the error bound we will perform about 10 'unnecessary' iterations for which

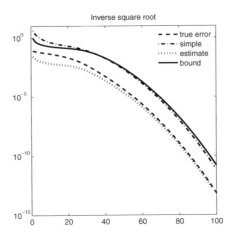

**Fig. 1.** Error and error bound for the inverse square root

the true error is already as small as desired while the error bound has yet to catch up.

*Example 2.* Our second experiment is with data stemming from an application in Quantum Chromodynamics; see [2]. We consider the approximation of $\mathrm{sign}(Q)b$, where $Q$ is the Hermitian Wilson fermion matrix which is highly indefinite. We took $Q = P(I - \frac{4}{3}\kappa_c D)$, where $\kappa_c = 0.15717$, the configuration matrix $D$ is available in the QCD collection of the matrix market [21] (matrix conf5.4-0018x8-2000.mtx), while $P$ is the so-called $\gamma_5$-matrix, a permutation matrix which symmetrizes $D$. The dimension of $Q$ is approximately $50\,000$ and $b$ is a random vector.

We first compute two numbers $0 < a_1 < a_2$ such that $\mathrm{spec}(Q) \subset [-a_2, -a_1] \cup [a_1, a_2]$. We then approximate $\mathrm{sign}(t)$ on $[-a_2, -a_1] \cup [a_1, a_2]$ using the Zolotarev rational approximation $Z$ for the inverse square root on $[a_1^2, a_2^2]$. To be specific, we approximate $\mathrm{sign}(Q)b$ as $Z(Q^2) \cdot Qv$. Note that this means that we perform the Lanczos process using the matrix $Q^2$, not $Q$. Let us mention that $g(t) = Z(t^2) \cdot t$ is an $\ell_\infty$ best approximation to the sign function on $[-a_2, -a_1] \cup [a_1, a_2]$; see [24].

To speed up computation, it pays off to compute $q$ eigenvalues of $Q$ which are smallest in modulus, $\lambda_1, \ldots, \lambda_q$, say, beforehand using a Lanczos procedure for $Q^2$. Denoting by $\Pi$ the orthogonal projector along the space spanned by the corresponding eigenvectors $w_i, i = 1, \ldots, q$, we then work with the matrix $\Pi Q \Pi$ and the vector $\Pi b$. In this manner, we effectively shrink the eigenvalue intervals for $Q$, so that we need fewer poles for an accurate Zolotarev approximation and, in addition, the linear systems to be solved converge more rapidly. The vector $\mathrm{sign}(Q)b$ can be retrieved as $\mathrm{sign}(\Pi Q \Pi)\Pi b + \mathrm{sign}(\mathrm{diag}(\lambda_1, \ldots, \lambda_q)) \cdot (I - \Pi)b$. In our computation we took $q = 30$, and the bounds $\ell_1, \ell_2$ for the spectrum of the matrix $(\Pi Q \Pi)^2$ were taken to be its smallest and largest nonzero eigenvalue, respectively. The number of poles $s$ in the rational approximation for this reduced interval was chosen such that the $\ell_\infty$-error was less than $10^{-7}$, that is $s = 11$.

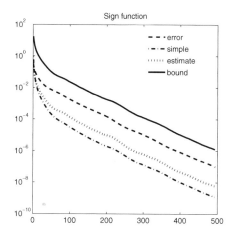

**Fig. 2.** Error and error bound for the sign function of the QCD matrix

Figure 2 shows the convergence curve and the error bound. Note that this time we compare with an 'exact' solution that has been computed beforehand by the Lanczos method. We see that the bounds for the error nicely reproduce the convergence behaviour and that they are about one order of magnitude larger than the true error. The estimate from [7] is again a lower bound in this example; the 'simple' estimate is also a lower bound, but a quite bad one.

*Example 3.* In this example we consider the Chebyshev rational approximation $g(A)b$ to the exponential function $\exp(-\tau A)b$, $\tau > 0$. The coefficients of the two polynomials of the same degree appearing in $g$ have been tabulated in [5] for several different degrees. It is known that the error associated with this approximation is $\max_{t \geq 0} |\exp(-t) - g(t)| = \mathcal{O}(10^{-s})$, where $s$ is the degree of the polynomials in the rational function; see [5], e.g. In this case, the poles $\sigma_i$ and the coefficients $\omega_i$ in the partial fraction expansion are complex, therefore pairing of the conjugate complex terms in the partial fraction expansion should be carried out when computing the error bound, as discussed in (8). For our example we took $A$ to be the standard 5 point discretization of the two-dimensional Laplacian on an equidistant grid of size $41 \times 41$. This results in a matrix of size $1600 \times 1600$ with eigenvalues $41^2 \cdot (4 - 2\cos(\pi/41 \cdot i) - 2\cos(\pi/41 \cdot j))$, $i, j = 1, \ldots, 40$. The time stepping parameter $\tau$ was chosen as 0.1. We then took $\ell_1, \ell_2$ as the smallest and largest eigenvalue of $\tau A$, respectively. The convergence history is given in the left plot of Figure 3. We note that there is an initial phase of slow convergence where during the first 20 iterations relatively small progress is made. This is a well-known phenomenon, see [6] and [13], e.g. This phase is reflected in the error bound. Throughout the whole iteration, the error bound is about two orders of magnitude larger than the true error. However, since convergence tends to be quite fast after the initial stagnation phase, we again do not perform prohibitively many additional iterations if we base our stopping criterion upon the upper bound. We note that for this example, where the norm of $A$ is relatively large,

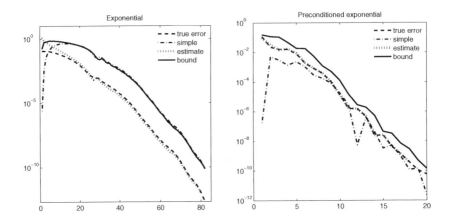

**Fig. 3.** Exponential function. Left: Standard Lanczos method. Right: SI-Lanczos method.

the *a priori* error bound from [13, Theorem 2] is not very useful since it is very far from the true error. For example, at iteration 80, the bound is just $\approx 0.1$.

To speed up the convergence of the Lanczos process when the number of iterations becomes excessive, acceleration procedures have been devised. Here we consider the Shift-and-Invert Lanczos (SI-Lanczos), as proposed in [15] and [20]. For a given real parameter $\mu > 0$, the procedure determines an approximation to $f(A)b$ within the Krylov subspace $\mathcal{K}_k((I - \mu A)^{-1}, b)$. This space is generated by a Lanczos recurrence, and requires a solve with $(I - \mu A)$ at each iteration. This procedure is therefore effecient only if one can solve these systems efficiently, e.g. using a multigrid method or a sparse direct solver.

For $f$ a rational function, SI-Lanczos corresponds to approximating each system solution $(A - \sigma_i I)^{-1} b$ in the partial fraction expansion by projecting the problem onto $\mathcal{K}_k((I - \mu A)^{-1}, b)$ and then imposing the Galerkin condition ([25, Proposition 3.1]). More precisely, let $\widehat{A} = (I - \mu A)^{-1}$, $\widehat{\sigma}_i = 1/(\sigma_i \mu - 1)$ and multiply both sides of $(A - \sigma_i I)x = b$ by $\widehat{A}$. Since $\widehat{A} \cdot (A - \sigma_i I) = \frac{1-\mu\sigma_i}{\mu}\left(\widehat{A} - \widehat{\sigma}_i I\right)$, for $i = 1, \ldots, s$, SI-Lanczos solves the systems

$$\left(\widehat{A} - \widehat{\sigma}_i I\right)\widehat{x} = \widehat{b}, \quad \text{with} \quad \widehat{x} = \frac{1 - \mu\sigma_i}{\mu}x, \ \widehat{b} = \widehat{A}b. \tag{10}$$

The linear systems in (10) have precisely the same shifted structure as those in the previous sections. Let $\widehat{x}_i^{(k)}$ be the Galerkin solution to system $i$ in $\mathcal{K}_k(\widehat{A}, \widehat{b})$, and let $x_i^{(k)} = \frac{\mu}{1-\mu\sigma_i}\widehat{x}_i^{(k)}$ be the corresponding approximate solution to the original system $(A - \sigma_i I)x = b$; see (10). Then

$$g(A)b - \sum_{i=1}^{s}\omega_i x_i^{(k)} = \sum_{i=1}^{s}\omega_i\big(x_i - x_i^{(k)}\big)$$

$$= \sum_{i=1}^{s} \frac{\mu \omega_i}{1 - \mu \sigma_i} (\widehat{x}_i - \widehat{x}_i^{(k)}) \equiv \sum_{i=1}^{s} \widehat{\omega}_i (\widehat{x}_i - \widehat{x}_i^{(k)}).$$

The procedure described in section 4 may thus be used to bound the error in the form given by the last expression. The right plot of Figure 3 contains the results for this approach, again for the 2D Laplacian on a $41 \times 41$ grid. Here we used $s = 14$ and $\mu = -1/\max_i |\sigma_i|$ (cf. [25]), so that now the interval $[\ell_1, \ell_2]$ is given by $\ell_1 = 1/(1 - \mu a_2)$, $\ell_2 = 1/(1 - \mu a_1)$, where $[a_1, a_2]$ is the interval containing $\text{spec}(\tau A)$.

As expected, the number of iterations to achieve a given accuracy is reduced substantially. A slow initial phase is no longer present and the error estimate almost coincides with the true error. Remarkably, our bound on the error is now much closer to the true error, too, being less than one order of magnitude too large.

# References

1. Alefeld, G., Herzberger, J.: Introduction to Interval Computation. Academic Press, London (1983)
2. Arnold, G., Cundy, N., van den Eshof, J., Frommer, A., Krieg, S., Lippert, T., Schäfer, K.: Numerical methods for the QCD overlap operator. II: Optimal Krylov subspace methods. In: Boriçi, et al. (eds.) [4]
3. Baker, G.A., Graves-Morris, P.: Padé Approximants, Encyclopedia of Mathematics and its applications. Cambridge University Press, Cambridge (1996)
4. Boriçi, A., Frommer, A., Joó, B., Kennedy, A., Pendleton, B. (eds.): Methods of Algorithmic Language Implementation. Lecture Notes in Computational Science and Engineering, vol. 47. Springer, Berlin (2005)
5. Carpenter, A.J., Ruttan, A., Varga, R.S.: Extended numerical computations on the 1/9 conjecture in rational approximation theory. In: Graves-Morris, P.R., Saff, E.B., Varga, R.S. (eds.) Rational Approximation and Interpolation. Lecture Notes in Mathematics, vol. 1105, pp. 383–411. Springer, Berlin (1984)
6. Druskin, V., Knizhnerman, L.: Two polynomial methods of calculating functions of symmetric matrices. U.S.S.R. Comput. Math. Math. Phys. 29, 112–121 (1989)
7. Frommer, A., Simoncini, V.: Stopping criteria for rational matrix functions of hermitian and symmetric matrices. SIAM J. Sci. Comput. 30, 1387–1412 (2008)
8. Gallopoulos, E., Saad, Y.: Efficient solution of parabolic equations by Krylov approximation methods. SIAM J. Sci. Stat. Comput. 13, 1236–1264 (1992)
9. Grimm, V., Hochbruck, M.: Rational approximation to trigonometric operators. BIT 48, 215–229 (2008)
10. Hairer, E., Lubich, C., Wanner, G.: Geometric numerical integration. In: Structure-preserving algorithms for ordinary differential equations. Springer Series in Computational Mathematics, vol. 31. Springer, Berlin (2002)
11. Hansen, E.R., Walster, W.G.: Global Optimization Using Interval Analysis, 2nd edn. Marcel Dekker, New York (2004)
12. Higham, N.J.: Matrix Functions – Theory and Applications. SIAM, Philadelphia (2008)
13. Hochbruck, M., Lubich, C.: On Krylov subspace approximations to the matrix exponential operator. SIAM J. Numer. Anal. 34, 1911–1925 (1997)

14. Hochbruck, M., Ostermann, A.: Exponential Runge-Kutta methods for parabolic problems. Applied Numer. Math. 53, 323–339 (2005)
15. Hochbruck, M., van den Eshof, J.: Preconditioning Lanczos approximations to the matrix exponential. SIAM J. Sci. Comput. 27, 1438–1457 (2006)
16. Horn, R.A., Johnson, C.R.: Topics in Matrix Analysis. Cambridge University Press, Cambridge (1994)
17. Kearfott, R.B.: Rigorous Global Search: Continuous Problems. Kluwer Academic Publishers, Dordrecht (1996)
18. Lopez, L., Simoncini, V.: Analysis of projection methods for rational function approximation to the matrix exponential. SIAM J. Numer. Anal. 44, 613–635 (2006)
19. The MathWorks, Inc., MATLAB 7 (September 2004)
20. Moret, I., Novati, P.: RD-rational approximations of the matrix exponential. BIT, Numerical Mathematics 44, 595–615 (2004)
21. National Institute of Standards and Technology, Matrix market
22. Neumaier, A.: Interval Methods for Systems of Equations. Cambridge University Press, Cambridge (1990)
23. Paige, C.C., Parlett, B.N., van der Vorst, H.A.: Approximate solutions and eigenvalue bounds from Krylov subspaces. Numerical Linear Algebra with Applications 2, 115–134 (1995)
24. Petrushev, P.P., Popov, V.A.: Rational Approximation of Real Functions. Cambridge University Press, Cambridge (1987)
25. Popolizio, M., Simoncini, V.: Acceleration techniques for approximating the matrix exponential operator. SIAM J. Matrix Analysis and Appl. 30, 657–683 (2008)
26. Ratschek, H., Rokne, J.: New Computer Methods for Global Optimization. Ellis Horwood, Chichester (1988)
27. Rump, S.M.: INTLAB – INTerval LABoratory. In: Csendes, T. (ed.) Developments in Reliabale Computing, pp. 77–104. Kluwer, Dordrecht (1999)
28. Saad, Y.: Analysis of some Krylov subspace approximations to the matrix exponential operator. SIAM J. Numer. Anal. 29, 209–228 (1992)
29. van den Eshof, J., Frommer, A., Lippert, T., Schilling, K., van der Vorst, H.A.: Numerical methods for the QCD overlap operator. I: Sign-function and error bounds. Comput. Phys. Commun. 146, 203–224 (2002)

# Error-Free Transformation in Rounding Mode toward Zero

Stef Graillat[1], Jean-Luc Lamotte[1], and Diep Nguyen Hong[2]

[1] CNRS, UMR 7606, LIP6, University Pierre et Marie Curie, 4 place Jussieu, 75252 Paris cedex 05, France
Stef.Graillat@lip6.fr, Jean-Luc.Lamotte@lip6.fr
[2] Laboratoire LIP, CNRS-ENSL-INRIA-UCBL, 46 alle d'Italie, 69364 Lyon Cedex 07, France
hong.diep.nguyen@ens-lyon.fr

**Abstract.** In this paper, we provide new error-free transformations for the sum and the product of two floating-point numbers. These error-free transformations are well suited for the CELL processor. We prove that these transformations are error-free, and we perform numerical experiments on the CELL processor comparing these new error-free transformations with the classic ones.

## 1 Introduction

For numerical computing, traditional processors are now in competition with new processors using new architecture.

Over the last 5 years, the main evolution of traditional processors has been towards multi-core architecture, but there is no new approach to design the floating-point unit. The power of the new processor is directly dependent on the number of cores.

On the other hand, new architectures are currently being used for specific numerical codes. The most popular are GPU (see http://www.gpgpu.org) and the CELL processor. These new possibilities are the result of the convergence between the multimedia system (mainly graphics operations) and numerical computation. These solutions offer huge power for numerical computation. The peak performance of traditional processors is around 50 Gflops and should be compared with the 200 Gflops of the CELL processors and the 500 Gflops of best graphic cards. Unfortunately, very often, their high level of performance is obtained with specific implementations of floating-point numbers which do not respect the IEEE 754 standard [1]. For example, on the CELL processor, the most powerful unit has only a rounding mode toward zero (truncated mode) and there are no subnormal numbers and no representation for infinity. In both architectures, to obtain a high level of performance, it takes a lot of hard works to find the dependencies of the numerical instructions and to use them carefully to write instructions that use the instruction pipeline fully. The algorithm study must take into account this situation: an algorithm which needs two or three

A. Cuyt et al. (Eds.): Numerical Validation, LNCS 5492, pp. 217–229, 2009.

times more operations can be more efficient if these operations can be easily pipelined.

More and more scientific applications need more accurate computations, whether for specific algorithms (accurate summation, accurate dot product) or for an entire method by using extended precision. One of the main way to achieve this higher precision is to use **Error-Free Transformation** (EFT). An EFT is an algorithm which transforms any arithmetic operation $\circ$ of two values $a$ and $b$ into a sum of two values $s$ and $e$, where $s$ is an approximation of the result and $e$ is an approximation of the error on the result. Such that $a \circ b = s + e$. A lot of publications have been written on EFT and their applications (see for example [2,3,4,5,6]) but most of the transformation algorithms use only the rounding mode to the nearest except for some papers by Priest [7]. With the new architectures, it is necessary to study the implementation of EFT on processors that perform computation with the rounding mode toward zero.

In this paper, the `TwoSum-toward-zero` proposed by Priest in [7] is studied from an implementation point of view. Its main limitation is found in the dependencies of its instructions. Another version is proposed which reduces the dependencies and allows a more efficient implementation. Concerning multiplication, we study a well-known algorithm that uses a rounding mode to the nearest and is based on FMA (Fused Multiply-Add). We prove that this algorithm is usable with a rounding mode toward zero.

The rest of the article is organised as follows. Section 2 gives a reminder of properties of floating-point numbers that will be used in the paper and results on EFT. In Section 3, we present the main characteristics of the CELL processor and motivates our work. Section 4 details the known EFT algorithms for the sum and the product with rounding mode toward zero. In Section 5, we provide a new EFT algorithm in rounding mode toward zero more suitable for the CELL processor; the proof is given in Section 6. Finally, Section 7 is devoted to performance measurements which show that our new algorithm is faster on the CELL processor.

## 2    Floating-Point Arithmetic and EFTs (Error-Free Transformations)

Let $\mathbb{F}$ denote the set of all floating-point numbers, and $x \in \mathbb{F}$ be a normalized floating-point number. It can be written as:

$$x = s \times \underbrace{x_0.x_1 \ldots x_{p-1}}_{\text{mantissa}} \times B^e, \quad 0 \leq x_i \leq B-1, \quad x_0 \neq 0, \qquad (1)$$

with $s = \pm 1$ the sign, $B$ the base, $p$ the precision, and $e$ the exponent of $x$. We can say that $x$ is a $p$-bit floating point number. The value $\texttt{eps} = B^{1-p}$ is the relative error of $x$.

The IEEE 754 standard [1] specifies the base $(B = 2)$, $x_0 = 1$ and two main representations: the single precision ($s = 1, p = 24$ bits with the hidden bit, and

$e = 8$) and the double precision ($s = 1, p = 53$ bits with the hidden bit, and $e = 11$).

Floating-point numbers are approximations of real numbers. Let $r$ be a real number. The approximation of $r$, denoted $\mathrm{fl}(r)$, in the floating-point set $\mathbb{F}$ is equal to $r$ if $r \in \mathbb{F}$. In the other cases, there are two consecutive floating-point numbers $f^-, f^+ \in \mathcal{F}$ such that: $f^- < r < f^+$, and then

$$\mathrm{fl}(r) \in \{f^-, f^+\}.$$

.

The value $\mathrm{fl}(r)$ is chosen between those two values depending on the current rounding mode. There are four rounding modes.

1. to the nearest: $\mathrm{fl}(r)$ is equal to the nearest floating point value of $r$.
2. toward $+\infty$: $\mathrm{fl}(r) = f^+$.
3. toward $-\infty$: $\mathrm{fl}(r) = f^-$.
4. toward zero: if $r < 0$ then $\mathrm{fl}(r) = f^+$ else $\mathrm{fl}(r) = f^-$.

The **approximation error** of $r$ is defined to be $\mathrm{err}(r) = r - \mathrm{fl}(r)$.

Another binary representation can be used to represent floating-point numbers. Let $x$ be a floating-point number with a binary representation. $x$ can be written as:

$$x = s \times 1.m \times 2^e,$$

where $s, m, e$ are respectively the sign, the mantissa coded with $p - 1$ bits and the exponent. Another representation of $x$ is

$$x = s \times 1m \times 2^{e-p+1},$$

where

- $1m$ is an integer such that $2^{p-1} \le 1m < 2^p$,
- $2^{e-p+1}$ is usually named $\mathrm{ulp}(x)$ (unit in the last place).

A bound of the relative error is $\mathsf{eps} = 2^{1-p}$. Since,

$$\mathrm{ulp}(x) = 2^e \mathsf{eps} = \frac{|x|}{1.m} \mathsf{eps},$$

it follows that

$$\frac{\mathsf{eps}}{2} |x| < \mathrm{ulp}(x) \le \mathsf{eps}|x|.$$

The following lemmas which can be found in [7] are used in this paper.

**Lemma 1.** Let $a = m \times \mathrm{ulp}(b)$ a floating-point number of p-bits, and $k$ an integer such as $|k| \le |m|$, then $k \times \mathrm{ulp}(b)$ is representable by a floating-point number of p-bits.

**Lemma 2.** Let $a$ and $b$ be two floating-point numbers of p-bits such that $1/2 \le a/b \le 2$, the difference of $a$ by $b$ is representable by a floating-point number of p-bits i.e. $\mathrm{fl}(a - b) = a - b$.

**Lemma 3.** Let $\circ$ be a floating-point operation. The following inequality is always true,

$$|\mathrm{err}(a \circ b)| < \mathrm{ulp}(\mathrm{fl}(a \circ b)) < \mathsf{eps}|a \circ b|.$$

# 3   The CELL Processor

The CELL processor [8] uses a new architecture optimized for multimedia applications. It can be used for scientific computation [9] as well. It implements two different cores. The main core is a PowerPC processor (named PPE) with some elements removed (for example, the reordering instruction mechanism) to free place for the 8 SPEs (Synergetic Processor Element) which provide the numerical computation power of the chip.

The PPE is a standard PowerPC processor. It manages the memory, the IO and runs the operating system. It is fully IEEE 754 compliant [1]. An SPE, on the contrary, is a small processor with a SIMD unit. It has only 256 KB of memory, for instructions and data, named the "local store" (LS) and 128 registers of 128 bits. All exchanges with the main memory are managed by the MFC (Memory Flow controller) through DMA access. The SIMD processor is based on a FMA (Fused Multiply-Add) and uses 128-bit registers. So, it performs 4 multiplications on single precision floating-point numbers in a single instruction. Another important characteristic is that it is fully pipelined. That means that it can provide 4 results of 4 FMA operations at each cycle. Its peak performance with a clock at 3.2 Ghz is around 25.6 Gflops. With the 8 SPE on a processor, the peak performance of the entire processor is around 200 Gflops. In double precision, the SIMD processor is not fully pipelined and the peak performance is only 1.8 Gflops/SPE.

The price we pay for the enhanced performance is the incompatibility with the IEEE 754 standard. For single precision, we should note that:

- There is no division.
- Only the 12 first bits of $\frac{1}{x}$ and $\frac{1}{\sqrt{x}}$ are exact.
- Inf and NaN are not recognized.
- Overflows saturate the largest representable values.
- There are no denormalized results.

Some SPE instructions will be explained in detail to facilitate the understanding of the algorithms. The variables correspond to a 128-bit registers which can contain 16 8-bit integers, or 8 16 bit integers, or 4 32-bit integers or 4 32-bit floating-point numbers or 2 64-bit floating point numbers. Let u,v and w be a 128-bits registers of integer or floating point variables and let comp be a field of 128 bits.

The instructions comp=spu_cmpabsgt(u,v) and comp=spu_cmpeq(u,v) compare the values of u and v. All the bits of comp are set to 1 if the corresponding elements of u and v are respectively greater or equal in absolute value. An example is provided in Table 1 on two vectors $u$, $v$ of 4 elements. Important instructions are:

- c=spu_sel(u, v, comp) selects the bits of u or v in relation to the bits of comp. Number of cycles: 2 (see table ).
- c=spu_add(u, v) adds the four values of u with the four values of v. Number of cycles: 6

**Table 1.** Example of the `spu_cmpabsgt` function result

| u | 1.0 | 1.0 | −1.0 | −1.0 |
|---|---|---|---|---|
| v | 0.5 | −2.0 | −0.5 | −2.0 |
| comp | 0xFFFFFFFF | 0x00000000 | 0xFFFFFFFF | 0x00000000 |

**Table 2.** Example of the `spu_sel` function result

| u | 1.0 | 1.0 | −1.0 | −1.0 |
|---|---|---|---|---|
| v | 0.5 | −2.0 | −0.5 | −2.0 |
| comp | 0xFFFFFFFF | 0x00000000 | 0xFFFFFFFF | 0x00000000 |
| v | 0.5 | 1.0 | −0.5 | −1.0 |

- `c=spu_sub(u, v)` subtracts the four values of u from the four values of v. Number of cycles: 6
- `c=spu_madd(u, v, w)` multiplies the four values of u with the four corresponding values of v and then adds the four values of w . Number of cycles: 6

The code optimisation on an SPE is very tricky. The SIMD programming is based on the Altivec system. The interested reader can visit the following website `http://www.freescale.com/altivec`. Just a specific note: with the compiler used by the CELL SDK (Software Development Kit), it is possible to have a good estimation of instruction orders that will be run on the processor. This estimation takes into account notably the number of cycles used by the instructions and the capabilities of the two pipelines. The estimation is given by the `SPU_TIMING` option of the compiler which indicates for each instruction the start cycle modulo 10 and the instruction cycle number. In this paper, the result of this option is slightly improved for a better understanding. Figure 1 shows how the instructions are run. On this program, the instruction `inst1` is run first and its duration is 6 cycles. The instruction `inst2` starts at the cycle 2. Its duration is 6 cycles. The instructions `inst3` and 4 start at cycle 8 on two separate pipelines. The sign − shows that no instruction can be run during these cycles due to variable dependencies between `inst2` and `inst3`. The cycle lost is also known as a pipeline bubble.

```
inst1 123456
inst2 234567
inst3 ------890123
inst4 ------89
```

**Fig. 1.** The left column shows the instructions and the right column the cycle number of each instruction and its start cycles

# 4    The "Error-Free Transformations" (EFT)

An EFT is an algorithm which transforms an arithmetic operation $\circ \in \{+, -, \times, /\}$ on two values $a$ and $b$ into a sum of two floating-point values $r$ and $e$ such that $a \circ b = r + s$. We also require that $r \approx \text{fl}(a \circ b)$ and $e \approx \text{err}(a \circ b)$. EFT are very useful to implement extended precision number [10,2] and accurate operators [4,3,5,6].

Let $a$ and $b$ be two floating-point numbers and $\circ$ any operation in $(+, -, \times, /)$ then we have

$$a + b = \text{fl}(a + b) + \text{err}(a + b),$$

where $\text{fl}(a \circ b)$ is a floating-point corresponding to the result and $\text{err}(a \circ b)$ is the rounding error.

It is known that the error obtained during the operation $a \circ b$ in the rounding mode to the nearest is a floating-point number for $\circ \in (+, -, \times)$. In that case, the result of an EFT must be $r = \text{fl}(a + b)$ and $e = \text{err}(a + b)$.

But it turns out that with other rounding modes, in most cases the error is a floating-point number but there are exceptions. For example, as noticed by Priest, with rounding toward zero, if we subtract a very small positive number from a very large positive number then the rounding error is not a floating-point number.

## 4.1    The Sum Operation

A set of algorithms has been proposed for the sum of two numbers in the rounding mode toward the nearest and used in a lot of libraries. We can cite TwoSum algorithm of Knuth [11] and FastTwoSum algorithm of Dekker [10],

For rounding mode toward zero, Priest proposed in [7] the following algorithm to compute the sum of two floating-point number:

```
1    TwoSum-toward-zero (a,b)
2    if (|a| < |b|)
3        swap(a,b)
4    s = fl(a + b)
5    d = fl(s - a)
6    e = fl(b - d)
7    if (e + d != b)
8        s = a, e = b
9    return (s,e)
```

If $[s, e] = \text{TwoSum-toward-zero}(a, b)$ then $a + b = s + e$ with either $s = e = 0$ or $|e| < \text{ulp}(c)$.

Figure 2 shows the implementation on the CELL processor of the TwoSum-toward-zero algorithm and how the code is run. The instruction running sequence has been given by the SPU_TIMING tool.

```
 1  TwoSum-toward-zero(a,b)              cycles
 2     comp = spu_cmpabsgt(b,a)          12
 3     a = spu_sel(a, b, comp)          -34
 4     b = spu_sel(b, a, comp)           45
 5     s = spu_add(a , b)               012345
 6     d = spu_sub(s , a)                  -678901
 7     e = spu_sub(b , d)                    ----234567
 8     tmp = spu_add(e , d)                    -----890123
 9     comp = spu_cmpeq(d, tmp)                          45
10     s = spu_sel(s, a, comp)                          -67
11     e = spu_sel(e, b, comp)                           89
12     return s,e)
```

**Fig. 2.** Implementation on the CELL processor of the TwoSum-toward-zero algorithm and its instruction running sequence. Cycle cost: 29.

This implementation is not efficient. It is obvious that there are important dependencies between the line 9 and lines 6, 7 and 8. The effect is clearly visible in the information generated by the SPU_TIMING tools. There are a lot of pipeline "bubbles" marked by the '-' character.

### 4.2   The Product Operation

For the product, there is an algorithm called TwoProduct in rounding mode to the nearest proposed by Veltkamp [10] using Dekker Split algorithm [10]. The Veltkamp algorithm is not efficient since it costs 17 floating point operations.

The TwoProduct algorithm can be re-written in a very simple way if a Fused-Multiply-and-Add (FMA) operator is available on the targeted architecture [12]. Some computers have a Fused-Multiply-and-Add (FMA) operation that enables a floating point multiplication followed by an addition to be performed as a single floating point operation. As a consequence, there is only one rounding error. The Intel IA-64 architecture, implemented in the Intel Itanium processor, has an FMA instruction as well as the IBM RS/6000 and the PowerPC before it and as the new Cell processor [13].

Thanks to the FMA, the TwoProduct algorithm can be re-written as follows, which costs only 2 operations.

```
1           TwoProductFMA ( a , b )
2           p = fl ( a * b )
3           e = FMA( a , b , -p )
4           return ( p , e )
```

The TwoProductFMA function is very efficient with only 2 operations in a rounding mode to the nearest. From a pipeline point of view, the TwoProductFMA is not as efficient as it looks because the two operations cannot be pipelined.

In spite of this bad characteristic, on most processors this algorithm is much
more efficient than the Veltkamp's algorithm.

## 5   A New Algorithm for the Sum

With rounding mode toward zero, Priest's `TwoSum-toward-zero` algorithm uses
a comparison between $e + d$ and $b$. This comparison should wait for the end of all
the previous instructions to be executed. We propose replacing this comparison
by another one which uses only the variables $b$ and $d$.

```
1        TwoSum−toward−zero2  (a,b)
2        if  (|a| < |b|)
3            swap(a,b)
4        s = fl(a + b)
5        d = fl(s − a)
6        e = fl(b − d)
7        if  (|2 * b| < |d|)
8            s = a, e = b
9        return (s,e)
```

There is not a lot of difference between our algorithm and those proposed by
Priest except that the instruction of line 7 relaxes the dependencies which allows
an increasing in performance. Figure 3 shows how the instructions are run on
the CELL. The cycle number is equal to 20 and should be compared with the
29 of the Priest algorithm.

The proof of this algorithm correctness is presented in the next section.

| 1 | TwoSum-toward-zero2(a,b) | cycles |
|---|---|---|
| 2 | comp = spu_cmpabsgt(b,a) | 12 |
| 3 | a = spu_sel(a, b, comp) | -34 |
| 4 | b = spu_sel(b, a, comp) | 45 |
| 5 | s = spu_add(a , b) | 012345 |
| 6 | d = spu_sub(s , a) | -678901 |
| 7 | e = spu_sub(b , d) | ----234567 |
| 8 | tmp = spu_mul(2 , b) | 789012 |
| 9 | comp = spu_cmpabsgt(d, tmp) | 34 |
| 10 | s = spu_sel(s, a, comp) | -56˙ |
| 11 | e = spu_sel(e, b, comp) | --89 |
| 12 | return s,e) | |

**Fig. 3.** Implementation on the CELL processor of the `TwoSum-toward-zero2` algorithm
and its instructions running sequence. Cycle cost: 20.

# 6   Proof

This section explains the proof in the rounding mode toward zero of the `TwoSum-toward-zero2` and the `TwoProductFMA` algorithms. The lines in the proof refer to the algorithm and not to its implementation on the CELL processor.

## 6.1   The Correctness Proof for the `TwoSum-Toward-Zero2` Algorithm

Let $a$ and $b$ be two floating-point numbers. After the two instructions of line 2 and 3 of algorithm `TwoSum-toward-zero2`, we have $|a| \geq |b|$. The proof will take into account the case $a > 0$. For the case $a < 0$, the proof is very similar.

When $a > 0$, we will study three cases carefully: $b \geq 0$, $-a \leq b \leq -a/2$ and $-a/2 < b < 0$.

$\boxed{\text{Case } b \geq 0}$

It is clear that $a + b > 0$. In rounding mode toward zero, $\mathrm{err}(a + b) \geq 0$ and $a + b = \mathrm{fl}(a + b) + \mathrm{err}(a + b)$ so we deduce that $b \leq a \leq \mathrm{fl}(a + b) \leq a + b$ and $0 \leq \mathrm{err}(a + b) \leq b$.

Let $b$ be equal to $h \times \mathrm{ulp}(b)$ with $h$ a positive integer. If $a > b > 0$ then $\mathrm{ulp}(a) = n \times \mathrm{ulp}(b)$ implies $a = k \times \mathrm{ulp}(b)$ with $k$ a positive integer. From line 4 of the `TwoSum-toward-zero2` algorithm, $s = \mathrm{fl}(a + b) \geq b$ hence $s = \mathrm{fl}(a + b) = l \times \mathrm{ulp}(b)$, $l$ being a positive integer. As a consequence

$$
\begin{aligned}
\mathrm{err}(a + b) &= a + b - \mathrm{fl}(a + b), \\
&= k \times \mathrm{ulp}(b) + h \times \mathrm{ulp}(b) - l \times \mathrm{ulp}(b), \\
&= (h + k - l) \times \mathrm{ulp}(b), \\
&= m \times \mathrm{ulp}(b).
\end{aligned}
$$

Moreover $0 \leq \mathrm{err}(a + b) \leq b$, hence $\mathrm{err}(a + b)$ is representable. This is a consequence of Lemma 1.

From line 5 of the `TwoSum-toward-zero` algorithm, it holds

$$
\begin{aligned}
d &= \mathrm{fl}(s - a), \\
&= \mathrm{fl}(a + b - \mathrm{err}(a + b) - a), \\
&= \mathrm{fl}(b - \mathrm{err}(a + b)), \\
&= \mathrm{fl}((h - m) \times \mathrm{ulp}(b)).
\end{aligned}
$$

As we have $0 \leq \mathrm{err}(a + b) \leq b$, it follows that $0 \leq b - \mathrm{err}(a + b) \leq b$ and therefore $b - \mathrm{err}(a + b) = (h - m) \times \mathrm{ulp}(b)$ is representable and $b = (h - m) \times \mathrm{ulp}(b)$ is the exact result.

To conclude

$$
\begin{aligned}
e &= \mathrm{fl}(b - d), \\
&= \mathrm{fl}(h \times \mathrm{ulp}(b) - (h - m) \times \mathrm{ulp}(b)), \\
&= \mathrm{fl}(m \times \mathrm{ulp}(b)), \\
&= \mathrm{err}(a + b),
\end{aligned}
$$

so $e$ is the exact result. Moreover

$$|d| = (h - m) \times \text{ulp}(b),$$
$$< h \times \text{ulp}(b),$$
$$< b,$$
$$< |2b|,$$

As a consequence, the comparison of line 7 of `TwoSum-toward-zero2` algorithm is not satisfied. Then the return result is: $(s = \text{fl}(a + b), e = \text{err}(a + b))$.

> Case $-a \le b \le -a/2$

We then have $1/2 \le -b/a \le 1$. As consequence, $a + b = a - (-b)$ is representable (by Lemma 2). So $s = \text{fl}(a + b) = a + b$, $d = \text{fl}(s - a) = b$ and $e = \text{fl}(b - d) = 0$. Then $d = b$ so the inequality of line 7 of the `TwoSum-toward-zero2` algorithm is not satisfied. The following result is returned: $(s = a + b, e = 0)$.

> Case $-a/2 < b < 0$

Hence $a > a + b > a/2 > |b| > 0$ and so $\text{err}(a + b) > 0$. We know that $a/2$ is a representable floating-point, so we have $\text{fl}(a + b) \ge a/2$. It follows that $a > s \ge a/2$, $1/2 \le s/a < 1$. Then $s - a$ is representable and so:

$$d = \text{fl}(s - a),$$
$$= s - a,$$
$$= a + b - \text{err}(a + b) - a,$$
$$= b - \text{err}(a + b),$$

and

$$e = \text{fl}(b - d);$$
$$= \text{fl}(b - (b - \text{err}(a + b))),$$
$$= \text{fl}(\text{err}(a + b)).$$

As $a > a + b > |b|$, we can deduce $a > s = fl(a + b) \ge |b|$, $a = h \times \text{ulp}(b)$, $s = k \times \text{ulp}(b)$, $b = -l \times \text{ulp}(b)$, $h, k, l$ being positive integers with $h > k > l > 0$. It follows that

$$\text{err}(a + b) = a + b - \text{fl}(a + b),$$
$$= h \times \text{ulp}(b) - l \times \text{ulp}(b) - k \times \text{ulp}(b),$$
$$= (h - l - k) \times \text{ulp}(b).$$

As $b < 0$ and $\text{err}(a + b) \ge 0$ the comparison of line 7 can be rewritten as follows:

$$|2b| < |d|,$$
$$< |b - \text{err}(a + b)|,$$

and so

$$2 * b > b - \text{err}(a + b),$$
$$|b| < \text{err}(a + b).$$

If the comparison of line 7 is satisfied, the returned result is $(s = a, e = b)$. As $0 < a + b < a$ we have

$$|e| = |b| < \text{err}(a + b) < \text{ulp}(\text{fl}(a + b)) \leq \text{ulp}(a) = \text{ulp}(s).$$

It is in that case that the error is not representable and so $s \neq \text{fl}(a + b)$.

If the comparison of line 7 is not satisfied, that means that $|b| \geq \text{err}(a+b) \geq 0$. Moreover $\text{err}(a+b) = (h-l-k) \times \text{ulp}(b)$, by Lemma 1 $\text{err}(a+b)$ is representable. Hence $e = fl(\text{err}(a + b)) = \text{err}(a + b)$. Therefore the returned result by this algorithm is $(s = \text{fl}(a + b), e = \text{err}(a + b))$.

In both cases, the equality $s + e = a + b$ and the inequality $e < \text{ulp}(s)$ are always correct if $s \neq 0$. So, the couple $(s, e)$ is the exact transformation of the sum of $a$ and $b$.

### 6.2   The Correctness Proof for the `TwoProductFMA` Algorithm

Let $a$ and $b$ be two floating-point numbers of $t$-bits. They can be written as $a = s_1 \times 1m_1 \times 2^{e1-t}$, $b = s_2 \times 1m_2 \times 2^{e2-t}$ with $2^t \leq 1m_1, 1m_2 < 2^{t+1}$.

The product $a \times b$ is equal to $(s_1 \times s_2) \times (1m_1 \times 1m_2) \times 2^{e1+e2-2t}$ As $2^t \leq 1m_1, 1m_2 < 2^{t+1}$, then we have $2^{2t} \leq 1m_1 \times 1m_2 < 2^{2t+2}$.

The intermediate result of the product $a \times b$ is a floating-point of $(2t + 1)$-bits without taking into account the first bit. In the rounding mode toward zero, the computed result of $a \times b$ is represented exactly by the $t + 1$ first bits of the intermediate result. Then the subtraction of $\text{fl}(a \times b)$ by $a \times b$ is exactly the $(t+1)$ last bits of the intermediate result. That means that $\text{err}(a \times b)$ is representable by a floating-point of $t$-bits and that $a \times b - \text{fl}(a \times b) = \text{err}(a \times b)$. This function is usable with two rounding modes: to the nearest and toward zero.

## 7   Performance Measurements

The performances have been measured on the sum of two vectors of 64 floating-point numbers. To have a accurate estimate, a sum of two 64 elements vector have been done $10^7$ times on 1 SPE, without memory exchange with the main memory.

Inside both code it is necessary to copy the data to registers. An empty program which contents only the load and store of the registers has been written. The cost of this part is around 10 cycles. In practice, the performance measurements show clearly that our algorithm is better than those proposed by Priest. If we remove the number of cycle due to the load and store of the registers, we find the theoretical performance. The performance of `TwoSum-toward-zero` and the `TwoSum-toward-zero2` algorithm are given in Table 3.

**Table 3.** Performance of the `TwoSum-toward-zero` and the `TwoSum-toward-zero2` algorithms on a CELL processor

| Algorithm | computation time in second | performance (MFLOPS) | cycle/operation |
|---|---|---|---|
| TwoSum-toward-zero | 7.93 | 80.7 | 39.65 |
| TwoSum-toward-zero2 | 6.13 | 104.4 | 30.65 |
| Only load-store registers | 2.15 | - | 10.75 |

## 8    Conclusion

In this paper, we have proposed an improvement of `TwoSum-toward-zero` algorithm which reduces the variable dependencies. It allows a better implementation on processors which use pipeline instructions.

Future work: the next step consists in using this algorithm to implement algorithms which use EFT on processors which compute only in rounding mode toward zero.

## Acknowledgements

The authors are very grateful to the CINES (Centre Informatique National de l'Enseignement Supérieur, Montpellier, France) for providing us access to their CELL blades.

## References

1. IEEE Computer Society: IEEE Standard for Binary Floating-Point Arithmetic, ANSI/IEEE Standard 754-1985. Institute of Electrical and Electronics Engineers, New York (1985); Reprinted in SIGPLAN Notices 22(2), 9–25 (1987)
2. Li, X.S., Demmel, J.W., Bailey, D.H., Henry, G., Hida, Y., Iskandar, J., Kahan, W., Kang, S.Y., Kapur, A., Martin, M.C., Thompson, B.J., Tung, T., Yoo, D.J.: Design, implementation and testing of extended and mixed precision BLAS. ACM Trans. Math. Softw. 28, 152–205 (2002)
3. Ogita, T., Rump, S.M., Oishi, S.: Accurate sum and dot product. SIAM J. Sci. Comput. 26, 1955–1988 (2005)
4. Graillat, S., Louvet, N., Langlois, P.: Compensated Horner scheme. Research Report 04, Équipe de recherche DALI, Laboratoire LP2A, Université de Perpignan Via Domitia, France, 52 avenue Paul Alduy, 66860 Perpignan cedex, France (2005)
5. Rump, S.M., Ogita, T., Oishi, S.: Accurate floating-point summation part I: Faithful rounding. Technical Report 07.1, Faculty for Information and Communication Sciences, Hamburg University of Technology (2007)
6. Rump, S.M., Ogita, T., Oishi, S.: Accurate floating-point summation part II: Sign, K-fold faithful and rounding to nearest. Technical Report 07.2, Faculty for Information and Communication Sciences, Hamburg University of Technology (2007)

7. Priest, D.M.: On Properties of Floating Point Arithmetics: Numerical Stability and the Cost of Accurate Computations. Ph.D thesis, Mathematics Department, University of California, Berkeley, CA, USA (1992),
ftp://ftp.icsi.berkeley.edu/pub/theory/priest-thesis.ps.Z
8. Kahle, J.A., Day, M.N., Hofstee, H.P., Johns, C.R., Maeurer, T.R., Shippy, D.: Introduction to the cell multiprocessor. IBM J. Res. Dev. 49(4/5), 589–604 (2005)
9. Williams, S., Shalf, J., Oliker, L., Kamil, S., Husbands, P., Yelick, K.: The potential of the CELL processor for scientific computing. In: CF 2006: Proceedings of the 3rd conference on Computing frontiers, pp. 9–20. ACM Press, New York (2006)
10. Dekker, T.J.: A floating-point technique for extending the available precision. Numer. Math. 18, 224–242 (1971)
11. Knuth, D.E.: The Art of Computer Programming, 3rd edn. Seminumerical Algorithms, vol. 2. Addison-Wesley, Reading (1998)
12. Nievergelt, Y.: Scalar fused multiply-add instructions produce floating-point matrix arithmetic provably accurate to the penultimate digit. ACM Trans. Math. Software 29, 27–48 (2003)
13. Jacobi, C., Oh, H.J., Tran, K.D., Cottier, S.R., Michael, B.W., Nishikawa, H., Totsuka, Y., Namatame, T., Yano, N.: The vector floating-point unit in a synergistic processor element of a cell processor. In: ARITH 2005: Proceedings of the 17th IEEE Symposium on Computer Arithmetic, Washington, DC, USA, pp. 59–67. IEEE Computer Society, Los Alamitos (2005)

# Fast (Parallel) Dense Linear System Solvers in C-XSC Using Error Free Transformations and BLAS

Walter Krämer and Michael Zimmer

Wissenschaftliches Rechnen/Softwaretechnologie,
Bergische Universität Wuppertal
Gaussstr. 20, 42097 Wuppertal, Germany
kraemer@math.uni-wuppertal.de, zimmer@math.uni-wuppertal.de

**Abstract.** Existing selfverifying solvers for dense linear (interval-) systems in C-XSC provide high accuracy, but are rather slow. A new set of solvers is presented, which are a lot faster than the existing solvers, without losing too much accuracy. This is achieved through two main changes. First, an alternative method for the computation of exact dot products based on the DotK-Algorithm is implemented. Then, optimized BLAS and LAPACK routines are used for the most costly parts, in terms of runtime, of the algorithm. Verified results are achieved by manipulating the rounding mode of the processor. Finally, an efficient parallel version of these solvers for distributed memory systems, based on ScaLAPACK, is presented, which allows to solve very large dense systems.

The new solver is compared to other solvers with respect to runtime and to numerical quality of the final result.

**Keywords:** Selfverifying methods, large linear interval systems, DotK methods, parallelization, block cyclic distribution, C-XSC, interval computations.

**AMS subject classification:** 65H10, 15-04, 65G99, 65G10, 65-04, 68W15.

## Some Notation

The set of floating point numbers with $t$ mantissa digits, base $b$ and exponents between $e_{\min}$ and $e_{\max}$ is denoted by $\mathbb{F} = \mathbb{F}(b, t, e_{\min}, e_{\max})$; operations in this set are denoted by a box around the corresponding operator (e. g. $\boxplus$, $\boxminus$, $\boxdot$). Sometimes floating point operations are alternatively denoted by $\mathrm{fl}(\cdot)$, for example, $\mathrm{fl}(\sum_{i=1}^{n} x_i)$ means $x_1 \boxplus x_2 \ldots \boxplus x_n$. All floating point operations in this paper adhere to the IEEE 754 standard. We assume that no overflow occurs but allow underflow. All other mathematical operations are meant to be exact. *eps* is the machine epsilon ($2^{-53}$ for double precision). If we want to emphasize that a quantity is a (machine) interval quantity, we surround it by brackets, for example $[C]$. Computing interval enclosures of expressions is sometimes indicated in the

A. Cuyt et al. (Eds.): Numerical Validation, LNCS 5492, pp. 230–249, 2009.

form $\diamond(\ldots)$, e. g. $[C] = \diamond(I - RA)$. The function $mid$ computes an approximation to the midpoint of an interval (componentwise for interval matrices and interval vectors). It is guaranteed that $mid([x]) \in [x]$. As condition number of a matrix $A$ we use the definition $cond(A) = ||A||_\infty ||A^{-1}||_\infty$.

# 1    Introduction

In this paper we discuss solvers that compute a verified solution $x$ of the problem

$$Ax = b, \qquad \text{(or } [A]x = [b])$$

where $A$ is a dense square matrix, while the right hand side $b$ and the solution $x$ are vectors of corresponding size. The elements of $A$ and $b$ can be real, complex, intervals or complex intervals. The solution $x$ is an interval vector or a complex interval vector whose diameter should be as small as possible.

There are already a number of selfverifying solvers available in C-XSC to attack this problem (see Section 1.1), however, time measurements show that these solvers are quite slow. For example, solving a system with a random floating point matrix $A \in \mathbb{R}^{n \times n}$ with Matlab's floating point solver, the selfverifying solver from Intlab [25], and the selfverifying solver from the C-XSC toolbox [8] on a Pentium 4, 2.8 GHz with 1 GB RAM, one gets the timings shown in Table 1.

**Table 1.** Time in s for solving a real $n \times n$ system

| $n$ | C-XSC toolbox | Intlab | Matlab |
|-----|---------------|--------|--------|
| 100 | 0.952 | 0.028 | 0.002 |
| 500 | 112.72 | 0.57 | 0.07 |
| 1000 | 797.15 | 3.72 | 0.48 |

The non-verifying Matlab solver of course is the fastest, but the difference between Intlab and C-XSC is huge, especially when considering that both solvers use basically the same algorithm [26]. The main reason is that the C-XSC solver uses the long accumulator [4] (see Section 2.1) throughout the algorithm to compute every dot product exactly, which of course has, if done without hardware support, a huge impact on the performance.

On the other hand, using exact dot products (the long accumulator) enables the C-XSC solver to compute results of very high accuracy. For example, solving a system with the ill-conditioned Hilbert-Matrix of dimension $n = 10$ and the first unity vector as right hand side yields the results shown in Figure 1 (here, the Hilbert-Matrix and the right hand side are scaled by the lowest common demoninator 232792560).

In this case, the C-XSC solver is able to compute the exact result [1]. Intlab computes an enclosure of the result, but loses about 7 digits, while the pure

---

[1] It holds $(Ax - b) = 0$ which can be checked in C-XSC using exact dot products componentwise.

| C-XSC toolbox | | | Intlab | | | Matlab | |
|---|---|---|---|---|---|---|---|
| + | 1.000000000000000 | E+2 | + | 1.000000000_____ | E+2 | + | 9.999989996685883 | E+1 |
| - | 4.950000000000000 | E+3 | - | 4.95000000_____ | E+3 | - | 4.949990494288593 | E+3 |
| + | 7.920000000000000 | E+4 | + | 7.92000000_____ | E+4 | + | 7.919978253948466 | E+4 |
| - | 6.006000000000000 | E+5 | - | 6.00600000_____ | E+5 | - | 6.005979106504940 | E+5 |
| + | 2.522520000000000 | E+6 | + | 2.52252000_____ | E+6 | + | 2.522509586181721 | E+6 |
| - | 6.306300000000000 | E+6 | - | 6.30630000_____ | E+6 | - | 6.306270330270943 | E+6 |
| + | 9.609600000000000 | E+6 | + | 9.60960000_____ | E+6 | + | 9.609549857202141 | E+6 |
| - | 8.751600000000000 | E+6 | - | 8.75160000_____ | E+6 | - | 8.751550319100756 | E+6 |
| + | 4.375800000000000 | E+6 | + | 4.37580000_____ | E+6 | + | 4.375773357049561 | E+6 |
| - | 9.237800000000000 | E+5 | - | 9.23780000_____ | E+5 | - | 9.237740322228931 | E+5 |

**Fig. 1.** Results of the different solvers for a real system with the Hilbert-Matrix, $n = 10$

floating point Matlab solver loses about 12 digits (and of course doesn't compute a verified enclosure).

Therefore, the goal was to develop new solvers in C-XSC that are considerably faster while maintaining a high accuracy in the numerical results. This has been achieved through the use of an alternative algorithm for (approximating) dot products (Section 2) and the use of BLAS and LAPACK libraries (Section 3).

Furthermore, to also allow large system matrices, an efficient parallelization of these new solvers is necessary. Such a parallelized solver for dense matrices is presented in Section 4.

## 1.1 Previous Work

There are a number of previous solvers with different purposes and features in C-XSC, some of which this work is based on:

- **LSS** [8]: A verified solver for real linear systems, which is part of the C-XSC Toolbox. This solver does not support over- or underdetermined systems, and does not use the second stage of the algorithm (see Section 3).
- **ILSS** [18,10]: A verified solver for real interval linear systems, which is available as additional software for C-XSC. It supports over- and underdetermined systems and also supports the second stage of the algorithm.
- **PILSS** [7]: A parallel version of the solver ILSS for distributed memory systems using MPI.
- **BLSS** [11]: A solver, specifically designed for system matrices with banded structure.

## 1.2 Some Remarks on the C-XSC Library

C-XSC is a C++ class library for verified scientific computing, developed mainly at the University of Karlsruhe and the University of Wuppertal. It provides many data types, especially interval data types, with corresponding operators. The basic data types are real, interval, complex and cinterval. For each of these datatypes, corresponding vector and matrix types are available as well. The result of every single operation in C-XSC, using the corresponding C-XSC operator, is computed with maximum precision , i. e. with only one final rounding (using the long accumulator, if necessary), see Section 2.1. To allow the exact result of more complex dot product expressions, this long accumulator is also available as an own datatype, `dotprecision`. C-XSC also contains an extensive toolbox with useful software routines for many mathematical problems. For further information, please see [13,9], or visit the XSC-languages website at `http://www.math.uni-wuppertal.de/wrswt/xsc-sprachen.html`

# 2    Exact/Accurate Dot Products

The ability to compute (enclosures of) dot products $x \cdot y = \sum_{i=1}^{n} x_i \cdot y_i$ in high(er) precision is very important, especially in verified numerics. C-XSC relies on a powerful algorithm for this task, the long accumulator [20,4], which is briefly explained in the next section. In Section 2.2 we present the implementation of an alternative algorithm in C-XSC, which allows to compute dot products in $K$-fold working precision, and which is (at least for small $K$) faster than the algorithm based on exact dot product computations (long accumulator).

## 2.1    Exact Dot Product Computations Using the Long Accumulator

The basic idea of this algorithm is to use a fixed-point accumulator (long accumulator) of sufficient length, in which all the computations of the dot product are performed. This fixed-point accumulator is shown in Figure 2.

| $g$ | $2e_{max}$ | $t$ | $t$ | $2|e_{min}|$ |

**Fig. 2.** Long accumulator

In this figure, $t$ is the length of the mantissa, $e_{min}$ and $e_{max}$ are the smallest and largest exponent, respectively and $g$ is a certain number of guard digits to prevent overflow. Inside the long accumulator, the value of a dot product of two floating point vectors can be computed and represented exactly. Only when converting the final result back to working precision, one final rounding has to be done.

It is important to note that, if realised in hardware, this method is even faster than ordinary floating point computation of the dot product by a loop [21]. However, this feature is not supported in current processors, and thus the long accumulator used in C-XSC has to be implemented in software leading to significant execution time penalties.

In C-XSC, the long accumulator is realised in four different classes. These are `dotprecision` for real results, `idotprecision` for interval results, `cdotprecision` for complex results and finally `cidotprecision` for complex interval results. It can be used in a relatively simple and self-explanatory way, as shown in the small example in Listing 1.

**Listing 1.** Example for the usage of the long accumulator in C-XSC

```
rvector  x,  y;            //floating  point  vectors
//...
dotprecision  accu(0.0);   //long  accumulator
accumulate(accu,  x,  y);  //compute  exact  result  of  x*y
real  result  =  rnd(accu); //final  rounding  to  nearest
```

The `accumulate` function computes the exact dot product inside the accumulator variable `accu`, while the function `rnd` rounds the current result stored inside the accumulator to the nearest floating point number.

### 2.2  The DotK Algorithm for Computing Dot Products in K-Fold Working Precision

The DotK algorithm [23] is an alternative algorithm for dot product computations. Based on error-free transformations it computes dot products in a simulated $K$-fold working precision.

Let us first discuss the basic error-free transformations [15,6,5]:

**Theorem 1.** *For all* $a, b \in \mathbb{F}$ *and* $\circ \in \{+, -, \cdot\}$ *there exists a* $y \in \mathbb{F}$ *with*

$$a \circ b = x + y,$$

*where* $x = a \boxdot b$.

This means that every single operation of the dot product can be transformed into a sum $x + y$ of floating point numbers, where $x$ is the floating point result of the operation under consideration and $y$ is the corresponding error. Thus, all information of the correct result is known.

These error-free transformations can be computed in pure floating point. For the transformation of a sum of two floating point numbers, the algorithm TwoSum [15,23] is used.

For the error-free transformation of a product of two floating point numbers, first the algorithm Split [6,23] is needed. Here, $factor$ is a constant with $factor := 2^s + 1$ and $s := \lceil t/2 \rceil$, where $t$ is defined by $eps = 2^{-t}$. So for **double** precision we get $t = 53$ and $s = 27$. This algorithm computes for a given floating point number $a$ two floating point numbers $x$ and $y$ with $a = x + y$, $|y| \leq |x|$ and non overlapping mantissas of $x$ and $y$.

With this an algorithm TwoProduct [6,23] for the error-free transformation of a product can be formulated (Algorithm 3).

**Data**: Two floating point numbers $a, b \in \mathbb{F}$
**Result**: Two floating point numbers $x, y \in \mathbb{F}$ such that $x = a \boxplus b$ and
$\qquad a + b = x + y$ hold
$x = a \boxplus b$
$z = x \boxminus a$
$y = (a \boxminus (x \boxminus z)) \boxplus (b \boxminus z)$

**Algorithm 1.** TwoSum

**Data**: One floating point number $a \in \mathbb{F}$
**Result**: Two floating point numbers $x, y \in \mathbb{F}$ with $a = x + y$
$c = factor \boxdot a$
$x = c \boxminus (c \boxminus a)$
$y = a \boxminus x$

**Algorithm 2.** Split

**Data**: Two floating point numbers $a, b \in \mathbb{F}$
**Result**: Two floating point numbers $x, y \in \mathbb{F}$ with $a \cdot b = x + y$
$x = a \boxdot b$
$[a_1, a_2] =$Split$(a)$
$[b_1, b_2] =$Split$(b)$
$y = a_2 \boxdot b_2 \boxminus (((x \boxminus a_1 \boxdot b_1) \boxminus a_2 \boxdot b_1) \boxminus a_1 \boxdot b_2)$

**Algorithm 3.** TwoProduct

With help of these algorithms it is possible to compute the dot product of two floating point vectors in two-fold working precision using the following Algorithm 4.

**Data**: Two floating point vectors $x, y \in \mathbb{F}^n$
**Result**: The result $res$ of the dot poduct $x \cdot y$ as if computed in two-fold
$\qquad$ working precision
$[p, s] =$TwoProduct$(x_1, y_1)$
**for** $i=2{:}n$ **do**
$\quad [h, r] =$TwoProduct$(x_i, y_i)$
$\quad [p, q] =$TwoSum$(p, h)$
$\quad s = s \boxplus (q \boxplus r)$
$res = p \boxplus s$

**Algorithm 4.** Dot2

This algorithm transforms a dot product of two floating point vectors of length $n$ into a sum of floating point values of length $2n$. Computing this sum in pure floating point leads to an approximation of the dot product as if computed in two-fold working precision. The proof of this statement can be found in [23]. Now, to achieve a result in $K$-fold working precision, the sum of length $2n$, into which the dot product is transformed in Algorithm 4, must be computed in a simulated higher precision. This finally leads to the desired algorithm for dot product computations in $K-$fold precision (Algorithm 5).

---

**Data**: Two vectors $x, y \in \mathbb{F}^n$, desired precision $K$
**Result**: The result $res$ of the dot poduct $x \cdot y$, as if computed in $K$-fold
working precision
$[p, r_1] = \text{TwoProduct}(x_1, y_1)$
**for** $i=2$:$n$ **do**
$\quad [h, r_i] = \text{TwoProduct}(x_i, y_i)$
$\quad [p, r_{n+i-1}] = \text{TwoSum}(p, h)$
$r_{2n} = p$
**for** $k=1$:$K$-$2$ **do**
$\quad$ **for** $i=2$:$2n$ **do**
$\quad\quad [r_i, r_{i-1}] = \text{TwoSum}(r_i, r_{i-1})$

$res = \text{fl}(\sum_{i=1}^{n-1} r_i + r_n)$

---

**Algorithm 5.** DotK

It can be shown (see [23]) that this algorithm computes the result of a dot product of two given floating point vectors, as if computed in $K$-fold working precision. As proven in [23], it is also possible to compute a reliable error bound for the achieved result, again only using pure floating point operations, resulting in the following algorithm Dot2err:

Thus, the only additional information needed to compute a valid error bound is the length $n$ of the dot product as well as the floating point sum of the absolute values of the computed error terms in the final summation.

There also exists a parallel version of this algorithm for shared memory architectures [24].

**Remarks on the Implementation.** The main goal of the implementation of the DotK algorithm in C-XSC was to provide a handling similar to the dotprecision-classes. Thus, four different DotK-classes have been implemented corresponding to the different four basic C-XSC datatypes:

- Class RDotK for dot products with real results
- Class IDotK for dot products with interval results
- Class CDotK for dot products with complex results
- Class CIDotK for dot products with complex interval results

Each of these new classes provides a set of useful constructors, operators and some basic set and get methods. More importantly, each class offers three essential

---

**Data**: Two vectors $x, y \in \mathbb{F}^n$
**Result**: The dot product $x \cdot y$, as if computed in two-fold working precision, as well as a strict error bound $err$ for the result

$[p, s] = \text{TwoProduct}(x_1, y_1)$
$e = abs(s)$
**for** $i=2:n$ **do**
$\quad [h, r] = \text{TwoProduct}(x_i, y_i)$
$\quad [p, q] = \text{TwoSum}(p, h)$
$\quad t = q \boxplus r$
$\quad s = s \boxplus t$
$\quad e = e \boxplus abs(t)$
$res = p \boxplus s$
$\delta = (n \boxdot eps) \boxslash (1 \boxminus 2n \boxdot eps)$
$\alpha = eps \boxdot abs(res) \boxplus (\delta \boxdot e \boxplus 3eta \boxslash eps)$
$err = \alpha \boxslash (1 \boxminus 2eps)$

---

**Algorithm 6.** Dot2err

methods: First a method `addDot`, with two floating point vectors as parameters, which computes the dot product of these vectors in the desired precision (denoted by a data member K of the class, which is changeable at runtime). Second, the two methods `res` and `res_enclosure`, which return either a result ignoring the error bounds or a reliable enclosure of the correct result using the error bounds.

To store the current intermediate result in this implementation of the DotK-algorithm a `dotprecision` variable of corresponding type is used. This has several advantages: It is possible to compute dot products seamlessly with the long accumulator using the DotK classes without having to change the source code. In the current implementation simply selecting precision $K = 0$ will let the DotK class compute dot products inside the `addDot` method using the long accumulator. Furthermore, this allows to add and substract single values from the intermediate result without introducing additional numerical errors. This special feature increases the accuracy of the new solvers presented below significantly.

For the interval, complex, and complex interval cases, the DotK algorithm has to be adapted appropriately. These changes are fairly easy, since these dot products can be reduced to (several) real dot products:

- A complex dot product of length $n$ can be computed as two real dot products of length $2n$
- An interval dot product of length $n$ can be computed as two real dot products of length $n$
- A complex interval dot product of length $n$ can be computed as four real dot products of length $2n$

Table 2 presents time measurements for our implementation[2]. These tests have been performed on a Pentium 4 with 3.2GHz and 2GB RAM. The speed

---

[2] When using the C-XSC interval operators for interval-types, the rounding mode is switched very often, which is very time-consuming. For complex types, the long accumulator is used internally for multiplication.

difference between the long accumulator and the DotK classes can vary depending on the used processor, since the speed of the accumulator largely depends on the integer unit of the CPU, while the speed of the DotK algorithm depends on the floating point performance of the processor. However, the DotK-algorithm has been faster for precision $K = 2$ on all tested machines (Pentium 4 2.8GHz, Pentium 4 3.2GHz, Core 2 Duo 2.4GHz, Itanium 2 1.6GHz). The performance of the C-XSC implementation of the DotK algorithm is highly dependend on the inlining capabilities of the compiler. With most compilers, corresponding optimization options must be set to activate inlining. On some systems, the compiler limits for inlining have to be tweaked to achieve satisfying results. The numerical results are not presented here but have been checked successfully to be of the expected $K$-fold precision.

**Table 2.** Timings for dot products, $cond = 10^{30}$, repeated 1000 times

| $n$ | Computed with... | real | interval | complex | cinterval |
|---|---|---|---|---|---|
| 1000 | C-XSC operators | 0.01 | 0.58 | 1.20 | 3.84 |
| | Accumulator | 0.19 | 0.40 | 0.72 | 1.64 |
| | DotK, K=2 | 0.03 | 0.12 | 0.20 | 0.47 |
| | DotK, K=3 | 0.09 | 0.21 | 0.37 | 0.87 |
| | DotK, K=4 | 0.12 | 0.27 | 0.47 | 1.07 |
| | DotK, K=5 | 0.14 | 0.32 | 0.57 | 1.28 |
| 10000 | C-XSC operators | 0.06 | 5.83 | 12.07 | 40.01 |
| | Accumulator | 1.85 | 4.02 | 7.05 | 16.22 |
| | DotK, K=2 | 0.35 | 1.16 | 2.03 | 4.64 |
| | DotK, K=3 | 0.98 | 2.27 | 4.02 | 9.56 |
| | DotK, K=4 | 1.24 | 2.79 | 5.04 | 11.62 |
| | DotK, K=5 | 1.49 | 3.30 | 6.07 | 13.70 |
| 100000 | C-XSC operators | 0.64 | 58.37 | 120.16 | 373.2 |
| | Accumulator | 18.65 | 40.32 | 70.73 | 161.82 |
| | DotK, K=2 | 3.53 | 11.66 | 20.41 | 46.46 |
| | DotK, K=3 | 9.86 | 24.57 | 41.48 | 97.83 |
| | DotK, K=4 | 12.44 | 29.76 | 51.91 | 118.75 |
| | DotK, K=5 | 15.02 | 34.95 | 62.34 | 139.64 |

## 3   The New Serial Solvers

With the help of the DotK classes a set of new solvers for linear (interval) systems has been implemented. These new solvers as well as existing solvers in C-XSC are based on the same well known algorithm described by Rump [26], which itself is based on the Krawczyk-Operator [22]. Algorithm 7 works (in slightly modified forms) for real point and interval systems, as well as for complex point and complex interval systems.

The last part of the algorithm, which uses an approximate inverse of double length $(R_1 + R_2)$, is also known as Rump's device and will be called part two or second stage of the algorithm in this paper.

---

**Data**: A square matrix $A$ und a right hand side $b$
**Result**: An interval enclosure of the solution of $Ax = b$
Compute approximate inverse $R$ of $A$
Compute approximate solution $\tilde{x} := Rb$
// Defect iteration
**repeat**
 | $\tilde{x} := \tilde{x} + R(b - A\tilde{x})$
**until** $\tilde{x}$ *accurate enough or max iterations reached*
// Compute enclosures of the residuum and the iteration matrix
$Z := R \diamond (b - A\tilde{x})$
$C := \diamond(I - RA)$
// Verification
$Y := Z$
**repeat**
 | $Y_A := blow(Y, \varepsilon)$ //$\varepsilon$-inflation
 | $Y := Z + C \cdot Y_A$
**until** $Y \subset interior(Y_A)$ *or max iterations reached*
// Check results
**if** $Y \subset interior(Y_A)$ **then**
 | Unique solution in $x \in \tilde{x} + Y$
**else**
 | **if** *Approximate inverse of double length not yet used* **then**
 | | //Second stage
 | | $R_1 := R$
 | | $S := R_1 \cdot A$
 | | Compute approximate inverse $S_1$ of $S$
 | | $S := S_1 \cdot R_1$
 | | $R_2 := S_1 \cdot R_1 - S$
 | | $R_1 := S$
 | | Restart algorithm with new approximate inverse $R = R_1 + R_2$ (sum must not be computed!)
 | **else**
 | | Algorithm failed, $A$ is singular or very ill-conditioned

---

**Algorithm 7.** Basic algorithm for selfverifying linear system solver (all operations in this algorithm are floating point operations)

The new solvers were designed to have the following basic features:

– Support for all basic C-XSC datatypes (`real`, `interval`, `complex`, `cinterval`)

– Support for over- and underdetermined systems
– Part two of the algorithm, using the inverse of double length, is available

Furthermore, in a first basic step, the required approximate inverse is computed using the well known Gauss-Jordan algorithm [27]. In the following, we compute the solution of systems with a random square system matrix of dimension $n = 1000$ and condition $10^{10}$ (see [28] for further details). With the basic solvers described above one gets the results shown in Table 3. Here, exact digits means an approximation of the average number of digits that are equal in the infimum and the supremum of the components of the solution vector. Intlab will be used as a reference point in the following measurements. The timings for Intlab contain some overhead due to interpretation and Matlab itself. However, this is not a serious drawback, because Matlab and thus Intlab use BLAS-routines for most computations, which are realized by native code.

**Table 3.** Timings for basic solvers

| What? | Solver | real | interval | complex | cinterval |
|---|---|---|---|---|---|
| Time | Intlab | 3.86 | 5.16 | 16.00 | 17.14 |
| | C-XSC | 435.15 | 901.84 | 5971.27 | 6335.61 |
| Exact Digits | Intlab | 6.09 | 0.93 | (6.67, 5.90) | (0.81, 0.05) |
| | C-XSC | 15.79 | 1.93 | (15.82, 15.78) | (1.71, 1.56) |

As a first step to improve the performance of these basic solvers, the DotK algorithm can be used for all dot products. This is a quite simple modification, as can be seen in the example in Listing 2 and Listing 3.

**Listing 2.** Computation of [C] = $\diamond$ (I-R*A) using the long accumulator

```
dotprecision  Accu;

for (i = 1; i <= n; i++) {
  for (j = 1; j <= n; j++) {
    Accu = (i == j) ? (real)1.0 : (real)0.0;
    accumulate(Accu,-R[i],A[Col(j)]);
    rnd(Accu,C[i][j]);
  }
}
```

Evidently, the required modifications are straight forward and rather small. Since the DotK-classes incorporate the accumulator, the programm can be "switched back" to ordinary C-XSC computations using the long accumulator without going back to the original source code, simply by setting the precision $K$ equal to 0. Then, the DotK classes will simply use the `accumulate` function of the long accumulator to compute the dot product exactly, thus leading to the same results as in the original C-XSC version.

**Listing 3.** Computation of `[C]` = `(I-R*A)` using the new DotK classes

```
RDotK  dot (K);

for  (i = 1;  i <= n;  i++) {
    for  (j = 1;  j <= n;  j++) {
        dot = (i == j) ? (real)1.0  :  (real)0.0;
        dot.addDot(−R[i],A[Col(j)]);
        C[i][j] = dot.res_enclosure ();
    }
}
```

The modifications described above result in a significant performance enhancement as shown in Table 4.

**Table 4.** Results after introducing DotK classes

| What? | Solver | real | interval | complex | cinterval |
|-------|--------|------|----------|---------|-----------|
|  | Intlab | 3.86 | 5.16 | 16.00 | 17.14 |
| Time | C-XSC, K=2 | 80.82 | 255.02 | 2914.91 | 3538.78 |
|  | C-XSC, K=3 | 91.09 | 324.55 | 2996.16 | 3923.15 |
|  | Intlab | 6.09 | 0.93 | $(6.67, 5.90)$ | $(0.81, 0.05)$ |
| Exact digits | C-XSC, K=2 | 13.99 | 1.93 | $(7.93, 7.93)$ | $(1.70, 1.55)$ |
|  | C-XSC, K=3 | 15.79 | 1.93 | $(15.82, 15.78)$ | $(1.71, 1.56)$ |

As can be seen, the precision of the results is only slightly worse than before. The solvers are now between three and four times faster using the DotK classes with $K = 2$ than with the long accumulator.

However, a lot of additional potential for optimization still lies in the matrix-matrix product when computing the interval matrix $[C]$ and in the computation of the approximate inverse $R$. To speed up these parts of the algorithm, optimized routines from the BLAS and LAPACK [2] are used. For the computation of the approximate inverse the corresponding LAPACK-routines `xgetrf` and `xgetri` can be used in a straightforward way. For the computation of $[C]$ however, an enclosure of the product $RA$ or $R[A]$, respectively, is needed. To achieve this with the ordinary BLAS-routine `dgemm`, manipulation of the rounding mode is used, in a similar way as in Intlab [25].

For this, a function `setround` is introduced, which sets the rounding mode of the processor to down (`setround(-1)`), up (`setround(1)`) or to nearest (`setround(0)`). With the help of this function, the enclosure of a real matrix-matrix product can be computed using Algorithm 8 (C-XSC like pseudocode).

---

**Data**: Two real matrices $A$ and $B$
**Result**: An interval enclosure of the matrix $C = AB$
setround(-1);
SetInf(C, A*B);
setround(1);
SetSup(C, A*B);
setround(0);

---

**Algorithm 8.** Computation of real matrix product using BLAS

The two matrix-matrix-products in this algorithm are computed using the corresponding BLAS routine `dgemm`. The algorithms for the interval and complex case follow the same basic idea and are not shown here. These are basically the algorithms presented in [25] with some minor adaptations.

Using the BLAS routines in this way, as well as the LAPACK routine for the computation of the approximate inverse and the DotK-algorithm and utilizing some other minor optimizations (see [28]) that are not detailed here, one finally gets the results shown in Table 5.

**Table 5.** Final results of the new solvers

| **What?** | **Solver** | **real** | **interval** | **complex** | **cinterval** |
|---|---|---|---|---|---|
| | Intlab | 3.86 | 5.16 | 16.00 | 17.14 |
| Time | C-XSC, K=2 | 3.96 | 5.34 | 15.82 | 18.88 |
| | C-XSC, K=3 | 4.38 | 5.65 | 16.80 | 19.02 |
| | Intlab | 6.09 | 0.93 | (6.67, 5.90) | (0.81, 0.05) |
| Exact digits | C-XSC, K=2 | 14.22 | 1.93 | (13.63, 12.87) | (1.86, 1.11) |
| | C-XSC, K=3 | 15.79 | 1.93 | (15.82, 15.78) | (1.86, 1.11) |

The new serial solvers are now a lot faster than the original C-XSC toolbox solver. For precision $K = 2$ they work roughly on the same speed as the Intlab solver `verifylss`, but they still maintain high accuracy, which in many practical cases are even the same as for the original C-XSC solvers. Furthermore, by increasing the precision of the DotK classes (increasing the value of K), the results shown in Table 5 often can be improved even more.

## 3.1   Some Numerical Results Concerning Ill-Conditioned Matrices

In this paragraph we use the so called Boothroyd/Decker matrices $A_n$ of dimension $n$ to compare the numerical quality of our new solver with the numerical quality of the Intlab solver `verifylss`. The ill-conditioned matrices $A_n$ are defined as follows

$$A_n = (a_{ij}) \text{ with } a_{ij} := \binom{n+i-1}{i-1}\binom{n-1}{n-j}\frac{n}{i+j+1}, i,j = 1,\ldots,n$$

For $n \leq 20$ all matrix elements are exactly representable as IEEE double numbers. As right hand side we use $b = (1, 1, \ldots, 1)^T$. Then, the exact solution vector is $x = (1, -1, 1, -1, \ldots)^T$.

Our new solver (using $K = 3$ for the DotK objects) returns for matrices up to order $n = 20$ either the exact solution vector or a tight enclosure of it whereas the solver `verifylss` breaks down for $n = 13$. The computed enclosure of the result vector in case of matrix order $n = 12$ is:

$$
\begin{array}{rr}
[ & 0.99999999982079, & 1.00000000016779] \\
[ & -1.00000000149304, & -0.99999999836399] \\
[ & 0.99999998842304, & 1.00000001074763] \\
[ & -1.00000004335473, & -0.99999995272265] \\
[ & 0.99999981774945, & 1.00000016863901] \\
[ & -1.00000048155897, & -0.99999947345126] \\
[ & 0.99999843469062, & 1.00000144278687] \\
[ & -1.00000335758376, & -0.99999630705000] \\
[ & 0.99999107401347, & 1.00000823290467] \\
[ & -1.00001753552019, & -0.99998078814825] \\
[ & 0.99994100039713, & 1.00005551901631] \\
[ & -1.00008847223671, & -0.99990482653736]
\end{array}
$$

This Intlab result is only accurate to about 4 decimals. Our new solvers compute the exact result in this case. If $n > 12$, Intlab produces NaNs for all the components of the solution vector.

The comparison shows clearly that the new C-XSC solver outperforms the solver coming with Intlab. We should mention that the original C-XSC toolbox solver produces the same numerical results as our new solver.

## 4   Parallelization

In the following we explain an efficient parallelization of these new solvers. The basic ideas of the serial solver, the usage of the DotK classes and of BLAS/LA-PACK routines, are carried over to this new parallel solver. Instead of LAPACK, the parallel version ScaLAPACK [3] is used.

For a more efficient approach than in the exisiting parallel solver PLSS, especially concerning memory, the matrices used in the algorithm are distributed equally among all processes. Every process saves certain parts of the matrices $A$, $R$ and $[C]$, which it stores throughout the algorithm, while the occurring vectors are stored completely in every process. All processes are involved in every step of the algorithm, so there is no root node (no master/slave or worker/manager approach) or a similar approach.

The matrices are distributed using a two dimensional block cyclic distribution scheme, the same distribution model used by ScaLAPACK. For this distribution model, the available processes are arranged in a two dimensional grid. The matrix is then distributed according to this grid and a predefined block size (see Figures 3 and 4). The optimal values for the number of rows and columns in the process grid, as well as the block size used, are hardware dependent and are not trivial to compute, because a balance between the costly communications and an equal work load has to be found. In our solvers, the number of rows and columns of the process grid is chosen to be equal or almost equal if possible (ideally, the number of processes should be $P = p^2, p \in \mathbb{N}$), while the block size can be set by the user when starting the solver (a value of about 256 delivered the best results in our tests).

| $P_0$ | $P_1$ | $P_2$ |
|-------|-------|-------|
| $P_3$ | $P_4$ | $P_5$ |
| $P_6$ | $P_7$ | $P_8$ |
| $P_9$ | $P_{10}$ | $P_{11}$ |

**Fig. 3.** Process grid for the two dimensional block cyclic distribution, 12 processes

| $P_0$ | $P_1$ | $P_0$ | $P_1$ |
|-------|-------|-------|-------|
| $P_2$ | $P_3$ | $P_2$ | $P_3$ |
| $P_0$ | $P_1$ | $P_0$ | $P_1$ |
| $P_2$ | $P_3$ | $P_2$ | $P_3$ |

**Fig. 4.** Distribution of a matrix in two dimensional block cyclic distribution using a $2 \times 2$ process grid based on 4 processes $P_i$

The inversion and the computation of the matrix-matrix product can now easily by computed using the corresponding ScaLAPACK routines in a similar way as in the serial case. However, the matrix vector products occurring in the algorithm also have to be parallelized. For this, so called MPI communicators are introduced for every row and every column in the process grid. With these communicators it is possible to perform a broadcast which is restricted to a specified row or column in the grid.

Every process then computes the parts of the occurring dot products for which it stores the needed matrix entries. All processes in one row in the process grid then have computed different parts of the same dot product. Thus, to compute a final result of this dot product, the data has to be broadcast inside their row in the process grid (using the MPI communicators). With the help of the long accumulator, the final result can then be computed in every single process.

Now, all processes in one row know the parts of the final result corresponding to their matrix rows. Since every process needs to know the complete result vector, these parts have to be exchanged with the processes corresponding to the other rows of the result. Thus, another broadcast, this time in the columns of the process grid, has to be performed to exchange these parts. After this step, all processes know the complete final result vector.

Thus, the parallelization of these matrix-vector products is quite complicate and communication intensive. But since it is only used in the $O(n^2)$ parts of the algorithm and the used data distribution reduces the memory needed in each process significantly, it is well worth the effort, as may be seen in the final results (Tables 6 and 7).

**Table 6.** Time measurements parallel solvers, $cond = 10^{10}$, $n = 5000$

| Computed with... | P | real | interval | complex | cinterval |
|---|---|---|---|---|---|
| DotK, K=2 | 1 | 265.30 | 363.88 | 1357.63 | 1723.44 |
| | 2 | 159.77 | 206.41 | 625.37 | 737.33 |
| | 4 | 99.98 | 128.77 | 365.58 | 411.14 |
| | 8 | 61.62 | 78.18 | 211.46 | 239.83 |
| DotK, K=3 | 1 | 279.64 | 383.29 | 1387.32 | 1801.44 |
| | 2 | 172.94 | 217.06 | 665.44 | 771.45 |
| | 4 | 104.13 | 134.21 | 379.01 | 427.99 |
| | 8 | 63.92 | 81.02 | 218.35 | 246.95 |

Stage two of the Alogrithm (approximate inverse of double length), if used for very ill-conditioned systems (which is indeed its main purpose), will in general not compute a verified solution when BLAS routines are used, since the results of the matrix-matrix-products will then have too wide diameters. Therefore, these products have to be computed using a higher precision dot product (using the DotK classes). This means that these products have to be manually parallelized, while maintaining the distribution of the matrix entries as described above. To achieve this, a special case of the two dimensional block cyclic distribution scheme is used, where the process grid has $P$ rows and one column, and the block size is $nb = \lceil \frac{n}{P} \rceil$. The matrix $A$ is then distributed as shown in Figure 5. If part one of the algorithm was executed first, the data now must be redistributed to fit this scheme (the cost of this redistribution is neglectable).

**Table 7.** Speedup parallel solvers, $cond = 10^{10}$, $n = 5000$

| Computed with... | P | real | interval | complex | cinterval |
|---|---|---|---|---|---|
|  | 1 | 1.0 | 1.0 | 1.0 | 1.0 |
| DotK, K=2 | 2 | 1.66 | 1.76 | 2.17 | 2.34 |
|  | 4 | 2.65 | 2.83 | 3.71 | 4.19 |
|  | 8 | 4.31 | 4.65 | 6.42 | 7.18 |
|  | 1 | 1.0 | 1.0 | 1.0 | 1.0 |
| DotK, K=3 | 2 | 1.62 | 1.77 | 2.08 | 2.34 |
|  | 4 | 2.69 | 2.86 | 3.66 | 4.21 |
|  | 8 | 4.37 | 4.73 | 6.35 | 7.29 |

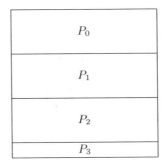

**Fig. 5.** Distribution of matrix entries for part two ($nb$ rows and $n$ columns per block)

**Table 8.** Time measurements parallel solvers, $cond = 10^{17}$, $n = 1000$

| Computed with... | P | real | interval | complex | cinterval |
|---|---|---|---|---|---|
|  | 1 | 432.53 | 706.16 | 1598.94 | 2699.34 |
| DotK, K=3 | 2 | 213.63 | 351.24 | 811.59 | 1335.43 |
|  | 4 | 109.95 | 178.41 | 410.44 | 679.90 |
|  | 8 | 61.36 | 100.33 | 214.68 | 349.62 |

The matrix-matrix-product is now computed as follows: Every process stores a horizontal block of matrix entries, both for the first and the second matrix. Now the dot products of the rows of the first matrix with the columns of second matrix have to be computed. Since every process already stores complete rows of both matrices, it only needs the missing data for the columns of the second matrix. To keep memory demands low, the computation is divided into several steps, where in each step the data for a $n \times nb$ block of the second matrix is broadcasted between the processes. Once this data has been sent, every process can compute

**Table 9.** Speedup parallel solvers, $cond = 10^{17}$, $n = 1000$

| Computed with... | P | real | interval | complex | cinterval |
|---|---|---|---|---|---|
| DotK, K=3 | 1 | 1.0 | 1.0 | 1.0 | 1.0 |
| | 2 | 2.02 | 2.01 | 1.97 | 2.02 |
| | 4 | 3.93 | 3.96 | 3.90 | 3.97 |
| | 8 | 7.02 | 7.04 | 7.45 | 7.72 |

a part of the result matrix for itself (the part of the result matrix computed is a part of the processes horizontal block of the result matrix and thus has not to be communicated in any way). As our timings show, this parallelization is quite efficient (Tables 8 and 9).

# 5    Conclusion and Future Work

With the new solvers described in this paper it is possible to compute a verified solution of a dense linear (interval-)system in C-XSC a lot faster than before without losing too much accuracy in the result (and in many practical cases without losing any accuracy at all compared to the original toolbox solvers). The speed of the new serial solver now compares very well to the speed of the corresponding Inlab solver but gives much better numerical results. In some cases it was not possible to compute a verified result using Intlab, whereas our new solver worked very satisfactory.

To attack very large linear systems some parallelization has to be done. To the authors knowledge there are no parallel selfverifying solvers available as open source software world wide. Intlab also does not support such an approach. The parallel version of our new solvers allows to compute the solution of very large dense systems (see also [17]) and it has been shown that it is very efficient. All software described in this paper will be made available as open source.

Additionally, our DotK classes are designed and integrated in C-XSC such that they and our matrix-matrix-product routines using BLAS can also be used in other C-XSC programs. The long accumulator (dotprecision variable) of C-XSC may be replaced by a DotK object to gain speed in dot product computations. But please keep in mind that the best way still would be to have hardware support for exact dot products [14]. This would give highest accuracy and optimal speed simultaneously!

The solvers presented in this paper are intended to solve dense systems and do not make use of any special structure of the matrix $A$ (banded, sparse, symmetric, positive definite, Toeplitz, Hankel, circulant, ...). While such systems of course can also be solved using our solvers, this approach would be quite inefficient and memory consuming. Thus, as further work, special solvers for these cases and especially for sparse systems will be investigated in general and implemented in C-XSC.

**Acknowledgement.** We would like to thank Gerd Bohlender, Werner Hofschuster, Rudi Klatte, and Mariana Kolberg for many fruitful discussions on the topic of this paper.

# References

1. Downloads: C-XSC library,
   http://www.math.uni-wuppertal.de/~xsc/xsc/cxsc.html
   Solvers, http://www.math.uni-wuppertal.de/~xsc/xsc/cxsc_software.html
2. Blackford, L.S., Demmel, J., Dongarra, J., Duff, I., Hammarling, S., Henry, G., Heroux, M., Kaufman, L., Lumsdaine, A., Petitet, A., Pozo, R., Remington, K., Whaley, R.C.: An Updated Set of Basic Linear Algebra Subprograms (BLAS). ACM Trans. Math. Soft. 28(2), 135–151 (2002)
3. Blackford, L.S., Choi, J., Cleary, A., D'Azevedo, E., Demmel, J., Dhillon, I., Dongarra, J., Hammarling, S., Henry, G., Petitet, A., Stanley, K., Walker, D., Whaley, R.C.: ScaLAPACK Users' Guide. Society for Industrial and Applied Mathematics, Philadelphia (1997)
4. Bohlender, G.: What do we need beyond IEEE Arithmetic? In: Computer Arithmetic and Self-validating Numerical Methods, pp. 1–32. Academic Press, San Diego (1990)
5. Bohlender, G., Walter, W., Kornerup, P., Matula, D.W., Kornerup, P., Matula, D.W.: Semantics for Exact Floating Point Operations. In: Proceedings, 10th IEEE Symposium on Computer Arithmetic, June 26-28. IEEE, Los Alamitos (1991)
6. Dekker, T.J.: A floating-point technique for extending the available precision. Numer. Math. 18, 224 (1971)
7. Grimmer, M.: Selbstverifizierende Mathematische Softwarewerkzeuge im High-Performance Computing. In: Konzeption, Entwicklung und Analyse am Beispiel der parallelen verifizierten Lösung linearer Fredholmscher Integralgleichungen zweiter Art. Logos Verlag (2007)
8. Hammer, R., Hochks, M., Kulisch, U., Ratz, D.: Numerical Toolbox for Verified Computing I: Basic Numerical Problems. Springer, Heidelberg (1993)
9. Hofschuster, W., Krämer, W.: C-XSC 2.0: A C++ Library for Extended Scientific Computing. In: Alt, R., Frommer, A., Kearfott, R.B., Luther, W. (eds.) Numerical Software with Result Verification (Dagstuhl Seminar 2003). LNCS, vol. 2991, pp. 15–35. Springer, Heidelberg (2004)
10. Hölbig, C., Krämer, W.: Selfverifying solvers for dense systems of linear equations realized in C-XSC. Technical Report BUW-WRSWT 2003/1 (2003)
11. Hölbig, C., Krämer, W., Diverio, T.A.: An Accurate and Efficient Selfverifying Solver for Systems with Banded Coefficient Matrix. In: Parallel Computing: Software Technology, Algorithms, Architectures and Applications, vol. 13, pp. 283–290. Elsevier Science B.V., Amsterdam (2004)
12. Kersten, Tim: Verifizierende rechnerinvariante Numerikmodule. Dissertation, University of Karlsruhe (1998)
13. Klatte, Kulisch, Wiethoff, Lawo, Rauch: C-XSC - A C++ Class Library for Extended Scientific Computing. Springer, Heidelberg (1993); Due to the C++ standardization (1998) and dramatic changes in C++ compilers over the last years this documentation describes no longer the actual C-XSC environment. Please refer to more accurate documentation available from the web site of our research group

14. Kirchner, R., Kulisch, U.: Hardware Support for Interval Arithmetic. Reliable Computing 12(3), 225–237 (2006)
15. Knuth, D.E.: The Art of Computer Programming: Seminumerical Algorithms, vol. 2. Addison-Wesley, Reading (1969)
16. Kolberg, M., Fernandes, L.F., Claudio, D.: Dense Linear System: A Parallel Self-verified Solver. International Journal of Parallel Programming, 0885-7458 (Print) 1573-7640, Online (2007)
17. Kolberg, M., Krämer, W., Zimmer, M.: A Noten on Solving Problem 7 of the SIAM 100-Digit Challenge Using C-XSC BUW-WRSWT 2008/2 (2008)
18. Krämer, W., Kulisch, U., Lohner, R.: Numerical Toolbox for Verified Computing II, Advanced Numerical Problems. Draft, about 400 pages, http://www.uni-karlsruhe.de/~Rudolf.Lohner/papers/tb2.ps.gz
19. Kulisch, U.: Computer Arithmetic and Validity - Theory, Implementation. De Gruyter, Berlin (2008) (to appear)
20. Kulisch, U., Miranker, W.: The arithmetic of the digital computer: A new approach. SIAM Rev. 28(1), 1–40 (1986)
21. Kulisch, U.: Die fünfte Gleitkommaoperation für Top-Performance Computer. Berichte aus dem Forschungsschwerpunkt Computerarithmetik, Intervallrechnung und numerische Algorithmen mit Ergebnisverifikation (1997)
22. Krawczyk, R.: Newton-Algorithmen zur Bestimmung von Nullstellen mit Fehlerschranken. Computing 4, 187–201 (1969)
23. Ogita, T., Rump, S.M., Oishi, S.: Accurate sum and dot product. SIAM Journal on Scientific Computing 26, 6 (2005)
24. Oishi, S., Tanabe, K., Ogita, T., Rump, S.M., Yamanaka, N.: A Parallel Algorithm of Accurate Dot Product (2007) (submitted)
25. Rump, S.M.: Intlab - Interval Laboratory. Developments in Reliable Computing, 77–104 (1999)
26. Rump, S.M.: Kleine Fehlerschranken bei Matrixproblemen. Dissertation, University of Karlsruhe (1980)
27. Stoer, J., Bulirsch, R.: Introduction to Numerical Analysis. Springer, New York (1980)
28. Zimmer, M.: Laufzeiteffiziente, parallele Löser für lineare Intervallgleichungssysteme in C-XSC. Master thesis, University of Wuppertal (2007)

# A Note on Solving Problem 7 of the SIAM 100-Digit Challenge Using C-XSC

Mariana Kolberg[1], Walter Krämer[2], and Michael Zimmer[2]

[1] Faculdade de Informática,
Pontifícia Universidade Católica do Rio Grande do Sul
Av. Ipiranga, 6681 Prédio 16 - Porto Alegre, Brazil
[2] Wissenschaftliches Rechnen/Softwaretechnologie,
Bergische Universität Wuppertal
Gaussstr. 20, 42097 Wuppertal, Germany
mkolberg@inf.pucrs.br,
{walter.kraemer,michael.zimmer}@math.uni-wuppertal.de

**Abstract.** This paper presents the usage of a reliable parallel linear system solver to compute the solution of problem 7 of the SIAM 100-digit challenge. Tests were executed on two different clusters: ALICEnext in Wuppertal and XC1 in Karlsruhe. An approach to find all the 100 digits of the exact solution with maximum accuracy is also discussed and tested.

**Keywords:** C-XSC, reliable computing, 100-digit challenge, reliable linear system solver, high performance computing, large dense linear systems.

## 1 Introduction

C-XSC is a powerful C++ class library which simplifies the development of self-verifying numerical software. It provides a lot of predefined highly accurate routines to compute reliable bounds for the solutions of standard numerical problems.

In this note we discuss the usage of a reliable linear system solver to compute the solution of problem 7 of the SIAM 100-digit challenge [23,24]. Of all the 100-digit challenge problems from SIAM, this is the problem most suitable for our parallel solver since to get the result we have to solve a $20\,000 \times 20\,000$ system of linear equations using interval computations. To perform this task we run our software on the advanced Linux cluster ALiCEnext located at the University of Wuppertal and on the high performance computer HP XC6000 at the computing center of the University of Karlsruhe.

The main purpose of this note is to demonstrate the power/weakness of our approach to solve linear interval systems with a large dense system matrix using C-XSC and to get feedback from other research groups all over the world concerned with the topic described. We are very interested to see comparisons concerning different methods/algorithms, timings, memory consumption, and different hardware/software environments. It should be easy to adapt our main

A. Cuyt et al. (Eds.): Numerical Validation, LNCS 5492, pp. 250–261, 2009.

routine (see Appendix below) to other programming languages, and different computing environments. Changing just one variable allows the generation of arbitrary large system matrices making it easy to do sound (reproducible and comparable) timings and to check for the largest possible system size that can be handled successfully by a specific package/environment.

Section 2 presents problem 7 of the SIAM 100-Digits Challenge. Section 3 describes the parallel verified solution using C-XSC with an accuracy of 16 digits. The results of this implementation are shown in Section 4. Section 5 presents an extension of the first solution which allows the computation of all the 100 digits for problem 7. Section 6 contains some concluding remarks. And finally in the appendix we present the source code for the implemented solution.

## 2    The Problem 7 of the Siam 100-Digit Challenge

Here comes the original problem [23]: Let $A = (a_{ij})$ be the $20\,000 \times 20\,000$ matrix whose entries are zero everywhere except for the primes 2, 3, 5, 7, ..., 224737 along the main diagonal and the number 1 in all the positions $a_{ij}$ with $|i - j| = 1, 2, 4, 8, \ldots, 16384$. What is the $(1, 1)$ entry of $A^{-1}$?

Later on we also solve this problem with dimension $n = 50.000$ and $n = 100.000$. In the $n = 50.000$ case the primes from 2 to 611953 are the diagonal entries and the number 1 is in all the positions $|i - j| = 1, 2, 4, 8, ..., 32768$ and in the $n = 100.000$ case the primes from 2 to 1299709 are the diagonal entries and the number 1 is in all the positions $|i - j| = 1, 2, 4, 8, ..., 65536$.

## 3    Implementation

Up to now there are no special linear system solvers for sparse system matrices available in C-XSC [21,8] (but see e.g. [15,11] for some first approaches). Thus we will solve the Problem 7 of the Siam 100-digit Challenge (see the next section) for dimensions 20.000, 50.000 and 100.000 with brute force using our parallel linear system solver for dense matrices [25,12,5]. In case of dimension $n = 20.000$ the matrix has 400.000.000, in case of $n = 50.000$ it has 2.500.000.000 and in case of $n = 100.000$ it has 10.000.000.000 entries. We do not store all these entries in one (master) process. Each process generates a matrix MyA, which stores only its part of the matrix, with the help of the function generateElementOfA (a pointer to this function is the first parameter when calling our new solver LSS). Matrices are stored according to the two-dimensional block cyclic distribution used by ScaLAPACK [17]. Internally the solver creates an approximate inverse $R$ of $A$ and also computes an enclosure (an interval matrix [C]) for $I - R \times A$. Because the solver does not exploit the sparse structure of the problem these matrices will be dense. Thus a lot of memory is needed. Nevertheless, using e.g. the cluster computer ALiCEnext at the University of Wuppertal or the high performance computer HP XC6000 at the computing center of the University of Karlsruhe we are able to solve the linear system $Ax = e_1$, where $e_1 = (1, 0 \ldots 0)^T$ denotes the first unit vector. Then, the first component of the solution vector $x$

gives an enclosure of the element at position $(1,1)$ of $A^{-1}$, which is the solution of the described problem.

In this note we do not give any details on the algorithm used to solve linear systems with interval matrices. We refer the reader to [7,22]. The use of BLAS and LAPACK for computing the verified solution of a linear system is described in [4]. The parallelization is described in [12,25]. A different approach (some kind of master-slave) for the parallelization has been used in [4,5,16] storing the complete system matrix (and/or some auxiliary matrices) on a single node (memory bottleneck). The new solver [12,25] overcomes this difficulty using a two dimensional block cyclic distribution of the matrices. It is based on BLAS, MPI [6,9], ScaLAPACK [17], so called error free transformations [19,18,2,10,20] and allows very large matrices.

Please note that until now we are only interested in an accurate enclosure of the true result within an interval with floating point numbers as bounds (i.e. roughly 15 decimal digits accuracy).

## 4     Interval Results and Some Timing Information

Our software has been developed and tested on two very different high performance cluster computers at the Universities of Wuppertal and Karlsruhe, on which also the final computations have been done.

The Clusters configuration are presented in Table 1.

**Table 1.** Cluster Comparison

|  | AliceNext | XC6000 |
| --- | --- | --- |
| Location | Wuppertal | Karlsruhe |
| CPU | AMD Opteron | Intel Itanium2 |
| Clock Frequency | 1.8 GHz | 1.5 GHz |
| Number of Nodes | 512 | 128 |
| Number of Cores | 2 | 2 |
| RAM per Node | 1 GB | 12 GB |
| Hard Disk | 2 x 250 GB | 146 GB |
| Network | 6 x Gigabit-Ethernet | Quadrics QsNet II interconnect |
| BLAS Library | AMD Core Math Library | Intel Math Kernel Library 10.0.011 |
| Compiler | Intel Compiler 9.0 | Intel Compiler 10.0 |

Let us first discuss the results obtained for the original problem ($n = 20.000$). We find the interval enclosure $A_{11}^{-1} = 0.72507834626840116746868771925116096886918059447950895787816476 9 \ldots \in$ [0.7250783462684010, 0.725078346268 4012]. This enclosure was reproduced in all cases on both machines even when using different numbers of processors. The value of $A_{11}^{-1}$ is known exactly as a rational number in which the numerator and denominator each have 97389 decimal digits, see [24] or http://www-m3.ma.tum.de/m3old/bornemann/challengebook/Chapter7

On AliceNext, solving the problem using 20 processors took about 1800 seconds and using 50 processors, it took about 870 sec. On the super computer HP XC6000 in Karlsruhe the corresponding timings were 620 and 280 seconds, respectively.

Table 2 presents the solver execution time in Wuppertal and Karlsruhe, when executing the linear system solver in case of a system matrix with dimension 20.000 and using 50 processors. Comparing these data gives deeper insight into which operations contribute most to the overall computing times. These main contributions are (as expected) on both machines

- computing the approximate inverse R,
- and computing the enclosure [C] of $I - R \times A$.

Computations on the XC6000 cluster where a lot faster than on ALICEnext, due to the faster Itanium2 CPUs. However, in the smaller $O(n^2)$ parts ALICEnext often is a little faster than the XC6000 cluster. The performance of these parts rely heavily on the inlining capabilities of the compiler. Since the Itanium2 processors require a very different compiler architecture, inlining might not yet work as efficient on these systems. Further investigations have to be done in that matter.

**Table 2.** Execution time in seconds

|  | AliceNext | XC6000 |
|---|---|---|
| Data distribution and initialization | 27.6 | 23.7 |
| Compute matrix R | 430.1 | 94.8 |
| Defect iteration | 3.8 | 3.4 |
| Computation of [z] | 3.6 | 4.4 |
| Computation of [C] | 402.0 | 149.2 |
| Verification | 2.1 | 2.3 |
| Overall time needed | 869.7 | 278.2 |
| Average number of exact digits | $1.581288580850802E + 001$ | $1.581288580850802E + 001$ |
| Result $A^{-1}[1,1]$ | $[7.250783462684010E - 001,$ $7.250783462684012E - 001]$ | $[7.250783462684010E - 001,$ $7.250783462684012E - 001]$ |

We also solved the problem for dimension 50.000 and 100.000 on the high performance computer in Karlsruhe. For the problem with dimension 50.000, we found the interval enclosure:

$$A_{11}^{-1} \in [7.250799024199662E\text{-}001, 7.250799024199664E\text{-}001].$$

Again the computed result does not depend on the number of processors used. The execution times using 50 and 100 processes are 3603 and 1958 sec, respectively.

For the problem with dimension 100.000, we found the interval enclosure:

$$A_{11}^{-1} \in [7.250806337086472E\text{-}001, 7.250806337086474E\text{-}001].$$

The time taken to solve this problem with 128 processes was 12118 seconds.

## 5   Solution with 100 Digits

With some small modifications we were also able to compute 100 digits of the exact result, as demanded in the original challenge. To achieve this, we solve the system seven times, setting the right hand side to

$$[b^{(i+1)}] = [b^{(i)}] - A \cdot \text{mid}([x^{(i)}]), \ i = 1, \ldots, 7$$

where $[b^{(1)}]$ is the first unity vector and $[x^{(i)}]$ is an enclosure of the solution of the system with right hand side $[b^{(i)}]$. Since the solver is already able to compute systems with multiple right hand sides, only small modifications were necessary for this approach and only the necessary computations were performed in each step ($R$ and $[C]$ were computed only once). To compute 100 digits of the exact result the sum

$$\sum_{i=1}^{6} \text{mid}([x_1^{(i)}]) + [x_1^{(7)}]$$

is computed inside the long fixed-point accumulator of C-XSC. We then get the exact result for the first 100 digits of $A_{11}^{-1}$ and dimension 20.000:

0.7250783462684011674686877192511609688691805944795
08957878164769207773189994596283573592392786478 2020.

This computation took 990 seconds on AliceNext using 50 processors, compared to 870 seconds for the computation of the normal interval enclosure.

## 6   Conclusion

Solving the Hundred-Dollar, Hundred-Digit Challenge Problem 7 is not very hard when using our parallel C-XSC solver. Even storing the sparse matrix A as a full matrix, because no special solver for sparse interval systems is available, the method leads to quite acceptable execution times.

We get bounds for the correct mathematical results. The correctness of these bounds is proved automatically by the computer using (machine) interval calculations. Our open source parallel C-XSC solver for linear interval systems is a very powerful tool. It is also able to handle system matrices and right hand sides with real or even with complex interval entries. The numerical results are always reliable. To the authors knowledge there is no other software available which is able to solve such large dense interval linear systems (please inform us if you are aware of other packages!). Of course, a lot of additional work has to be done to create algorithms and to implement corresponding software packages which are able to exploit sparsity. This is a very challenging task.

## Acknowledgement

We want to thank Gerd Bohlender, Rudolf Lohner and Holger Obermaier for helping us to get our programs to run on the parallel machine at the Computing Center of Karlsruhe University.

# References

1. Hölbig, C., Krämer, W.: Selfverifying solvers for dense systems of linear equations realized in C-XSC. BUW-WRSWT (2003/1) (2003)
2. Dekker, T.J.: A floating-point technique for extending the available precision. Numerische Mathematik 18(3), 224–242 (1971)
3. Anderson, E., Bai, Z., Bischof, C., Blackford, S., Demmel, J., Dongarra, J., Du Croz, J., Greenbaum, A., Hammarling, S., McKenney, A., Sorensen, D.: LAPACK Users' Guide, 3rd edn. Society for Industrial and Applied Mathematics, Philadelphia (1999)
4. Kolberg, M., Bohlender, G., Claudio, D.: Improving the Performance of a Verified Linear System Solver Using Optimized Libraries and Parallel Computation. In: Palma, J.M.L.M., Amestoy, P.R., Daydé, M., Mattoso, M., Lopes, J.C. (eds.) VECPAR 2008. LNCS, vol. 5336, pp. 13–26. Springer, Heidelberg (2008)
5. Grimmer, M.: Selbstverifizierende Mathematische Softwarewerkzeuge im High Performance Computing. In: Konzeption, Entwicklung und Analyse am Beispiel der parallelen verifizierten Lösung linearer Fredholmscher Integralgleichungen zweiter Art. Logos Verlag (2007)
6. Grimmer, M., Krämer, W.: An MPI extension for verified numerical computations in parallel environments. In: Arabnia, et al. (eds.) Proceedings to Int. Conf. on Scientific Computing (CSC 2007, Worldcomp 2007), Las Vegas, pp. 111–117 (2007)
7. Hammer, R., Hocks, M., Kulisch, U., Ratz, D.: Numerical Toolbox for Verified Computing I: Basic Numerical Problems. Springer, Heidelberg (1993)
8. Hofschuster, W., Krämer, W.: C-XSC 2.0: A C++ library for extended scientific computing. In: Alt, R., Frommer, A., Kearfott, R.B., Luther, W. (eds.) Numerical Software with Result Verification (Dagstuhl Seminar 2003). LNCS, vol. 2991, pp. 15–35. Springer, Heidelberg (2004)
9. Karniadakis, G., Kirby II., R.M.: Parallel Scientific Computing in C++ and MPI. Cambridge University Press, Cambridge (2003)
10. Knuth, D.E.: The Art of Computer Programming, 3rd edn. Seminumerical Algorithms, vol. 2. Addison-Wesley, Reading (1997)
11. Hölbig, C., Krämer, W., Diverio, T.: An accurate and efficient selfverifying solver for systems with banded coefficient matrix. In: Parallel Computing: Software Technology, Algorithms, Architectures and Applications, 1st edn., pp. 283–290. Elsevier Science B.V., Amsterdam (2004)
12. Krämer, W., Zimmer, M.: Fast (parallel) dense linear interval systems solving in C-XSC using error free transformations and BLAS. In: Cuyt, A., Krämer, W., Luther, W., Markstein, P. (eds.) Numerical Validation in Current Hardware Architectures (Dagstuhl Seminar 2008). LNCS, vol. 5492, pp. 203–249. Springer, Heidelberg (2008)
13. Kulisch, U.: Computer Arithmetic and Validity. de Gruyter, Berlin (2008)
14. Kulisch, U.W., Miranker, W.L.: The arithmetic of the digital computer: A new approach. SIAM Rev. 28(1), 1–40 (1986)
15. Krämer, W., Kulisch, U., Lohner, R.: Numerical Toolbox for Verified Computing II: Advanced Numerical Problems. Springer, Heidelberg (2006)
16. Kolberg, M., Fernandes, L.F., Claudio, D.: Dense Linear System: A Parallel Self-verified Solver. International Journal of Parallel Programming (2007)
17. Blackford, L.S., Choi, J., Cleary, A., D'Azevedo, E., Demmel, J., Dhillon, I., Dongarra, J., Hammarling, S., Henry, G., Petitet, A., Stanley, K., Walker, D., Whaley, R.C.: ScaLAPACK Users' Guide. Society for Industrial and Applied Mathematics, Philadelphia (1997)

18. Yamanaka, N., Ogita, T., Rump, S.M., Oishi, S.: A parallel algorithm of accurate dot product. http://www.ti3.tu-harburg.de/paper/rump/RuZi07.pdf
19. Ogita, T., Rump, S.M., Oishi, S.: Accurate sum and dot product. SIAM Journal on Scientific Computing 26(6), 1955–1988 (2005)
20. Bohlender, G., Walter, W., Kornerup, P., Matula, D.W.: Semantics for exact floating point operations. In: Proceedings, 10th IEEE Symposium on Computer Arithmetic, pp. 26–28. IEEE, Los Alamitos (1991)
21. Klatte, R., Kulisch, U., Wiethoff, A., Lawo, C., Rauch, M.: C-XSC - A C++ Class Library for Extended Scientifix Computing. Springer, Heidelberg (1993)
22. Rump, S.M.: Kleine Fehlerschranken bei Matrixproblemen. Ph.D thesis, Universität Karlsruhe (1980)
23. Trefethen, N.: A Hundred-Dollar, Hundred-Digit Challenge. SIAM, Philadelphia (2002)
24. Bornemann, F., Laurie, D., Wagon, S., Waldvogel, J.: The SIAM 100-Digit Challenge - A Study in High-Accuracy Numerical Computing. SIAM, Philadelphia (2004)
25. Zimmer, M.: Laufzeiteffiziente, parallele Löser für lineare Intervallgleichungssysteme in C-XSC. Master's thesis, Universität Wuppertal (2007)

# Appendix

### Source Code to Create the System Matrix and to Call the Parallel Solver

In this appendix we show the source code of the program to create the matrix and right hand side. It calls the parallel solver LSS for dense linear interval systems available in C-XSC [25,12].

```
/*
 * Solving problem 7 of the SIAM 100-digit challenge using C-XSC
 *
 * The problem: A=a_ij is the 20000x20000 matrix (in this program,
 * the dimension can be altered) whose entries are zero everywhere except
 * for the primes 2,3,5,7,... along the main diagonal and the number 1 in
 * all position a_ij with |i-j|=1,2,4,8,...
 * What is the entry (1,1) of the inverse of A?
 *
 * Here this problem is solved by computing the solution of the linear system
 * A*x=b, where b is the first unit vector, with a fast parallel dense linear
 * system solver using C-XSC. (Note: Since A is a sparse matrix, using a
 * dense solver is not very efficient).
 *
 * Author: Michael Zimmer
 *
 */


//Headerfiles for output streams(logfile)
#include <iostream> #include <fstream> #include <sstream>
//Headerfile for MPI functions
```

```
#include "mpi.h"

//Headerfile for time mesurements
#include "sys/time.h"
//Headerfile for the solver
#include "lss_par.hpp"

using namespace cxsc; using namespace std;

//Dimension of the interval matrix A
const int dim = 20000;
//All primes between 1 and dim
int primes[dim];
//Directory for logfile of each node
const string datadir = "/data/mzimmer";
//Directory to which all logfiles will be copied at the end
const string targetdir = "/home/mzimmer/Upload/bin/output";

//Get current timer value in s
double getTime() {
   struct timeval _tp;
   gettimeofday(&_tp,0);
   return _tp.tv_sec + _tp.tv_usec / 1000000.0;
}

//Logarithm of base 10
real log10(real x) {
  return ln(x) / ln(real(10.0));
}

//Logarithm of base 2
real log2(real x) {
  return ln(x) / ln(real(2.0));
}

//Determines if an integer n is a prime
bool isPrime(int n) {
  if(n == 2)
    return true;
  else if(n < 2  ||  n%2 == 0)
    return false;

  bool prime = true;

  for(int i=3 ; i<=(int)sqrt((double)n) ; i++) {
    if(n%i == 0) {
      prime = false;
      break;
    }
  }
```

```
    return prime;
}

//Generates all primes between 1 and dim and stores them in the
//array primes
void generatePrimes() {
  int p = 0;
  int i = 0;

  while(p < dim) {
    i++;
    if(isPrime(i)) {
      primes[p] = i;
      p++;
    }
  }
}

//Determines if an integer n is a power of two
bool isPowTwo(int n) { //works well in the range were we use it
  real l = log2(n);
  return l == (int)_double(l);
}

//Function defining elements of A. The reference parameter r
//will be overwritten with the value of element (i,j) of matrix
//A.
void generateElementOfA(int i, int j, real& r) {
  if(i==j)
    r = primes[i-1];
  else if(isPowTwo(cxsc::abs(i-j)))
    r = 1.0;
  else
    r = 0.0;
}

//Computes an approximate of the average number of
//exact digits (the number of digits equal in the
//infimum and the supremum)
real computeNumberOfExactDigits(ivector &x) {
  dotprecision accu(0);

  for(int i=1 ; i<=VecLen(x) ; i++) {
    real d = diam(x[i]);
    if(d == 0) {
      accu += 1e16;
    } else {
      accu += abs(mid(x[i])) / d;
    }
```

```
  }

  return abs(log10(rnd(accu)/VecLen(x)));
}


int main (int argc, char** argv) {
  //MPI process ID
  int myId;
  //Number of processes
  int np;
  //Dimension of the matrix A
  int m=dim, n=dim;
  //Right hand side of the system
  rvector b(m);
  //Computed solution
  ivector x(n);
  //Precision to be used for computation of dot products
  //(K-fold working precision)
  int K=2;
  //Number of threads used for computation of dot products
  int threads=0;
  //Variables for error codes
  int comErr, err;
  //Blocksize for ScaLAPACK
  int nb=256;
  //Variables for the measurement of the time needed
  double start, stop;

  //Initialise MPI
  MPI_Init(&argc,&argv);

  //Determine the number of processes
  MPI_Comm_size(MPI_COMM_WORLD, &np);

  //Determine own process ID
  MPI_Comm_rank(MPI_COMM_WORLD, &myId);

  //Prepare output of process data into a logfile
  ostringstream s;
  s << datadir << "/" << "output" << myId << ".txt";
  ofstream out(s.str().c_str());

  //Write some information to the logfile
  out << SetPrecision(23,15) << Scientific;   // Output format
  out << "K=" << K << endl;
  out << "m=" << m << endl;
  out << "n=" << n << endl;

  //Generate all needed prime numbers
```

```
generatePrimes();

//Right hand side is the first unit vector. Will be broadcast
//by process 0 to the other processes
if(myId==0) {
  b = 0.0;
  b[1] = 1.0;
}

//Start the solver
//
//Parameters are:
//generateElementOfA: A pointer to a function which generates
//                    Element (i,j) of the matrix A
//b: Right hand side of the system
//x: Solution of the system (will be overwritten by the solver)
//m: Number of rows of matrix A
//n: Number of columns of matrix A
//np: Number of available processes
//myId: Own process id
//nb: Block size for ScaLAPACK
//err: General error variable
//comErr: Communication-error variable
//out: Output stream to write status messages to
//K: Precision for dot products
//threads: Number of threads used for dot products
//LSS_ONLY_PART_ONE: A pre-defined constant determining that only
//                   part one of the solver should be executed
//                   (other possibilities: LSS_ONLY_PART_TWO, LSS_BOTH_PARTS)

start = getTime();

LSS(generateElementOfA,
    b, x, m, n, np, myId, nb, err, comErr,
    out, K, threads, LSS_ONLY_PART_ONE);

stop = getTime();

//Write overall time needed to logfile
out << endl << "Overall time needed:  " << stop-start << "s" << endl;

//Write result or error message to logfile
if(myId == 0) {
  if (!err) {
      out << "Average number of exact digits: "
      << computeNumberOfExactDigits(x) << endl;
      out << "Result: " << x[1] << endl;
  } else {
      out << "Error: " << LinSolveErrMsg(err) << endl;
  }
```

```
  }

  //Close the logfile and move it to the targetdir
  out.close();
  string syscmd_mvres= "mv "+ s.str() + " " + targetdir;
  system(syscmd_mvres.c_str());

  //End the program
  MPI_Finalize();

  return 0;
}
```

# Author Index